FEMALE LABOR SUPPLY:
THEORY AND ESTIMATION

A RAND CORPORATION RESEARCH STUDY

A list of other Rand publications
appears at the back of this book.

FEMALE LABOR SUPPLY:
THEORY AND ESTIMATION

JAMES P. SMITH, EDITOR

WITH CONTRIBUTIONS BY

JOHN COGAN

GIORA HANOCH

JAMES HECKMAN

T. PAUL SCHULTZ

JAMES P. SMITH

PRINCETON UNIVERSITY PRESS
PRINCETON, NEW JERSEY

WILLIAM MADISON RANDALL LIBRARY UNC AT WILMINGTON

Copyright © 1980 by The Rand Corporation

Published by Princeton University Press, Princeton, New Jersey
In the United Kingdom: Princeton University Press, Guildford, Surrey

All Rights Reserved

Library of Congress Cataloging in Publication Data will be found on the last printed
page of this book

Clothbound editions of Princeton University Press books are printed on acid-free
paper, and binding materials are chosen for strength and durability.

Printed in the United States of America by Princeton University Press, Princeton,
New Jersey

HD6053
.F4

To my Mother and Father,
and Sandy

208679

CONTENTS

PREFACE

Labor economics has undergone (at least) two revolutions in the last two decades. First, there was the explicit recognition that human skills are both malleable and durable. This led to much work on "investments in human capital." Second, labor economists discovered women!

This book is devoted exclusively to women, to determinants of their market wages and values of home time and to factors affecting labor supply, i.e., market work. Men are in the background, just as women are in the early work on human capital. One does not have to delve too deeply to see female/male employment ratios are rising and one does not have to think too long about many actual and proposed welfare schemes to realize that evaluation of alternatives will hinge on labor supply effects and that women may provide much of the basis for differentiation. Hence, systematic analysis of female labor supply is in order.

Whether these studies fill the order is uncertain, but they surely make a first course and this course represents the state of the art. The evidence, much of the analysis, and estimation techniques are new. Examine this work knowing that although it does not exhaust all of the recent advances, nonetheless, it represents a significant departure from most of what has gone before.

All of the work presented here is by staff of Rand's Labor and Population Studies Program. In addition to emphasis on labor supply, work in the program is more or less equally divided between human resource problems of the U.S. and those of less-developed economies. The work on economic development spans human fertility and determinants of full (market and nonmarket) income distributions and even touches on technical change in agriculture and associated distributional repercussions. The U.S. work also emphasizes income distributions, especially race differentials, and extends to migration and human fertility.

Paul Schultz, now of Yale, was the initial program director and retains an affiliation as a collaborator. John Cogan and Jim Smith are economists on the research staff. Giora Hanoch (Hebrew University of Jerusalem) and Jim Heckman (University of Chicago) conducted their research as resident consultants.

Schultz's initial work was supported by the National Institutes of Health. The original research for everything else is a product of grants to Rand from the Office of the Assistant Secretary for Planning and Evaluation, Department of Health, Education and Welfare.

FINIS WELCH
Labor and Population Studies
January 1979

FEMALE LABOR SUPPLY:
THEORY AND ESTIMATION

INTRODUCTION

JAMES P. SMITH

THE RAND CORPORATION

In the last decade, research on female labor supply has expanded at a rate which even exceeds the remarkable rate of growth of the female labor force. The initial intellectual impulse was the work of Jacob Mincer (1962) who contributed a powerfully simple explanation of discrepancies between time series and cross-sectional market work patterns for white married women using the standard decomposition of income and price effects of traditional price theory. In his seminal paper on the allocation of time (1965), Gary Becker generalized the role of time in economic activity, so that time became a central element in decisions affecting fertility, health, location, and many other things. Becker's theory served also as the foundation for the household production model that became so popular in the early 1970's. Since the work of Mincer and Becker, several substantive methodological advancements have been made. The proposals for a National Income Maintenance Plan produced a number of small-scale negative income tax experiments that not only provided additional data sources for analysts, but raised questions about the usefulness of experimental versus nonexperimental data and the ability of economists to predict the potential impact of a national long-term income maintenance program. The simple model of labor supply choice was also extended in a number of dimensions. These included issues related to the family and the ability of husbands and wives to substitute their time in the market and nonmarket sectors; life-cycle patterns of time allocation; the interrelationship between life-cycle decisions regarding human capital accumulation and the consumption of market goods and leisure; uncertainty; and difficulties encountered with a corner solution when the majority of married women elect to work zero hours in the market. More recently, research has increasingly focused on the appropriate method of estimation. This trend is best characterized by the work of Gronau (1974) on selectivity bias, and of Heckman (1974b) on the joint distribution of hours and wages within censored samples.

Although this recent work has clearly extended the research frontier, the theory of labor supply and its related econometric methodology still contains many unresolved issues. The essays included in this volume address themselves to an important subset of these theoretical and econometric problems. The range of subjects covered is indeed impressive. In addition to the problems encountered with censored samples in estimating wage and hours functions, the topics include the choice between linear and nonlinear methods of estimation, the availability of alternative definitions of labor supply (participation, weeks worked, and annual hours), the role of time and money costs in the decisions to work and the extent of work, and the ability of the life-cycle approach to interpret otherwise anomalous empirical estimates. In each paper, theoretical models are tested empirically using a variety of existing micro-data sets.

This introduction has a threefold purpose. The first goal is to relate this volume to the existing literature so that the reader is better able to appreciate the motivation for these essays, the problems they are attempting to resolve, and their departure from conventional methods of analysis. Since much of the work concentrates on estimation techniques, I will summarize briefly the insights and problems associated with those articles that are the direct intellectual antecedents of the research contained in this book. The second purpose is to highlight the main theoretical and econometric innovations of the individual essays, so that the interested reader can see the forest from the midst of a fascinating but complex array of trees. Finally, I attempt to synthesize the principal empirical findings with an eye toward identifying the major similarities and differences emerging from the separate papers.

Until recently, the standard practice in empirical research was to estimate labor supply functions over samples of working women only. This was done either directly by confining the analysis exclusively to labor force participants or indirectly by imputing a wage to nonworking women from a wage equation estimated over a sample of workers. This restriction was forced by the absence of data on the value of time for women who were not working. Much of the econometric work on labor supply during the past five years has dealt with alternative methods of estimating wage and labor supply functions that are free of this censoring bias.

The first step toward resolving the censoring problem involved a clearer understanding on the nature of the decision to participate in the labor force. Economists frequently used alternative definitions of labor supply—annual hours, weekly hours, weeks worked, and labor force participation rates—interchangeably in empirical work. This practice was correctly criticized in papers by Ben-Porath (1973a) and Lewis (1972). They both argued that labor force participation involves a comparison between market wage offers ("W_m") and the value of home time at zero hours of work (the reservation wage "W_r"). A participation rate of 40 percent indicates simply that 40 percent of the women have market wages that exceed their reservation wages.

Ben-Porath considered two alternative interpretations of observing 40 percent of women in the labor force at any particular time. In the first, the 40 percent represents an estimate of the average desired fraction of time to spend in the labor force for every woman in that group. In any given week only some of these women will be labor force members (due to transitory and short-run factors). But over a sufficiently long time interval, each woman will spend 40 percent of her available time in the labor force. If this were an accurate characterization of the world, the standard Slusky interpretation of coefficients for wages and other variables in a participation equation as conveying information about income and substitution effects and as being qualitatively similar to hours of work equations would have some validity. There would, in fact, be little reason to distinguish among alternative definitions of labor supply. The second view suggested by Ben-Porath is that labor force participation rates reflect persistent differences among women. In this case, the participation rate indicates that 40 percent of the women desire in some long-run sense to be labor force members, while the other 60 percent do not. The difference in the interpretation we give to participation equations can be illustrated simply. Let there be no variation in market wages, but variation only in female home wages. Labor force participation rates would then measure the cumulative density of the women's reservation wage distribution up to the market wage. Since the slope of labor force participation rates with respect to the market wage is simply the reservation wage density function, the responsiveness of participation rates to wages depends directly on the tightness of the distribution of home wages.

Ben-Porath argued that the strong serial correlation observed over time in the probability that a given woman works is strong evidence that this second view is a much closer description of reality.

The insights of Ben-Porath and Lewis set the stage for the important work of Gronau. In a series of papers (1973a, 1973b, 1974), Gronau developed more formally the interpretation of the participation equation suggested by Ben-Porath and Lewis. The probability of participation was seen as depending upon whether offered market wages exceed reservation wages where

$$W_m = \alpha X + u_1$$

$$W_r = \beta Y + u_2$$

so that the probability of participation can be written as

$$\frac{\alpha X - \beta Y}{\sigma_p} > \frac{u_2 - u_1}{\sigma_p} = \frac{u_p}{\sigma_p}.$$

X and Y are the systematic determinants and u_1 and u_2 are normally distributed errors in the market and reservation wages equations, respectively. Since the participation error (u_p) is distributed as a standardized normal, probit estimation of this probability was appropriate. Although participation probabilities had been estimated before the work of Gronau, the interpretation placed on the coefficients was now quite different. For example, instead of using the wage coefficient to retrieve income and substitution parameters, it was now an estimate of $1/\sigma_p$ (the inverse of standard deviation of errors about the probability of participation). Gronau's initial interest was in deriving the unobserved potential market wage and home wage (the value of time) for nonworkers. However, without some additional strong a priori assumptions, he could not identify all the unknown parameters necessary to calculate the value of time with the participation equation alone. Since we observe only the wage of workers (the wage conditional on $W_m > W_r$), it was impossible to identify the full set of unobserved means and variances of the market and reservation wages for women. The assumptions Gronau invoked to estimate the value of time were indeed heroic. He proceeded by examining extreme cases in which the system was identified. First, he assumed that all women within a given education and age group expect the same wage, i.e., that there exists zero variance in residual market wage offers. Thus, differences in the participation of women within that group represent *only* differences in their reservation wages. One can then calculate the mean and standard deviation of the reservation wage distributions that would result in the observed labor force participation rate and mean wage of working women. The second alternative he considered was zero dispersion in home wages, so that labor force participation rates mirror only variation in market wages. By a similar procedure, he used the observed participation rate and wages of workers to deduce the implied mean and dispersion in market wages.

In closely related work, Gronau raised the issue of censoring or selectivity bias in the wage generating function for women. The difficulties encountered in estimating labor supply and wage equations are closely linked because identical sample censoring issues arise. The expected wage for workers may be written as

$$E(W_m) = \alpha X + E\left(u_1 \,\middle|\, \frac{\alpha X - \beta Y}{\sigma_p} > \frac{u_2 - u_1}{\sigma_p}\right).$$

If one estimates a wage equation using samples of working women, biases result because the same sets of variables that determine wages enter in as a criterion for sample eligibility. The estimated wage function confounds the true behavioral wage function with the rules for sample inclusion. The issue is illustrated in Figure I.1

For simplicity, let education be the sole variable determining market wages and assume further that education does not affect reservation wages. The solid line in Figure I.1 represents the true relation between education and market wages. However, by restricting the analysis to workers, our sample includes only women in the shaded area. In the

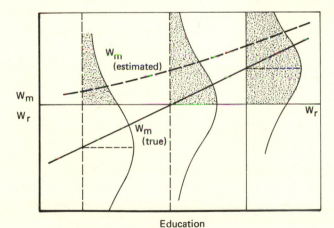

Education

FIGURE I.1   Illustration of selectivity bias

case illustrated above, the rate of return to education will be underestimated (the dotted line) because of the negative correlation introduced over the censored sample between education and the true residual in the wage equation. As Gronau pointed out, in making comparisons between groups of people who differ in their labor force participation rates (i.e., men and women, black females and white females), some of the observed differences may have little to do with behavioral dissimilarities but merely reflect sample censoring.

James Heckman's "Shadow Prices, Market Wages, and Labor Supply" (1974b) was a seminal methodological contribution in labor supply estimation. It extended the work of Gronau in a number of dimensions. First, it relaxed some of Gronau's restrictive assumptions by allowing for residual variation in both market and reservation wages and for correlation between their residuals. More importantly, it integrated into one consistent framework decisions regarding wages, hours, and participation. One limitation of Gronau's framework was that he focused on individual equations in the system in isolation—the probability of participation or the wage equation. Furthermore, he ignored completely the information available from the extent of hours worked among participants. Heckman's approach allows one to estimate a common set of parameters which underly the function determining the probability that a woman works, her hours of work, her observed wage rate, and her shadow wage. His conceptual framework rests on two behavioral relations—the market wage and the shadow wage functions. The shadow wage is defined as the marginal value placed on a woman's leisure evaluated at each unit of leisure (and hence hours of work). Heckman's model can be written as

$$W_s = b_1 H + BY + u_2$$
$$W_m = \alpha X + u_1.$$

A woman works if $W_m > W_{s|h=0}$ (her market wage exceeds her shadow wage at zero hours of work). For working women, shadow and market wages are equated at the margin so that one can solve for the hours equation.

$$H = \frac{1}{b_1}(W_m - BY) - \frac{u_2}{b_1} \quad \text{if} \quad \alpha X - BY > u_2 - u_1.$$
$$H = 0 \quad \text{if} \quad \alpha X - BY < u_2 - u_1.$$
$$W_m = \alpha X + u_1 \quad \text{if} \quad \alpha X - BY > u_2 - u_1.$$
$$W_m \text{ unobserved if } \alpha X - BY < u_2 - u_1.$$

Heckman writes out the likelihood function for the observed sample distribution of hours and wages for K workers and $N - K$ nonworkers as

$$\prod^{K} \frac{P(H, W_m)}{P(W_m > W_{s|h=0})} P(W_m > W_{s|h=0}) \prod^{N-K} P(W_m < W_{s|h=0}),$$

where $P(H, W_m)$ is the unconditional distribution of hours and wages and $P(W_m > W_{s|h=0})$ and $P(W_m < W_{s|h=0})$ are the probabilities of observing a woman working and not working. By differentiating this likelihood function with respect to all the unknowns ($\alpha, B, \sigma_1, \sigma_2, \sigma_{12}$), Heckman solves for the complete set of parameters, using nonlinear estimation. Although Heckman's work represents a significant methodological advance, it was computationally quite expensive and his technique was, therefore, never adopted in applied research.

These articles by Gronau and Heckman set the stage for that component of our research concerned primarily with econometric methodology. Because they were written prior to the other essays that treat statistical issues, the papers by Paul Schultz and John Cogan are placed first in this volume. This arrangement was also chosen because their papers contain a simple exposition and critique of the conventional methods of estimating labor supply equations.

Paul Schultz's "Estimating Labor Supply Functions for Married Women" summarizes informally many of the problems inherent in empirical work on labor supply. He includes a comprehensive discussion of the difficulties associated with the wage variable in particular. In addition to the censoring issue, biases may result from measurement error, simultaneity if hours and wages are determined jointly with other economic choices, the confounding and perhaps separate influences of transitory and permanent wage variation, and nonlinearities due to income tax rates. Schultz argues that the appropriate estimation method depends in part on the relative importance of these alternative sources of bias. For example, if measurement error in wages is the dominant factor, creating an instrumental variable for the wage rate using a sample of working women would not be a bad strategy to pursue. Since the purged residual variation about the wage equation would in this instance have no relation to the decision to participate in the market, sample censoring could be safely ignored. Because the other essays concentrate on the selectivity question,

Shultz's cataloging of other perhaps equally important problems should serve as a useful caveat.

Using the 1967 Survey of Economic Opportunity, Schultz estimates labor supply functions for samples of married spouse-present women stratified into age groups and race. These functions are estimated by several alternative econometric techniques identifying, it is hoped, situations in which alternative methods yield basically identical estimates and those cases in which considerable care must be exercised in choosing among them. First, a labor supply function is estimated across all women using both Tobit and OLS and an instrument for the market wage calculated from the sample of working women. The second strategy consists in running a separate participation equation (using an OLS linear probability and a logistic model) and an OLS hours function over a sample of workers. Finally a reduced form Tobit for all women is estimated abandoning the possibility of retrieving any structural parameters.

In his paper, "Married Women's Labor Supply: A Comparison of Alternative Estimation Procedures," Cogan investigates more formally the biases inherent in some conventional labor supply functions. He deals first with the two traditional methods: (1) estimating over samples of working women, and (2) using the full sample of women but imputing a wage to nonworkers from a wage equation using the sample of workers. Cogan illustrates with great clarity the reasons why each approach is flawed. In so doing, he also clarifies the assumptions necessary to justify the use of either. He next critiques in detail the econometric methodology underlying Gronau's models, making explicit the statistical assumptions necessary to estimate the value of home time. He shows that if either of the two extremes considered by Gronau were, in fact, appropriate, then one of the traditional methods of estimating labor supply functions would also be correct. Since the traditional methods provide more information than Gronau's procedures, the usefulness of Gronau's techniques for applied empirical work is questionable.

Finally, Cogan compares estimates obtained with the two traditional methods with those reported by Heckman based on his maximum likelihood estimation. The 1967 National Longitudinal Survey is used in his empirical work. Systematic differences in the estimated parameters are substantial between Heckman's approach and the procedure of using only the subsample of working women. Systematic, but much smaller, differences are found between Heckman's method and the alternative of imputing wages to all women and estimating the hours equation over the complete sample of women. If Heckman's estimates are taken as the benchmark, the direction of the bias with the two traditional models is consistent with a priori expectations.

Even after the distinction is made between labor force participation and the extent of work-given participation, several measures of labor supply exist and have been used in empirical work—hours per week, weeks per year, annual hours. Labor supply can be specified over any time interval and within that interval many indices of the extent of work are possible. Theory provides little guidance about the "correct" supply concept to choose or about any relationships and constraints that may exist among them. From the perspective of preferences, the conventional model is couched in terms of aggregrate leisure time. An individual selects some total amount of leisure and market goods but the distribution of these leisure hours throughout the year is left open. But people do care for a variety of reasons about the timing of their leisure consumption. Leisure hours are clustered during particular days in a week and spread out during the weeks within a year. This problem of alternative definitions of labor supply is the subject of Giora Hanoch's "Hours and Weeks in a Theory of Labor Supply." Most of the work differentiating labor supply definitions has relied on fixed costs of work. Hanoch's model takes a very different perspective by assuming that within preference functions, individuals are not indifferent between the types of leisure they consume and when it is consumed.

Hanoch develops a theoretical model in which the nonperfect substitution between different types of leisure is explicit. He permits an individual to choose between leisure in a week that he does work and leisure in a week that he does not work. Based on this formulation, Hanoch derives a simultaneous multivariate model of wages, labor force participation, and annual hours and weeks worked. In particular, a consistent set of labor supply functions for both weeks worked and annual hours is derived and the relationship between them clarified. Hanoch shows that within his framework, using hours worked per week as a supply definition would be inappropriate, since it represents the ratio of two demand functions and permits no clear interpretation.

Perhaps Hanoch's real contribution is that his model possesses the flexibility to analyze a number of distinctions between units of leisure that the individual does not regard as perfect substitutes. The specific form adopted was clearly geared to justifying an empirical model that had both annual hours and weeks worked as potential dependent variables. But researchers interested in other sets of definitions of the extent of work can easily adapt the model to their purposes.

Until recently, economists viewed labor-leisure choice in a single-period framework. While this was clearly suited to explaining lifetime measures of average market participation in terms of long-run or permanent values of wealth and wage rates, individuals are faced with temporal variations in wage rates and other variables that could elicit timing responses about long-run desired levels. Moreover, the data indicated a clear age pattern to work time for both men and women. Male work age profiles have an inverted U shape with a peak in market hours occurring around age 45. The profiles for women are less easy to characterize, but they seem to be double-peaked with two periods of declining participation—one during childbearing and the other immediately before retirement. Ghez and Becker (1975) and Heckman (1971) formulated the basic theoretical structure for analyzing life-cycle timing patterns of market work. Their models explain timing decisions in terms of differences between rates of interest and time preference and life cycle movements in wage rates. Most recent research dealing with life-cycle labor supply has been predominantly theoretical, employing the techniques of optimal control to integrate a wider set of choice variables into life-cycle decision-making. Although the primary emphasis in this work concerns human capital investment patterns, the corresponding optimal age-consumption patterns of market goods and leisure have also been derived (Blinder and Weiss, 1975; Heckman, 1974c). Life-cycle models have also been used with some success to interpret empirical results of the income maintenance experiments (Metcalf, 1974; Smith, 1975) and retirement decisions, especially those connected with social security. Since the experiments were all limited in duration, they clearly induced timing behavior that contaminated their usefulness in predicting the potential impact of a permanent income maintenance plan.

The only essay in this volume that deals explicitly with life-cycle issues is James Smith's "Assets and Labor Supply." In empirical work, researchers have used variables measuring nonlabor income or assets to estimate pure wealth effects. The empirical difficulty was that estimated coefficients on assets were typically positive or, if negative, so small in absolute value that compensated labor supply elasticities were often negative. This problem also plagues many of the other essays in this volume (Cogan, Hanoch, Heckman). Using a life-cycle framework, Smith examines in detail the expected relationship between the observed asset levels of families and their labor supply. He argues that, to a large extent, assets at any age represent accumulated past savings and, hence, reflect desired consumption and income profiles. Smith demonstrates that economic theory suggests little of an unambiguous nature about the expected relationship between assets and labor supply. Rather, they are both simultaneously determined by similar economic variables over the life cycle, so that the empirical relationship should not be interpreted as reflecting a causal sequence from assets to market work.

In his empirical work, Smith uses the 1967 Survey of Economic Opportunity which contains information on assets, wages, and labor supply of family members. The implications of the life-cycle model for the savings and labor supply of each family member are tested. Although the quality of the asset data in the SEO is not ideal, his empirical results basically support the predictions of the theory.

In June 1975, James Heckman circulated to the Rand staff a five-page draft note on sample censoring that forms the nucleus of his paper, "Sample Selection Bias as a Specification Error." Building on the work of Amemiya (1973b) Heckman advanced the simple, neat view of censoring bias as another variant of specification error. Using well-known theorems involving truncated normal distributions he proves that the expected wage and hours for a sample of workers can be written as

$$E(W_m) = \alpha X + \frac{\sigma_{1p}}{\sigma_p} \lambda$$
$$E(h) = B_0(\alpha X - BY) + \sigma_p \lambda,$$

where λ is the ratio of height of the density to the right tail area, σ_{1p} is the correlation between the errors in the participation and wage equations, and σ_p is the standard deviation of the participation error. Therefore, the bias in estimating wage and hours over samples of working women results from the omission of the variable λ. If one knew or could estimate λ, then it would be possible to obtain consistent wage and hours equations with samples of workers. Heckman suggests estimating λ from a first-stage probit on the probability of participation. His formulation of the problem also clarifies the nature of the biases involved in using samples of working women. The bias depends on the sign of λ in the relevant equation as well as the sign of the coefficients in the auxilliary regression between λ and the variables in X and Y. Since λ is a negative function of the probability of participation, the issue reduces to whether variables in the X and Y vectors increase or decrease participation. The real value of this technique is its simplicity. The censoring correction can be estimated with inexpensive statistical programs easily available to applied researchers. Heckman's model clearly can be applied to a wider scope of censoring problems than just labor supply. It has already been used in the analysis of migration, unionism, educational choice, and the effects of welfare programs. For his empirical work, Heckman uses a sample from the 1967 National Longitudinal Survey for Mature Women. In interpreting his results, he proposed a modification of the labor supply function as an alternative to the fixed costs model of Hanoch and Cogan. Heckman argues that the issue is not so much fixed costs, but the limited availability of low-cost child care. These are conceptually distinct models and their implications are contrasted.

Giora Hanoch's "A Multivariate Model of Labor Supply: Methodology and Estimation," is a tour de force in dealing with a wide variety of estimation problems. In addition to incorporating Heckman's correction for participation selectivity bias, he considers a number of issues previously ignored or not included in a fully integrated system. First, based on his theoretical model in "Hours and Weeks in a Theory of Labor Supply," Hanoch's econometric method allows for the simultaneous joint determination of the supply of annual hours and weeks of work. The common practice in empirical research had been to treat these separately as two alternative, but unrelated, definitions of labor supply. The most fundamental contribution of this paper involves the impact of fixed costs of work. Since fixed time or money costs of work will impart a discontinuity in the supply function, the reservation wage at which an individual enters the market occurs at a positive quantity of working hours. If fixed costs are important, estimates of labor supply functions that ignore this discontinuity would seriously overestimate the measured wage elasticity of labor supply. In spite of the emphasis given to the zero truncation of working hours, there are probably corner limits that are as pervasive. One obvious restriction is that individuals cannot work more than 52 weeks per year. This 52 week limit imposes constraints on the responsiveness of the supply of weeks and annual hours as individuals approach the point of full-time work. Hanoch suggests methods that deal with this upper truncation in the estimation of labor supply. Finally, he considers the survey week selectivity bias that is ignored in all other research. In many data sets, information on hours worked during a week is only available for individuals who worked during the survey week. Because of this, analysts have restricted their empirical studies to those who have positive weeks and positive hours of work in the survey week. But survey week workers are not a random sample of all workers. If the survey week is a random week during the year, the people most likely to be found working are those with the largest weeks worked in the previous year. Hence, the probability of working during the survey week should be proportional to the fraction of weeks in a year that one works. Hanoch develops a statistical technique that controls for this bias. Instead of estimating his complex model with fully efficient, but expensive, methods, Hanoch outlines a step-by-step estimation procedure that is less costly to execute and quite feasible with existing computer programs. His model is estimated using a subsample of white married women from the 1967 Survey of Economic Opportunity.

The effect of time and money costs on labor supply is treated in greater depth in John Cogan's "Labor Supply with Costs of Labor Market Entry." The standard theoretical treatments of these costs analyze separately the impact of exogenous fixed time and money costs. Both time and money costs impart a discontinuity to the labor supply function, but they have different predictions about the extent of work among participants. Fixed money costs of work increase the hours worked of participants while fixed time costs reduce observed hours of workers. More realistically, Cogan contends that individuals have the potential to trade off time and money costs and that this choice depends in part on their earning capacity. The decision of where to live relative to place of work, the type and form of child-care arrangements, and the mode of transportation to work all indicate that such substitution possibilities exist. Cogan constructs a theoretical model in which people are confronted not with rigidly determined time or money costs, but rather with a locus of points representing all possible combinations of time and money costs of work. An individual chooses not only his desired bundle of leisure and market goods, but he must also minimize the cost of engaging in work. The comparative statics of this model are developed and the close link that exists between the labor supply function and the function describing the trade-off between time and money costs of work is illustrated. Cogan outlines a statistical method for estimating a labor supply function with endogenous time and money costs. The data used in Cogan's empirical analysis is taken from the 1976 Survey of the Michigan Panel of Income Dynamics.

The large quantity of empirical work presented in the volume precludes any attempt to summarize it completely. Instead, I will highlight those results relating to the two behavioral functions that form the core of our research—the wage and labor supply equations. The hope is to identify the major similarities and differences emerging from the separate papers.

Four of the papers offer evidence on the importance of selectivity bias in female wage functions. Cogan (Chapter 2) contrasts OLS wage regressions with those obtained with Heckman's maximum likelihood procedure, while Heckman (Chapter 5), Hanoch (Chapter 6), and Cogan (Chapter 7) employ the censoring correction proposed by Heckman (Chapter 5). Although each study adopts a different specification of the wage function using three separate data sets, a strikingly consistent story emerges. Any evaluation of the impact of sample censoring depends partly on the underlying reason for estimating a wage function. One may be interested primarily in predicting wages for women, in retrieving structural parameters in the wage functions, or simply in obtaining an instrument to be used in another equation (i.e., labor supply). The general consensus appears to be that sample censoring is a real but not overwhelming issue in the estimation of female wage functions. The estimated coefficients on λ are nontrivial (from .087 to .1282), but only in Hanoch's essay is the statistical significance impressive. All four studies report that OLS overpredicts wages of all women by a moderate amount. Evaluated at the mean characteristics in the respective samples, the OLS point estimates exceed the true average wage offer for women by 5.3 to 11.1 percent.[1] However, since OLS predicts the same wage for women independent of their current labor force status, this bias becomes considerably more severe when

---

[1] In the individual studies, the OLS wage prediction exceeds the mean wage offer by 5.3 percent (Cogan, Chapter 7), 5.5 percent (Heckman), 7.8 percent (Cogan, Chapter 2), and 11.1 percent (Hanoch).

imputing wages to nonworking women. For example, the studies by Heckman and Hanoch imply that OLS overstates wages for nonparticipants by over 20 percent. If wage equations are not corrected for censoring bias, the potential wages of nonworking women will apparently be substantially exaggerated.

Cogan and Heckman present OLS equations alongside the censored adjusted wage regressions. These comparisons, which are summarized in Table I.1, can be used to detect the magnitude of the sample-selection bias on individual parameters. The effect of sample censoring on the education coefficient appears to be very minor, producing only a slight underestimate. Ironically, it was partly the concern over a potential bias in the return to schooling that motivated the original research on censoring. In contrast, the coefficient on market experience does differ markedly. The OLS estimates of the return to market experience range from 15 percent (Cogan, Chapter 7) to 29 percent (Cogan, Chapter 2) below the true parameter, with Heckman's 22

TABLE I.1: Comparison of Female Wage Equations
(*standard errors in parentheses below coefficients*)

	Cogan, Chapter 2 Corrected[b] for Censoring	OLS	Heckman, Chapter 5 Corrected for Censoring	OLS	Cogan,[a] Chapter 7 Corrected for Censoring	OLS
Education	.0879 (.0074)	.0854 (.0073)	.0779 (.0057)	.0763 (.0056)	.096 (.007)	.092 (.007)
Experience	.0259 (.0046)	.0184 (.0030)	.0207 (.0035)	.0167 (.0021)	.251[c] (.042)	.213 (.026)
Constant	−.8761 (.206)	−.7176 (.191)	−.515	−.401	−.212 (.136)	−.113 (.105)
λ				.0878 (.059)	.088 (.076)	
Data Source	1967 National Longitudinal Survey		1967 National Longitudinal Survey		Michigan Income Dynamics	

[a] Cogan also included variables for southwest residence and age which were not altered by the selectivity correction.

[b] Based on Heckman's maximum likelihood procedure developed in Heckman (1974b).

[c] Cogan's variable is the log of market experience.

percent in an intermediate position. Apparently, selectivity bias produces a serious underestimate of the true impact of market experience on female wages. This sensitivity of the experience variable is not surprising in view of the high correlation of past market experience with the current participation decision. Finally, OLS systematically overestimates the intercept in all three studies. The difference in intercepts alone implies that OLS overstates the mean wage offer by 10 to 20 percent.

The only study that offers any evidence of the use of an OLS instrumental wage is Cogan's (Chapter 2). Cogan estimates a labor supply function for all women, using an instrumental wage from an OLS regression. The resulting measured wage elasticity exceeds the Heckman maximum likelihood estimate by 25 percent. This was expected, since OLS tends to overstate wages more for low-wage women thereby compressing the wage differences among women. However, none of the coefficients on the other variables in the labor supply function appear to be affected by the use of the wage instrument. Additional experimentation will be necessary before any final assessment on the use of the instrumental wage can be obtained.

While the similarity among these studies is encouraging, one should be cautious before extrapolating our results to other data sets and demographic groups. Because of the nonlinear nature of Heckman's censoring technique, wage equations estimated from other samples with different average economic and demographic characteristics may be quite different from those included in this volume. Moreover, the censoring correction is derived from the behavioral participation function. Schultz's evidence in Chapter 1 suggests that participation equations differ significantly across race and age groups. In view of this, it would not be surprising if future research provides a different view of the effect of censored samples on female wage functions.[2]

In contrast to the general uniformity of estimates for the wage equation, there is much more disagreement among the essays on the appropriate labor supply function. This partially reflects a dispute concerning the appropriate structural labor supply model, and also is a result of some sticky statistical problems in identification. The main theoretical contention concerns the possible existence of a discontinuity in the labor supply function due to fixed costs, as argued by

---

[2] For example, Smith (1979) reports a negative coefficient for λ in a sample of black women.

Cogan and Hanoch. I will summarize the results in the three main areas that deal with labor supply functions: the choice of linear and nonlinear methods of estimation, the importance of selectivity bias, and the existence of fixed costs.

Schultz reports experiments contrasting simple linear (OLS) and nonlinear maximum likelihood estimates. The Tobit expected value locus and the OLS supply function (estimated over all women) produce quite similar results at the sample means, indicating that OLS is a good linear approximation to Tobit. As one might suspect, they diverge significantly as we move away from the sample means. The conceptual advantage of Tobit is that one can also derive the index function. Although the expected value locus by incorporating the zero truncation of hours is the aggregrate labor supply function, the coefficients of the Tobit index reflect the parameters of the individual's utility function, in particular income and substituting effects. For some purposes, we are more interested in testing hypotheses about these utility parameters. Similarly, Schultz's OLS and logistic participation equations are almost identical when evaluated at the means. Apparently, these computationally less expensive linear methods provide useful guidance to the applied researcher in searching for an appropriate model specification, at least in situations where the data are not bunched at one of the extremes (mostly zeros or ones). The advantages of the nonlinear Tobit and logit (or probit) are mainly increased reliability of predictions for demographic groups that are not representative of the sample means. This general conclusion appears to be consistent with applied research reported in areas other than labor supply.

To fix ideas on selectivity bias and fixed costs, Figures I.2 and I.3 present labor supply functions with and without a discontinuity. In Figure I.2, the true supply function for the individual is the index line. However, because of the truncation of hours at zero (the decision of some women not to participate in the labor force), the expected number of working hours per female can be obtained from the expected value locus. This is the labor supply function in the sense that it measures at each wage the average amount of work effort per woman. Finally, an OLS labor supply function for workers will approximate the means of these distributions conditional on positive hours of work. The distance between the OLS function for workers and the index line measures the extent of selectivity bias at each wage. In

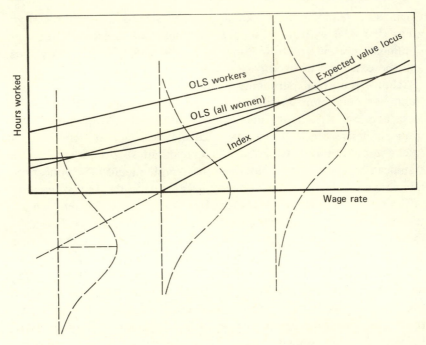

FIGURE I.2   Labor supply function without discontinuity

Figure I.3, the labor supply model with fixed costs is graphed. Because fixed costs eliminate the close link between the parameters of the participation and hours function (the parameters are proportional without fixed costs), the point at which the reservation wage equals the market wage can occur at a positive quantity of hours. If the discontinuity is large, the zero truncation will in fact be relatively unimportant for workers, and the slope of an OLS function over workers will closely approximate the index function. Thus the importance of selectivity may be severely diminished when the discontinuity is sufficiently large. For illustrative purposes, I have also placed in Figure I.3 the estimated index function that results from ignoring the discontinuity (and hence imposes an inappropriate constraint). Clearly this function can be considerably more elastic than the true index.

The papers by Schultz and Cogan (Chapter 2) were written prior to the work on fixed costs so they, of course, do not test the validity of the constraints imposed by ignoring a possible discontinuity in the labor supply function. Within the context of a no fixed costs model

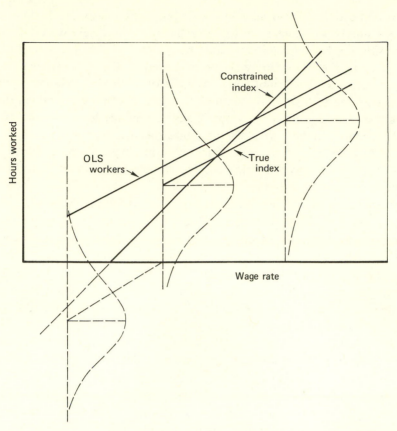

FIGURE I.3   Labor supply function with discontinuity

(Figure I.2), both studies provide evidence on the appropriateness of
the two conventional methods of estimating labor supply functions—
OLS over a sample of workers, and by the full sample of women with
an instrumental OLS wage. Their OLS labor supply equations estimated over the sample of working women have substantially smaller
wage elasticities than corresponding functions using the full sample of
women. As is evident from Figure I.2 (where the OLS line is less
steep), this is consistent with an important role for selectivity bias in
the labor supply function. Cogan also reports that the OLS function on
workers underpredicts reservation wages (which Cogan estimates as
often being negative), so that nearly every woman is predicted to be a
market participant. When an OLS instrumental wage is used in a Tobit

function estimated over all women, Cogan's estimates indicate the true labor supply wage elasticity is overestimated. Intuitively we are compressing the horizontal (wage) axis by the use of this instrument and overstating the labor supply elasticity. Based on these two studies, it is clear that when we do not allow for a discontinuity in the labor supply function, the data strongly support the presence of a significant censoring bias in labor supply functions. Conventional methods of estimating labor supply relations will seriously bias the true response.

Unfortunately, the story becomes more muddled when the possibility of a discontinuity is considered. The three essays that allow both for selectivity bias and fixed costs are Heckman, Hanoch (Chapter 6), and Cogan (Chapter 7). The divergence between the estimates reflects the trade-off in the data between a discontinuous labor supply function and sample censoring. Heckman finds little support for the fixed costs model, but an important role for selectivity bias in labor supply functions. In contrast, the discontinuity in Cogan's labor supply equation is quite large (1,151 hours) so that for women who work, the zero truncation of hours is unimportant. Because of this, an OLS function estimated over workers may closely approximate the individual labor supply function. Hanoch reports evidence in favor of both fixed costs and selectivity. The minimum entry hours estimated by him are smaller (870 annual hours), allowing for an independent role for censoring. Both Hanoch and Cogan report relatively small wage elasticities in an individual's supply function, indicating that much of the adjustment in hours worked occurs through the participation response. Particularly intriguing in this regard is that, according to Hanoch, at high female wages when women work full-time work years, the labor supply function becomes backward bending resembling those estimated for males. In contrast, the wage response in the individual labor supply function estimated by Heckman is much larger. Heckman argues for an alternative definition of hours worked based on dividing earnings by the wage rate. This definition apparently fills out the hours density at low wages and partially accounts for the absence of a discontinuity in his paper.

Even if there were no disagreement about the correct structural labor supply model, the statistical problems in identifying labor supply functions alone would be severe. The major defect is that we have no strong a priori information for distinguishing between factors affecting participation decisions and those that affect hours, given participation.

As such, the estimated λ normally includes the same variables as those included directly in the individual labor supply function. Although λ is not ordinarily a linear function of these variables, the potential for collinearity is there. In practice, this has evidently presented estimation problems, and thus the inability of the data to enable us to discriminate clearly between alternative structural labor supply models may not be surprising.

With a problem as complex and far-reaching as labor supply and wages, the final chapter will never be written. Although we believe that these essays may have advanced the state of the art, many issues are unresolved and puzzles abound. Even within these essays, there is disagreement about the relative importance of sample censoring and fixed costs. Many fundamental methodological questions relating to experimental design and estimation of the data from the income maintenance experiments remain unanswered and are not even touched upon in this volume. The sensitivity of some of the estimation techniques advanced here to alternative specifications of the model is open to serious scholarly question. A limitation in all this work is that we do not take advantage of the longitudinal information available from many recent panel data sets. Panel data have considerable potential for addressing issues that are impossible to analyze with individual cross-sectional data sets. The question of persistent and transitory components of labor force participation over time and the estimation of life-cycle models using panel data require major statistical and theoretical innovations. But all that must remain the subject of future work.

ACKNOWLEDGMENTS

I am indebted to The Rand Corporation for supporting the rewriting and editing necessary to turn the original manuscripts into a book.

CHAPTER 1

ESTIMATING LABOR SUPPLY
FUNCTIONS FOR MARRIED WOMEN

T. PAUL SCHULTZ
YALE UNIVERSITY

I. INTRODUCTION

There are ample reasons to refine nonexperimental cross-sectional
estimates of labor supply parameters in light of continuing advances in
conceptual and statistical methodology (Cain and Watts, 1973). First,
from a policy standpoint, more precise parameters of long-run labor
supply functions would help in the design and administration of
welfare reform legislation.

Second, and central to the research strategy of this investigation,
there is a growing awareness that many aspects of family decision-
making over the life cycle are interrelated, implying that unexplained
deviations or disturbances in individual behavior are related over time
and across different behavioral outcomes (Nerlove and Schultz, 1970).
Problems of simultaneous equation bias in disentangling behavioral
relations underlying labor market behavior are undoubtedly more
severe in the case of married women than of married men. For
example, age at marriage, cumulative fertility, the presence of young
children in the household, prior experience in the labor force, and
market wage offers are all behaviorally interrelated with a wife's
current labor supply decisions, and all are probably influenced by
common exogenous factors. Inclusion of these relatively endogenous
and in certain instances error-prone variables directly in the conditional analysis of labor market behavior is likely to have biased past
estimates of the long-run responsiveness of married women's labor
supply.[1] To evaluate the consequences of proposed welfare reforms,

---

[1] Heckman in Chapter 5 proposes a test of the endogenous nature of the wife's prior
labor market experience in accounting for current labor supply, and provides evidence of
its endogeneity.

for example, it is necessary to estimate not only short-run adjustments of labor supply conditioned on these endogenous variables, but also to consider long-run repercussions, allowing these other aspects of household behavior to adapt to new institutional and economic environments. Since the identification problems involved in this approach are formidable, it may be necessary to settle on estimating partially reduced form equations in which such outcomes as fertility or family composition are implicitly solved out of the estimation equation.

Third, many statistical problems in estimating labor supply functions call for special treatment, and though they have often been neglected in the study of men, they cannot be ignored in the study of married women. These problems occur because a large proportion of married women do not participate in the market labor force, and occupy a corner solution in their allocation of time between market and nonmarket activities. This volume addresses some of these issues: the discrete labor force entry decision, complicated by noncontinuous costs of entry; a distribution of market job options that is not independent over hours and wages; the time allocation process as essentially multidimensional in character, admitting to a variety of measurement conventions such as hours per day and week, and days and weeks per year. Nonlinear maximum likelihood estimation techniques seem more appropriate than ordinary linear regression to the analysis of dichotomous decisions, such as labor force participation, and limited dependent variables, such as hours worked. However, with these nonlinear models, simultaneous equation estimation techniques do not always have well-established statistical properties. Subsequent studies in this book address this problem at greater length, and develop estimation and computational techniques.

Where firm theoretical or convincing empirical guidance is now lacking, the specification and estimation of labor supply models will remain controversial. For example, how is one to choose among identifying restrictions? The choice of instruments to identify one relationship may merely introduce other endogenous variables resulting in biased and unstable parameter estimates. Where are nonlinearities and discontinuities important, and how should predictive errors be compared across methodologies? Which variables are appropriately treated in a particular context as endogenous and which as exogenous or at least predetermined? I suspect that the answers to these questions will emerge only as alternative approaches to new sources of survey data begin to evidence regularities that are insensitive to seemingly minor matters of variable definition, sample composition, and estimation technique. Much work remains to be done before this stage of consensus is achieved, but there has also been palpable progress in this direction, as documented in this volume.

To estimate labor supply parameters that could be useful to policymakers, a number of relatively strong assumptions are needed. If simple and sophisticated formulations of the labor supply model lead to essentially the same outcome, those sources of bias implicit in the simple approach can be pragmatically neglected, while refinement of model specification and estimation proceeds in those areas where different approaches imply substantial differences in policy-relevant parameter estimates.

Section II of this paper presents the time-allocation-labor supply framework and explores alternative specifications for the underlying structural equations determining market demand and individual supply functions. Section III discusses the empirical specification of the model and the data used to obtain the estimates reported in Section IV. The fifth and final section sums up how these empirical findings differ from earlier studies and discusses their implications for policy and further research.

II. The General Framework and Problems of Estimation

The objective of any labor supply study is to explain the decision of the wife whether to participate in the market labor force, P, and if she does, the number of hours to work in this activity per year, H. The expected supply of labor, L, can then be expressed as the product of the expected probability of participation and the expected hours worked, conditional on participation. Consumer demand theory, when simplified to a single period framework without uncertainty, implies that an individual's demand for time to engage in nonmarket activities can be expressed as a function of his own market wage offer, market prices, nonearned market income, and peculiar tastes and talents that are initially assumed to be distributed randomly across populations.[2]

---

[2] These are later interpreted as a difference of unobserved factors affecting market and nonmarket productivities and tastes. Cogan, Chapter 2, examines at a more formal level how simplifying assumptions widely made in the empirical literature can bias parameter estimates.

To extend this framework to a two-person household, in particular that of a husband and wife, only one additional market price variable, the wage offer available to the other spouse, must be added to the list of factors determining the reduced-form demand equations for nonmarket time if both spouses engage in some market activity (Heckman, 1971; Ashenfelter and Heckman, 1973).

This classical demand approach to labor supply functions yields several well-known predictions. The income-compensated own-wage effect of either spouse on the household's demand for his nonmarket time is negative (i.e., own-price effect). The influence of increased real income, holding household technology, market wage offers, and prices constant, is to increase or to decrease demand for nonmarket activities depending on whether the final (unobserved) composite product of nonmarket activities is a normal or inferior good. The income-compensated cross-wage effect, namely, the compensated effect of one spouse's market wage offer on the household's demand for the *other* spouse's nonmarket time, is positive or negative depending on whether nonmarket time of one spouse is a substitute or complement for the nonmarket time of the other spouse in the household. Regardless of the sign, symmetry conditions imply equality for both compensated cross-wage effects. When one estimates the mirror image of the demand for nonmarket time, or the supply of labor to the market, all of the above signs of the effects are, of course, reversed.

SPECIFICATION OF THE STRUCTURAL MODEL

The labor supply behavior of each spouse is determined by two relationships: (1) the market wage offer or *market demand function, W,* and (2) the shadow value of time in nonmarket activities or the *individual's supply function, S.*

$$W = f(Z, \varepsilon_1), \tag{1.1}$$

$$S = g(X, \varepsilon_2), \tag{1.2}$$

where Z and X are vectors of possibly overlapping endogenous and exogenous variables that affect the market demand wage, W, and the individual supply wage, S, respectively, and ε_1 and ε_2 are two, not necessarily independent, normally distributed random disturbances that undoubtedly embody errors in measurement, the effects of many minor omitted variables, and purely stochastic variability. Both of these relationships are probably a function of the number of hours worked in the market. The inclusion of at least one variable among the Z's that is excluded from the X's, and vice versa, permits one to identify statistically the supply from the demand functions in the household labor market.

An interior equilibrium occurs if the schedules intersect and the slope of the individual supply wage function, with respect to hours worked, exceeds (positively) the slope of the market demand wage function.

If the two wage functions are assumed linear, as illustrated in Figure 1.1, we have the following

$$W_i = \alpha_0 + \alpha_1 H_i + \alpha_2 Z_i + \varepsilon_{1i} \qquad (1.3)$$
$$S_i = \beta_0 + \beta_1 H_i + \beta_2 X_i + \varepsilon_{2i} \qquad i = 1, \ldots, n \qquad (1.4)$$

where i refers to individuals and the α's and β's are parameters to be estimated.

When no market work is undertaken, the reservation or supply wage for entry into market work is denoted S_0, where $H = 0$. The market offer provided for the first hour worked in the market is similarly denoted W_0. The individual participates in the labor force if W_0 exceeds S_0, and works some amount, say H^*, in Figure 1.1, where the marginal value of time in market and nonmarket activities is equal. For these interior equilibria $W^* = W = S$ for the observed H^*. The individual does not participate if $W_0 < S_0$, and in this case the levels of both the supply and the demand functions are not directly observed.

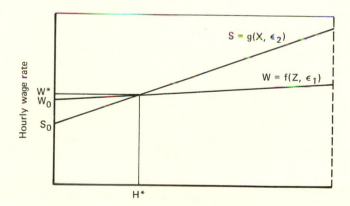

FIGURE 1.1   Hours supplied to the market

Solving equations 1.3 and 1.4 for the labor supply, one obtains

$$H_i = \frac{1}{\beta_1 - \alpha_1}(\alpha_0 - \beta_0 + \alpha_2 Z_i - \beta_2 X_i) + \frac{\varepsilon_{1i} - \varepsilon_{2i}}{\beta_1 - \alpha_1}, \qquad (1.5)$$

if
$$\alpha_0 - \beta_0 + \alpha_2 Z_i - \beta_2 X_i > \varepsilon_{2i} - \varepsilon_{1i}, \qquad (1.6)$$

and otherwise,

$$H_i = 0.$$

Market participation occurs if inequality 1.6 obtains, in which case the number of hours worked in the market is determined by equation 1.5. Otherwise, hours worked is definitionally zero for nonparticipants.

Expected hours worked is proportional to the difference between the systematic components of the individual's demand and supply functions, if this difference is positive, where the factor of proportionality, $1/(\beta_1 - \alpha_1)$, is the slope of this excess labor demand schedule with respect to hours worked in the market. Illustrated in Figure 1.2, this framework lends itself to maximum likelihood estimators proposed by Tobin (1955, 1958).

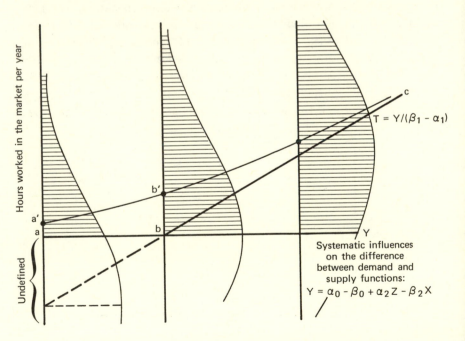

FIGURE 1.2   The distribution of hours worked in the market

Unexplained individual deviations in the hours worked decision (about the Tobit Index, T) are reduced to the composite disturbance

$$v_i = \frac{\varepsilon_{1i} - \varepsilon_{2i}}{\beta_1 - \alpha_1},$$

that is assumed normally distributed with zero mean, constant variance, and, of course, distributed independently of X and Z.[3]

The expected value locus of H given Y, when there is no residual variance, i.e., $\sigma_v^2 = 0$, is two line segments abc. But allowing disturbances, i.e., $\sigma_v^2 > 0$, the expected value locus of hours worked per person, which is the market labor supply, becomes a nonlinear function of Y, approximately $a'b'c$ in Figure 1.2. Individuals do not enter the market labor force if $T_i > -v_i$. At point b, where the Tobit index equals zero, half of the population participates in the market labor force, and participants work, on average, twice as many hours as expected for the entire population.

This general framework is used here for interpreting labor market behavior. Though not always expressed in precisely these terms, most previous attempts to estimate "labor supply functions" can be viewed as imposing particular restrictions on this general model in order to obtain parameter estimates that describe one or both dimensions of the labor supply phenomenon.

MEASUREMENT PROBLEMS WITH MARKET WAGE RATES

From an economist's perspective, the most important explanatory variable in a labor supply equation is the market wage rate. In this section, I discuss some problems in using available information on

[3] The normal random disturbance assumption is, of course, valid if the component errors, ε_1 and ε_2, are independent and normally distributed. At the opposite extreme, if the two component errors are perfectly positively correlated with identical variances, the errors in the supply and demand functions would cancel out and exert no net influence on the participation and hours worked decisions. Efforts to estimate with full information techniques the supply and demand functions for married women have yielded large positive correlations between these two errors, suggesting that omitted factors influence in the same direction productivity in market and nonmarket activities. Heckman (1974b) obtained estimates of .65 and .83 for white women age 35 to 44, depending upon the unit of time considered, respectively, hours or weeks worked per year. Olsen (1974) obtained estimates ranging from .75 to .99 for alternative age groups with various identifying restrictions. The magnitude of the error variances from Heckman's model were almost identical, particularly when weeks worked per year is used as the measure of labor supply. Olsen's error variance estimates were more diverse.

market wage rates. First, observed wage rates are derived in most data sources by dividing market earnings by hours worked in the labor force during the relevant period, either a year or a week. Errors in reporting hours worked are thereby transmitted inversely to the measured market wage rate, biasing down directly estimated effects of the measured wage rate on labor supplied to the market.[4]

A second problem in obtaining an adequate measure of wages for secondary workers is the simultaneous equations bias. Past decisions regarding labor market participation and market- or nonmarket-specific training will be reflected over time in current market wage offers. But since these earlier decisions are jointly and simultaneously determined with current labor market behavior, the current market wage outcome is itself endogenous. To estimate long-run labor supply response parameters, an appropriate exogenous wage rate would be wage opportunities available to an individual at the outset of the marriage and adult life-cycle planning period. This source of parameter bias implies that for at least older married women, the direct relation between an error-free measure of current market wages and market labor supply would be positively biased (overstated) from the "true" relation that is sought here between life-cycle wage opportunities and labor supply.

A third and related source of parameter bias stressed by Mincer (1962) is the confounding effect of transitory variation in market wages, which would also appear to bias up (positively) compensated own-wage effects and bias down the wealth or pure income effects embodied in the effect of current wages on current labor supply.

Finally, variation in marginal taxes on market earnings and prices (the market purchasing power of money) may systematically affect the real market wage across the sample, adding additional potentially endogenous complications to measuring the appropriate market wage variable.

These problems of measuring, without systematic error, permanent (life-cycle) market wage opportunities may be resolved, or at least alleviated, by replacing the observed market wage rate with an instrumental variable estimator inferred from the sample of workers for whom market wages are observed (see Hall, 1973). This auxiliary instrumental variable equation might be interpreted, under certain

---

[4] More precisely, biasing the estimated elasticity of labor supply with respect to own wages toward minus one.

assumptions, as the market demand structural equation 1.3, having been estimated by single equation techniques. Gronau (1974) has stressed that this interpretation neglects selectivity bias, for unexplained variation in market wages will tend to be associated with condition 1.6, and hence, with inclusion of the observation in the working sample.[5] In this case, the parameter estimates of the instrumental variable market wage equation do not provide a consistent or asymptotically unbiased basis to infer market wage offers for the population of workers or nonworkers.

SELECTIVITY BIAS

But how serious is this bias? If the residual variation in the correctly specified equation 1.3, namely, $\sigma^2_{\varepsilon_1}$, could be entirely attributed to errors in measuring wages, and therefore, were independent of the selection of the observation for the "working" sample, there would be no selectivity bias. Also, as labor force participation within a group became universal, the bias would vanish as the observed wage for any Z approached the expected value of the market wage offer for that Z. Other things being equal, the bias would therefore appear more serious in the analysis of secondary workers such as married women than for the study of market wages of males between the ages of 25 and 55.

More generally, if an instrumental variable in the market wage equation is correlated with the probability of participation, its coefficient in the market wage equation will tend to be biased by the systematic censorship of data.[6] Moreover, since supply determinants, in addition to demand determinants, might plausibly influence observed market wages, it is not clear whether a market demand wage equation or a reduced form equation inclusive of both demand and supply factors should be estimated. Several examples of different sources of selectivity bias may illustrate the problem.

[5] See Cogan, Chapter 2, for a discussion on the direction of bias.

[6] See Cogan, Chapter 2: a way to evaluate selectivity bias for some variables, Z^*, among Z but not X, is to include them in the estimation of the labor market behavior equation (1.5), in addition to the instrumental estimate of the market wage rate based on Z. If these demand variables exert an independent effect on labor "supply" in addition to that "transmitted" via their effect on the instrumental market wage variable, selectivity bias in coefficients for Z^* in the instrumental market wage equation is indicated. Alternatively, this could be interpreted as suggesting that Z^* is also among the supply determinants.

Some variable in Z might be omitted from the estimated demand function, such as ability (Griliches and Mason, 1972; Hause, 1972), quality of schooling (Welch, 1973), or taste for market work, and persons with this "ability" might be offered higher market wages and be more frequently found in the "working" sample, other things being equal. Even if this "ability" is uncorrelated with explanatory variables included in the market demand function, intercept estimates based on the censored "working" sample are biased because the criterion for censorship depends positively on "ability." In this instance, the "predicted" market wage offer for nonworkers would tend to exceed the "expected" market wage offer. Observed proxies for "ability" might be used, or information on individuals over time assembled, in order to infer the nature of the covariance structure between unobserved components in the residual disturbances.[7]

More complex characterizations of the market clearing process might provide additional explanations for selectivity bias related to *supply determinants*. Suppose an individual faces not a single market wage offer but a distribution of wage offers (Ben-Porath, 1973a; Lewis, 1972; Gronau, 1974), and the time he is willing to search for the highest paying job depends directly on his household's physical net worth. The expected market wage offer *accepted*, and hence observed in the working sample, becomes a positive function of his household's net worth under rather general assumptions (Danforth, 1974).

Bias resulting from estimating market wages as though they were determined only by the demand function, without reference to the supply function, can be appraised in an unrigorous but simple way by comparing demand and reduced form specifications. In this study, the instrumental variable market wage equation based first only on the demand determinants and then with the additional supply determinants was estimated. The F ratio was then calculated to test whether the additional supply determinants reduce the residual variance of wage rates by a statistically "significant" amount. The null hypothesis of no supply effects is sustained in two out of three cases, suggesting that the reduced form model for market wage rates is not a significant improvement over the naive demand model used later in this chapter.

---

[7] Several studies, although they have not yet dealt directly with the censorship problem, have identified structural models containing unobserved factors by restricting how these unobserved factors enter into the determination of several different relations. See Goldberger (1972b), Griliches (1973).

In this investigation, the problems associated with error-prone measures of market wages are likely to be of greater quantitative significance than the selectivity bias from the censored information available only from workers. Therefore, the strategy followed here will be to estimate for the sample of persons with reported wages an instrumental variable wage equation by single equation methods, and use these estimates to impute market wage offers to all persons within the stratified group (see Appendix A).

Yet further complications must be faced if the effect of taxation on the family joint supply of labor is deemed important. This would seem particularly relevant to a married woman, whose marginal tax on market earnings depends to a considerable extent on her husband's wage and hours worked, and her household's other income. Imputed market wage offers obtained from the instrumental variable wage equation are, therefore, multiplied by one minus the estimated marginal tax rate for the household, and adjusted for differences in relative prices by region, area of residence, and income class of the family (see Appendix B).[8] Both the tax rate and the region of residence are to some degree choice variables, but are for simplicity treated here as exogenous. This seemingly appropriate adjustment for taxes and price level has no distinct effect on the labor supply parameter estimates reported later.

APPROACHES TO ESTIMATION OF THE LABOR MARKET MODEL

Heckman (1974b) provides the most general and attractive exposition of, and estimation approach to, the labor market. He assumes that the market demand wage function is independent of hours worked, in other words, $\alpha_1 = 0$—a strong assumption, but one implicit in most studies of earnings functions (e.g., Mincer, 1974). If condition 1.6 obtains, and labor force participation occurs, then two reduced form equations follow:

$$W_i = \alpha_0 + \alpha_2 Z_i + \varepsilon_{1i} \tag{1.7}$$

$$H_i = \frac{1}{\beta_1}(\alpha_0 - \beta_0 + \alpha_2 Z_i - \beta_2 X_i) + v_i, \tag{1.8}$$

otherwise, $H_i = 0$, and W_i is not observed.

[8] Nonemployment income should also be deflated by the price level, but probably not by the full marginal tax rate. The appropriate tax rate is unclear and no adjustment is performed in the empirical treatment of either nonemployment income or the stock form of this variable-net worth.

A likelihood function is formed using conditional information on both workers and nonworkers. Nonlinear iterative search methods are applied to maximize this function, and parameters are obtained to the joint underlying structural equations. Aside from the computational burden of Heckman's original (1974b) full information maximum likelihood estimation approach, his empirical specification treats the prior labor market experience of the woman, and the number of children under six in the household (or recent fertility), as exogenous. A main objective of this study is to treat women's market wages, their accumulated labor force experience, and fertility as all endogenous to the long-run labor market behavior of wives.[9] The remainder of this section explores several simplifications of the labor market model that permit the application of single equation methods to estimate the parameters of the labor market model.

Two issues underlie the alternative estimation approaches: (1) whether to seek estimates of the structural supply and demand equations at the cost of admitting selectivity bias by imputing market wages according to single equation instrumental variable methods, or to obtain less ambitious but consistent estimates of the reduced form equation for the labor market; and (2) whether to assume that the participation and hours worked decisions are determined by separable functions, or that both outcomes arise from an integrated censoring process, as implied by the Tobit framework presented earlier.[10]

I. The first approach simplifies Heckman's model by estimating equations 1.7 and 1.8 sequentially, and assumes that the market demand wage equation 1.7 estimated for those with reported wages is an adequate basis for imputing wage rates to those with and without observed wages. The second stage estimates of labor market behavior can be based on the assumption that the participation and hours

---

[9] It should be noted that Heckman in his subsequent analysis of this problem presented in Chapter 5 concludes that there is statistical evidence for the endogenous treatment of labor market experiences, and indeed more plausible parameter values are obtained under that working assumption. However, Cogan, Heckman, and Hanoch in their various subsequent chapters all rely upon the number of preschool-aged children in the household as an exogenous variable to determine the shadow value of nonmarket time of the reservation wage. One might conclude that their estimates are, therefore, likely to approximate short-run responses, holding reproductive behavior constant.

[10] Olsen has proposed a general maximum likelihood formulation for study of the participation and hours decision, that includes the Tobit as a special homogeneous case.

worked decisions arise from a single Tobit framework:

$$H_i = \frac{1}{\beta_1}(\hat{W}_i - \beta_0 - \beta_2 X_i) + \varepsilon_{2i}/\beta_1, \tag{1.9}$$

if
$$\beta_0 + \beta_2 X_1 - \hat{W}_1 > \varepsilon_{2i}; \tag{1.10}$$

otherwise, $H_1 = 0$, where

$$\hat{W}_i = \hat{\alpha}_0 + \hat{\alpha}_2 Z_i \quad \text{for} \quad i = 1, 2, \ldots, m, \ldots, n. \tag{1.11}$$

In this case, one of the variables in X would be this instrumental variable imputed wage for the husband. Estimates of the market demand equation 1.11 are potentially subject to selectivity and specification bias, but on the other hand, they permit one to disentangle the demand and supply functions simply. As indicated earlier, this scheme is beyond reproach only in the deterministic case where the variance in market wages unexplained by the instruments is caused by errors in measurement, and hence there is no stochastic disturbance ε_1.[11]

Estimates from this Tobit framework can be readily compared to ordinary least squares estimates of equation 1.9 that neglect the censorship bias and provide a linear approximation for nonlinear expected value locus of H given Y. However, the Tobit framework implies not only the aggregate expected supply of labor, but also the participation rate. The Tobit index parameters can also be readily transformed into the individual supply equation 1.4.

II. The same empirical specification can be adopted as in formulation I, but the participation decision and hours worked decision are estimated separately, in the first case for the entire population (n), and in the second case only for labor force participants (m).

$$P_i = \frac{1}{\beta_1}(\hat{W}_i - \beta_0 - \beta_2 X_i) + v_i \quad \text{for} \quad i = 1, 2, \ldots, m, \ldots n. \tag{1.12}$$

$$H_i = \frac{1}{\beta_1^*}(\hat{W}_i - \beta_0^* - \beta_2^* X_i) + v_i^* \quad \text{for} \quad i = 1, 2, \ldots, m. \tag{1.13}$$

If the Tobit framework is appropriate, the sign and statistical significance of the related parameters should be similar. The relative magnitude of the participation and hours elasticities would also depend on

---

[11] Subsequent studies by Cogan in Chapter 2 and Heckman in Chapter 5 suggest that selectivity bias in the estimation of the market wage equation is probably not serious, at least in comparison with selectivity or censoring bias in estimating the labor supply equation. It is unclear, however, whether including among the instruments linear and squared terms in "children less than six" does not simply open the door to other closely related life-cycle *endogenous* variables that confound the purpose of the test reported by Heckman in Table 5.2 of Chapter 5.

the level of participation in the group. Since the dependent variable in equation 1.12 is dichotomous, equal to one if the individual is currently in the market labor force and zero otherwise, ordinary least squares estimates of this equation are not ideal.[12] The more realistic logistic model is assumed, therefore, and maximum likelihood estimates calculated.

The product of the estimated values of equations 1.12 and 1.13 is equal to the expected value of the entire population's labor supply if the disturbances across equations, v_1 and v_1^*, are uncorrelated in the probability limit with the explanatory variables.[13] It is more plausible to anticipate that the disturbances will be positively correlated with one another, and the estimates of equation 1.13 will, therefore, not be consistent or unbiased estimates of the parameters for the entire population.[14] The quantitative importance of this censorship bias in the study of labor supply behavior has not been documented, to my

[12] See studies of linear probability functions to explain participation rates, by Bowen and Finnegan (1969), Cain (1966), and Boskin (1973). For discussion of the improved properties of the logistic model, see Cox (1970), Nerlove and Press (1973).

[13] The elasticity of the expected labor supply, $E(L)$, with respect to any of its exogenous determinants, X^*, is the sum of the respective elasticities of the expected participation probability, $E(P)$, and the expected hours worked conditional on participation, $E(H)$, where P and H are assumed to contain independent stochastic elements.

$$L = P \cdot H,$$
$$E(L) = E(P) \cdot E(H),$$
$$\eta_{E(L),X^*} = \left[\frac{dE(H)}{dX^*} E(P) + \frac{dE(P)}{dX^*} E(H) \right] \frac{X^*}{E(P) \cdot E(H)},$$
$$\eta_{E(L),X^*} = \eta_{E(P),X^*} + \eta_{E(H),X^*},$$

where η_{yx} is the elasticity of y with respect to x. Clearly if $\eta_{E(P),X^*}$ and $\eta_{E(H),X^*}$ are of the same sign, as is widely presumed, the response elasticity of H among the working sample will tend to understate, in absolute value, the response elasticity of the full labor supply, since it neglects the related participation decision. Empirical evidence on the adequacy of this approximation is later presented in Table 1.6.

[14] The nature of parameter bias resulting from the censorship problem can be illustrated with reference to Fig. 3. Assume that persons with a given set of characteristics X and Z are observed to work on average 50 percent of the time, and work H^* hours per year, if they do work. The reduced form model implies that an individual with a positive deviation from his group's average propensity to participate, $\varepsilon_{1i} - \varepsilon_{2i}$, will also exhibit a positive deviation in his hours worked, v_i, and thus find himself in the upper tail of the group's hour's distribution (i.e., above the index T in Fig. 3). As the proportion of the group working declines, the observed average value of H becomes an increasingly upward biased predictor of T for the entire population of workers and nonworkers. If market participation is positively (negatively) associated with the determinant of the excess demand curve, say Y^*, the slope parameter estimated for Y^* from equation 1.13 will be biased downward (upward) from the "true" parameter for the entire population.

knowledge. If the unexplained variance in equations 1.12 and 1.13 were purely errors in measurement, they might be unrelated across equations and hence the censoring bias would be negligible. In addition, if omitted variables, such as barriers to labor force entry and institutional inflexibilities in adjusting hours of work once employed, differed across equations 1.12 and 1.13, this source of censorship bias might be less severe. Regardless, the unconditional estimates of equation 1.12 are consistent, although they neglect seemingly relevant information contained in the hours worked decision.

III. An unrestricted reduced form equation can be estimated for equation 1.5 and implicitly 1.6, in which market wages are replaced by the instruments that are thought to determine market wages in formulation I and II. Loss of efficiency is presumed to occur, but selectivity bias and specification bias caused by the wage computation procedure are eliminated, and consistent estimates are obtained. Information on income tax rates and price variation is lost in the process. The problem of combining simultaneous equation methods with the Tobit (or logit) nonlinear estimation approach is avoided, for the explanatory variables are now all exogenous. Reduced form equations could also be estimated for the participation and hours worked decisions separately, although these will not be presented.

Unrestricted reduced form estimates of labor market behavior have, of course, numerous shortcomings. All of the parameter estimates contain a factor of proportionality, $1/(\beta_1 - \alpha_1)$. More important, the structural relationships determining market and nonmarket effects are inseparable, and no inferences can be drawn regarding how labor market behavior responds to policy changes operating through market wage rates, taxes, or subsidies. In addition, variables that might enter both the demand and supply function, such as schooling, are revealed only as *net* effects.

The next section discusses which variables are included among Z, the determinants of the market demand wage equation, and among X, the determinants of the individual supply equation, and explores the bases for discriminating between exogenous and endogenous variables in the context of estimating long-run labor market models.

III. The Empirical Specification of the Model and the Data

The models of labor market behavior presented in the previous section are based on a static, certain, single-period decision-making framework. Nonetheless, the empirical objective of this study is to estimate the magnitude of long-run or life-cycle labor supply responses to permanent changes in the factors that constrain how couples allocate their time and form their families. The distinction must, therefore, be carefully drawn between explanatory variables viewed as exogenous constraints to household life-cycle behavior and those viewed as endogenous factors affected by decisions made jointly and simultaneously within the household over its life cycle.

Where endogenous variables might seemingly function as current determinants of labor market behavior, two methods of empirical analysis are available. Either the endogenous explanatory variable is "replaced" by a simultaneous equation estimator in the structural equation estimated, or it is replaced by its exogenous determinants and a reduced form or final form equation is estimated. Empirical studies of labor market behavior have in general applied direct least squares or maximum likelihood methods, treating all explanatory variables as exogenous.[15] This strategy has undoubtedly increased the "explanatory power" (i.e., raised R^2) of these exercises but has probably also distorted estimated response parameters that are central to the design of sound long-run social policy.

EXOGENOUS VARIABLES

In this study the following list of variables will be treated as exogenous: the educational attainment of both husband and wife, their health, age, race, region, size of their city of residence, the household's nonearned income, and for black males, whether or not they lived in the south at age 16.

The explanatory variable in the above list that is most overtly endogenous is the flow of unearned income or its stock counterpart, the household's nonhuman wealth. Just as parents are assumed to determine their children's human capital stock, it would be desirable to know their *inherited* nonhuman capital stock (current and anticipated). But such information is generally not available. Household nonearned income, therefore, may be related to past family savings and associated with past and current labor force behavior. Nonearned income also

---

[15] The number of children a woman bears and the labor force experience she accumulates are two variables that have proved helpful in explaining a married woman's market wage rate and current labor force behavior. But they appear themselves endogenous to the long-run behavioral processes that are explored here. See Mincer and Polachek (1974), Cain (1966), Bowen and Finnegan (1969), and Heckman (1974b).

contains transfers, many of which are more or less contingent upon labor market behavior. Such transfers as private and public welfare, unemployment benefits, workmen's compensation, pensions and social security are, therefore, excluded from *nonemployment* income in this study.

Until a satisfactory theory of life-cycle savings has been developed and combined with a model of labor market behavior, it is difficult to treat nonemployment income as an endogenous variable.[16] Yet some of the problems that arise when nonemployment income is treated as exogenous can be alleviated if labor market behavior is analyzed within relatively narrow (i.e., ten-year) age cohorts. The disaggregation by age moderates the presumed correlation between life-cycle accumulation of wealth that is associated with aging, and systematic variation in labor market behavior across phases of the life cycle.

There are other reasons for not combining age cohorts of married women in the United States: they have experienced different phases of the business cycle, benefited from schooling of different quality, acquired different amounts and types of labor market experiences, and borne different numbers of children. Within an age cohort the effect on labor market behavior of differences in nonemployment income could then be attributed to three remaining factors: inheritance, savings and asset management behavior, and luck or random variation in returns on nonhuman wealth. The first and last effects might be treated as exogenous, but savings and asset management behavior remains intractably endogenous to the household sector, and a potential source of simultaneous equation bias in this investigation.

ENDOGENOUS VARIABLES

A model of the labor market behavior of married women might contain the following endogenous variables: the wife's market wage, the husband's market wage, the husband's market hours worked decision, and the family's composition. A number of measurement problems were noted in analyzing observed current market wage rates.

[16] Heckman's (1971) discussion of the problem is useful. In one chapter he constructs a full market income variable including nonearned income. Treating this full market income as an endogenous variable, he estimates the labor "supply" equation by applying a two-stage simultaneous equation method. The wage parameters obtained are full market income compensated wage effects, in contrast to the traditional uncompensated wage effects obtained in the next section. Smith (Chapter 4) discusses at greater length how the endogeneity of savings and nonhuman wealth might bias estimates of life-cycle models of family labor market behavior.

The solution adopted here is to impute permanent market wage rates to husbands and wives on the basis of estimated market demand wage equations. Since these equations can be estimated only for persons reporting a current hourly wage, a selectivity bias may be introduced by this procedure. This two-stage method replaces the endogenous wage variables by an imputed combination of exogenous instruments.

The husband's hours worked decisions may be solved out of the traditional reduced form labor supply equation, since the husband's labor market behavior is a function of the same exogenous variables as is the wife's (Heckman, 1971).

The composition of the family has been used frequently to account for the labor market behavior of married women.[17] Mincer (1962), Cain (1966), and others have attributed the labor supply effect of young children in the household to their role in increasing the opportunity value of a mother's time in the home. These investigations have essentially held "fertility" constant by including variables for children in the labor supply function, and thereby estimated wage and income effect on labor supply under the assumption that current fertility patterns and the relative price and quality of child care substitutes for the mother's time were exogenously given.

There are grounds to argue that fertility is endogenous to the family's life-cycle allocation of time, and is the most important discretionary factor influencing the wife's labor market behavior. But the economic theory of fertility (or surviving family size) says little about the determinants of the timing and spacing of childbearing. Since it is not the number of children the woman will bear that directly affects her current labor supply, but the current presence of preschool-aged children in the household,[18] the relationship between family composition variables in the labor supply function and completed fertility remains elusive.

[17] Others have proposed the hypothesis that in households which contain older children and other nonworking adults, mothers have access to lower-cost and perhaps better-quality child-care substitutes for their own time, and will therefore work more in the labor market. In general this reasonable hypothesis has been weakly confirmed by U.S. data. See Sweet (1973), and Cain (1966).

[18] The evidence suggests that the substitution of market goods and services for the mother's own time in child care is least satisfactory when the child is very young (see estimates by Leibowitz, 1972, Smith, 1972, and others). These differential effects of children by their age and number are seen for all education and race groups. Sweet (1973) explores from a sociological viewpoint the consequences of family composition and other endogenous variables, such as marital history, for current labor market behavior of married women, using standard multiple regression techniques.

Even without a satisfactory theory of the economic determinants of family composition, this class of variable is very likely to be endogenous to the long-run determination of married women's labor market behavior. In addition, when the tempo and patterns of fertility are in flux, as they are today in the United States, it is not advisable to hold fertility variables artificially constant, unless the long-run effects of the family's price and income variables on fertility are jointly estimated (Schultz, 1974, 1976).

Therefore, in the labor market model estimated in the next section, family composition variables are explicitly omitted. The estimated effects on labor supply of wage, income, health, and residence variables can, in the implicit reduced form equation, be assumed to operate both directly in the labor market and indirectly through their long-run impact on fertility and family composition. It is hypothesized that the inclusion of family composition variables in past studies of the labor market behavior of married U.S. women has biased toward zero the estimated labor supply effects of wage and income variables, particularly among young women for whom children are closely related to labor supply behavior.

FINAL EMPIRICAL SPECIFICATION OF DEMAND AND SUPPLY EQUATIONS

Combining observations on the nature of the process determining long-run labor market behavior, the market demand wage equation (1.1) and the individual supply wage equation (1.2) are assumed to be of the following form:

$$W_i = \alpha_0 + \alpha_2 E_i + \alpha_3 X_i$$
$$+ \alpha_4 X_i^2 + \alpha_5 F_i + \alpha_6 D_i + \alpha_7 Z_i + \varepsilon_{1i}, \qquad (1.1')$$

$$S_i = \beta_0 + \beta_1 H_i + \beta_2 \hat{W}_i + \beta_3 N$$
$$+ \beta_4 F_i + \beta_5 D_i + \varepsilon_{2i}, \qquad (1.2')$$

where the new symbols are defined:

E_i: Years of education completed, treated as a spline or integer variable;

X_i: Years of *experience* since approximate age of leaving school;

X_i^2: *Experience squared*, divided by ten;

F_i: Dummy variable equal to one if respondent is *resident on a farm*, zero otherwise;

D_i: Dummy variable equal to one if respondent reports a major health *disability*, zero otherwise;

Z_i: A vector of four dummy variables defining whether the respondent currently *resides* in (1) an SMSA, (2) small city, (3)
large city, and (4) the southern region;

$\hat{W}_j$: The spouses's instrumental variable estimate of his after-tax
real permanent *market wage* rate in dollars per hour;

N_i: The household's flow of *nonemployment income* in hundreds of
dollars last year.

From the demand side, market wages are assumed to be determined
by a semi-log earnings function (Mincer, 1974), with arguments for
years of schooling, a quadratic in experience, farm residence, health
disability, and regional labor market characteristics. From the supply
side, nonmarket wages are assumed to be determined by hours worked
in the market by the wife, husband's permanent wage rate, nonemployment income, farm residence, and health disability. It should be
noted that schooling, aging, and regional labor market characteristics
enter *only* the market demand wage equation. Conversely, wife's hours
worked, husband's wage, and nonemployment income enter *only* the
individual supply wage equation. Since these restrictions may be viewed
as arbitrary, alternative restrictions might be investigated.

Equation 1.1 is first estimated from the subsample of persons who
report hourly wage rates (Appendix A). The parameter estimate
obtained for various sex, race, and educational strata of the population
are used to impute a market tax and price adjusted wage rate to all
persons, regardless of labor force status (Appendix B).

Substituting the imputed wage rates into equations 1.9 and 1.10, the
labor market equation may be estimated by ordinary least squares,
admitting to truncation bias, or by Tobit techniques. The individual
supply equation can be derived from the Tobit parameter estimates by
changing their sign and multiplying each by the reciprocal of the
estimate on the wife's own-wage variable.

Alternatively, equations 1.12 and 1.13 can be estimated to obtain
independent evidence of the responsiveness of participation and hours
worked to the different explanatory variables. Again, the estimates of
equation 1.13, based on the subsample of persons working positive
hours, need not be representative of the full population. This selectivity bias would be a function of the covariance between the true errors
in those two equations, v_i and v_i^*. If these errors were independent,
the censorship bias would be negligible and the sum of the elasticities

of P and H with respect to any explanatory variable should approach the elasticity of the labor supply, L, obtained from the Tobit formulation. Estimates of equation 1.12 can be transformed into a supply equation, and the reservation wage calculated by setting P equal to one-half.

Lastly, either the Tobit or the separate participation and hours worked equations can be estimated as unrestricted reduced form equations. In this case, the wife's wage is replaced by the wife's characteristic variables that enter the market demand equation 1.1 but do not enter the individual supply equation 1.2.[19]

THE DATA

The data examined in this study are from the 1967 U.S. Survey of Economic Opportunity. In the spring of 1967 detailed economic, labor supply and demographic information was collected by the Census Bureau for the Office of Economic Opportunity from some 26,000 sampled household units. By design, it overrepresents black and low-income families in the U.S. population.

Only married women between the ages of 14 and 64 with husbands present are analyzed here. Observations were discarded on a few units where the core questions regarding education, age, and residence were incomplete for both spouses. Units were also eliminated if the husband was a full-time student or in the armed forces, where it was assumed that unobserved constraints might be responsible for divergent labor force behavior. Nonwhite non-Negro units were also excluded from the study population. The full sample consisted of 14,113 wife-husband units, approximately three-fourths white and one-fourth black.[20] Table 1.1 provides more detail on the size and character of the age and race cohorts within which labor market behavior is studied.

---

[19] Because of the cost of the Tobit estimates with many explanatory variables, the husband's imputed wage is not replaced by his schooling, age quadratic, and disability variables. Exploratory estimates using ordinary least squares did not indicate that the other reduced form coefficients were sensitive to this substitution, and hence the husband's imputed wage remains included in the "unrestricted" reduced form Tobit estimates reported in the next section.

[20] In order to use information in the survey on net physical worth (not reported here in detail), 10 to 20 percent of the full sample had to be omitted, because their asset and liability schedules were incomplete. The differential effect of this net worth restriction, by race and age of wife, on the size of the sample is seen by comparing the last two rows of Table 1.1.

TABLE 1.1: Unweighted Means and Standard Deviations of Variables Used in Labor Supply Regressions by Race and Age Samples[a]

Variable	White Families Age of Wife					Black Families Age of Wife				
	14–24	25–34	35–44	45–54	55–64	14–24	25–34	35–44	45–54	55–64
Wife's tax-adjusted imputed hourly wage	1.37 (.266)	1.58 (.281)	1.67 (.311)	1.62 (.348)	1.46 (.370)	1.22 (.325)	1.33 (.423)	1.33 (.491)	1.15 (.471)	1.05 (.385)
Husband's tax-adjusted imputed hourly wage	1.98 (.393)	2.49 (.513)	2.77 (.652)	2.61 (.691)	2.31 (.636)	1.73 (.361)	1.91 (.431)	1.95 (.486)	1.79 (.484)	1.69 (.445)
Nonemployment income (hundreds of dollars per year)	.815 (3.46)	1.68 (6.52)	2.92 (10.3)	5.55 (24.5)	6.21 (21.5)	.324 (2.47)	.681 (3.27)	.741 (3.46)	1.71 (6.60)	1.64 (5.05)
Farm residence[b]	.0399 (.196)	.0482 (.214)	.0756 (.264)	.104 (.306)	.102 (.325)	.0360 (.186)	.0529 (.224)	.0641 (.245)	.0780 (.268)	.0633 (.244)
Wife's disability[b]	.0335 (.180)	.0651 (.247)	.115 (.319)	.184 (.388)	.257 (.437)	.0620 (.241)	.0987 (.298)	.154 (.361)	.150 (.433)	.389 (.488)
Husband's disability[b]	.0654 (.247)	.0748 (.263)	.126 (.332)	.209 (.407)	.292 (.455)	.0660 (.249)	.107 (.309)	.136 (.342)	.236 (.425)	.322 (.468)

Wife's participation[b,c]	.336	.261	.334	.368	.264	.308	.421	.466	.453	.380
	(.472)	(.439)	(.472)	(.482)	(.441)	(.462)	(.494)	(.499)	(.498)	(.486)
Husband's participation[b,c]	.868	.840	.780	.685	.588	.868	.845	.797	.752	.648
	(.338)	(.366)	(.414)	(.464)	(.492)	(.339)	(.362)	(.403)	(.432)	(.478)
Wife's hours market work per year	480.	363.	513.	612.	437.	386.	623.	708.	655.	530.
	(781.)	(721.)	(831.)	(898.)	(812.)	(704.)	(855.)	(887.)	(876.)	(822.)
Husband's hours market work per year	1884.	1909.	1752.	1509.	1247.	1723.	1722.	1612.	1482.	1232.
	(997.)	(1014.)	(1071.)	(1129.)	(1152.)	(885.)	(934.)	(961.)	(995.)	(1044.)
Full sample size	1254	2595	2857	2522	1142	500	983	1107	821	332
Sample size with complete net worth information	1101	2113	2162	1804	780	452	860	899	657	276

[a] Beneath the mean value of the variable in the full sample is its standard deviation (not corrected for degrees of freedom).

[b] Variable is a dummy variable equal to one if the condition or characteristic is applicable to the observation. Thus, the participation variables indicate the average sample frequency of market labor force participation or more precisely when the individual reported a number of hours worked greater than zero (see definitions). The standard deviation in these cases can also be derived directly from the mean (m) according to formula: $sd = \sqrt{m(1-m)}$.

[c] Participation is defined for the purposes of this study to mean those working a positive number of hours during the week preceding the survey and working a positive number of weeks last year. Hence, the product of these two responses, or estimated annual hours worked, is also positive.

The subsample of "working" couples is defined to include only units where both husband and wife reported three items: working a positive number of hours in the week preceding the survey; working a positive number of weeks last year; and receiving earnings last week. Labor force participation is, thus, defined as working last week a positive number of hours and working last year a positive number of weeks. This is a narrower definition of labor force participation than commonly adopted. The traditional assumption is that the most comprehensive and useful single summary measure of labor supply is the number of hours worked per year, which must be constructed from the SEO file as the product of last week's hours worked and last year's weeks worked. This will be the dependent variable in equations 1.9 and 1.13. The hourly wage rate is defined, as already noted, as last week's earnings divided by last week's hours worked. Since an instrumental variable estimate of the market wage replaces the observed wage, the definitional shortcoming of this wage variable is eliminated by the adopted two-stage estimation procedure.

The means and the standard deviations of the variables entering the labor market equations are reported for the full sample in Table 1.1 by age and race group. The variables are defined in greater detail and the market demand wage equations are discussed and estimates reported in Appendix A. Although the SEO is not a representative sample for the U.S. population, having been designed to overrepresent low-income and black units, the weighted means differ remarkably little within age and race groups from the unweighted values reported here.

IV. ESTIMATES OF THE LABOR MARKET MODEL FOR MARRIED WOMEN

THE LABOR FORCE PARTICIPATION DECISION

Estimates of equation 1.12 are first presented, where the dependent variable is equal to one if the married woman worked in the market labor force last week and last year, and zero otherwise. Earlier studies, such as Bowen and Finnegan (1969), have analyzed this dichotomous dependent variable with ordinary linear regression techniques. Estimates of this linear probability function (OLS) are reported in the first row of Table 1.2. The second row contains maximum likelihood estimates of the parameters to the logistic model (MLL).[21]

---

[21] See footnote b to Table 1.2 for functional form of logistic or log-linear model.

MLL estimates are preferable to the OLS estimates for three reasons. The unrestricted or untransformed OLS model can predict for outliers a negative or greater than one probability of labor force participation, which is awkward. The OLS estimates are, in addition, less efficient than the MLL estimates because of heteroskedasticity in the disturbances. Finally, the standard errors of the OLS parameters are not consistent, and conventional t tests are suspect, whereas asymptotic efficiency and consistency are well established properties of the MLL estimates (Nerlove and Press, 1973; Cox, 1970; Malinvaud, 1970).

Table 1.2 shows that the estimated elasticities at the expected value of the dependent variable in the two models (i.e., OLS and MLL) are similar when the t statistics are substantial. In all white and virtually all black cases, elasticities and t statistics increase in absolute value for the logit formulation. But the improvement is not large except where variables exhibit substantial variability, such as for nonemployment income (e.g., whites aged 45 to 54).[22] As anticipated from earlier studies, wages of wives and husbands are closely associated with the wife's labor force entry. All race age groups, except white wives aged 35 to 44, exhibit a pronounced tendency to work more often if their instrumental variable wage is greater. Own-wage elasticities of whites and blacks are largest among the young and old, reaching a low of .2 for whites aged 35 to 44 and a low of .4 for blacks aged 35 to 54.

Wives tend to enter the labor force less often as their husbands' instrumental wage level rises, except for the youngest age cohort, where the effect is different from zero at only the 5 percent level. This tendency for the elasticity of participation with respect to husbands' wage to rise sharply after age 24 is consistent with Mincer's (1962) and subsequent studies that document the diminished "income" effect before the onset of childbearing. In noting the higher participation elasticities with respect to wages for whites in comparison with blacks, it should be noted that the average level of participation for blacks is 30 percent greater than for whites.

Labor force participation is not notably responsive to nonemployment income flows (or net physical worth that is not reported here) except perhaps among white wives between the ages of 35 and 54.

[22] One reason that the MLL elasticities are greater than those obtained from the OLS model is that the logit expected value of participation conditional on the sample means was in all ten cases less than the sample means of the dependent variable, which is the expected value in the OLS model that is used to calculate point estimates of elasticities.

TABLE 1.2: Regression on Labor Force Participation of Married Women[a]
(Spouse-present married couples by race and age of wife: SEO 1967)

Worker	Estimation Technique	Constant Term	Wife's Wage	Husband's Wage	Nonemployment Income	Farm Residence	Own Disability	R^2 (SEE)	Chi-Squared with 5 Degrees of Freedom (−Log Likelihood)
WHITE, AGE 14–24 (n = 1254):									
Wife	OLS[b]	.0299 (.37)	.367 (6.14) [1.500]	−.0652 (1.61) [.385]	.0001 (.04) [.0003]	−.162 (2.36) [.0193]	−.0645 (.87) [.0064]	.0423 (.463)	
Wife	MLL[b]	−2.34 (6.19)	1.67 (5.92) [1.542]	−.309 (1.62) [.412]	.0005 (.03) [.0003]	−1.03 (2.41) [.0276]	−.437 (1.07) [.0098]		55.2 (772.7)
WHITE, AGE 25–34 (n = 2595):									
Wife	OLS[b]	.319 (5.74)	.161 (4.27) [.9777]	−.123 (5.96) [1.177]	.00067 (.51) [.0043]	−.113 (2.72) [.0209]	−.0311 (.87) [.0078]	.0163 (.436)	
Wife	MLL[b]	−.705 (2.42)	.856 (4.32) [1.006]	−.673 (5.85) [1.247]	.00341 (.50) [.0043]	−.639 (2.66) [.0229]	−.186 (.92) [.0090]		43.8 (1467.)
WHITE, AGE 35–44 (n = 2857):									
Wife	OLS[b]	.621 (11.6)	.0324 (.89) [.1619]	−.109 (6.20) [.9032]	−.00173 (2.04) [.0152]	−.181 (5.19) [.0410]	−.179 (6.29) [.0614]	.0348 (.464)	

Wife	MLL[b]	.654 (2.56)	.159 (.92) [.1793]	-.519 (6.08) [.9704]	-.0105 (1.93) [.0207]	-.893 (5.03) [.0455]	-.937 (6.11) [.0725]	106.4 (1766.)

WHITE, AGE 45–54 (n = 2522):

Wife	OLS[b]	.526 (10.0)	.144 (4.23) [.6352]	-.123 (6.97) [.8759]	-.00132 (3.46) [.0199]	-.206 (6.22) [.0585]	-.219 (8.69) [.1097]	.0636 (.467)
Wife	MLL[b]	.0863 (.36)	.719 (4.52) [.7529]	-.560 (6.62) [.9472]	-.0154 (3.59) [.0553]	-.993 (5.98) [.0671]	-1.12 (8.36) [.1334]	181.8 (1568.)

WHITE, AGE 55–64 (n = 1142):

Wife	OLS[b]	.194 (3.07)	.291 (6.93) [1.615]	-.128 (5.00) [1.123]	-.00086 (1.47) [.0203]	-.186 (4.42) [.0849]	-.126 (4.20) [.1225]	.0806 (.424)
Wife	MLL[b]	-1.35 (3.89)	1.52 (6.56) [1.690]	-.697 (4.58) [1.223]	-.00722 (1.36) [.0346]	-1.18 (4.20) [.1071]	-.864 (4.45) [.1683]	98.2 (609.6)

BLACK, AGE 14–24 (n = 500):

Wife	OLS[b]	.287 (2.50)	.223 (2.59) [.883]	-.138 (1.64) [.778]	-.0042 (.50) [.0044]	-.110 (.90) [.0129]	-.100 (1.17) [.0202]	.0190 (.460)
Wife	MLL[b]	-.893 (1.62)	1.01 (2.51) [.860]	-.639 (1.57) [.769]	-.0274 (.48) [.0062]	-.563 (.88) [.0141]	-.547 (1.17) [.0236]	9.53 (303.9)

TABLE 1.2: Continued

Worker	Estimation Technique	Constant Term	Wife's Wage	Husband's Wage	Nonemployment Income	Farm Residence	Own Disability	R^2 (SEE)	Chi-Squared with 5 Degrees of Freedom (−Log Likelihood)
BLACK, AGE 25–34 (n = 983):									
Wife	OLS[b]	.467 (5.70)	.260 (5.31) [.818]	−.194 (3.67) [.879]	.00165 (.35) [.0027]	−.168 (2.12) [.0211]	−.122 (2.32) [.0286]	.0405 (.485)	
Wife	MLL[b]	−.116 (.33)	1.12 (5.00) [.861]	−.839 (3.59) [.932]	.00699 (.35) [.0028]	−.749 (2.10) [.0230]	−.561 (2.31) [.0322]		40.9 (648.7)
BLACK, AGE 35–44 (n = 1107):									
Wife	OLS[b]	.620 (8.84)	.136 (3.38) [.388]	−.144 (3.23) [.605]	.0101 (2.42) [.0161]	−.284 (4.22) [.0391]	−.271 (6.66) [.0893]	.0745 (.481)	
Wife	MLL[b]	.532 (1.75)	.597 (3.27) [.429]	−.636 (3.19) [.673]	.0518 (2.25) [.0208]	−1.38 (4.13) [.0477]	−1.28 (6.13) [.106]		89.6 (719.9)
BLACK, AGE 45–54 (n = 821):									
Wife	OLS[b]	.729 (9.34)	.143 (2.67) [.364]	−.191 (3.38) [.754]	−.00290 (1.14) [.0110]	−.387 (5.42) [.0666]	−.254 (6.48) [.140]	.0859 (.4777)	

Wife	MLL[b]	1.01 (2.93)	.639 (2.58) [.409]	-.853 (3.28) [.848]	-.0123 (1.08) [.0117]	-1.88 (5.06) [.0816]	-1.14 (6.19) [.158]	75.8 (527.6)

BLACK, AGE 55–64 ($n = 332$):

$$P = \alpha_0 + \alpha_1 X_1 + \alpha_2 X_2 + \cdots + \alpha_n X_n + \varepsilon,$$

Wife	OLS[b]	.517 (4.35)	.220 (2.07) [.607]	-.143 (1.50) [.635]	-.00232 (.45) [.0101]	-.175 (1.46) [.0293]	-.289 (5.29) [.295]	.1247 (.458)
Wife	MLL[b]	.140 (.25)	1.01 (1.98) [.681]	-.689 (1.46) \[.747]	-.0111 (.41) [.0118]	-1.11 (1.52) [.0450]	-1.39 (4.96) [.346]	44.5 (198.2)

[a] Beneath each (regression) coefficient in parentheses is the absolute value of the ratio of the coefficient to its (asymptotic) standard error. And in brackets is the absolute value of the elasticity of the expected value of participation with respect to variation about the mean in each explanatory variable.

[b] The OLS rows are ordinary least squares estimates of the linear probability function with a dummy dependent variable:

where P is the probability of labor force participation, α's are the OLS parameters reported, X's the explanatory variables, and ε the disturbance. The MLL are maximum likelihood estimates of the logistic model:

$$P = 1/(1 + \exp -[\beta_0 + \beta_1 X_1 + \beta_2 X_2 + \cdots + \beta X_n + u],$$

where exp is the base of natural logarithms, β's are the reported parameter estimates for the explanatory variables, X's, and u the disturbance. Consequently, the value of α's and β's are not directly comparable, although the t's and elasticities are analogous.

TABLE 1.3: Estimates of the Reservation Wage Derived from Labor Force Participation Equation[a]

Age of Wife	(1) Actual Mean Imputed After Tax Wage Rate ($/hour)	(2) OLS Estimates (Table 1.2)	(3) Logit Estimates (Table 1.2)	(4) Logit Estimates but Means of Other Race[b]	(5) Ratio Actual to Logit Reservation (1)/(3)[c]	(6) Participation Rate (%)
			WHITES			
14–24	1.37	1.82	1.78	1.74	.77	.34
25–34	1.58	3.07	2.16	2.11	.73	.26
35–44[d]	1.67	6.80	6.22	3.57	.27	.33
45–54	1.62	2.53	2.46	1.81	.66	.37
55–64	1.46	2.27	2.22	1.94	.66	.26
			BLACKS			
14–24	1.22	2.08	2.04	2.20	.60	.31
25–34	1.33	1.63	1.61	2.02	.83	.42
35–44	1.33	1.58	1.60	2.23	.83	.47
45–54	1.15	1.48	1.52	2.64	.76	.45
55–64	1.05	1.60	1.64	1.99	.64	.38

[a] Derived from the labor force participation equation coefficients reported in Table 1.2 by solving for the value of the "Wife's Wage" that is required to obtain a participation probability of one-half given the sample mean values of the other explanatory variables, i.e., husband's wage, nonemployment income, farm residence, and health disability (see Table 1.1).

[b] Derived as in note (a) except the sample mean values of the explanatory variable are those of the other race group. This exercise provides some indication of how much of the race difference in estimated reservation wages is due to the different levels of the conditioning variables of the two groups, and how much is due to different estimates of the response coefficients.

[c] The ratio of the actual to the reservation wage indicates approximately the extent to which market after-tax wages reached the median reservation wage for the group. It is anticipated that this ratio and the actual participation rate would tend to move up and down together, as it appears to do for blacks.

[d] The wife's wage coefficient for the white 35–44 age group is not asymptotically statistically different from zero at the 10 percent level. The reservation wage derived for this group from the estimated equation is not defined with any precision.

Finally, farm residence and health disabilities restrict the supply of labor market entrants, holding constant the effect of residence and disability on the market demand wage variables.

The equilibrium characterization of the labor market model implies that the coefficient on the wife's wage rate is positive, i.e., $1/\beta_1 > 0$, and this is confirmed in all race and age groups. The individual supply function may then be derived from the estimates of the participation equations in Table 1.2 by dividing all of the remaining coefficients by the reciprocal of the wife's wage coefficient and reversing their sign. If we assume that the disturbance is symmetric and has zero expected value about the linear or logistic function, then the expected value of the individual supply wage at which half of the cohort enters the labor market can be called the median reservation wage.[23]

This reservation wage, conditional on the sample means of the explanatory variables in the supply equation (i.e. husband's wage, nonemployment income, farm residence, and health disability), is calculated for the linear (OLS) and logistic (MLL) estimates and is compared in columns 2 and 3 of Table 1.3 with the mean value of the instrumental variable market wage (after taxes) in column 1. Replacing the sample mean values of the conditioning supply equation variables by those for the other race sample, column 4 indicates how much of the differences in participation between white and black wives is accounted for by the level of supply wage determinants, and how much must be residually attributed to different response parameters. For the 14–24 age groups, the differences in reservation wages widens when supply variables are "held constant." At all other ages, the white reservation wage is substantially greater than the black, and the differences in the mean levels of the supply determinants accounts for about half of the gap, on average.

THE HOURS WORKED DECISION AMONG THE WORKING

Estimates of equation 1.13 are presented in the first two rows of Table 1.4. The sample is restricted to couples where *both* husband and wife reported earnings in the previous week and also reported positive hours worked last week and positive weeks worked last year. The first ordinary least squares (OLS) regression is based on the observed market wage rate, derived by dividing weekly earnings by hours worked last week. The second OLS regression replaces the market wage rate by its instrumental variable prediction (for both spouses), adjusted for marginal income taxes and price level differences.[24]

---

[23] The OLS equation is simply solved for the dependent variable being .5. In the case of the logit model the dependent variable is the natural logarithm of the odds ratio, in other words $\ln((P)/(1-P))$, which equals zero when P is .5.

[24] Hall (1973), having obtained what is essentially an instrumental variable (IV) estimate of wage rates (for participation), divides annual earnings by his IV wage to calculate annual labor supply.

TABLE 1.4: Regressions on Annual Hours Worked in the Labor Market by Currently Married Women by Age and Race[a]

Subsample and Regression Number	Sample Composition (Size)	Estimation Technique	Explanatory Variables								Constant Term	R^2 (MSE)[d]
			Own Wage Rate		Spouse Wage Rate		Non-employment Income[c]	Farm Residence	Own Disability			
			Observed	Predicted[b]	Observed	Predicted[b]						
WHITE AGE 14–24												
1	Labor Force[e] (356)	OLS	12.0 (.36) [.017]		−44.8 (1.20) [.082]		−15.2 (1.26) [.0078]	233. (.68) [.0018]	109. (.39) [.0013]		1536.	.0121 (.451 E6)
2	Labor Force[e] (356)	OLS		23.8 (.16) [.024]		33.3 (.31) [.047]	−17.0 (1.41) [.0087]	303. (.88) [.0024]	112. (.40) [.0013]		1342.	.0087 (.452 E6)
3	All Persons[f] (1255)	OLS		551. (5.56) [1.58]		−55.1 (.82) [.228]	−2.34 (.37) [.0040]	−183. (1.60) [.0153]	−87.8 (.72) [.0061]		−155.	.0356 (.590 E6)
4	All Persons[f] (1255)	Tobit		1633. (5.88) [1.83]		−235. (1.23) [.382]	−1.65 (.09) [.001]	−921. (2.35) [.030]	−488. (1.22) [.013]		−2429.	— (.590 E6)
BLACK AGE 14–24												
1	Labor Force[e] (135)	OLS	171. (1.47) [.238]		−4.51 (.08) [.0082]		61.7 (.85) [.012]	58.5 (.11) [.0007]	−211. (.57) [.0052]		923.	.0304 (.525 E6)
2	Labor Force[e] (135)	OLS		32.6 (.13) [.034]		−135. (.51) [.195]	76.8 (1.02) [.0150]	−65.9 (.12) [.0008]	−260. (.70) [.0064]		1393.	.0131 (.534 E6)
3	All Persons[f] (500)	OLS		358. (2.73) [1.13]		−257. (2.00) [1.15]	−1.30 (.10) [.0011]	−115. (.61) [.0107]	−203. (1.55) [.0326]		411.	.0213 (.490 E6)

No.	Group (N)	Method	(1)	(2)	(3)	(4)	(5)	(6)	(7)
4	All Persons[f] (500)	Tobit	1028. (2.68) [1.12]	−689. (1.76) [1.06]	−20.9 (.40) [.006]	−430. (.71) [.014]	−661. (1.47) [.036]	−832.	— (.485 E6)
WHITE AGE 25–34									
1	Labor Force[e] (573)	OLS	4.17 (.19) [.0067]	−73.3 (3.24) [.165]	5.62 (.82) [.0062]	−185. (.82) [.0025]	−510. (3.45) [.0165]	1645.	.0404 (.536 E6)
2	Labor Force[e] (573)	OLS	82.9 (.66) [.0945]	−265. (3.34) [.463]	6.72 (.77) [.0074]	−239. (1.06) [.0033]	−511. (3.44) [.0165]	1939.	.0427 (.534 E6)
3	All Persons[f] (2595)	OLS	214. (3.45) [.930]	−218. (6.43) [1.49]	2.19 (1.01) [.0101]	−176. (2.59) [.0234]	−149. (2.54) [.0267]	582.	.0200 (.511 E6)
4	All Persons[f] (2595)	Tobit	909. (4.12) [1.16]	−819. (6.40) [1.65]	6.41 (.80) [.009]	−725. (2.77) [.028]	−406. (1.79) [.021]	−607.	— (.510 E6)
BLACK AGE 25–34									
1	Labor Force[e] (357)	OLS	98.9 (2.37) [.120]	−40.6 (1.03) [.0660]	3.91 (.37) [.0015]	−32.6 (.17) [.0008]	−356. (2.19) [.0119]	1442.	.0307 (.447 E6)
2	Labor Force[e] (357)	OLS	227. (2.31) [.209]	−262. (2.12) [.334]	6.52 (.61) [.0025]	−218. (1.03) [.0053]	−311. (1.90) [.0104]	1713.	.0316 (.477 E6)
3	All Persons[f] (983)	OLS	493. (5.85) [1.05]	−391. (4.31) [1.20]	−.29 (.04) [.0003]	−310. (2.27) [.0263]	−296. (3.27) [.0469]	764.	.0534 (.695 E6)
4	All Persons[f] (983)	Tobit	1020. (5.53) [1.08]	−836. (3.98) [1.28]	4.00 (.23) [.002]	−756. (2.31) [.032]	−718. (3.16) [.057]	136.	— (.693 E6)
WHITE AGE 35–44									
1	Labor Force[e] (764)	OLS	45.0 (1.73) [.0624]	−45.1 (2.69) [.0976]	−4.42 (1.51) [.0061]	−7.74 (.0587) [.0002]	−313. (2.84) [.0115]	1608.	.0245 (.492 E6)

TABLE 1.4: Continued

Subsample and Regression Number	Sample Composition (Size)	Estimation Technique	Own Wage Rate Observed	Own Wage Rate Predicted[b]	Spouse Wage Rate Observed	Spouse Wage Rate Predicted[b]	Non-employment Income[c]	Farm Residence	Own Disability	Constant Term	R^2 (MSE)[d]
2	Labor Force[e] (764)	OLS		-41.2 (.39) [.0448]		-216. (3.81) [.383]	-3.13 (1.08) [.0043]	-121. (.906) [.0031]	-329. (2.96) [.0121]	2311.	.0434 (.482 E6)
3	All Persons[f] (2859)	OLS		49.2 (.77) [.160]		-227. (7.39) [1.23]	-2.99 (2.00) [.0170]	-311. (5.08) [.0459]	-357. (7.17) [.0799]	1134.	.0444 (.661 E6)
4	All Persons[f] (2859)	Tobit		198. (1.08) [.254]		-653. (7.08) [1.40]	-10.8 (2.14) [.024]	-984. (5.26) [.057]	-1122. (7.00) [.099]	957.	— (.661 E6)
					BLACK AGE 35-44						
1	Labor Force[e] (422)	OLS	58.7 (1.71) [.0675]		18.2 (.63) [.0301]		.508 (.06) [.0003]	-211. (1.11) [.0042]	-443. (3.52) [.0205]	1421.	.0520 (.434 E6)
2	Labor Force[e] (422)	OLS		225. (2.80) [.201]		-44.7 (.48) [.0579]	.779 (.09) [.0005]	-250. (1.26) [.0050]	-405. (3.22) [.0188]	1349.	.0642 (.428 E6)
3	All Persons[f] (1107)	OLS		320. (4.48) [.598]		-247. (3.14) [.681]	19.5 (2.65) [.020]	-458. (3.85) [.045]	-502. (6.98) [.109]	858.	.0873 (.721 E6)
4	All Persons[f] (1107)	Tobit		552. (3.93) [.590]		-493. (3.11) [.776]	36.1 (2.49) [.022]	-1207. (4.33) [.062]	-1280. (7.41) [.158]	471.	— (.717 E6)

#									
			WHITE AGE 45–54						
1	Labor Force[e] (658)	OLS	−18.7 (1.03) [.0250]	−49.6 (3.34) [.101]	−1.85 (.78) [.0036]	−16.0 (.12) [.0003]	−427. (4.90) [.0232]	1899.	.0555 (.403 E6)
2	Labor Force[e] (658)	OLS	71.5 (.80) [.0719]	−177. (3.33) [.282]	−2.66 (1.12) [.0051]	−72.0 (.51) [.0015]	−414. (4.61) [.0725]	2041.	.0517 (.405 E6)
3	All Persons[f] (2522)	OLS	288. (4.54) [.761]	−273. (8.30) [1.16]	−2.30 (3.26) [.0209]	−340. (5.52) [.0579]	−433. (9.27) [.131]	987.	.0698 (.751 E6)
4	All Persons[f] (2522)	Tobit	784. (4.74) [.946]	−676. (7.60) [1.32]	−15.9 (3.98) [.066]	−1032. (5.98) [.080]	−1317. (9.54) [.181]	370.	— (.748 E6)
			BLACK AGE 45–54						
1	Labor Force[e] (286)	OLS	113. (2.71) [.130]	−27.9 (1.10) [.0458]	−4.61 (.34) [.0035]	−189. (.73) [.0036]	−390. (3.13) [.035]	1399.	.0658 (.514 E6)
2	Labor Force[e] (286)	OLS	325. (3.06) [.271]	4.66 (.04) [.0059]	−7.41 (.56) [.0056]	−2.83 (.01) [.0001]	−346. (2.82) [.0323]	1110.	.1035 (.493 E6)
3	All Persons[f] (821)	OLS	406. (4.34) [.714]	−289. (2.92) [.789]	−7.03 (1.58) [.0183]	−506. (4.06) [.0603]	−458. (6.67) [.175]	868.	.0985 (.696 E6)
4	All Persons[f] (821)	Tobit	674. (3.58) [.647]	−640. (3.10) [.952]	−12.7 (1.33) [.018]	−1509. (4.97) [.098]	−1109. (7.04) [.231]	687.	— (.691 E6)
			WHITE AGE 55–64						
1	Labor Force[e] (180)	OLS	29.0 (1.29) [.0421]	−24.4 (1.27) [.0531]	4.15 (.73) [.0128]	15.8 (.049) [.0003]	−412. (2.48) [.0305]	1757.	.0497 (.509 E6)

TABLE 1.4: Continued

Subsample and Regression Number	Sample Composition (Size)	Estimation Technique	Own Wage Rate Observed	Own Wage Rate Predicted[b]	Spouse Wage Rate Observed	Spouse Wage Rate Predicted[b]	Nonemployment Income[c]	Farm Residence	Own Disability	Constant Term	R^2 (MSE)[a]
2	Labor Force[e] (180)	OLS		280. (1.81) [.284]		-124. (1.10) [.190]	2.11 (.38) [.0065]	-1.52 (.005) [.0003]	-389. (2.33) [.0288]	1466.	.0490 (.510 E6)
3	All Persons[f] (1142)	OLS		577. (7.50) [1.93]		-254. (5.41) [1.34]	-1.67 (1.55) [.023]	-314. (4.06) [.086]	-271. (4.93) [.159]	298.	.0932 (.601 E6)
4	All Persons[f] (1142)	Tobit		1860. (7.09) [2.09]		-866. (4.95) [1.54]	-10.4 (1.60) [.050]	-1359. (4.34) [.125]	-1177. (5.32) [.231]	-1567.	— (.596 E6)
			BLACK AGE 55–64								
1	Labor Force[e] (88)	OLS	97.9 (.96) [.099]		9.29 (.26) [.0153]		5.04 (.29) [.0063]	-1240. (1.63) [.0099]	-91.3 (.37) [.0083]	1280.	.0595 (.567 E6)
2	Labor Force[e] (88)	OLS		142. (.46) [.115]		237. (.80) [.297]	1.77 (.10) [.0022]	-935. (1.20) [.0075]	-38.6 (.16) [.0034]	850.	.0891 (.549 E6)

			478.	-222.	-5.55	-332.	-456.	611.	.1369
3	All Persons[f] (332)	OLS	(2.69)	(1.39)	(.64)	(1.64)	(4.97)		(.591 E6)
			[.945]	[.707]	[.0172]	[.0394]	[.334]		
4	All Persons[f] (332)	Tobit	1003.	-603.	-14.8	-1281.	-1335.	116.	—
			(2.37)	(1.52)	(.64)	(2.03)	(5.52)		(.578 E6)
			[.950]	[.919]	[.022]	[.073]	[.469]		

---

[a] Beneath each regression coefficient in parentheses is the absolute value of the ratio of the coefficient to its (asymptotic) standard error and, in brackets, the elasticity of annual hours worked with respect to that variable evaluated at the unweighted sample means. The properties of the calculated t ratio for the "All Persons" sample are not known because of the imputation procedure. The elasticities for the Tobit estimates are with respect to the expected value locus (not the Tobit index) and are therefore analogous with the OLS elasticities from regression 3.

[b] Predicted wage based on market wage determination equation (see Appendix A) adjusted for marginal federal income taxes and cost of living price deflator (see Appendix B).

[c] Nonemployment income is defined as nonearned income excluding work-related income flows: unemployment compensation, pensions, social security, workman's compensation, and welfare.

[d] Mean squared error.

[e] The "Labor Force" is a sample of couples for whom both spouses had a defined hourly wage rate (excluding armed forces, self-employed without a salary, and unemployed) and worked some hours last week and some weeks last year. The hourly wage is obtained by dividing weekly earnings by hours worked last week. If either spouse was a full-time student, or the wife was a part-time student, the couple was excluded from the working sample of currently married women in the labor force. Hence, by an oversight, some husbands in the working samples may be part-time students.

[f] "All Persons" is a sample of couples for whom both spouses provided sufficient information to impute an hourly wage rate and for whom it was possible to estimate hours worked last year (including zero). In other words, all the explanatory variables in the market wage determination equation (see Appendix A) were defined, such as age, race, sex, education, etc., and hours worked last week and weeks worked last year were answered. Armed forces personnel and full-time students were excluded from both samples.

Replacement of the observed by the instrumental variable wage rate has a number of consequences for parameter estimates, as discussed earlier, but unfortunately, it is not possible to predict the sign or magnitude of the sum of these effects on any of the parameter estimates.

Substituting the instrumental variable wage for the observed market wage does not generally reduce the explanatory power (R^2) of the hours worked equations, even though the wage imputations accounted for only a third to a fourth of the observed variation in hourly wages (Appendix A).[25] The hours worked equation accounts for only 1 to 10 percent of the variation in hours worked, although F tests of overall statistical significance are by conventional standards satisfactory for all samples, except for the youngest.

Within all of the samples of working white wives, hours worked is related neither to the observed nor to the instrumental own-wage rate. In contrast, black wives, at least from the age of 25 to 54, exhibit a pronounced tendency to work longer hours if *they* are themselves observed to receive higher wage rates. This positive hours worked responsiveness to own market wages is increased severalfold when instrumental variable wages are used.

Conversely, working white wives are more responsive to their *husbands' wage rate* than are black wives, and the estimated negative magnitude of this spouse-wage effect is three to five times larger (in absolute value) when the observed wage is replaced by the instrumental variable. This tendency is particularly clear among white wives between the ages of 25 and 54 and also appears among black wives aged 25 to 34.

In no case does the regression coefficient on the nonemployment income variable exceed twice its standard error. There is no evidence within the "working" sample, therefore, to show how nonemployment income affects, if at all, the hours worked in the market by working married women. This result differs from most previous studies that find the negative effect of nonearned household income on wives' labor supply greater than that of the husband's earned income or wage rate. The reason for this new finding may be traced to the more appropriate definition of "nonemployment income" used here, which excludes work conditioned transfers, or to the instrumental variable treatment of the husband's permanent wage as endogenous.

[25] Comparison of R^2 between OLS and 2SLS estimation equations is not an appropriate test of statistical significance. See Dhrymes (1969).

TOTAL LABOR SUPPLY: EXPECTED HOURS WORKED IN THE MARKET
BY ALL PERSONS

Ordinary least squares (linear) estimates of the total labor supply equation 1.9 are reported in row 3 of Table 1.4. These estimates, based on the full sample of all persons, neglect the censorship bias imparted by the limited nature of the dependent variable, hours worked. Tobit (nonlinear) estimates of the total labor supply equation 1.9 are reported in row 4 of Table 1.4. The estimates refer to the parameters of the Tobit index (i.e., T in Figure 1.2 or bc), their asymptotic t statistics, and the elasticity of the expected value locus ($a'b'c$) evaluated at sample means. The market wage variables for husband and wife are based on the instrumental variable wage equations.

As anticipated, in every age and race group, the own-wage effect (and elasticity) is increased (positively) when the sample is expanded from the restricted "labor force" group to "all persons." The husband's wage effect is also increased (negatively), with the exception of the youngest age group. In most cases the t statistics rise, often dramatically.[26]

The effects of nonemployment income flows, however, continue to vacillate in sign and statistical significance. There is some suggestion that for the expanded "all persons" sample a negative income (or wealth) effect increases during the last half of the life cycle.[27]

The last set of regressions in Table 1.4 refer to the nonlinear Tobit formulation of equation 1.9. The mean squared error of the nonlinear

[26] As noted earlier, if P and H (among workers) are related to any exogenous variable in the same direction, then the elasticity of total labor supply (among all persons) will tend to exceed (in absolute value) the elasticity with respect to H, hours worked among workers. Intuitive arguments can also be offered to explain why expanding the sample severalfold to include nonparticipants in the labor force (as defined in this study) increases the magnitude of estimated labor supply response parameters.

[27] The nonemployment income flow variable was replaced by the net physical wealth stock variable, and additional OLS and Tobit estimates of the labor market equation were obtained based on the reduced sample, for which wealth information in the SEO was complete (see Table 1.1, last row). All but one of the "income" coefficients shifted in the negative direction (t's increased negatively or, if positive, decreased toward zero). In two out of ten cases the Tobit coefficient on the stock variable was still positive, whereas in five out of ten cases the Tobit coefficient on the flow variable was positive. The statistically significant *positive* (perverse) parameter for nonemployment income in the Tobit regression for black wives aged 35 to 44 reversed sign when net physical wealth was used to measure other sources of household income. As in the results reported here, the only evidence of a pronounced wealth-induced reduction in labor supply was among white wives between ages 45 and 64; in other words, in these cases the t statistics exceeded 2.5 on the net physical wealth coefficient.

model about the expected value locus (reported in parentheses in the last column) is less than the mean squared error about the linear regression line, but the differences are not large.[28] There are a few substantial discrepancies between the elasticities and t statistics obtained from the Tobit formulation and the ordinary least squares (OLS) linear model, though in general the elasticity estimates of nonemployment income (or net physical wealth) are somewhat greater in absolute value.[29]

In summary, expanding the analysis from those currently working in the labor force to all married women narrows the apparent differences between the race groups in their participation and hours worked responsiveness to own-wage and their husband's wage. According to either the OLS or logit estimates, the husband's wage clearly affects black wives in their decision whether to participate in the labor force, but only marginally influences how much they decide to work once in the labor force, particularly between the ages of 35 and 64. On the other hand, their own-wage response is evident in both decisions but is stronger regarding the participation decision from ages 14 to 34 and 55 to 64. Conversely, both decisions of white wives are more affected by their husband's wage, though the hours worked decision is only sensitive between the ages of 25 and 54. Own market wage opportunities exert a more pronounced effect on the decision of white wives to participate at all ages than they do on how many hours are worked once they enter the labor force.

The individual supply equation may be derived from the Tobit formulation in the same manner as from the participation equation. The expected reservation wage implied by the Tobit estimates is reported in Table 1.5, conditional, in column 1, on the relevant sample means for the four supply determinants, and in column 2, on the sample means for the opposite race group. Column 3 shows the percentage of the gap between black and white reservation wages that is accounted for by the different population means, assuming the same parametric structure for the labor supply equation. Between the ages

---

[28] Since the Tobit estimates of the expected value of the dependent variable, average hours worked, are not necessarily unbiased, the mean squared error of the Tobit regressions may exceed those of the ordinary least squares regression.

[29] Note that, as with the logistic model, the Tobit coefficients are not directly comparable to the OLS coefficients, although the t ratios and elasticities are analogous. These patterns are also noted when physical net worth is substituted for nonemployment income. See footnote 28 above for more detail on these results not reported here.

TABLE 1.5: Estimates of the Reservation Wage
Derived from Estimates of the Tobit Formulation
of Labor Market[a]

Age Group	Tobit Estimates Own Race Means[a]	Tobit Estimates Other Race Means[b]	Percentage of Race Differences Explained by Group Means[c]
	WHITES		
14–24	1.81	1.77	−18
25–34	2.83	2.47	28
35–44[d]	5.49	2.82	64
45–54	2.33	1.63	68
55–64	2.20	1.93	40
	BLACKS		
14–24	2.03	2.19	−73
25–34	1.54	1.98	34
35–44	1.34	1.86	13
45–54	1.30	2.10	78
55–64	1.52	1.86	50

[a] Derived from the labor market Tobit index parameters reported in regression 4 of Table 1.4 by solving for the value of "own wage" that is implied to obtain a Tobit index value of zero (one-half participating), given the sample mean values of the other explanatory variables, i.e., spouse wage, nonemployment income, farm residence, and own disability (see Table 1.1).

[b] Derived as in note (a) except that the sample mean values of the explanatory variables are those of the other race group.

[c] This indicates what percentage of the difference between the Tobit estimates of the reservation wage for whites and blacks is explained by the different levels of the explanatory variables (i.e., spouse's wage, nonemployment income, farm residence, and own disability) for the two race groups. A negative percentage implies that the adjustment to the other race group's means widens rather than narrows the implied difference in reservation wages in the youngest age group.

[d] The "own wage" coefficient for white married women aged 35–44 is not asymptotically statistically different from zero at the 10 percent confidence level. Therefore, the reservation wage calculated for this group is not defined by these estimates with any notable precision.

TABLE 1.6: Comparison of Elasticity Estimates of Labor Supply According to Alternative Estimating Procedures and Models

Variable	(1) Participation Probability (all persons) MLL[a]	(2) Hours Worked (H > 0) OLS[b]	(3) Expected Labor Supply (1) + (2)	Combined Labor Supply Model (all persons)		(6) Asymptotic t for (5) Tobit[d]
				(4) OLS[c]	(5) Tobit[d]	
WHITE WIVES						
AGE 14–24						
Own Wage	1.542	.024	1.57	1.58	1.83	(5.88)
Husband's Wage	−.412	.047	−.365	−.228	−.382	(1.23)
Nonemp. Income	.0003	−.0087	−.0084	−.0040	−.001	(.09)
AGE 25–34						
Own Wage	1.006	.095	1.10	.930	1.16	(4.12)
Husband's Wage	−1.247	−.463	−1.71	−1.49	−1.65	(6.40)
Nonemp. Income	.0043	.0074	.0117	.0101	.009	(.80)
AGE 35–44						
Own Wage	.1793	−.0448	.135	.160	.254	(1.08)
Husband's Wage	−.9704	−.383	−1.35	−1.23	−1.40	(7.08)
Nonemp. Income	−.0207	−.0043	−.0250	−.0170	−.024	(2.14)
AGE 45–54						
Own Wage	.7529	.0719	.825	.761	.946	(4.74)
Husband's Wage	−.9472	−.282	−1.23	−1.16	−1.32	(7.60)
Nonemp. Income	−.0553	−.0051	−.060	−.0209	−.066	(3.98)
AGE 55–64						
Own Wage	1.690	.284	1.97	1.93	2.09	(7.09)
Husband's Wage	−1.223	−.190	1.41	−1.34	−1.54	(4.95)
Nonemp. Income	−.0346	.0065	−.0281	−.023	−.050	(1.60)
BLACK WIVES						
AGE 14–24						
Own Wage	.860	.034	.894	1.13	1.12	(2.68)
Husband's Wage	−.769	−.195	−.964	−1.15	−1.06	(1.76)
Nonemp. Income	−.0062	.0150	.0088	−.0011	−.006	(.40)
AGE 25–34						
Own Wage	.861	.209	1.07	1.05	1.08	(5.53)
Husband's Wage	−.932	−.334	−1.27	−1.20	−1.28	(3.98)
Nonemp. Income	.0028	.0025	.0053	−.0003	.002	(.23)
AGE 35–44						
Own Wage	.429	.201	.630	.598	.590	(3.93)
Husband's Wage	−.673	−.0579	−.731	−.681	−.776	(3.11)
Nonemp. Income	.0208	.0005	.021	.020	.022	(2.49)

See footnotes at end of table.

TABLE 1.6: Continued

| Variable | (1) Participation Probability (all persons) MLL[a] | (2) Hours Worked (H > 0) OLS[b] | (3) Expected Labor Supply (1) + (2) | Combined Labor Supply Model (all persons) | | (6) Asymptotic t for (5) Tobit[d] |
				(4) OLS[c]	(5) Tobit[d]	
AGE 45–54						
Own Wage	.409	.271	.680	.714	.647	(3.58)
Husband's Wage	−.848	.0059	−.842	−.789	−.952	(3.10)
Nonemp. Income	−.0117	−.0056	−.017	−.018	−.018	(1.33)
AGE 55–64						
Own Wage	.681	.115	.796	.945	.950	(2.37)
Husband's Wage	−.747	.297	−.450	−.707	−.919	(1.52)
Nonemp. Income	−.0118	.0022	−.0096	−.017	−.022	(.64)

[a] Maximum likelihood estimates for the Logistic Model. Obtained from second row of Table 1.2.
[b] Ordinary least squares linear regression estimates of hours worked, based on "labor force" subsample. Obtained from second row of Table 1.4.
[c] Ordinary least squares linear regression estimates of hours worked based on "all persons" sample. Obtained from third row of Table 1.4.
[d] Maximum likelihood estimates of model with truncated normal dependent variable (Tobit). Obtained from fourth row of Table 1.4.

of 45 and 64, about half of the race differences in reservation wages can again be explained by the different levels of the supply determinants.

Reservation wages vary a great deal with age. For white wives the reservation wage increases sharply from ages 14–24 to 25–34, and is essentially undefined for the subsequent decade, suggesting a very high reservation wage when the total number of children in the household reaches its maximum. Thereafter, as child-care responsibilities decline, the reservation wage for white wives declines abruptly. For black wives the age pattern is smoother, but falls from the first age cohort until it rises slightly again in the last age cohort.

Though black wives begin childbearing earlier than do whites, differences in family composition would appear only partly to explain the different age pattern of black reservation wages. One might hypothesize that, in addition to the aging and life-cycle effects of family formation, there is also a strong vintage (Welch, 1973) effect present for black wives, given the much lower quality of schooling they received in the past than in the present. Recent improvements in the schooling of younger cohorts may have increased both their market (see Table 1.3, column 1) and nonmarket productivity.

COMPARISONS OF EMPIRICAL RESULTS ACROSS MODEL FORMULATIONS

If one makes the strong assumption of independence in the disturbances in the market participation and hours worked equations 1.12 and 1.13, the sum of the elasticity of participation and the elasticity of hours worked conditional on participation should approximately equal the Tobit elasticity of the expected value locus of the labor supply. Table 1.6 compares these elasticity estimates across models for the three central economic variables. Where the underlying response coefficients are estimated with considerable confidence, i.e., the Tobit asymptotic t statistics are substantial, the sum of the elasticities obtained from the stepwise equations is similar to the Tobit elasticity.[30] The simple stepwise approach appears to yield, more often than not, a slight underestimate of the Tobit elasticity; this might be due to the positive correlation anticipated between the disturbances in equations 1.12 and 1.13 and postulated within the Tobit framework. Nonetheless, the simple stepwise approach appears to be closer to the Tobit estimates than the linear approximation (column 4) for the labor supply function that neglects the limited dependent variable bias.

In Figures 1.3 and 1.4, the differences between the linear (OLS) and nonlinear (Tobit) estimates of the relations between wife's wage and husband's wage and the market labor supply are plotted, holding the other variables in equation 1.9 constant at the sample means. The cohort plotted is white wives aged 45 to 54. It is again evident that in the vicinity of the sample means (i.e., husband's wage = $2.61; wife's wage = $1.62) the slopes of the OLS regression line and the Tobit expected value locus (or labor supply) are similar. But for outlying observations, several standard deviations from the mean, they diverge.

---

[30] With respect to the wife's elasticities, the sum of the stepwise estimates is on average about 15 percent from the Tobit elasticity estimates; for the husband's wage elasticity estimates the figure is only 4 percent, on average. These comparisons are restricted to those coefficients for which the asymptotic t statistics in the Tobit equation exceed in absolute value two. In eight out of ten cases, the wife's wage elasticity estimates are less than the Tobit ones, and the same is true of nine out of ten cases for the husband's wage elasticities.

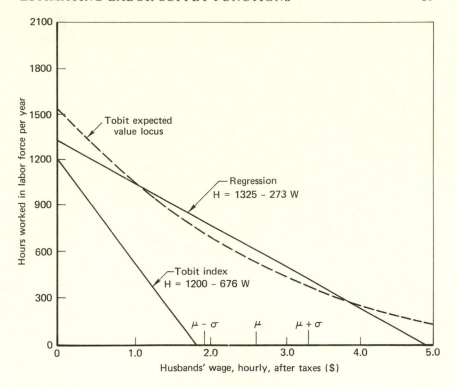

FIGURE 1.3 Comparison of linear regression and Tobit nonlinear estimates of the relationship between husband's wage and hours worked for all currently married white women, 45–54 years of age

NOTE: Other explanatory variables in the relationship reported in Table 1.4 are held constant at unweighted sample means. Wage is expressed in hourly wage rate adjusted for the incidence of federal income tax and differences in price level. See Appendices A and B for explanation. The sample unweighted mean of the wage is indicated by μ and one standard deviation range is indicated by $\mu \pm \sigma$.

One methodological conclusion supported by these calculations is that neglecting truncation bias does not seriously bias point estimates at the sample means but does limit the value of the estimates for predicting behavior over a wide range of conditioning variables. Also, the Tobit framework permits one to solve for the component participation rate (and hours worked by participants), and reservation wage, whereas the linear regression provides information only on the slope of the combined labor supply.

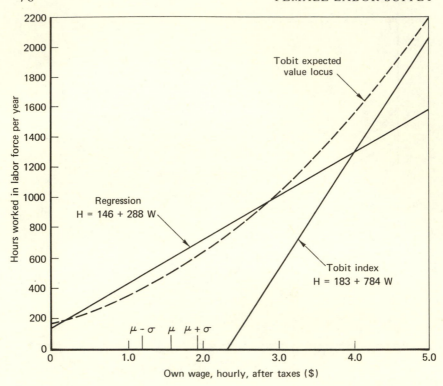

FIGURE 1.4 Comparisons of linear regression and Tobit nonlinear estimates of the relationship between own wage and hours worked for all currently married white women, 45–54 years of age

NOTE: Other explanatory variables in relationship reported in Table 1.4 are held constant at unweighted sample means. Wage is expressed in hourly wage rate adjusted for the incidence of federal income tax and differences in price level. See Appendices A and B for explanation. The sample unweighted mean of the wage is indicated by μ, and one standard deviation range is indicated by $\mu \pm \sigma$.

UNRESTRICTED REDUCED FORM ESTIMATES

The preceding estimates of the labor market model assumed that unexplained variability in the observed market hourly wage across the "labor force" subsample was due to errors in measurement and independent of condition 1.6. A market demand wage equation was, therefore, directly estimated by single equation methods and applied to impute permanent wages to the entire sample. Relaxing this strong assumption, Tobit estimates of the unrestricted reduced form equation 1.5 are reported in Table 1.7. These reduced form estimates are free of "selectivity bias" or nonlinear simultaneous equation bias, but do not identify whether an exogenous variable exerts its effect on labor market behavior through its influence on the market demand equation, or the individual supply equation, or both.[31]

The reduced form estimates may only be compared unrigorously with those in row 4 of Table 1.4 in terms of (1) their explanatory power; (2) their estimates of two common variables that do not enter the market demand function, i.e., husband's permanent wage rate and nonemployment income; and (3) the role attributed in equations 1.9 and 1.11 to variables directly (in the labor supply equation) and indirectly (market wage equation) and the sum of these effects that is presumably captured in the reduced form equation 1.5.

The mean average square error (MSE) of the reduced form equations is on the average 5.4 percent smaller than for the restricted labor supply model, despite the net addition of ten explanatory variables to the estimation equation. Yet the calculated F ratio indicated that if the model is assumed linear (not reported), this loss of ten degrees of freedom is sufficiently offset by the reduction in the MSE to be statistically significant at the 1 percent confidence level in all age and race cohorts, except the smallest, viz. blacks age 54–64.[32]

For every race and age group the (negative) effect of the husband's wage rate increases in magnitude in the reduced form equations, compared with the previously estimated expected labor supply functions. The estimated effect of nonemployment income on labor supply is also generally strengthened in the reduced form equation and shifts in the negative direction, although these nonemployment income effects remain larger in magnitude and more frequently statistically significant for whites than blacks.

Farm residence decreases the market labor supply of wives by a greater amount according to the reduced form estimates than according to the structural equation models of the labor market. This is

[31] Several differences should be noted between the estimates summarized in Table 1.6 and those in Table 1.7. First, the instrumental variable market wage equation (Appendix A) is fitted with the dependent variable in logarithmic form. The Tobit reduced form assumes that all right-hand-side variables linearly determine the Tobit index. Second, the instrumental variable estimates of the market wage offer are adjusted for marginal taxes and differences among households in the costs of living. Such a nonlinear (multiplicative) adjustment is not incorporated into the Tobit reduced form estimates reported in Table 1.7.

[32] See Johnston, 1972, pp. 198–204, for F constrained ratio test of statistical significance of constraints in a linear statistical model.

TABLE 1.7: Tobit Estimates of the Reduced Form Equation of Annual Hours Worked in the Labor Market by Currently Married Women (Beneath the Tobit Index Slope Coefficient is its Asymptotic *t* Statistic in Parentheses, and Elasticity of the Expected Value Locus in Brackets)

| | Currently Married Women | | | | | | | | | |
| | Age 14–24 | | Age 25–34 | | Age 35–44 | | Age 45–54 | | Age 55–64 | |
Variables	White	Black	White	Black	White	Black	White	Black	White	Black
1. Spouse Wage ($/hour)	−375.[a] (1.91) [.646]	−771.[a] (1.84) [1.32]	−1206.[a] (8.82) [2.52]	−1003.[a] (4.31) [1.62]	−949.[a] (9.85) [2.08]	−677.[a] (3.99) [1.10]	−908.[a] (9.87) [1.81]	−971.[a] (4.22) [1.49]	−1113.[a] (6.02) [2.05]	−643. (1.54) [1.03]
2. Nonemployment Income ($/year)	−4.83 (.27) [.003]	−35.9 (.71) [.011]	.87 (.11) [.001]	3.54 (.21) [.002]	−14.7[a] (2.84) [.034]	29.3[a] (2.05) [.018]	−21.2[a] (5.13) [.090]	−9.81 (1.04) [.014]	−15.8[a] (2.27) [.078]	−24.4 (1.08) [.038]
3. Farm Residence	−1316.[a] (3.34) [.046]	111. (.18) [.004]	−1002.[a] (3.80) [.040]	−537. (1.50) [.024]	−1175.[a] (6.14) [.070]	−1027.[a] (3.60) [.055]	−1174.[a] (6.57) [.093]	−1369.[a] (4.47) [.092]	−1505.[a] (4.66) [.144]	−1409.[a] (2.25) [.085]
4. Disability	−490. (1.48) [.017]	−866. (2.01) [.053]	−525.[a] (2.42) [.029]	−740.[a] (3.42) [.062]	−1129.[a] (7.30) [.103]	−1288.[a] (6.60) [.165]	−1391.[a] (10.4) [.196]	−1085.[a] (7.02) [.233]	−1224.[a] (5.69) [.251]	−1328.[a] (5.66) [.490]
5. Years Elementary Schooling	1126.[a] (2.96) [.661]	−92.8 (.30) [.082]	52.0 (.52) [.029]	280.[a] (2.36) [.296]	310.[a] (4.40) [.270]	191.[a] (2.93) [.344]	163.[a] (2.49) [.209]	−53.5 (1.11) [.144]	8.11 (.08) [.016]	−39.0 (.50) [.127]
6. Years Secondary Schooling	443.[a] (5.93) [.944]	503.[a] (5.20) [1.15]	273.[a] (4.13) [.544]	415.[a] (6.00) [.734]	164.[a] (3.10) [.290]	128.[a] (1.93) [.168]	92.8[a] (1.68) [.134]	189.[a] (2.20) [.181]	457.[a] (4.18) [.542]	12.2 (.038) [.009]

Variable										
7. Years Higher Schooling	164. (1.55) [.055]	18.3 (.07) [.003]	400.[a] (4.87) [.189]	422.[a] (3.82) [.112]	288.[a] (3.72) [.108]	96.8 (.96) [.032]	188.[a] (2.47) [.069]	381.[a] (3.01) [.083]	434.[a] (3.08) [.164]	543.[a] (2.00) [.129]
8. Secondary School Dummy	8410.[a] (2.79) [6.59]	-547. (.23) [.471]	548. (.72) [.414]	1352. (1.48) [.931]	2367.[a] (4.30) [1.56]	1225.[a] (2.33) [.673]	1213.[a] (2.29) [.697]	-1107.[a] (2.60) [.448]	-838. (.96) [.432]	-188. (.26) [.067]
9. Higher School Dummy	2141.[a] (4.99) [.282]	3163. (4.56) [.263]	1137.[a] (3.28) [.193]	1637.[a] (3.96) [.160]	550.[a] (1.79) [.072]	855.[a] (2.28) [.089]	429. (1.40) [.055]	-420. (.76) [.027]	496. (.87) [.067]	-477. (.66) [.044]
10. Post-Schooling Experience (yrs.)	-162.[a] (1.83) [.357]	259.[a] (2.34) [.744]	95.0[a] (1.70) [.757]	34.1 (.52) [.310]	139. (1.56) [2.24]	-197.[a] (2.03) [3.53]	-127. (.98) [2.93]	-216. (1.38) [6.05]	-28.9 (.09) [.918]	519. (1.33) [20.9]
11. Post-Schooling Experience (yrs. squared/10)	329.[a] (2.41) [.341]	-84.6 (.61) [.123]	-.390 (.01) [.004]	15.3 (.51) [.173]	-19.9 (.91) [.679]	46.1[a] (2.04) [1.87]	15.4 (.73) [1.11]	24.1 (1.02) [2.25]	-9.70 (.25) [1.24]	-70.0 (1.56) [12.1]
12. City Size 1 Residence	208. (.73) [.013]	83.6 (.17) [.004]	333.[a] (3.80) [.040]	87.5 (.29) [.004]	-91.6 (.47) [.006]	296. (1.07) [.055]	406.[a] (1.93) [.022]	-247. (.71) [.008]	61.0 (.16) [.004]	-732. (1.17) [.025]
13. City Size 2 Residence	440. (2.06) [.158]	-228. (.78) [.146]	404.[a] (2.23) [.157]	262. (1.25) [.143]	-72.0 (.49) [.027]	-7.55 (.044) [.004]	232. (1.49) [.080]	9.60 (.05) [.005]	330. (1.19) [.112]	3.29 (.01) [.002]
14. South Residence	397. (2.95) [.128]	147. (.65) [.077]	475.[a] (4.29) [.132]	123. (.83) [.056]	249.[a] (2.64) [.070]	12.9 (.10) [.006]	95.4 (.93) [.025]	-181. (1.13) [.094]	-220. (1.19) [.060]	117. (.48) [.063]
15. Residence Outside of SMSA	345. (1.69) [.118]	-843.[a] (2.34) [.148]	137. (.78) [.041]	-388. (1.61) [.060]	-300.[a] (2.05) [.081]	-399.[a] (2.01) [.062]	121. (.78) [.033]	-636.[a] (2.84) [.136]	97.7 (.35) [.030]	-179. (.47) [.033]

See footnote at end of table.

TABLE 1.7: Continued

	Currently Married Women									
	Age 14–24		Age 25–34		Age 35–44		Age 45–54		Age 55–64	
Variables	White	Black	White	Black	White	Black	White	Black	White	Black
Constant	−10213. (3.37)	−728. (.30)	−1120. (1.46)	−1583. (1.60)	−2677. (2.96)	2046. (1.92)	3021. (1.62)	7147. (2.72)	3941. (.65)	−7869. (.92)
Mean Squared Error (about E(Hours))	.557 E6	.433 E6	.491 E6	.643 E6	.638 E6	.683 E6	.728 E6	.655 E6	.573 E6	.542 E6
Mean of Hours Worked	479.5	385.5	363.2	623.1	512.5	707.8	612.3	654.5	437.4	530.2
Standard Deviation—Hours Worked	780.9	704.5	721.2	854.6	831.1	886.6	897.7	875.8	812.1	821.6

[a] Asymptotic t suggests a 5 percent or better confidence can be expressed for the coefficient being nonzero. Variables are defined in Table 1.11.

particularly noticeable among whites, for whom the market wage equation consistently prescribes lower market demand for the labors of farm residents. The labor supply effects of a health disability, on the other hand, are similar in size in the reduced form equation and in the structural equation model, even though disabilities appear to exert a depressing effect on market demand. The labor supply effect of health disabilities increases considerably with age in both the reduced form and the structural equation model.

Educational attainment in the reduced form equation generally increases market work. This is anticipated from the positive coefficient attached to years of schooling in the market wage demand equation. What is perhaps more interesting than the rule are the exceptions. Primary schooling is *not* observed to increase, to a statistically significant degree (i.e., $t > 1.7$), the labor supply among whites aged 24 to 35 and 55 to 64, nor among blacks aged 14 to 24 and 45 to 64. Secondary and higher education has a more consistent positive effect across ages, but even these diminish among older black cohorts, for whom the quality of schooling may have been much inferior.

Schooling may increase an individual's productivity in both market and nonmarket activities, but not necessarily by the same proportion, and affect the level and composition of goods demanded through wealth and price effects. The differences in these potentially offsetting effects of education might be called education's productivity bias toward market or nonmarket activities. Among whites aged 14 to 24, primary schooling has an overall market bias, and this bias emerges clearly again after age 35 when white wives begin to return from child-rearing activities to the market labor force. For blacks the market bias of primary schooling is evident only from age 25 to 44, when this group is most active in the labor force.

Each additional year of secondary or higher education, on the other hand, is associated with greater market work among both races and most age groups, according to the unrestricted reduced-form estimates (Table 1.7). In terms of derivatives of the Tobit expected value locus, an additional year of secondary or higher education is directly associated with an increase of 75 to 200 hours of market work per year (derived from Table 1.7). Neglecting progressive tax effects, the structural equation model associates an 8 to 15 percent increase in market wage rates with each added year of education, implying an increase in expected labor supply of about 25 to 75 hours per year. Schooling

TABLE 1.8: Direct Estimates of the Effects of Children on Annual Hours Worked in the Labor Supply Force by Currently Married Women by Age

Regression Number	Subsample Characteristics (Size)	No. Children by Age 0–4	5–13	14–17	Wife's Wage[a]	Husband's Wage[a]	Non-employment Income	R^2
			WHITE					
	Age 14–24							
1	All	−322.	−29.6		344.	16.6	−.0426	.1705
	(1259)	(14.0)	(.67)		(3.66)	(.26)	(.73)	
2	All				577.	−61.6	−.0165	.0358
	(1259)				(5.62)	(.91)	(.27)	
	Age 25–34							
1	All	−242.	−73.7	68.0	220.	−206.	.0189	.1145
	(2608)	(15.5)	(7.01)	(1.88)	(3.71)	(6.40)	(.92)	
2	All				212.	−217.	.0212	.0199
	(2608)				(3.44)	(6.44)	(.98)	
	Age 35–44							
1	All	−221.	−117.	−.185	137.	−223.	−.0385	.1117
	(2879)	(8.19)	(9.95)	(.01)	(2.22)	(7.52)	(2.75)	
2	All				53.8	−231.	−.0297	.0444
	(2879)				(.85)	(7.53)	(2.05)	
	Age 45–54							
1	All	−266.	−131.	−5.07	307.	−261.	−.0229	.0849
	(2538)	(2.29)	(5.47)	(.28)	(4.90)	(8.00)	(3.27)	
2	All				289.	−273.	−.0231	.0694
	(2538)				(4.59)	(8.35)	(3.28)	
	Age 55–64							
1	All	835.	−188.	−3.93	576.	−260.	−.0146	.0967
	(1146)	(1.51)	(1.62)	(.12)	(7.52)	(5.53)	(1.53)	
2	All				576.	−256.	−.0164	.0931
	(1146)				(7.52)	(5.49)	(1.53)	
			BLACK					
	Age 14–24							
1	All	−157.	−26.6		258.	−118.	−.0146	.0806
	(504)	(5.58)	(.59)		(1.98)	(.91)	(.12)	
2	All				360.	−255.	−.0136	.0214
	(504)				(2.76)	(1.99)	(.11)	
	Age 25–34							
1	All	−208.	−36.5	−34.0	415.	−356.	−.00225	.1289
	(988)	(8.34)	(2.27)	(.71)	(5.00)	(4.03)	(.03)	
2	All				483.	−389.	−.00207	.0515
	(988)				(5.74)	(4.29)	(.03)	
	Age 35–44							
1	All	−194.	−59.4	22.8	313.	−215.	.153	.1418
	(1113)	(5.45)	(3.49)	(1.18)	(4.48)	(2.80)	(2.13)	
2	All				317.	−244.	.195	.0877
	(1113)				(4.46)	(3.11)	(2.64)	

Regression Number	Subsample Characteristics (Size)	No. Children by Age 0–4	5–13	14–17	Wife's Wage[a]	Husband's Wage[a]	Non-employment Income	R^2
	Age 45–54							
1	All	−64.2	−58.2	11.3	414.	−293.	−.0730	.1064
	(828)	(.53)	(1.68)	(.45)	(4.56)	(3.01)	(1.64)	
2	All				421.	−308.	−.0690	.1018
	(828)				(4.64)	(3.17)	(1.55)	
	Age 55–64							
1	All		61.7	24.0	512.	−207.	−.0697	.1386
	(335)		(.55)	(.51)	(2.87)	(1.28)	(.80)	
2	All				502.	−202.	−.0660	.1367
	(335)				(2.84)	(1.26)	(.76)	

[a] Tax adjusted imputed hourly wage rate.

TABLE 1.9: Number and Age Composition of Children by Race and Age Subsamples

Age of Wife	Number of Children less than Age 18 (by Age) 0–4	5–13	14–17	All Ages
	WHITE			
14–24	1.04	.16	.01[a]	1.21
25–34	.92	1.49	.10	2.51
35–44	.26	1.33	1.02	2.61
45–54	.02	.38	.89	1.29
55–64	.00	.03	.37	.40
	BLACK			
14–24	1.41	.33	.10[a]	1.75
25–34	1.03	1.94	.22	3.19
35–44	.41	1.54	1.25	3.20
45–54	.04	.51	.93	1.48
55–64	.00	.08	.48	.56

[a] There is no way to be certain from the SEO file whether the children are the mother's own. Hence one suspects that the seven white and four black wives age 14–24 with a child age 14–17 were caring for children other than their own. Sample sizes may be obtained from Table 1.8.

beyond the primary level is, therefore, associated with a much greater increase in wives' market work than can be attributed to education's effect operating on market wages alone. Variation in the traditional "price of time" variable, the market wage, provides only half the explanation of why education, after primary school, alters so dramatically the allocation of a married woman's time between market and nonmarket activities.

The other regional and experience variables added to the unrestricted reduced form equation in Table 1.7 do not exhibit pronounced or consistent effects on expected labor supply across age and race groups.

SIMULTANEOUS EQUATION BIAS AND FAMILY COMPOSITION

It is now possible to consider briefly how family composition or fertility variables influence estimated labor "supply" response parameters. Table 1.8 compares estimates reflecting variables with and without the inclusion of three variables reflecting the size and age composition of the family. These estimates are comparable to the linear regressions on expected labor supply reported as regression 3 in Table 1.4.[33] The means of the family composition variables are reported in Table 1.9.

As widely observed, the presence of preschool-aged children is associated with wives' labor market behavior in both racial groups from age 14 to at least 44. These family composition variables explain more of the variation in labor market behavior among the younger cohorts than do the "economic" variables. Of particular interest is the effect of these family composition variables on the wife's and husband's wage coefficients. As predicted, for the youngest age cohort, for whom young children tend to reflect higher fertility goals, the inclusion of the family composition variables reduces the size of the wife's wage coefficient 38 percent for whites and 28 percent for blacks, and the husband's wage effect decreases in absolute value by more than half for whites, and even reverses sign for blacks. But by the second age group, 25–34, the family composition variables do not alter appreci-

---

[33] Farm residence and health disability were included for comparability with the earlier estimates, but not reported here, for simplicity. The slight differences in sample size noted are related to the variables included in the working sample for the study of fertility behavior.

ably the wage coefficients for whites (up 4 percent on wife's wage and down 5 percent on husband's wage) and reduce the size of the wage coefficients for blacks by much smaller amounts, 14 and 8 percent, respectively. In later age cohorts the inclusion of family composition variables influences the wage coefficients in seemingly erratic ways.

One might interpret these findings to suggest that the timing of early childbearing is jointly and simultaneously related to a wife's labor market plans in her younger married years. Market wage opportunities are allowed too small a long-run effect on the labor supply of wives in the youngest age cohort unless fertility patterns are also permitted to respond to the level of market earnings opportunities available to husbands and wives. Holding constant family composition as though it were in the long run exogenous to the allocation of the family labor supply ignores the substantial extent to which fertility also responds to the same wage and income variables as does the wife's labor supply. These results imply, moreover, that the past practice of including family composition variables in labor supply functions for wives over age 34 has probably not substantially biased (downward) the estimated wage and income response parameters. Among the youngest cohort aged 14 to 24, much greater labor market responsiveness may be anticipated than has heretofore been estimated. This may explain the unexpected growth in the young female labor force in the last decade and the equally unanticipated decline in birth rates as young women's wage rates have been rising relative to men's.

V. SUMMARY AND CONCLUSIONS

INTERPRETATION OF THE PARAMETER ESTIMATES

Several empirical regularities emerge independent of model specification and estimation method. Studies of married women have noted lower levels of labor supply associated with household income from sources other than the wife's own earnings. This is often interpreted as evidence of the normal income effect demand for leisure. This result is replicated here, but only with respect to the husband's wage (Table 1.6, column 5). The "pure" income effect, to the extent that nonemployment income in a cross-section measures exogenous variation in physical wealth, is close to zero.[34] The labor supply elasticity with respect to husband's wage is always substantial, and increases sharply at the start of the marriage life cycle, increasing from age 14–24 to 25–34 from −.4 to −1.6 for whites and from −1.1 to −1.3 for blacks. This pattern of cross-wage effects is consistent with the strong substitutability of time of husband and wife in nonmarket activity during the child-rearing years, with somewhat greater complementarity of sharing activities at the start and end of the marriage cycle.

Conversely, the wife's labor supply elasticity with respect to her own wage is largest at the start and end of the life cycle, fluctuating for whites from 1.8 to .3 to 2.1, and for blacks from 1.1 to .6 to 1.0. Mincer (1962, p. 67) was the first to speculate that since it was more difficult to find substitutes (market goods and services) "for mother's care of small children" than for her other nonmarket activities "such as food preparation and physical maintenance of the household," the income effect on their hours of market work would be greater (negatively larger) when small children are present in the household than at other times in the life cycle. Though the empirical regularity is observed here, it would appear that the possibilities for substitution of the wife's nonmarket time for market income declines during the years of child rearing, but that this response is not readily attributed to income effects. The own-wage elasticity reaches a minimum somewhat later for school-aged children (Table 1.9); and older children may also generate substantial time demands, particularly among higher wage, better educated white women (Leibowitz, 1972; Smith, 1972).

According to these estimates of uncompensated own and cross-wage elasticities, any increase in an income tax borne proportionately by both husband and wife would not greatly alter the overall participation rate or hours worked by married women, although it might elicit a moderate change in the age composition of women working. A surtax

---

[34] Evidence from subsequent studies of labor supply of married women have generally confirmed this regularity. Heckman's inclusion of assets also obtains a statistically insignificant coefficient (Chapter 5, Tables 5.1 and 5.3), as it did in my restricted SEO sample for white net worth. See also Cogan's results in Chapter 3, Table 3.3 and Chapter 7, Table 7.2, Table 7.4. Hanoch's estimates in Chapter 6 cast no light on this issue, for he combines work contingent transfers in "nonemployment income" (Appendix B), and then adds husband's actual earnings. He is thus returning to the practice of Kosters (1966) of assuming that the compensated cross wage response of wives to husband's wages is zero, and neglecting the definitional inverse dependency of pensions, unemployment compensation, etc., on labor supply.

would increase hours worked among white and black married women aged 14–24 and over 55, and decrease it among women in the intervening age groups. Age stratification in the analysis of labor market behavior of married women, therefore, appears fully justified by these systematic parameter differences by age among both racial groups.

CONCLUSIONS

In two situations, nonlinear estimation procedures have been proposed above as improvements over traditional linear regression techniques. In the case of analyses of the labor force participation decision, the dichotomous nature of the dependent variable suggests that the linear probability function should be replaced by a logit or probit model. The comparison of response elasticities (Table 1.2) and implicit reservation wages (Table 1.3) obtained from the linear and nonlinear approaches did not reveal any major surprises, although the confidence intervals about the point estimates appear to be tighter in the statistically defensible case of the nonlinear logit formulation.

Analyses of the number of hours worked by all persons also suggest the need for a nonlinear estimation procedure because of the truncation of observations at a lower limit of zero hours worked. The Tobit framework is preferable to the ordinary least squares for the additional reason that it explicitly estimates the variance of the disturbances about the Tobit index, and the Tobit framework thereby provides estimates of the two components of the expected labor supply: the participation rate and hours worked conditional on participation.

In the actual empirical results, the Tobit procedure, in comparison with the linear ordinary least squares method, accounts for only a slightly increased share of the variance of hours worked and implies similar estimates of response elasticities at sample means. But again, an improvement is noted in tighter confidence limits based on the Tobit framework, and in more plausible values for predicted behavior away from the sample means. In sum, the Tobit technique seems a warranted application of more costly nonlinear estimation procedures to the study of labor market behavior. As a first approximation, however, linear methods are not likely to lead one far astray.

Finally, there is the issue of whether the estimation of expected labor supply behavior should be treated as two separate decisions regarding participation and hours worked conditional on participation, or whether these two decisions are appropriately viewed as generated by the same linear function that is simply truncated at zero hours. Two questions are involved. First, does estimating the two decision equations separately introduce a serious selectivity bias, since the working wives may not be representative of nonworking wives? The striking similarity in response elasticities obtained from the sum of the two decision functions and that obtained from the integrated Tobit framework (Table 1.6, columns 3 and 5) suggests that this source of selectivity bias is not very important in the context considered here.

The second question is whether the imposition of a homogeneous process to generate the participation and hours worked outcomes may be an undesirable restriction on the way these very different decisions are actually made. While retaining the joint estimation approach implicit in the Tobit framework, there is reason to reformulate the likelihood function in such a manner as to test statistically whether the joint decisions to participate in the labor force and to work a specific number of hours once in the labor market are determined by the same linear combination of factors.

ACKNOWLEDGMENTS

Contract NIH-71-2211 from the Center for Population Research of the National Institute of Child Health and Human Development permitted me to explore alternative methodological approaches to the study of labor supply, while grant NE-G-00-3-0212 from the National Institute of Education assisted me in writing this paper and performing the final computations at the University of Minnesota.

This work benefited from critical readings of drafts by J. Cogan, J. DaVanzo, D. N. De Tray, D. H. Greenberg, J. Hause, J. J. Heckman, S. Hoenack, H. D. Mohring, R. Olsen, T. W. Schultz, R. Shishko, and C. Sims. J. P. Smith helped in compressing the Rand report into its current form. They share no responsibility for remaining shortcomings, but credit is due for improvements in content and presentation. For research assistance I am indebted to K. Van Riesen, T. Turner, and R. Shakotko.

ESTIMATION OF MARKET DEMAND WAGE EQUATIONS

In this appendix an equation is specified analogous to equation 1.1′ that accounts for variation across individuals in market wage rates. Subsequently, ordinary least squares estimates of the parameters to this equation are obtained for several populations of labor force participants defined by sex, race, schooling, and regional origins. The first issue is the choice of determinants of market wage rate offers that are to be treated as exogenous to individual labor market behavior.

The market demand wage rate equations estimated for persons reporting an hourly wage are shown in Tables 1.10 and 1.11. The rationale for disaggregating the population according to demographic and economic characteristics is explained below. The variables are defined following Table 1.11 in terms of the information collected by the 1967 Survey of Economic Opportunity.

DEFINITIONS OF VARIABLES AND SYMBOLS IN WAGE EQUATION
(TABLES 1.10 AND 1.11)

> Wage = Hourly wage last week (Spring 1967), equal to last week's earnings divided by last week's hours worked (in dollars).
>
> Farm = Dummy variable equals one if respondent lives on a farm, zero otherwise.
>
> Not SMSA = Dummy variable equals one if respondent does not live in a Standard Metropolitan Statistical Area (Census definition).
>
> City Size (1) = Dummy variable equals one if respondent lives in a city with a population between 250,000 and 499,999.
>
> City Size (2) = Dummy variable equals one if respondent lives in a city with a population of 500,000 or more.

TABLE 1.10: Hourly Wage Rate Equation: Males[a]

Sample Composition	Farm	Not SMSA	City Size (1)	City Size (2)	South	Dis-ability	Educa-tion (Yrs.)	Work Experi-ence	Work Experi-ence (Sq.)	Constant	N	R²	(MSE)
WHITE													
EDUCATION													
0–8 yrs.	−.308 (7.77)	−.100 (3.33)	.0248 (.54)	.0971 (3.19)	−.0854 (4.13)	−.136 (4.99)	.0474 (9.24)	.0509 (19.6)	−.0075 (15.6)	−.173	2098	.294	(384)
9–12 yrs.	−.199 (6.77)	−.0556 (2.85)	.0243 (.002)	.109 (5.81)	−.0894 (6.87)	−.144 (7.07)	.0774 (14.9)	.0488 (29.7)	−.0081 (21.3)	.351	5351	.290	(929)
13+ yrs.	−.228 (3.32)	.0325 (.85)	.115 (2.33)	.272 (7.83)	−.0348 (1.52)	−.159 (3.51)	.0550 (10.5)	.0455 (15.5)	−.0101 (11.4)	.667	2468	.224	(609)
BLACK: SOUTH AT AGE 16													
EDUCATION													
0–8 yrs.	−.401 (10.4)	−.176 (5.13)	.0364 (.60)	.201 (5.97)	−.215 (6.34)	−.116 (3.35)	.0251 (4.78)	.0296 (8.06)	.0043 (6.97)	.120	1587	.387	(294)
9–12 yrs.	−.120 (1.90)	−.192 (5.07)	−.0530 (1.12)	.136 (4.44)	−.245 (9.49)	−.132 (2.90)	.0439 (4.82)	.0246 (8.22)	−.0050 (6.19)	.483	1322	.308	(185)
13+ yrs.	−.209 (.78)	−.0903 (.71)	.198 (1.55)	.389 (4.49)	−.104 (1.67)	−.201 (1.68)	.103 (6.35)	.0227 (2.65)	−.0060 (2.38)	.405	272	.278	(51.9)
BLACK: NON-SOUTH AT AGE 16													
EDUCATION													
0–8 yrs.	−.839 (−2.52)	−.283 (1.33)	.270 (1.47)	.0564 (.46)	−.164 (1.43)	−.204 (2.60)	.0285 (2.14)	.0183 (1.92)	−.0026 (1.68)	.357	259	.156	(38.7)
9–12 yrs.	−.677 (1.74)	.0115 (.11)	.130 (1.19)	.0779 (1.24)	−.132 (1.40)	−.103 (1.99)	.0551 (4.21)	.0312 (8.22)	−.0064 (6.44)	.447	739	.135	(100)
13+ yrs.	−.427 (1.01)	−.158 (.80)	.0993 (.33)	.0238 (.19)	−.196 (1.81)	−.156 (1.17)	.0634 (3.26)	.0317 (3.50)	−.0092 (3.37)	.811	180	.204	(25.0)

[a] See variable definitions in Statistical Appendix A below. T statistics are presented in parentheses beneath the regression coefficients.

TABLE 1.11: Hourly Wage Rate Equation: Females[a]

Sample Composition	Farm	Not SMSA	City Size (1)	City Size (2)	South	Disability	Education (Yrs.)	Work Experience	Work Experience (Sq.)	Constant	N	R² (MSE)
WHITE												
EDUCATION												
0–8 yrs.	-.0494	-.196	-.0052	-.0631	-.143	-.0941	.0102	.0403	-.0069	-.0513	860	.160
	(.65)	(3.44)	(.060)	(1.14)	(3.76)	(1.83)	(.97)	(8.76)	(8.03)	(.41)		(212)
9–12 yrs.	-.106	-.0911	-.0134	.150	-.0677	-.156	.0832	.0219	-.0043	.116	3658	.149
	(2.80)	(3.48)	(.37)	(5.96)	(3.96)	(5.02)	(11.26)	(11.36)	(8.53)	(3.19)		(772)
13+ yrs.	.0053	-.0321	.173	.158	-.0795	-.0236	.0903	.0175	-.0038	.458	1286	.136
	(.069)	(.60)	(2.53)	(3.16)	(2.45)	(.35)	(10.1)	(4.56)	(3.27)	(8.10)		(321)
BLACK												
EDUCATION												
0–8 yrs.	-.0359	-.308	.0048	.226	-.304	-.0525	.0200	.0144	-.0028	-.0675	1169	.346
	(.56)	(7.40)	(.077)	(5.89)	(8.79)	(1.44)	(2.69)	(2.92)	(3.45)	(.68)		(238)
9–12 yrs.	.0729	-.100	.0803	.280	-.244	-.0790	.0843	.0075	-.0017	-.0190	1980	.280
	(1.04)	(2.44)	(1.62)	(9.03)	(11.7)	(2.37)	(9.79)	(3.00)	(2.63)	(.417)		(335)
13+ yrs.	-.0618	-.0245	.0078	.178	-.181	-.164	.151	.0141	-.0052	.400	508	.320
	(.37)	(.28)	(.08)	(2.98)	(4.20)	(2.16)	(12.6)	(2.69)	(3.27)	(5.49)		(845)

[a] See variable definitions in Statistical Appendix A below. T statistics are presented in parentheses beneath the regression coefficients.

South = Dummy variable equals one if respondent lives in Southern Census Region.

Disability = Dummy variable equal to one if respondent reported he had a major health disability.

Education = Years of schooling completed in the educational level considered: 0–8 for those with elementary or less schooling completed; 1–4 for those with some high school but no college; 1–8 for those with some years of college or post-high-school education completed.

Work Experience = Difference in years between respondent's age and age when he is assumed to have entered the market or nonmarket labor force. The age of labor force entry by years of schooling completed is derived from Hanoch (1965b, p. 54) and Mincer (1974) and is as follows:

Age of Entry into Labor Force	Schooling Grade Completed
10	<5
14	5–7
16	8
18	9–11
20	12
23	13–15
26	16
28	17–20

Work Experience Squared = The value of the work experience variable squared, divided by ten.

N = Number of observations in sample.

R^2 = Coefficient of determination.

MSE = Mean squared error.

PROCEDURES USED TO ADJUST IMPUTED MARKET WAGE FOR FEDERAL INCOME TAXES AND COST OF LIVING DIFFERENCES

ADJUSTMENT OF PREDICTED WAGE RATES

From the permanent market offer wage rate predicted by the hourly wage equation (discussed in Tables 1.10 and 1.11), an approximation is sought for the individual's valuation at the margin of labor market activity. The predicted wage is adjusted, *first* for the incidence of federal income taxes (which is assumed to be a simplified function of the predicted wages and actual hours worked of all household members; household nonearned income; and numbers of dependents), and *second* for regional and income class differences in relative price levels that affect the purchasing power of market income.

LINEARIZED BUDGET CONSTRAINT

It is assumed that the market demand wage offer is independent of hours worked, implying that the market income budget constraint is a linear function of hours worked. Under a continuously progressive income tax, the slope of the *after-tax* market income budget constraint would monotonically decrease as the number of hours worked increased (see Hall, 1973). The fundamental problem of joint determination of tax rates and hours worked is not resolved here, and has been analyzed directly only under restrictive assumptions (Wales, 1973; Olsen, 1974).

IMPUTATION OF TAX RATES

Studies of labor supply behavior have frequently neglected the differential effect of taxes, but this procedure is certainly not justified for the study of secondary workers, whose marginal tax rate is not a simple increasing function of their own wage rate. There will soon be available a merged file, based on the 1967 SEO and 1966 IRS tax file prepared by Okner (1972), that may provide better estimates of income tax liability for the survey units considered here.

As a first approximation, I have in the interim proceeded to use a much simplified procedure of imputation, which is summarized by the following assumptions:

1. All married couples currently living together file a tax return jointly;
2. Other persons with dependent children file tax returns as "head of household";
3. Otherwise, persons with income in excess of $600 in 1966 file tax returns as single;
4. All nonearned income of a household is attributed to the head of household;
5. Gross taxable income is set equal to the product of imputed wage rates and actual hours worked (and those of the spouse, if any), or if self-employed, farm and business income, plus nonearned income if the individual is the head of household;
6. Net taxable income is set equal to gross taxable income minus the standard deduction of 10 percent and $600 personal exemptions for self, spouse, and own children, if any;
7. The appropriate tax table for 1966 federal income taxes was consulted and the total tax liability and marginal tax rate were determined.

The least satisfactory step in this procedure, from a conceptual point of view, is the use of the hybrid of an imputed wage and the actual hours worked (an endogenous variable) in step 5. Using predicted hours worked might have been preferable, but with the limited explanatory power of a reduced form hours equation, this procedure was not adopted here. From a practical point of view, the standard deduction assumption and the neglect of capital gains benefits undoubtedly overstates tax rates for the high-income units; and my inability always to attribute dependents to the appropriate tax unit, except for children, may distort the tax estimates for middle- and lower-middle-income units.

Nonpecuniary market rewards for work may be another important inducement to participate and work in the market (Morgan, 1974, II, chapter 6). Even the most readily measured nonwage rewards, such as fringe benefits, are not available in the SEO file for study here.

COST OF LIVING ADJUSTMENT

The purchasing power of market income differs substantially across regions of the United States. Moreover, these differences in cost of living by residental location are not uniform with regard to the basket of goods and services purchased by households at different income levels. Cost of living indexes for 1967 are, therefore, distinguished for 24 groups defined in Table 1.12 by metropolitan or nonmetropolitan residence in four census regions (Northeast, North Central, South, and West), divided into three income size classes. The methodology used to construct the "basket of goods" by income level assumed a family of four with a typical age composition. To assign each of the SEO households (not tax return units) to an income size class, total actual market income per capita of the household is multiplied by four. Economies of scale are regrettably neglected here in allocating the family unit. Metropolitan residence was assumed to imply residence within a standard metropolitan statistical area (SMSA), and census region of residence was reported directly. The marginal after-tax wage rate for all individuals in the household was then divided by the appropriate cost of living index.

TABLE 1.12: Cost of Living Adjustment Factors by Region
and Family Income Level

Total Family Income ($)[a]	Northeast		North Central		South		West	
	Metro. Areas[b]	Non-Metro. Areas[b]	Metro. Areas[b]	Non-Metro. Areas[b]	Metro. Areas[b]	Non-Metro. Areas[b]	Metro. Areas[b]	Non-Metro. Areas[b]
7,000 or less	102	96	102	98	95	88	105	103
7,001 to 11,000	106	99	101	94	93	86	103	98
11,001 or over	108	95	100	92	94	84	103	95

SOURCE: U.S. Bureau of Labor Statistics, *Three Standards of Living, Spring 1967* (1970), Table 3, p. 35.

[a] Cost of living indexes are based on income levels for a family of four persons. Therefore, the SEO family unit's income is divided by $n/4$, where n is the number of individuals in the family.

[b] Metropolitan Areas are defined as within a Standard Metropolitan Statistical Area (SMSA).

CHAPTER 2

MARRIED WOMEN'S LABOR SUPPLY: A COMPARISON OF ALTERNATIVE ESTIMATION PROCEDURES

JOHN COGAN

THE RAND CORPORATION

I. Introduction

A central problem in estimating married women's labor supply functions is that no market wage is observed for women who do not work. Several empirical approaches have been devised to deal with this problem. One approach (Kalachek and Raines, 1970; Boskin, 1973; Schultz, Chapter 1) is to use only those women who work as the sample for estimation. Another approach (Hall, 1973; Leibowitz, 1972; and Schultz, Chapter 1) uses the entire sample of observations. Both of these conventional procedures, hereafter termed Models I and II, respectively, use a predicted wage, obtained from an auxiliary wage equation estimated on the subsample of working women, as a right-hand-side regressor. The usual justification for the imputed wage in Model I is that the observed wage is either jointly determined with hours of work or measured with error. The justification for the computed wage in Model II is usually that the failure to observe wages for nonworking women is a problem in "missing variables." Recently, Heckman (1974b) has proposed a maximum likelihood estimator which effectively resolves the problem.

This chapter presents a methodological and empirical comparison of these three alternative methods of estimation. A fourth procedure, developed by Gronau (1973b) is added to the methodological evaluation. Beginning with a general framework, the examination brings into sharp focus the restrictive assumptions implicit in the two conventional approaches. We also consider the directions of bias in the estimated parameters of these two models that result if these implicit assumptions are violated in the data.

Each of the estimation procedures is applied to data from the 1967 National Longitudinal Survey of Mature Women. Comparisons of estimated wage and hours of work parameters across procedures are made. The comparisons reveal systematic and, in some cases, large biases in the parameter estimates of the conventional models. Comparisons of predicted reservation wages, probabilities of working, and predicted versus actual labor force participation rates are also given.

II. STATISTICAL LABOR SUPPLY MODELS

All procedures analyzed in this paper use a common framework as the theoretical foundation for their empirical models. This framework has its origins in the work of Mincer (1962) and Kosters (1966). As will be shown, differences among procedures may be traced to differences in assumptions regarding the nature of the underlying distributions of market and reservation wages. To bring these differing assumptions into clear view, it will be instructive to begin by outlining a general formulation of the estimation problem.

We may express the labor supply function as[1,2]

$$h_i = \text{MAX}(0, h(W_{1_i} - W_{2_i})), \quad \text{where} \quad h(\cdot) \geq 0 \quad \text{and} \quad h'(\cdot) > 0 \tag{2.1}$$

The side conditions of equation 2.1 indicate the nature of the labor force participation decision. If the market wage offered the married woman exceeds her reservation wage, she spent some time in the labor force and h will be positive. If the market wage she is offered is less than her reservation wage, she will reject this wage offer and allocate all of her time to nonmarket activities, in which case time worked will be zero and no market wage will be observed.

The relations determining the married woman's offered market wage and reservation wage can be written as

$$W_{1_i} = j(Z_i, \varepsilon_{1_i}), \tag{2.2}$$

$$W_{2_i} = g(Q_i, \varepsilon_{2_i}), \tag{2.3}$$

[1] An important assumption implied in equation 2.1 is that any fixed costs associated with market work are assumed to be nonexistent. See Chapters 6 and 7 for a treatment of fixed costs of work.

[2] The labor supply function is presented in deterministic form solely for simplicity. One could add a disturbance term to reflect differences in functions among individuals, but this would not affect the analysis that follows.

where Z represents a vector of observable market-related attributes of the married woman, and Q denotes a vector of her nonmarket related attributes; Q and Z will, in general, have some elements in common. ε_1 and ε_2 are random deviations in W_1 and W_2, respectively. Each is assumed to have mean zero, constant variance, and to be uncorrelated with the elements of Z and Q. ε_1 may be regarded as reflecting the effect of unobservable factors on the offered wage rate (such as the wife's ability, the quality of her education, etc.). Similarly, ε_2 may be viewed as measuring the effect of unobservable factors on her reservation wage (her nonmarket skills and tastes for nonmarket activities).

If we assume that the true relationships among the wife's labor supply, her market wage, her reservation wage, and their respective determinants are linear, we may write the labor supply model as[3]

$$h_i = \delta_1(W_{1_i} - W_{2_i}) \tag{2.4}$$

$$W_{1_i} = Z_i\beta + \varepsilon_{1_i}, \tag{2.5}$$

$$W_{2_i} = Q_i\alpha + \varepsilon_{2_i} \tag{2.6}$$

These equations yield important insight into the problem of estimation. Clearly, since W_2 is unobservable for all women, and W_1 is unobservable for nonworking women, the parameters δ_1, β, and α cannot be estimated. The best one can do is to estimate the reduced-form parameters of the system. The reduced-form labor supply equation is given by

$$h_i = Z_i\pi_1 + Q_i\pi_2 + V_i, \tag{2.7}$$

where $\pi_1 = \delta_1\beta$, $\pi_2 = -\delta_1\alpha$, and $V = \delta_1(\varepsilon_1 - \varepsilon_2)$. As equation 2.7 indicates, the reduced form yields estimates of the parameters of the reservation wage equation up to an unknown linear transformation.

Alternatively, one may impose some restrictions on the model. Labor Supply Models I and II may be characterized by the restrictions imposed on the stochastic disturbances of the market and reservation wage equations. These restrictions may be viewed as the classical technique of identifying the structural parameters through constraints on the variance-covariance matrix of disturbances.

---

[3] The assumption of linearity is made for expository convenience. Under this assumption, δ_1 is simply the inverse of the slope of the labor supply function. The side condition that hours-of-work has a lower bound of zero is hereafter dropped for purposes of exposition.

LABOR SUPPLY MODEL I

We may derive the typical empirical labor supply equation of Model I by substituting the reservation wage equation (2.6) into the deterministic labor supply function (2.4):

$$h_i = \delta_1 W_{1_i} + Q_i \pi_2 + \varepsilon_{2_i}^*, \tag{2.8}$$

where $\pi_2 = -\delta_1 \alpha$ and $\varepsilon_2^* = -\delta_1 \varepsilon_2 \sim N(0, \delta_1^2 \sigma_{\varepsilon_2}^2)$.

The distinctive feature of Model I is that the parameters of the labor supply equation are estimated by using a sample comprised solely of working women. This feature, however, is its primary shortcoming. Since ε_2 is a systematic determinant of labor supply, selecting a sample comprising only working women is equivalent to selecting ε_2. Consequently, in the resulting sample, the distribution of ε_2 is truncated, and the parameter estimates obtained are generally biased and inconsistent. Formally, a woman will be in the sample if

$$W_2 = Q\alpha + \varepsilon_2 < W_1 = Z\beta + \varepsilon_1 \tag{2.9}$$

or equivalently if

$$\varepsilon_2 < Z\beta + \varepsilon_1 - Q\alpha. \tag{2.10}$$

Since all women for whom the above inequality does not hold (i.e., for those who are not working) are excluded from the sample, the conditional expectation of the disturbance term (denoted ε_2^*) in equation 2.8 may not be assumed to be zero. Under the assumption of normally distributed disturbances the conditional expectation of the disturbance term of the labor supply equation is[4]

$$E(\varepsilon_2^* \mid h > 0) = \delta_1 \left(\frac{\sigma_2^2 - \sigma_{12}}{\sigma_u} \right) \frac{f(I)}{P(I)}, \tag{2.11}$$

where σ_{12} is the covariance between market and reservation wage disturbances; σ_u is the standard deviation of the disturbance $\varepsilon_2 - \varepsilon_1$; and $f(I)$ and $P(I)$ are the density and distribution functions of the unit normal distribution evaluated at I. I is defined as

$$I = \frac{X\beta - Q\alpha}{\sigma_u}.$$

---

[4] This result is derived by Rosenbaum (1961). For the original analysis of this problem in the labor supply context, see Heckman (Chapter 5).

Equation 2.11 indicates that the expected value of the disturbance term of the censored sample is functionally related to all the right-hand-side regressors of Model I.

While, in general, calculation of the direction of the consequent bias is a nontrivial task, we may, with an eye toward the estimates presented in Section III, speculate on the probable signs of these biases.

First, consider the expectation of hours of work conditional upon working:

$$E(h \mid Z, Q, h > 0) = \delta_1(E(W \mid Z, Q, h > 0)) + Q\pi_2 + \frac{\delta_1(\sigma_2^2 - \sigma_{12})}{\sigma_u} \frac{f(I)}{P(I)}$$

$$= \delta_1 \hat{W} + Q\pi_2 + \delta_1 \left(\frac{\sigma_2^2 - \sigma_{12}}{\sigma_u}\right) \frac{f(I)}{P(I)}. \tag{2.12}$$

Substituting equation 2.12 into the hours of work equation, we have a "true" supply equation:

$$h = \delta_1 \hat{W} + Q\pi_2 + \delta_1 \left(\frac{\sigma_2^2 - \sigma_{12}}{\sigma_u}\right) \frac{f(I)}{P(I)} + V_1, \tag{2.13}$$

where V_1 has zero mean over the subsample of working women. The estimated labor supply equation in Model I, on the other hand, is given by equation 2.8, except that an instrumental variables estimate of the wage replaces the actual wage rate.[5]

The error term in the estimated equation is the sum of the last two terms in equation 2.13. If the correlation among right-hand-side variables is zero, the direction of bias in the estimated effect of any variable depends upon the sign of the correlation between that variable and the error term in the estimating equation.[6] This sign of the correlation may be inferred by partially differentiating the disturbance term with respect to an element in Q. Differentiating with respect to

[5] The instrumental variable estimate of the wage is usually obtained from an OLS wage equation also estimated on the subsample of working women. This instrumental variable will in general be a good approximation of the expected value of wages conditional upon working.

[6] Typically in micro data these correlations are small and the results reported in Section IV indicate that they are empirically unimportant. However, to the extent that these correlations are nonzero, biases in the estimates are, from a theoretical point of view, ambiguous in sign.

the Kth element in Q yields:

$$\frac{\partial E(\varepsilon_2^* \mid h > 0)}{\partial Q_K} = -\delta_1 \left(\frac{\sigma_2^2 - \sigma_{12}}{\sigma_u} \right) \pi_K \left[\frac{f(I)P(I) + f(I)^2}{P(I)^2} \right]. \qquad (2.14)$$

The term inside the brackets is necessarily positive. Therefore the bias in the estimate Q_K depends upon the magnitudes of the variance in reservation wages (σ_2^2) and the covariance between market and reservation wages (σ_{12}). Heckman (1974b) indicates that σ_2^2 exceeds σ_{12}. If so, estimates of parameters that negatively affect the wife's labor supply will be biased in a positive direction, and vice versa.

The probable direction of bias in the wage coefficient is more difficult to determine because the wage is an estimated wage rate. However, $f(I)/P(I)$ varies inversely with $P(I)$, the probability of participation. If predicted wage rates covary positively with the probability of participation, then $\hat{W}$ and $f(I)/P(I)$ will be negatively correlated. A strong positive correlation between $\hat{W}$ and the probability of participation was found by Gronau (1973a) and is found in the estimates to be discussed in Section IV of this chapter. If σ_2^2 exceeds σ_{12} this positive correlation will impart a negative bias in the wage coefficient of Model I.

The question naturally arises as to the conditions under which Model I yields consistent estimates of the labor supply parameters. Clearly, if $\sigma_2^2 = \sigma_{12}$ consistent estimates can be obtained. The fact that the wage equation parameters are estimated with bias k, in this case, is irrelevant for the hours of work equation.

Also, if one is willing to assume that all women with a particular set of nonmarket attributes (defined by the elements of Q) have identical reservation wages, then the parameter estimates of Model I are consistent. Under this assumption the reservation wage equation becomes

$$W_{2_i} = Q_i \alpha. \qquad (2.15)$$

The condition for labor force participation is then given by

$$\varepsilon_1 > Q\alpha - Z\beta. \qquad (2.16)$$

Equation 2.16 indicates that since ε_1 is the stochastic component of the market wage offer, differences in the participation decision among women with identical characteristics (i.e., identical Q and Z vectors) are assumed to result from only unobservable factors that affect the market's demand for their time. Selecting only working women as the sample for estimation under these conditions will not result in biased parameter estimates, because the selection of the sample is assumed to be based on market demand factors (ε_1), rather than on stochastic supply factors. Note, however, the restrictiveness of this assumption. As equation 2.3 implies, differences in tastes and nonmarket productivities imply differences in reservation wages. Therefore, the assumption that all women with a given Q have identical reservation wages amounts to assuming away any differences in tastes or nonmarket productivities.

If we adopt this assumption and substitute equation 2.14 into 2.4, we obtain Model I:

$$h_i = \delta_1 \hat{W}_{1_i} + Q_i \pi_2 + V_{1_i}^*, \tag{2.17}$$

where the disturbance term reflects errors in approximating the expected value of the wage offer equation among the sample of workers. By the construction of the OLS estimator, these errors must have mean zero.

In summary, then, the assumptions that are necessary to obtain consistent estimates of the labor supply and reservation wage parameters under Model I are either that: (1) the variance in reservation wages due to unobservable factors equals the covariance between market wages and reservation wages that results from unobservable factors; (2) that all women with a given set of observable nonmarket characteristics have identical tastes and nonmarket productivities.

LABOR SUPPLY MODEL II

Model II differs from Model I in that the entire sample of married women, both working and nonworking, is used to obtain the parameter estimates of the labor supply function. Since no wage rates are observed for nonworking women, "potential" wages must be assigned to these women. The standard procedure in assigning or imputing wage rates is to obtain an instrumental variable estimate of the wage by using a sample of women with wage rates. This estimate is then assigned to all women, working or not. Although the specification of the labor supply function under Model II is identical to that of Model I, the implicit justification of Model II is quite different.

The standard specification of Model II may be obtained by substituting the reservation wage equation into the hours of work equation and replacing the wage offer with the imputed market wage:

$$h_I = \delta_1 \hat{W}_{1_i} + Q_i \pi_2 + V_{2_i}. \tag{2.18}$$

If the OLS wage equation is a good approximation to the expected value of wages conditional upon working, then we may write Model II's estimating equation as

$$h_i = \delta_1 \left[Z_i \beta + \left(\frac{\sigma_1^2 - \sigma_{12}}{\sigma_u} \right) \frac{f(I)}{P(I)} \right] + Q_i \pi_2 + V_{2_i}^*. \tag{2.19}$$

The "true" equation over the entire sample of women may be written as[7]

$$h = \delta_1 (Z\beta) + Q\pi_2 + \varepsilon_1^*. \tag{2.20}$$

Comparing equations 2.19 and 2.20, the disturbance term V_2^* has the interpretation

$$V_2^* = \varepsilon_1^* - \delta_1 \left(\frac{\sigma_1^2 - \sigma_{12}}{\sigma_u} \right) \frac{f(I)}{P(I)}, \tag{2.21}$$

the expectation of which is nonzero and in general correlated with the right-hand-side variables. Thus, estimates of Model II will be biased. This bias may be viewed as arising out of the fact that an inappropriate constraint has been imposed. In the "true" equation, $f(I)/P(I)$ has a zero coefficient. In Model II the constraint that the coefficient on this variable is not zero has been imposed.

The biases in the parameter estimates of Model II may be inferred from partially differentiating the expected value of the disturbance with respect to each of the right-hand-side variables. The partial derivative with respect to an element in Q, denoted Q_K, is

$$\frac{\partial E(V_2^*)}{\partial Q_K} = \delta_1 \pi_K \left(\frac{\sigma_1^2 - \sigma_{12}}{\sigma_u} \right) \left[\frac{f(I)P(I) + F(I)^2}{P(I)^2} \right]. \tag{2.22}$$

Assuming that $\sigma_1^2 > \sigma_{12}$ the bias in the estimated π_K is the same as the signs of the true population parameter. Thus, the estimated parameters of π_2 in Model II will overstate (in absolute value) the true population parameters.

---

[7] In the derivation that follows we ignore the fact that hours of work cannot be negative. This does not affect the conclusion drawn, so long as the hours of work equation is estimated taking into account this constraint on hours worked.

As was the case in Model I, the direction of bias in the wage coefficient is in general indeterminant because the partial correlation between expected wages conditional upon work ($\hat{W}$) and $f(I)/P(I)$ is indeterminant. If, however, $\hat{W}$ and the probability of participating are positively correlated, the expectation of the disturbance term V_2^* and $\hat{W}$ will be positively correlated. This will impart a positive bias in the estimate of the wage coefficient, tending to overstate the effect of wage rates on hours of work.

The conditions under which Model II's estimates are consistent are easily derived from the preceding analysis. Obviously, if the unexplained variation in market wage offers (σ_1^2) equals the covariance between market and reservation wage disturbances (σ_{12}) then the inappropriate constraint is not binding and the estimates are consistent.

Alternatively, if one assumes that all women with a given set of observed market-related attributes face identical wage offers, then labor supply parameter estimates of Model II are consistent. Under this assumption we rewrite the labor supply and market wage equations as

$$h_i = \delta_1 \hat{W}_{2_i} + Q_i \pi_2 + \varepsilon_{1_i}^*, \qquad (2.23)$$

$$W_{2_i} = Z_i \beta + \mu_{2_i}, \qquad (2.24)$$

where it is assumed that μ_2 reflects errors of measurement that are not systematically related to the labor supply decision. These errors of measurement are, of course, assumed to be distributed with mean zero and independently of the elements of Z. This assumption guarantees that estimates of β are consistent.

Note, however, the restrictiveness of this assumption. It implies that differences in labor force participation among women with identical observed characteristics result solely from unobserved differences in tastes and nonmarket productivities.

By defining $\hat{W}_1$ as $\hat{\beta}Z$, and imputing this wage to all women in the sample, one could estimate the parameters of the labor supply equation by ordinary least squares. But while the disturbance term μ_2 is distributed normally with mean zero and constant variance, the range of values that the independent variable (h) can take on is limited. Specifically, h cannot be negative. A more appropriate estimate procedure, under these circumstances, is the Tobit procedure. (See Schultz, Chapter 1.)

Gronau's approach is confined to estimating reservation wages (the intercept of the labor supply equation on the wage axis). His method consists of using labor force participation rates rather than relying on hours of work. Two polar or extreme cases are considered. Case A assumes that all married women within a given age-education-income group face the same market wage offer but differ randomly in their reservation wages. Case B assumes that all married women within this given group have the same reservation wage, but differ randomly in the wage rates offered to them in the marketplace. Gronau estimates mean reservation wages of particular groups of married women under each set of assumptions. Before we examine each of these cases in detail it will be instructive to outline the general problem of estimation as formulated by Gronau.

For convenience we write the market and reservation wage equations as

$$W_1 = \bar{W}_1 + \varepsilon_1, \tag{2.25}$$

$$W_2 = \bar{W}_2 + \varepsilon_2. \tag{2.26}$$

Gronau, in designing the general problem of estimation, assumes that market and reservation wages are jointly distributed within a given age-education-income class. He then obtains the following expression for the mean reservation wage of a particular class:

$$\bar{W}_2 = \frac{1}{1-P} \int_{-\infty}^{\infty} \int_{W_1}^{u} W_2 f(W_1, W_2) \, dW_2 \, dW_1, \tag{2.27}$$

where P is the labor force participation rate, i.e., the probability that $W_1 > W_2$ and $f(W_1, W_2)$ constitute the joint density function of market wage offers and reservation wages. In general, these parameters are unknown. The problem is to estimate them.

As a first step, Gronau assumes that market wage offers and reservation wages are independently distributed and that their joint distribution is bivariate normal. This permits him to express the mean observed market wage rate of working women ($\hat{W}_1$) as an explicit function of the unknown mean reservation wage ($\bar{W}_2$), the unknown mean of the market wage offer distribution ($\bar{W}_1$), the unknown variances in reservation wages (σ_2^2) and in market wage offers (σ_1^2), and the observed labor force participation rate. That is,

$$\hat{W}_1 = \bar{W}_2 + \sigma_1 \left\{ \frac{1}{P} \left(2\pi \frac{\sigma_1^2 + \sigma_2^2}{\sigma_1^2} \right)^{-1/2} \exp \left[-\frac{1}{2} \frac{\bar{W}_1 - \bar{W}_2}{\sigma_1^2 + \sigma_2^2} \right]^2 \right\}. \quad (2.28)$$

The assumption of a bivariate normal distribution has, in effect, reduced the moments to be estimated to the means and variances of the marginal distributions of W_1 and W_2, and a covariance term. The assumption of independence has eliminated this covariance term from the model. Still, knowledge of the mean wage rate of working women and of the participation rate does not provide enough information to determine the parameters of the joint density function. Some further restrictive assumptions are necessary. Gronau adopts two that lead to the two cases described earlier.

In Case A, the assumption is that the variance in wage offers (σ_1^2) within a given age-education class equals zero. In terms of equation 2.25, this implies that ε_1 equals zero and, hence, that $\hat{W}_1 = \bar{W}_1$. Under this assumption, differences in labor force participation decisions among women in the same age-education-income class result from differences in reservation wages. In Case B, the assumption is that the variance in reservation wages (σ_2^2) is zero. In terms of equation 2.26, this implies that ε_2 equals zero and, consequently, that $\hat{W}_2 = \bar{W}_2$. In Case B, differences in labor force participation among women within a given class are assumed to result from differences in offered market wages. In both cases it is assumed that the mean market wage offer varies only with the wife's age and education and that the mean reservation wage varies solely with the husband's income.

Gronau has been criticized for assuming that market and reservation wages are independently distributed. (See Heckman, 1974b.) This criticism seems somewhat misdirected in view of the two restrictive assumptions mentioned above. In his general formulation, Gronau could have allowed for a nonzero covariance between the market and reservation wages within a given class and lost nothing. Equation 2.28, the outcome of Gronau's general formulation of the problem under the assumption of independence, already contains too many unknown parameters to be estimated. Relaxing the assumption of independence only adds one more unknown parameter (the covariance term) to this equation. Once Gronau imposes the restrictive assumption that either the variance in market wage offers or the variance in reservation wages is zero, the question of independence between the two wages becomes irrelevant.

Under the assumption of Case A, Gronau expresses the mean wage of a woman in the ith income group and jth market wage class as

$$\bar{W}_{1_{ij}} \equiv W_{1_{ij}} = \bar{W}_{2_i} + \sigma_2 I_{ij}, \tag{2.29}$$

where I_{ij} is a standard normal variate representing the number of standard deviations separating $\bar{W}_{1_{ij}}$ and $\bar{W}_{2_i}$. Given the labor force participation rate of women in income group i and market wage group j, I_{ij} is calculated from the tables of the normal distribution.

Gronau then assumes a linear relation between the mean reservation wage and the level of income. That is,

$$\bar{W}_{2_i} = \alpha_0 + \alpha_1 Y_i. \tag{2.30}$$

Substituting equation 2.30 into 2.29, one obtains

$$\bar{W}_{1_{ij}} = \alpha_0 + \alpha_1 Y_i + \alpha_2 I_{ij}. \tag{2.31}$$

Gronau uses equation 2.31 to obtain estimates of the mean reservation wage of married women belonging to each income group and the within group variance in reservation wages ($\sigma_2 = \hat{\alpha}_2$). Note, however, that there is no disturbance term associated with this equation (and Gronau does not mention any). Since equation 2.29 is an identity, there can be no disturbance term associated with it. This leaves us with equation 2.30. If we assume that the linear relationship between income and mean reservation wage is not perfect, then we may add a disturbance term, V_{ij}, to equation 2.30. Substituting this relationship into equation 2.29, we obtain

$$W_{1_{ij}} = \alpha_0 + \alpha_1 Y_i + \alpha_2 I_{ij} + V_{ij}. \tag{2.32}$$

Gronau estimated the parameters of 2.32 by ordinary least squares and calculated the mean reservation wage for a particular income group i by

$$W_{2_j} = \bar{W}_{1_{ij}} - \hat{\alpha}_2 I_{ij}. \tag{2.33}$$

Two objections may be raised regarding his Case A procedure. The first stems from some methodological considerations. The assumption underlying the derivation of Case A's estimating equation 2.32 was that all women with a given set of market-related attributes[8] face

---

[8] In Gronau's work, the market-related attributes are age and education.

identical market wage offers. Recall that it was this assumption that enabled us to identify the labor supply parameters in Model II. Although both procedures make the same restrictive assumptions, Model II generates more information than Gronau's Case A. With Gronau's procedure, we can obtain estimates of the parameters of the reservation wage function. But with Model II, we can obtain estimates of the parameters of the reservation wage function and of the labor supply and shadow wage functions as well.[9] Moreover, Gronau requires a grouping of observations, whereas Model II does not. Since important intragroup variations in behavioral variables are lost when observations are grouped, Gronau's procedure is less efficient than that of Model II.

The second objection to Gronau's Case A is that the empirical model is misspecified. In particular, the mean market wage offer, the dependent variable in the empirical equation 2.32 is, according to the assumptions of his theoretical model, an exogenous variable. On the other hand, the standard normal variate, I, a right-hand-side regressor in the empirical model, is the endogenous variable of his theoretical work. Recall that the market wage offer (W_1) was assumed to have zero variance within a given age-education-income group. Under this assumption, it is determined independently of reservation wages and the participation rate. Stated alternatively, it is determined outside the model. The variate I_{ij}, however, is determined within the model. It is functionally related to the labor force participation rate, which is, in turn, dependent on the distribution of reservation wages, hence V_{ij}.

The foregoing suggests that the correct specification of Gronau's empirical model would be obtained if equation 2.29 were rewritten as

$$I_{ij} = \frac{\bar{W}_{1_{ij}}}{\sigma_2} - \frac{\hat{W}_{2_i}}{\sigma_2}. \qquad (2.34)$$

Assuming the inexact relation between reservation wages and income, we obtain

$$I_{ij} = \frac{1}{\sigma_2} \bar{W}_{2_{ij}} - \frac{1}{\sigma_2} (\alpha_0 + \alpha_1 Y_i + \mu_{ij}) \qquad (2.35)$$

[9] As we show in Section IV, Labor Supply Model II may also be used to generate the probability that a woman with a given set of observable characteristics will participate in the labor force.

or, equivalently,

$$I_{ij} = \beta_0 + \beta_1 I_i + \beta_2 \bar{W}_{2_{ij}} + \mu_{ij}^*, \tag{2.36}$$

where

$$\beta = \frac{-\alpha_0}{\sigma_2}, \qquad \beta_1 = -\frac{\alpha_1}{\sigma_2}, \qquad \beta_2 = \frac{1}{\sigma_2}, \quad \text{and} \quad \mu_{ij}^* = \frac{-\mu_{ij}}{\sigma_2}.$$

Since, by the assumptions of the model, both income and the market wage offer are uncorrelated in the probability limit with μ_{ij}^*, ordinary least squares can be used to obtain consistent estimates of the β_k. These estimates can be used to calculate reservation wages by the formula

$$\hat{W}_{2_i} = \frac{(\hat{\beta}_0 + \hat{\beta}_1 Y_i)}{\hat{\beta}_2}. \tag{2.37}$$

In Case B, Gronau assumes that all women within a given age-education-income-group have identical reservation wages. Under this assumption, σ_2 equals zero, and the mean observed market wage offer may be written as

$$\hat{W}_{1_{ij}} = \bar{W}_{2_i} + I_{ij}^* \sigma_1, \tag{2.38}$$

where I_{ij}^* is again a standard normal variate defined for given values of the labor force participation rate. Assuming the inexact relationship between income and the mean reservation wage, we obtain Gronau's Case B regression equation

$$\hat{W}_{1_{ij}} = \gamma_0 + \gamma_1 Y_i + \gamma_2 I_{ij}^* + \mu_{ij}. \tag{2.39}$$

The objections that were raised regarding Gronau's Case A procedure are similar to those we now raise against Case B. Briefly, our chief objection is that it is, on methodological grounds, inferior to Model I. The assumption underlying Case B—that all women with a given set of nonmarket-related characteristics have identical reservation wages—is the same one that enabled us to identify the labor supply parameters in Model I. The two models, in effect, make identical assumptions, but Model I provides more information regarding labor supply behavior and more efficient estimates of the relevant parameters at a lower cost than does Case B. Hence, Model I is superior to Gronau's Case B procedure. Also, Gronau's empirical equation 2.39 is deficient on statistical grounds. Given the assumptions underlying its derivation, both the observed mean wage rate and the variate I^* are endogenous variables. The variate I^* is a function of the participation rate, which is, in turn, systematically related to the mean reservation wage. Since the disturbance term μ_{ij} is a component of the reservation wage, it cannot be assumed to be uncorrelated with the participation rate, hence I^*. The endogeneity of $\hat{W}_2$ follows directly from its definition. $\hat{W}_2$ is defined as $E(W_1 \mid W_1 > W_2)$ or, equivalently, as $E(W_2 \mid W_2 > \alpha_0 + \alpha_1 Y + \mu)$. Thus, the Case B empirical model (2.39) contains one equation and two endogenous variables and, as a consequence, is statistically incomplete.

In summary, we have argued that the Gronau procedure is methodologically inferior to the labor supply procedures. We have also argued that it is deficient on statistical grounds. For these reasons we have excluded the Gronau approach from our empirical comparisons of the alternative estimators of reservation wages in Section III.

THE HECKMAN PROCEDURE

The procedure developed by Heckman in his seminal 1974 *Econometrica* article was a substantial improvement over those described previously. Recall that in Labor Supply Models I and II, and in the Gronau procedure, estimation of the reservation wage required the strong assumption that either ε_1, the stochastic disturbance of the market wage equation, or ε_2, the stochastic disturbance of the reservation wage equation, is zero. Heckman allows for both stochastic disturbances to exist and permits correlation between them.

Heckman derives the shadow wage equation, which is written as

$$W_{S_i} = \left(\frac{1}{\delta_1}\right) h_i + Q_i \Gamma + \varepsilon_{2_i}. \tag{2.40}$$

The market wage equation is written as

$$W_{1_i} = Z_i \beta + \varepsilon_{1_i}, \tag{2.41}$$

and the disturbances ε_1 and ε_2 are assumed to be jointly normally distributed, each with mean zero.

For working women, the shadow wage equals the market wage. Also, for working women, we can rearrange equations 2.40 and 2.41 to obtain the following two equation systems:

$$h_i = \delta_1 (Z_i \beta - Q_i \Gamma) + (\varepsilon_{1_i} - \varepsilon_{2_i}) \delta_1 \tag{2.42}$$

and

$$W_{1_i} = Z\beta + \varepsilon_{1_i}. \tag{2.43}$$

For nonworking women, the shadow wage at zero hours of work (W_2) exceeds the wage that could be earned in the market (W_1), and h equals zero.

The observed marginal distributions of hours and wage rates are conditional upon the decision of whether to work or not. As a first step toward obtaining consistent estimates of the parameters of equations 2.42 and 2.43, Heckman expresses the conditional joint distribution of observed hours and wages as a function of the unconditional joint distribution of hours and wages. That is,

$$j[(h, W_1) \mid W_1 > W_2] = \frac{n(h, W_1)}{P(W_1 > W_2)}, \tag{2.44}$$

where $n(h, W_1)$ is the unconditional distribution, $P(W_1 > W_2)$ is the probability that a woman works, and $j[(h, W_1) \mid W_1 > W_2]$ is the conditional distribution of hours and wages.

Using this relation between the conditional and unconditional distributions of hours and wages, Heckman then forms the likelihood function for a sample consisting of, say, K women who work and $(T - K)$ who do not. The likelihood function can be written as

$$L = \prod_{i=1}^{k} n(h_i, W_{1_i}) \prod_{i=k+1}^{T} P(W_{1_i} < W_{2_i}). \tag{2.45}$$

By maximizing this function with respect to the parameters of the model (i.e., α's, β's, σ_1^2, σ_2^2, and cov $(\varepsilon_1 \varepsilon_2)$), one may obtain consistent, asymptotically unbiased, and efficient parameter estimators.

Heckman's procedure is, statistically, far superior to either of the Labor Supply Models. It is, however, substantially more costly to implement. If either of the conventional Labor Supply Models yielded estimates similar to those obtained with the Heckman procedure, then the large cost differential would dictate the use of Model I or II. Various factors could account for similarity among these alternative estimators. If, for instance, the unobservable nonmarket characteristics of the wife were unimportant in determining the quantity of labor she supplies to the market, then Model I would yield estimates close to those obtained by Heckman's procedure. If, however, the unobservable factors that are presumed to affect market wage offers are, in reality, unimportant, then the estimates of Model II would closely approximate Heckman's. These statements are made assuming, of course, that the specification of the empirical model is correct. Misspecification of the empirical model, errors of measurement, or joint determination of the relevant variables could produce similarities or dissimilarities in estimates independent of the validity of the maintained assumptions of each of the procedures.

III. COMPARISON OF EMPIRICAL RESULTS

In this section, estimates from Models I and II are compared with those obtained by the Heckman procedure. Both labor demand and labor supply are considered. Comparisons of demand estimates employ market wage function parameter estimates and predicted market wages, while those involving supply are made on the basis of estimated labor supply parameters and predicted reservation wages. Estimated demand and supply functions are then brought together to enable us to compare the three procedures relative to both predicted and actual labor force participation rates.

The sample used for the comparisons was selected from the 1967 National Longitudinal Survey and consisted of approximately 2,300 white married women whose husbands were present at the time of the interview. The following specification of the labor supply and market wage functions was adopted for each technique.

$$h = \delta_0 + \delta_1 W_1^* + \delta_2 E + \delta_3 Y + \delta_3 A + \delta_4 C + \delta_5 C_2 + \delta_6 C_3 + \varepsilon,$$
$$(2.46)$$

$$W_2^* = \beta_0 + \beta_1 E + \beta_2 M + u, \quad \text{where} \qquad (2.47)$$

h is the wife's annual hours of market work,
W_1^* is the logarithm of the wife's hourly wage rate,
Y is the husband's yearly income,
E is the wife's level of education,
A is the household's level of assets minus its level of debts,
C_1 is the number of children in the household less than 6 years of age,
C_2 is the number of children in the household ages 6–13,
C_3 is the number of children in the household ages 14–17,
M is the married woman's previous labor market experience, defined as the number of years in which the wife worked at least six months in a given year.

The means and standard deviations of the variable are reported in Appendix Table 2.9.

Model I was estimated by ordinary least squares using a sample consisting of only working women. Model II was estimated using Tobit analysis. Both models used a predicted market wage, obtained from an OLS wage equation estimated on the subsample of working women. Estimates of Heckman's model were obtained with maximum likelihood described in the preceding section.

LABOR MARKET DEMAND COMPARISONS

Market wage parameter estimates are given in Table 2.1. The ordinary least squares (OLS) estimates are obtained from a sample comprised solely of labor force participants during the year preceding the survey. The Heckman estimates are obtained from the entire sample of women, regardless of their labor force status during the year preceding the interview. The dependent variable is the natural logarithm of the wife's market wage rate. Hence, one should interpret the coefficients as percentage increases in the market wage rate for unit increases in the independent variables. The standard errors of the coefficients are given in parentheses.[10]

TABLE 2.1: Market Wage Parameter Estimates[a]

Procedure	Constant	Education	Experience
OLS	−.7176	.0854	.0184
	(.191)	(.0073)	(.0030)
Heckman	−.8761	.0879	.0259
	(.206)	(.0074)	(.0046)

[a] The dependent variable is the natural logarithm of the wife's hourly wage rate. The standard errors of the coefficients are given in parentheses.

[10] Strictly speaking, comparisons between the estimates of the standard errors across the different models are not valid. The standard errors of the conventional Labor Supply Models are correct only if their respective assumptions regarding the stochastic disturbances are true. If the assumptions regarding the disturbance matrix do not hold, then the estimates of the standard errors are biased downward. The standard errors are presented only to facilitate comparisons with previous estimated labor supply parameters that make similar assumptions.

Surprising, perhaps, is the small difference between the estimated education coefficients of the two procedures. The OLS estimate differs from the Heckman estimate, using the standard error of the Heckman coefficient, by less than one standard deviation. The effect of sample censoring, which would bias the OLS estimate toward zero, appears to be trivial, at least with this data base. Further evidence of the magnitude of the sample-selection bias of the education coefficient may be obtained from the partial correlation between education and the labor force participation rate in the sample. A zero correlation between these two variates would imply a zero correlation between education and the disturbance term of the wage equation. The correlation in the sample is 0.02.

The coefficients on years of labor market experience do, however, differ markedly. The Heckman estimate of the effect of experience on the wife's wage offer is 41% larger than the OLS estimate. Here it appears that the "selectivity bias" has a substantial effect. Indeed, the high partial correlation between the experience variable and labor force participation (0.44) indicates that this bias should be of a substantial magnitude.[11] The largest difference in the estimates is between the constant terms. The difference alone implies that OLS overstates the estimated mean wage offer by 16%.

The smaller estimated effects of education and experience and the larger constant term in the OLS equations are attributable to sample selection bias. The direction of bias in the wage equation is determined by two factors: the partial correlation between the variable in the wage equation and the probability of participating in the labor force; and the sign of the difference between σ_1^2 and σ_{12}. If both the correlation and the difference are the same sign, the bias is opposite in direction of the true population parameters. Estimates of the covariance matrix of disturbances, reported in Table 2.4, indicate that σ_1^2 exceeds σ_{12}, hence the expected direction of bias is negative in both coefficients.

Predicted market wages by level of education and years of labor market experience are given in Table 2.2. These estimates provide further indication of the effect of the selectivity bias on estimated market wage rates. The difference between the estimates appears to be substantial in all cases. The results indicate that it is important to control for "selectivity bias" in estimating wage equations—especially

[11] See Heckman (Chapter 5) for a treatment of the case where market experience is endogenous.

TABLE 2.2: Predicted Market Wages

Years of Experience	Procedure	Years of Education Completed		
		0	8	16
0	OLS	1.00	1.40	1.98
	Heckman	.83	1.19	1.69
4	OLS	1.07	1.51	2.13
	Heckman	.93	1.32	1.87
8	OLS	1.16	1.62	2.29
	Heckman	1.03	1.46	2.07

if the purpose of the estimates involves wage differentials between white women and other demographic groups. The correlation between the predicted log wage rates of the two estimation procedures is 0.98. This correlation is significantly different from zero and not significantly different from 1 at conventional levels.

Finally, predicted wage rates are often used as regressors in household demand functions, such as fertility equations. The selectivity bias in wage equation estimates may result in a bias in the estimate of these demand functions. If, however, the correlation between the predicted wages estimated with selectivity bias and predicted wages estimated correcting for selectivity bias is close to unity, the resulting bias in demand function should be small.

LABOR SUPPLY COMPARISONS

We demonstrated in Section II that if the correlations among the right-hand-side variables are small, the direction of bias in each estimated coefficient of Models I and II depends upon the sign of the difference between σ_2^2 and σ_{12} and the partial correlation between each regressor and the probability of participation. Estimates of the covariance matrix of disturbances obtained from Heckman's procedure (reported in Table 2.4) show that σ_1^2 exceeds σ_{12}. The signs of the partial correlations may be obtained by inspecting the estimated coefficients of a labor force participation regression that uses the same regressors as the hours of work function.

TABLE 2.3: Probit Index Coefficient of Wife's Labor Force
Participation Equation

Variable	Coefficient	Standard Error	Sign of Model I	Sign of Bias Model II
Constant	2.013	.418	—	—
Wife's Predicted Wage	3.20	2.27	−	+
Wife's Education	−.162	.021	+	−
Husband's Earnings ($1,000)	−.074	.009	+	−
Children <6	−.521	.046	+	−
Children 6–13	−.002	.024	+	−
Children 14–17	.296	.048	−	+

The coefficients of the participation equation, reported in column 1 of Table 2.3, provide the signs of these partial correlations. Columns 3 and 4 translate these partial correlations into expected directions of bias in the estimates of Models I and II. The directions of bias in the corresponding coefficients of Models I and II are opposite one another. Thus, Model I should understate the effect of any variable on the wife's hours of work and Model II should overstate its effect.

This expectation is borne out dramatically in the labor supply estimates of each model reported in Table 2.4. Every estimated parameter in Model I understates the corresponding estimate in Heckman's model and every estimated parameter in Model II overstates the corresponding estimate in Heckman's model. The differences in estimates between Model I and Heckman's are the largest. The education and wage coefficients in Model I are 40% of Heckman's estimates, the husband income coefficient is one-third Heckman's, and the coefficients on the youngest and oldest children variables are about 20% of Heckman's estimates.

The differences in estimates between Model II and Heckman's procedure, though systematic, are less striking. Only the estimated effects of education and the wage rate differ by any noteworthy magnitude. Model II's estimates of these effects exceed the corresponding estimates of Heckman's model by about 25%.

Table 2.4: Labor Supply Parameter Estimates[a]

Variable	Model I	Heckman	Model II (Tobit)
Education	−117.84	−273.0	−339.27
	(17.36)	(21.2)	(25.54)
Husband's Income	−.0194	−.0536	−.056
	(.0055)	(.007)	(.0073)
Children under 6 years	−136.57	−651.27	−660.27
	(38.51)	(47.9)	(48.50)
Children 6–13	−69.72	−76.15	−94.29
	(19.84)	(27.4)	(27.76)
Children 14–17	43.69	255.96	241.68
	(30.59)	(43.0)	(43.58)
Log Wife's Wage	1571.0	3892.0	4805.27
	(177.04)	(197.9)	(262.68)
Intercept	2345.4	4671.93	4694.92
	(294.2)	(406.89)	(419.60)

[a] The standard errors of the coefficients are given in parentheses.
Maximum Likelihood Estimates of Covariance Matrix

$$\begin{array}{c} & \varepsilon_1 & \varepsilon_2 \\ \varepsilon_1 & .487 & .136 \\ \varepsilon_2 & & .201 \end{array}$$

The systematic differences across empirical procedures are indicative of the importance of accounting for the sample selection bias in estimating married women's wage and hours equations. It appears that unmeasured factors that affect the wife's hours of work and her market wage offer also strongly influence the probability of her working. Hence, the implicit assumptions underlying conventional procedures for estimating wage and hours equations are violated.

The estimated hours of work equations are translated into estimates of reservation wages for further comparisons of the estimation procedures. The predicted reservation wages of Model I never exceeded 20 cents and, as a result, are deleted from the comparisons. Table 2.5

TABLE 2.5: Predicted Reservation Wages[a]

Number of Children under 6 Years	Procedure	Years of Education Completed		
		8	12	16
0	Heckman	.97	1.28	1.70
	Model II (Tobit)			
1	Heckman	1.15	1.52	2.01
	Model II (Tobit)	1.27	1.68	2.23
2	Heckman	1.36	1.80	2.38
	Model II (Tobit)	1.46	1.93	2.56

[a] The predicted reservation wages are evaluated at the sample means of the data. The reservation wages were computed by taking the exponential of the predicted natural logarithm of the reservation wage.

compares predictions from Model II and Heckman's procedure for various levels of education and number of young children in the home. The predicted reservation wages of Model II exceed those of Heckman's approach by 16 cents on average. The correlation between the predicted reservation wages over the entire sample is .92. This correlation is significantly different from zero but not significantly different from 1 at .05 level.

LABOR FORCE PARTICIPATION PREDICTIONS

In Table 2.6, we bring together supply and demand predictions to calculate the probability that a woman with a given set of market and nonmarket attributes will work at some point over the year. These probabilities may be interpreted as point estimates of yearly labor force participation rates. For comparative purposes, we also present predictions of a probit regression of labor force participation on the set of determinants of reservation wages and market wages.

The probability of working is simply the probability that the market wage offer exceeds the reservation wage. Under the assumption of normally distributed disturbances, the probability of working is:

$$P = \frac{1}{\sqrt{2\pi}} \int_{-\infty}^{T} e^{-1/2t^2} \, d_t, \qquad (2.48)$$

TABLE 2.6: Predicted Probabilities of Working

Number of Children under 6 Years	Procedure	Years of Education Completed		
		8	12	16
0	Probit	.52	.61	.70
	Model I	.91	.92	.93
	Model II	.55	.63	.71
	Heckman	.55	.63	.71
1	Probit	.31	.40	.49
	Model I	.88	.90	.91
	Model II	.35	.43	.52
	Heckman	.35	.43	.52
2	Probit	.15	.21	.28
	Model I	.85	.87	.88
	Model II	.18	.25	.32
	Heckman	.18	.24	.32

where

$$T = \frac{\ln \hat{W}_F - \ln \hat{W}_R}{\hat{\sigma}_2^2}.$$

To calculate this probability for Models I and II we need estimates of σ_u^2. Under the implicit assumptions of Model I the distribution of reservation wages conditional upon the wife's characteristics is degenerate. Therefore an estimate of σ_u^2 is the residual variance in the wage equation. Under the implicit assumption of Model II the variance in market wage offers is assumed to be degenerate. The residual variance in hours worked estimated from the Tobit equation has the interpretation of $\delta_1^2 \sigma_{\varepsilon 2}^2$. Therefore, to calculate σ_u^2 we divide the variance from the Tobit equation by the estimate of the wage coefficient.

The probabilities of working predicted by Model II and Heckman's procedure are identical across the education and young children levels reported in Table 2.6. These predictions are marginally above the probabilities predicted by the probit model, which uses no information

on hours of work. The probabilities of working predicted by Model I
are extremely high due to low estimated reservation wages.

In Table 2.7, we compare actual labor force participation rates with
those predicted by each of the models. To make these comparisons,
observations in the sample were grouped into 9 cells, which were
defined according to the wife's education level (0–8, 9–12, and 13+
years) and the number of children under 6 years of age (0, 1, 2).
Actual and predicted labor force participation rates were computed for

TABLE 2.7: Predicted and Actual Labor Force Participation Rates

Number of Children under 6 Years	Procedure	Years of Education Completed		
		0–8	9–12	> 12
	Actual	.54	.60	.63
	Probit	.46	.63	.70
0	Model II	.56	.74	.76
	Heckman	.53	.72	.75
	Cell Size	213	962	238
	Actual	.33	.31	.34
	Probit	.16	.24	.31
1	Model II	.22	.27	.34
	Heckman	.17	.26	.34
	Cell Size	69	413	119
	Actual	.10	.23	.40
	Probit	.0	.08	.08
2	Model II	.0	.06	.08
	Heckman	.05	.09	.10
	Cell Size	20	142	60

Entire Sample

Actual	.48
Probit	.45
Model I	1.0
Heckman	.51
Cell Size	2301

each cell. The predicted participation rates for each procedure were computed by assigning both a predicted market wage and a predicted reservation wage to each woman. For those women whose predicted market wage exceeded their predicted reservation wage, a 1 was assigned for predicted labor force participation status. All others were assigned a zero.

The predicted labor force participation rates of Model I were unity in each cell and, hence are omitted from the table. Comparing the predictions among the remaining models reveals small differences. The largest difference is between the Probit and Model II predictions in the cell containing women with 0–8 years of schooling and no preschool children in the home.

These predictions cannot be used to discriminate among models. But they do indicate that there is some misspecification of the functional form of the hours of work equation. All models overpredict the participation rate among women with no preschool children, and underpredict the participation rate, among women with preschool children. It appears that the effect of children is overstated in all models.

Finally, we consider the probability of a successful prediction of a woman's labor force status. We compare the actual labor force status of each woman in the 9 cells with that predicted by each of the procedures. The proportion of successful predictions was then calculated by summing the number of successful predictions in each cell and dividing by the number of women in the cell. These proportions are shown in Table 2.8.

All procedures, except Model I, appear to predict labor force status equally well. Over the entire sample, the three procedures correctly classify 70 percent of the observations in the data. Model I, on the other hand, is no better in classifying observations than flipping a coin.

V. Conclusions

This chapter has examined four methods of estimating the parameters underlying married women's labor supply functions. The implicit restrictive assumptions concerning the disturbance structure of two conventional empirical approaches are brought to light. Gronau's (1973b) approach of estimating reservation wages is compared with conventional methods and judged to be inferior on methodological grounds.

TABLE 2.8: Proportions of Successful Predictions of Labor Force
Status

Number of Children under 6 Years	Procedure	Years of Education Completed		
		0–8	9–12	> 12
	Probit	.72	.72	.74
	Model I	.54	.60	.63
0	Model II	.67	.67	.72
	Heckman	.69	.70	.74
	Cell Size	213	962	238
	Probit	.62	.71	.71
	Model I	.33	.31	.34
1	Model II	.59	.69	.66
	Heckman	.61	.69	.67
	Cell Size	69	413	119
	Probit	.90	.76	.68
	Model I	.10	.23	.40
2	Model II	.90	.76	.65
	Heckman	.85	.76	.67
	Cell Size	20	142	60

Entire Sample

Probit	.72
Model I	.48
Model II	.69
Heckman	.70
Cell Size	2301

Using the same restrictive assumptions as the two conventional approaches, it generates less information concerning the determinants of married women's labor supply function.

Empirical comparisons are made among the two conventional methods and Heckman's 1974 maximum likelihood method. The selectivity bias in estimating wage offer equations is important for the intercept and the return to prior labor market experience, but small for the return to education. Large and systematic differences in the estimated parameters of the hours of work equation are found between Heckman's approach and the conventional procedure of using only the subsample of working women (Model I). Systematic, but relatively small differences in estimated hours of work parameters (except for the wage coefficient) are found between Heckman's method and an alternative conventional approach of imputing wages to all women and estimating the hours of work equation over the entire sample of observation (Model II). Comparisons of predictions among the procedures reveal a striking similarity between Heckman's prediction of these methods and Model II, but large differences between the other approaches and Model I.

In conclusion, much of the recent empirical work on married women's labor supply has been undertaken with the objective of estimating substitution and income effects for use in evaluating response to alternative negative income tax programs. The relatively large difference in estimated wage effects between Heckman's method and Model II suggests that the higher cost of the former procedure may be justified by the advantages of obtaining a more accurate estimate. If, however, the estimates are used to predict reservation wages (for use as an estimate of the value of time) or labor force participation rates, the small differences between the two approaches suggest that the simpler and cheaper conventional approach may be preferred.

APPENDIX TABLE 2.9

Sample Statistics

	Total	*Nonworkers*	*Workers*
Central City	.212	.216	.209
	(.409)	(.412)	(.406)
South	.362	.353	.370
	(.480)	(.478)	(.483)
Education	11.41	11.28	11.56
	(2.57)	(2.61)	(2.52)
Age	37.23	36.89	37.59
	(4.38)	(4.41)	(4.32)
Husband's Earnings	7060.0	7553.6	6527.6
	(4697.6)	(5191.7)	(4031.6)
KIDS 0–5	.545	.765	.308
	(.806)	(.894)	(.616)
KIDS 6–13	1.40	1.56	1.22
	(1.22)	(1.22)	(1.20)
KIDS 14–17	.532	.476	.593
	(.748)	(.737)	(.755)
Experience	7.30	5.07	9.70
School–67	(6.06)	(4.71)	(6.42)
Logwage			.480
			(.650)
Annual Hours	660.91		1373.77
	(872.09)		(775.59)
Sample Size	2301	1194	1107

CHAPTER 3

HOURS AND WEEKS IN THE THEORY OF LABOR SUPPLY

GIORA HANOCH

HEBREW UNIVERSITY, JERUSALEM

I. Introduction

The basic static model of labor supply determination has been widely used, both theoretically and empirically. It is characterized by many simplifying assumptions: one individual, one period, two commodities ("consumption" and "leisure"), no uncertainty; and a time constraint, a nonwage income, and a fixed wage rate, all given exogenously.[1]

In recent literature, various extensions and modifications of this basic model have been offered to account for presumed or observed deviations of its simplifying features from the real world, and to integrate it into broader contexts, such as family and household decisions, lifetime human and nonhuman capital accumulation, occupational choice and mobility, income distribution, and unemployment.[2] At the same time, significant advances have been made in econometric applications of the model and in its extensions to empirical observations.[3]

Nevertheless, the theory of labor supply and its related econometric methodology are still in a primitive stage, with many important aspects either completely neglected or analyzed very superficially.

---

[1] For formulations and discussions of the basic model, see Robbins (1930) and Lewis (1956). See also Ashenfelter and Heckman (1973) and Hanoch (1965a).

[2] For the family model, see Mincer (1962), Becker (1965), Cain (1966), Kosters (1966), Muth (1966), and Gronau (1973b). For extensions to life-cycle models, see Smith, Chapter 4, Blinder and Weiss (1975), and Heckman (1974c). For various other extensions and modifications, see Barzel (1973), Lindsay (1971), Michael (1973), and Stigler (1962).

[3] See Hall (1973) and Gronau (1973b, 1974); Schultz, Chapter 1; and in particular, Heckman (1974a, 1974b).

One such aspect is the treatment of various time dimensions of labor supply, such as hours of work (per week or per year) and annual weeks of work. Some studies employ these as alternative measures of labor supply, using one or the other as a dependent variable in the labor supply equation.[4] Others ignore the weeks-per-year dimension and employ weekly data rather than annual data, thus defining persons not working during a given survey week as nonparticipants in the labor force.[5] However, both approaches are inconsistent and incomplete, because the two variables (annual hours and annual weeks) must be jointly and simultaneously determined within a multidimensional labor/leisure context.

The primary novel feature of the model presented here is that the different types of leisure (nonmarket time) are distinguished by their corresponding time dimensions. For simplicity, the analysis considers only two dimensions (hours and weeks). However, as shown in Section VI, the extension of the analysis to other dimensions, such as days, months, or years, is analogous and straightforward.

Measuring time in hours, and assuming the horizon for individual labor supply decisions to be one year, the total number of annual hours of work is certainly a major variable in the labor supply decision. However, the distribution of these hours over the year is still to be determined. For example, one is generally not indifferent to a choice of working 100 hours weekly during 20 consecutive weeks (and staying off the labor market the rest of the year) or working 40 hours weekly during 50 weeks, though both supply an equal annual total of 2,000 hours of work.

This conceptual framework suggests that these two alternatives involve different combinations of two distinct commodities: "leisure during working weeks" (L_1) and "leisure during nonworking weeks" (L_2), which are separate arguments in the utility function, and are thus not perfect substitutes. Using the framework of the individual household production function, the two types of leisure are distinct, since they are inputs into different leisure activities. For example, a given number of hours would be used differently on a long vacation than after work and on the weekend.

[4] See, for example, Kosters (1966), and Kalachek and Raines (1970). In some cases, the independent wage variable is also different, using weekly wages in the weeks equation and thus ignoring the hours-per-week decision—e.g., Heckman (1974b).

[5] As in Greenberg and Kosters (1970), and others. See also notes 8 and 9 below.

Continuing this example, assume that 8 hours daily (56 weekly) are required for self-maintenance (sleep, meals, etc.), that no time is spent on travel to work, and that a year consists of exactly 52 weeks. Then the first alternative provides 240 ($= (7 \times 16 - 100) \times 20 = 12 \times 20$) annual hours of L_1, and 3,584 ($= 112 \times 32$) hours of L_2; whereas the second alternative implies $L_1 = 3,600$ ($= (112 - 40) \times 50$); and $L_2 = 224$ ($= 112 \times 2$). In both cases, therefore, the sum $L_1 + L_2$ equals 3,824 annual hours of leisure. If the hourly wage is independent of the distribution of hours over time, then the two alternatives also yield equal incomes. The choice of the preferred combination, however, determines annual weeks (20 versus 50) in addition to annual hours.

An elegant feature of this formulation is that, although the *product* (weeks per year times hours per week) measures annual hours of work supplied, the two types of leisure combine additively to give the total (composite) leisure demanded. "Composite leisure" is a valid and meaningful variable, because both types of leisure have equal shadow prices (i.e., the wage rate W). However, the two are not perfect substitutes in utility, as implied by the common one-dimensional analysis of labor supply. The present analysis thus shows (even after introducing fixed weekly time costs of going to work) the validity of the one-dimensional model of labor supply measured in annual hours and viewed as a mirror image of leisure demand. On the other hand, this model is incomplete, being merely one part of a simultaneous model in which the determination of weeks worked is another essential part.

Empirical evidence tends to corroborate this view. In some groups, such as married women, a large proportion of individuals work part time (in terms of weeks worked annually) for many years. The number of weeks worked seems to vary over time and among individuals, in response to the same variables affecting hours worked, such as own wage rate, spouse's wage rate, income from other sources, number and ages of children, and age of worker.[6] Despite qualitative similarities, however, the effects of these variables on weeks worked tend to differ from their effects on hours, and therefore require a separate explanation.

Viewing the number of weeks worked as a labor supply variable subject to choice affects the empirical treatment of data. Consider a sample of observations collected in a given survey during one week.[7] If

[6] See Kosters (1966), Heckman (1974b), and others.

[7] As in census data, or in the 1967 Survey of Economic Opportunity (SEO).

an individual normally works K weeks per year, the probability of finding him (her) working during the survey week is $K/52$ (if the survey week is considered a random drawing from the year's 52 weeks). The subsample of weekly participants (those with positive hours of work in the survey week) thus overrepresents individuals with relatively large K, and underrepresents those with relatively low K, the representation being proportional to K. An important selectivity bias is thus implied by the very definition of the subsample.[8]

A serious bias related to this problem is due to the procedure, used in some studies, of defining the annual-hours labor supply variable as the product of hours worked during the survey week times number of weeks worked last year.[9] This procedure imputes zero annual hours to all individuals who have a positive K (and are therefore annual labor force participants), but who happen to be out of work during the survey week. Clearly, total labor supply is thus biased downward; but, no less important, the probability of this downward bias is negatively related to the individual's K, since it is proportional to $(52 - K)$.

Another implication of this simple analysis is more constructive. Classifying the sample into groups, we can simply estimate the mean number of weeks worked during the current survey year in any given group from the number in the group working during the survey week (which is an estimate of the mean probability $\bar{K}/52$).[10] Relating estimated current weeks to last year's weeks may help in evaluating the direction of changes in participation for different groups, as well as in estimating the transitory component in the variance of weeks worked.[11]

---

[8] For example, in a sample of 6,515 white married couples from the SEO, 3,071 women worked a positive number of weeks in 1966, averaging 35.4 weeks. However, only 2,109 of these worked during the survey week, averaging 41.5 weeks worked in 1966.

[9] Suppose $K_t = \bar{K} + u_t$, where u_t is a random annual transitory component. Then, classifying groups by intervals of K_{t-1}, estimating $\hat{K}_t$ in each group from the number working (as in note 10 below), and regressing $\hat{K}_t$ on K_{t-1}, we get a least squares regression coefficient that is a consistent estimate of $(1 - (\sigma_u^2/\sigma_k^2))$. For example, in the sample of white women in note 8, this procedure yielded the estimate $\sigma_u^2/\sigma_k^2 = 0.175$ ($R^2 = .98$).

[10] As in Greenberg and Kosters (1970), and Schultz, Chapter 1.

[11] For example, for the white women in the sample mentioned in note 8 above, the average number of weeks for the total sample was 16.7 in 1966. Estimating the current (1967) number of weeks from the number working in the survey week (and in 1966) gives $(2,109/6,515) \times 52 = 16.9$.

Additional implications of this two-dimensional analysis of labor supply are detailed in the following sections, but these few examples should indicate the importance of this approach.

In addition to restricting the analysis to just two dimensions, the present model also ignores all considerations of clustering and timing of work periods. For example, if the decision is made to work five 8-hour days weekly, the model does not determine which two days are the rest days, or whether they are consecutive. Similarly, a given number of vacation weeks may be clustered together, or split into two or more vacation periods, with their timing indeterminate as well.

In many instances, however, decisions about timing and clustering may be regarded as either determined exogenously by employers, social norms, or law, or determined independently of quantity. Scale and cost considerations would tend to induce clustering; hence, we may conveniently assume that all weekly leisure hours are clustered in consecutive days, that nonworkweeks are clustered together (allowing also a nonintegral number of workweeks), and that timing is either determined exogenously or does not affect the choice of L_1 and L_2. Since empirical data on hours and weeks do not usually include any clustering or timing information, these simplifying assumptions are appropriate for most empirical applications.

A similar assumption is made regarding hours per day. For any given amount of weekly hours, the distribution of hours over days of the week is assumed to be determined independently or exogenously. Additional simplifying assumptions are listed and explained below.

Section II presents the basic two-dimensional model for the individual, incorporating fixed weekly time costs of work. The relations between the utility function and the supply of hours and weeks are explained analytically, as well as diagrammatically. Section III deals with corner solutions or exogenous restrictions, with respect to either weeks per year or hours per week. Section IV generalizes the model to a two-worker family context, and provides examples of intrafamily effects. Section V introduces fixed weekly money costs of participation, using duality relations to simplify the formal derivation. Section VI suggests extensions to other time dimensions. The appendix derives the relations used in computing the numerical examples, based on Cobb–Douglas utility functions.

II. Outline of the Basic Model

DEFINITIONS AND SYMBOLS

The following definitions and symbols are used throughout:

T = Maximum potential leisure hours per nonworkweek ($T \leq 168$).

$(1-\theta)T$ = Weekly time costs of going to work ($0 < \theta \leq 1$).

$\theta T = \begin{cases} \text{Maximum potential workhours per week.} \\ \text{Maximum potential leisure hours per workweek.} \end{cases}$

N = Maximum potential workweeks per year ($N \leq 52$).

H = Hours worked per workweek ($H \leq \theta T$).

K = Weeks worked per year ($K \leq N$).

L_1 = Leisure consumed during workweeks (in annual hours):

$$L_1 = K(\theta T - H); \qquad 0 \leq L_1 \leq \theta NT. \qquad (3.1)$$

L_2 = Leisure consumed during nonworkweeks (in annual hours):

$$L_2 = (N - K)T; \qquad 0 \leq L_2 \leq NT. \qquad (3.2)$$

Y = Annual nonwage income.

W = Hourly wage rate.

X = Consumption per year (other than leisure).

A = Annual workhours ($A = KH$).

F = Full income ($F = Y + W\theta NT$).

$U(X, L_1, L_2)$ = The individual's utility function. U is assumed (as in usual static demand theory under certainty) to be ordinal, increasing and quasiconcave for nonnegative (X, L, L_2), with continuity and differentiability as conveniently required, and with X a normal good.

THE BASIC MODEL

The individual's budget constraint is

$$X = Y + WKH = Y + WA. \qquad (3.3)$$

His optimization problem, under this basic model, is then

$$\text{Max } U(X, L_1, L_2) \quad \text{subject to eqs. 3.1, 3.2, and 3.3,} \qquad (3.4)$$

where N, T, θ, Y, and W are given.

EXPLANATIONS OF ASSUMPTIONS

Before analyzing this model, a few explanations are in order regarding the underlying assumptions.

1. X represents both value and quantity of consumption, taken as a composite good and measured in units of money. This implies, first, that relative prices of consumption goods are assumed constant, thus permitting aggregation into one composite good; and, second, that the price of the composite good X is constant and equals 1.[12] Variation in consumption among weeks (e.g., between work and nonworkweeks) is ignored by assuming utility to depend on the total annual magnitude of X.

2. Variations in hours worked among workweeks are also ignored by defining H as a scalar (endogenous) variable, to be interpreted as average weekly hours of work.

3. Allowing N and T to be smaller than their physical maxima $(N < 52;\ T < 168)$ implies two types of fixed "committed time expenditures" required for subsistence or for personal maintenance: first, $(168 - T)$ hours required per week; and, second, $(52 - N)$ weeks subtracted from both work and leisure activities per year. Since N and T are assumed to be given to an individual, it is immaterial whether or not these committed time expenditures appear explicitly in the specification of the utility function.

4. "Leisure" should be interpreted, in the spirit of the modern household production approach, as nonmarket time, available either for direct consumption as true leisure; or for use in other nonmarket activities that enhance utility directly or indirectly. In defining the utility function, we thus assume implicitly that both L_1 and L_2 are allocated optimally among their respective nonmarket activities (in addition to the exogenous committed time expenditures).

5. Allowing θ to be less than 1 introduces an important new element into this model—namely, weekly time costs associated with working, for transportation, preparation, additional rest requirements, etc. Every workweek, $(1 - \theta)T$ hours are "lost" since they are included neither in L_1, which is what appears in the utility function,

---

[12] Some extensions of the model, particularly those analyzing income tax effects, must modify the assumption $P_X = 1$ to allow the effective price of consumption to be different from 1 and to vary with the tax rate.

nor in H, which is the hours remunerated. The decision to participate in the labor force thus involves time costs of $(1-\theta)KT$ annual
hours, proportional to the number of weeks worked K, but independent of weekly hours H. This time cost specification serves as a
realistic generalization of the model without affecting its desirable
simple properties. The introduction of money costs of participation,
however, in addition to time costs, may complicate matters somewhat.[13]

6. As explained in the introduction, the basic feature of this model is
   its distinction between two types of leisure, L_1 and L_2, which
   cannot be regarded as perfect substitutes. This distinction permits
   their joint determination, analogous to any other pair of consumption goods, which yields in turn a joint determination of K and H
   (or K and A), with some implied constraints relating their separate
   behavior. On the other hand, the model does assume perfect
   substitutability of hours of work from the point of view of the
   demand for labor, as the wage rate is assumed independent of total
   hours $A = KH$, as well as of their allocation between K and H.

ANALYSIS OF THE MODEL

Proceeding with the analysis of the model, equation 3.1 may be
rearranged to give

$$A = KH = \theta KT - L_1. \tag{3.5}$$

Similarly, equation 3.2 gives

$$KT = NT - L_2. \tag{3.6}$$

Substituting equation 3.6 into the right side of 3.5,

$$A = KH = \theta NT - \theta L_2 - L_1; \tag{3.7}$$

and substituting equation 3.7 into 3.3 gives the budget constraint

$$X = N + W\theta NT - \theta WL_2 - WL_1.$$

Transferring the terms involving endogenous variables to the left now
gives the budget constraint in the familiar form:

$$X + W \cdot L_1 + \theta W \cdot L_2 = Y + W\theta NT = F. \tag{3.8}$$

---

[13] See Section V. Time and money costs constitute one source of stochastic variation in
labor supply equations, if assumed given to individuals but unobserved and variable
among individuals.

The consumer maximization may now be reformulated as an ordinary three-commodity competitive demand model, i.e.

$$\text{Max } U(X, L_1, L_2) \quad \text{s.t.} \quad P_X X + P_1 L_1 + P_2 L_2 = F \qquad (3.9)$$

under given income $F = (Y + W\theta NT)$ and prices

$$\mathbf{P} = (P_X, P_1, P_2) = (1, W, \theta W).$$

This formulation requires some interpretation. The individual's total time available for work is θNT, valued at $W\theta NT$, so that full income $F = Y + W\theta NT$ is the potential maximum income. The preceding formulation views the individual as purchasing both types of leisure (as well as consumption X) with this full income, where L_2 may be bought at a lower price than L_1: $\theta W < W$, since no time costs of going to work are required for L_2. Substituting L_2 for L_1 on the margin involves a fixed rate of substitution $1/\theta$, which is larger than 1 because of the corresponding proportional reduction in time costs $(1-\theta)KT$ associated with the reduction in $L_1 = K(\theta T - H)$.

The optimal solutions to the optimization equation (3.9) are the three ordinary demand functions $X(\mathbf{P}, F)$, $L_1(\mathbf{P}, F)$, and $L_2(\mathbf{P}, F)$. These satisfy the usual restrictions of demand theory. For example, they satisfy the budget constraint in equation 3.9 as an identity; they are homogeneous of degree zero in $(\mathbf{P}, F)$; their matrix of substitution effects is negative semidefinite and symmetric; and they satisfy the Engel and Cournot aggregation restrictions.[14] They also provide a convenient, well-recognized framework for completely specifying preferences, i.e., the relevant parameters of the utility function. Thus, the nature of preferences may be characterized sufficiently by specifying the income and price elasticities and the shares in full income of these three demand functions. (Actually, because of the budget identity, specifying the parameters of any two demand functions is sufficient.)

Two specific elements of this particular model require further analysis. First, since the focus of the model is on labor supply rather than on demand for leisure, we must relate the demands L_1 and L_2 to the supply variables K and H, or K and A, which are uniquely determined by L_1 and L_2 (as in equations 3.6 and 3.7). Second and more important, however, full income F and the two leisure prices P_1 and P_2 depend linearly on the same wage rate W, thus providing many specific implications in addition to those of standard demand theory.

[14] See Brown and Deaton (1972).

The supply of annual weeks K is a mirror image of the demand for leisure L_2 (save for a change of units given by the fixed coefficient T as in equation 3.6). This relation is similar to that between the leisure demand and labor supply in the classical one-dimensional labor supply model. Regarding K as a function of the exogenous variables W and Y, the derivatives of $K(W, Y)$ may be expressed in terms of the partial derivatives of the demand function $L_2(P, F)$ as follows:

$$\frac{\partial K}{\partial Y} = -\frac{1}{T}\frac{\partial L_2}{\partial Y}\bigg|_w = -\frac{1}{T}\frac{\partial L_2}{\partial F} \quad \left(\text{since } \frac{\partial F}{\partial Y}\bigg|_w = 1\right), \qquad (3.10)$$

with $\partial K/\partial Y$ negative if (and only if) L_2 is a normal good in consumption. Also,

$$\frac{\partial K}{\partial W} = -\frac{1}{T}\frac{\partial L_2}{\partial W}\bigg|_Y = -\frac{1}{T}\left[\frac{\partial L_2}{\partial P_1} + \theta\frac{\partial L_2}{\partial P_2} + \theta NT\frac{\partial L_2}{\partial F}\right] \qquad (3.11)$$

(since $\partial P_1/\partial W = 1$, $\partial P_2/\partial W = \theta$, and $\partial F/\partial W = \theta NT$).

The sign of $\partial K/\partial W$ is indeterminate, with a "backward-bending" supply curve for K possible: if L_2 is a normal good, then $\partial L_2/\partial F$ is positive, $\partial L_2/\partial P_2$ negative, and $\partial L_2/\partial P_1$ negative or positive, depending on whether L_1 and L_2 are gross complements or substitutes, respectively, in demand.

When analyzing the supply of annual hours A, the two types of leisure may be aggregated into one composite good, since their relative price is constant: $P_2/P_1 = \theta W/W = \theta$. Composite leisure is defined as

$$L = L_1 + \theta L_2 = \theta NT - A \qquad (3.12)$$

by equation 3.7 and the price of L is W, as seen by substituting 3.12 into the budget equation (3.8):

$$X + WL = Y + W\theta NT = F. \qquad (3.13)$$

By Hicks' composite-good theorem,[15] the individual's utility level may be expressed as a function of X and L alone:

$$u^* = U^*(X, L), \qquad (3.14)$$

with U^* manifesting the usual behavior; namely, it is monotone increasing and quasiconcave in its arguments. However, since the consumer's problem is to maximize equation 3.14 subject to 3.13, it is identical in all respects to the familiar one-dimensional static problem

[15] See Hicks (1946).

of leisure-consumption choice, with $A = (\theta NT) - L$ yielding that simple model's labor supply.

Thus, one may argue, a full circle is completed, achieving nothing new: using annual hours A as a measure of labor supply (which indeed is a common practice), the naive model with one-dimensional leisure may be applied and estimated. But this apparent futility is misleading. First, the present model justifies the aggregation of the two types of leisure *not because they are perfect substitutes*, as is assumed explicitly or implicitly in the literature, but rather *because their relative prices are constant* (proportional to W). However, if this did not have any operational implications, it would be just a cosmetic improvement. The second and main point, which is the very reason for the present formulation, is that the equation for annual hours A is not a complete model. The simple model of hours labor supply is just one equation in a simultaneous model with two equations, where the weeks supply function $K(W, Y)$ discussed above is the second equation.

The individual's complete optimization process may be viewed as a two-stage process (as in any composite-good case, where relative prices among the components are constant). The first stage determines the optimal allocation of a given L between L_1 and L_2, holding both X and L constant; that is,

$$\underset{(L_1, L_2)}{\text{Max}} \ U(X, L_1, L_2) \quad \text{s.t.} \quad L_1 + \theta L_2 = L. \tag{3.15}$$

The first-order conditions for optimum are $(\partial U / \partial L_2)/(\partial U / \partial L_1) = \theta$ and $L_1 + \theta L_2 = L$, yielding the solutions $L_1(X, L)$ and $L_2(X, L)$. Substituting these functions in the utility function gives

$$u^* = U[X, L_1(X, L), L_2(X, L)] = U^*(X, L), \tag{3.16}$$

where the function $U^*(\ )$ is the utility function relevant for the *second stage* of the optimization, defined as equations 3.13 and 3.14. In this second stage, L and X are determined as functions of W and F, and $A = \theta NT - L$ gives the hours labor supply $A(W, Y)$. But the allocation of L between L_1 and L_2, accomplished by the often-overlooked first stage (equation 3.15), underlies the weeks labor supply $K(W, Y) = N - (1/T)L_2$, through the determination of L_2.

Diagrammatic analysis gives additional insights into this joint determination of the two dimensions of labor supply by a two-stage process.

Figure 3.1 depicts the first stage. The two leisures (L_1, L_2) are measured on the axes. The budget line, corresponding to a given L, $L = L_1 + \theta L_2$, intersects the horizontal L_1-axis at $(L, 0)$ and the vertical L_2-axis at $(0, L/\theta)$. Its slope is

$$\frac{\partial L_2}{\partial L_1}\bigg|_L = -\frac{1}{\theta} = -\frac{P_1}{P_2}.$$

The individual's optimal point is $\ell = (L_1, L_2) = [K(\theta T - H), (N - K)T]$, where the indifference curve $U(X, L_1, L_2) = u^*$ (defined for X fixed at its optimal level) is tangent to the budget line. The horizontal (broken) line through ℓ (and through $(0, L_2)$) is a line of *constant K*, corresponding to the optimal level of K at ℓ. (K is constant when L_2 is constant,

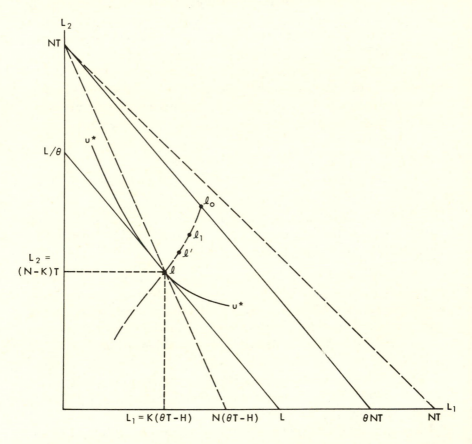

FIGURE 3.1 Allocation of leisure between two types and determination of hours and weeks

since N and T are fixed.) The negatively sloped (broken) line through ℓ and $(0, NT)$ is a line of *constant H*, as may be verified by eliminating K between equations 3.1 and 3.2, giving

$$L_1 T + L_2(\theta T - H) = NT(\theta T - H). \tag{3.17}$$

For constant H, this is a linear equation in (L_1, L_2), satisfied by the points $(0, NT)$, $[N(\theta T - H), 0]$, and $\ell = [K(\theta T - H), (N - K)T]$. The optimal number of weekly hours H may be measured by the intersection of this constant-H line with the L_1-axis, equal to $N(\theta T - H)$, determining H (since N and θT are fixed).

As annual work hours decrease (such as in the case of decreased wage W and positively sloped supply of A), L increases ($L = \theta NT - A$), and the budget line shifts upward (maintaining a constant slope $-1/\theta$). On each new budget line, a new optimal point such as ℓ' is determined similarly. The indifference map is also shifting, however, since in general X also varies with W, and the utility function and its related $L_1 | L_2$ indifference curves depend on X.

One special case leaves the indifference map invariant: suppose the utility function is *separable*, of the form $U[X, \psi(L_1, L_2)]$. Then the $L_1 | L_2$ indifference curves correspond to $\psi(L_1, L_2) = $ constant, and are independent of X. (However, the utility *level* associated with each curve varies with X, since $u = U(X, \psi)$.) Even in the nonseparable case, however, one may expect a continuous curve (such as the broken curve through ℓ and ℓ') to represent the locus of all optimal allocations of L corresponding to variations in W.

Variations in Y, with W constant, will result in a similar analysis and a similar locus of optimal points, but in general the locus for variations in Y is different from the locus corresponding to variable W, unless U is separable and the indifference map invariant, in which case the locus is a regular two-commodities expansion path, or income-consumption curve, and is fixed.

The limiting budget line as A or H approaches zero (but K remains positive), is the line of maximum $L = \theta NT$. However, if H actually reaches zero, participation in the labor force is terminated, the fixed time costs $(1 - \theta)TK$ related to work are eliminated, and K also becomes zero by definition. That is, the individual is switched to the point $(0, NT)$, corresponding to $H = K = 0$, rather than actually reaching the limiting point ℓ_0, where $H = 0$ but $K > 0$.

However, if $\theta < 1$, then H will never approach zero, and participation will cease at an earlier stage, switching to $H = K = 0$ from a point such as ℓ_1, where both H and K are positive. In other words, the reservation wage W_0 will be higher than the point of intersection of the extended supply curve $A(W)$ with the W-axis. This effect may be seen in Figure 3.2, which describes the second-stage maximization, where X and L are determined given the reduced utility function $U^*(X, L)$ and the budget line $X + WL = Y + W\theta NT$. The indifference curve corresponding to nonparticipation is that through the point $B = (NT, Y)$, where the level of utility is $u_0^* = U^*(Y, NT)$. The reservation wage W_0, below which the individual quits the labor force, is the wage that yields tangency of the budget line CC (which passes through $(\theta NT, Y)$) to the indifference curve u_0^*. At the quitting point $Q_0 = (L_0, X_0)$, the utility

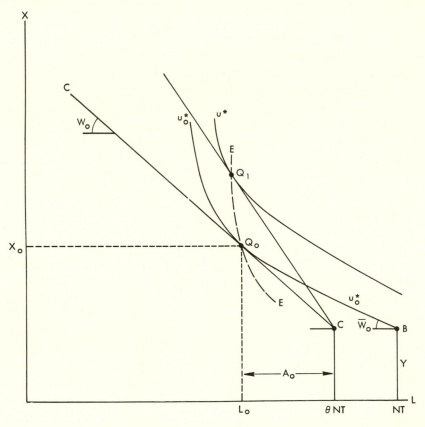

FIGURE 3.2   Effect of time costs on reservation wage and choice of composite leisure

level equals $u_0^* = U(X_0, L_0)$ and hours are positive: $A_0 = \theta NT - L_0 > 0$. Thus, the part of the expansion path EE that lies below the point Q_0 is irrelevant, since it corresponds to a utility lower than u_0^*, the utility level associated with nonparticipation.

In the special case $\theta = 1$ (no time costs of work), the reservation wage $\bar{W}_0$ will be the slope of the indifference curve u_0^* at the point $B = (NT, Y)$, corresponding to zero annual hours of work. Inspecting this case in Figure 3.1, we find that normally the quitting point will be a point such as ℓ_0, where hours are zero but weeks are still positive. Only in cases where the point ℓ_0 lies on the L_2-axis between 0 and NT will K approach 0 before H. Expressed somewhat differently, this result implies that the weeks reservation wage (where the extended supply curve $K(W)$ intersects the W-axis) is normally below the hours reservation wage, and therefore it is not effective: participation in the labor force involves a minimum number of workweeks, which is positive and bounded away from zero, and the supply of weeks $K(W)$ is discontinuous at $\bar{W}_0$.

Figure 3.3 gives an example of these relations for a specific utility function ($u = X^{1-a-b} L_1^a L_2^b$), and demonstrates the effects of time costs ($\theta < 1$). For $\theta = 1$ (zero time costs), the hours supply curve intersects the axis at $\bar{W}_0 = 1$, but the weeks supply curve is discontinuous ($K_0 = 25$). With positive time costs ($\theta < 1$), the reservation wage increases above $\bar{W}_0$, the supply of hours becomes discontinuous, and the minimum supply of weeks increases.

This analysis provides testable hypotheses regarding labor force participation behavior and the expected distribution of hours and weeks worked. If hours (due to time costs of work) and, especially, weeks labor supplies exhibit a strong discontinuity at the reservation wage, one would expect few individuals to be working small numbers of weeks annually, with higher proportions at either zero weeks proper (nonparticipants) or above a positive minimum number of weeks. The discontinuity of the weeks labor supply may be tested directly in estimating a properly specified model. It also has implications for the choice of a proper estimation procedure.[16]

---

[16] Models that assume the supply curve to be continuous at the reservation wage thus seem to give extremely biased estimates of the supply elasticity, if minimum quantity supplied is relatively large—even when sophisticated estimation methods are applied to correct the sample's selectivity bias, as in Heckman (1974b). See Hanoch, Chapter 6, for the appropriate specification and estimation methods in this case.

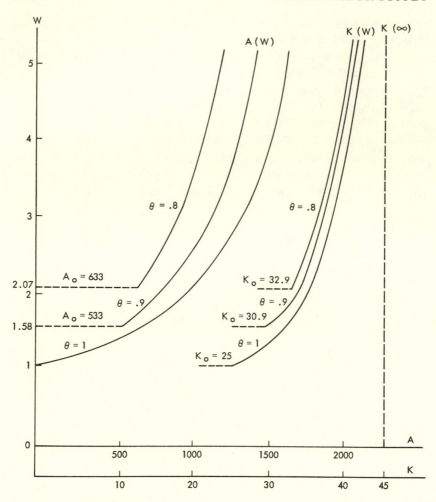

FIGURE 3.3 Example of hours and weeks labor supplies and effects of time costs
$(u = X^{.8}L_1^{.1}L_2^{.1};\ T = N = 50;\ Y = 10{,}000;\ \theta = 1,\ 0.9,\ \text{or}\ 0.8)$

Although the diagrammatic analysis is powerful in some respects,
certain features of the model, which are more quantitative and general,
are more easily derived mathematically. Returning to the second-stage
problem for the determination of hours A, as defined in equations 3.13
and 3.14, the supply function for A, which mirrors the demand for
composite leisure L, is given by

$$A(W, Y) = \theta NT - L(W, F) = \theta NT - L(W, Y + W\theta NT), \quad (3.18)$$

with the following nonwage-income and wage effects:

(i) $\quad \dfrac{\partial A}{\partial Y} = \dfrac{-\partial L(W, F)}{\partial F}$;

(ii) $\quad \dfrac{\partial A(W, Y)}{\partial W} = \dfrac{-\partial L(W, F)}{\partial W} - \dfrac{\partial L(W, F)}{\partial F} \cdot \theta NT.$ $\qquad$ (3.19)

Again, if the demand for L is normal, $\partial L/\partial F > 0$ and $\partial L/\partial W < 0$ (negatively sloped demand), and therefore $\partial A/\partial Y$ is negative, but $\partial A/\partial W$ is of indeterminate sign.

Using equation 3.7 or 3.12, or the supply of A may be related to the separate demands for L_1 and L_2, the components of L, in terms of price and income effects, as follows:

(i) $\quad \dfrac{\partial A}{\partial Y} = \dfrac{-\partial L_1}{\partial Y}\bigg|_{\mathrm{w}} - \theta \dfrac{\partial L_2}{\partial Y}\bigg|_{\mathrm{w}} = \dfrac{-\partial L_1}{\partial F} - \theta \dfrac{\partial L_2}{\partial F}$;

(ii) $\quad \dfrac{\partial A}{\partial W} = -\dfrac{\partial L_1}{\partial W}\bigg|_{Y} - \theta \dfrac{\partial L_2}{\partial W}\bigg|_{Y}$

$\qquad = -\left[\dfrac{\partial L_1}{\partial P_1} + \theta \dfrac{\partial L_1}{\partial P_2} + \theta NT \dfrac{\partial L_1}{\partial F} \right] - \theta \left[\dfrac{\partial L_2}{\partial P_1} + \theta \dfrac{\partial L_2}{\partial P_2} + \theta NT \dfrac{\partial L_2}{\partial F} \right].$

$$\qquad (3.20)$$

If both L_1 and L_2 are normal, the full-income effects are both positive, the own-price effects on each demand negative, and the cross-effects $\partial L_1/\partial P_2$ and $\partial L_2/\partial P_1$ of unknown equal sign, such that the wage effect on each part of equation 3.20 separately is of unknown sign.

Since the supply of A depends on both demands, whereas the supply of K is related to L_2 alone, we can compare their slopes with respect to W and Y. Substituting from equations 3.10 and 3.11, which give the effects on K, into equation 3.20 (or, alternatively, using equation 3.5 directly) gives

(i) $\quad \dfrac{\partial A}{\partial Y} = -\dfrac{\partial L_1}{\partial F} + \theta T \dfrac{\partial K}{\partial Y}$;

$$\qquad (3.21)$$

(ii) $\quad \dfrac{\partial A}{\partial W} = -\dfrac{\partial L_1}{\partial W}\bigg|_{Y} + \theta T \dfrac{\partial K}{\partial W}.$

Measuring the effects on K on an annual hours basis by using potential annual hours of work θTK, equation 3.21 implies

$$1. \quad -\frac{\partial A}{\partial Y} > -\frac{\partial(\theta TK)}{\partial Y} > 0,$$

if both L_1 and L_2 are normal goods; and

$$2. \quad \frac{\partial A}{\partial W} > \frac{\partial(\theta TK)}{\partial W} > 0,$$

if both

$$\left.\frac{\partial L_1}{\partial W}\right|_Y \quad \text{and} \quad \left.\frac{\partial L_2}{\partial W}\right|_Y$$

are negative (that is, if substitution effects dominate income effects of the change in W in the demands for both L_1 and L_2). Conversely, if both

$$\left.\frac{\partial L_1}{\partial W}\right|_Y \quad \text{and} \quad \left.\frac{\partial L_2}{\partial W}\right|_Y$$

are positive, the supplies of A and K are backward-bending, and

$$3. \quad -\frac{\partial A}{\partial W} > -\frac{\partial(\theta TK)}{\partial W} > 0,$$

with the effect on A again stronger in absolute magnitude (because of the additional effect, assumed to be in the same direction as for L_2, of demand for L_1, which affects A but not K).

A reasonable special case, for which these results obtain necessarily, is that mentioned above, where the utility function is *separable* (that is, weakly separable between consumption X and leisures L_1 and L_2: $u = U[X, \psi(L_1, L_2)]$), and where both L_1 and L_2 are normal with respect to the subutility function $\psi(L_1, L_2)$. This case implies, first, that the solutions to the first-stage maximization (3.15) are independent of X: $L_1(L)$ and $L_2(L)$ (the indifference map in Figure 3.1 is thus invariant with respect to variations in either W or Y); and, second, that $L_1(L)$ and $L_2(L)$ are increasing in L (so that the optimum expansion locus in Figure 3.1 is stable and positively sloped). In this case, both L_1 and L_2 necessarily move in the same direction as L for any variation in W or in Y (or both), and the magnitude of the response of A is always greater than the response of θTK, and in the same direction (as in the example used for Figure 3.3, since the Cobb–Douglas utility function is separable).

In the general nonseparable case, the effects of W on L_1 and L_2 (under constant Y) may have opposite signs, resulting in a reversal of magnitudes or even opposite signs for the two slopes $\partial A/\partial W$ and $\partial K/\partial W$.

Although either supply curve (or both) may be backward-bending, the magnitude of each negative slope (at a given W) is bounded by the corresponding income effect of the change in W, since the substitution effects are necessarily positive.

The income effects are proportional to annual hours A, *for both* A *and* K. This result is verified as follows. The Slutsky equations for $\partial L_2/\partial P_i$ and $\partial L/\partial W$ are given by[17]

$$\frac{\partial L_2}{\partial P_i}=\frac{\partial L_2}{\partial P_i}\bigg|_u-L_i\frac{\partial L_2}{\partial F}\qquad(i=1,2)$$

and

$$\frac{\partial L}{\partial W}=\frac{\partial L}{\partial W}\bigg|_u-L\frac{\partial L}{\partial F},$$

where the first term in each equation is the pure substitution effect along a given indifference surface. Substituting these demand relations in the supply equations 3.11 for K and 3.19 for A gives

$$\frac{\partial K}{\partial W}=-\frac{1}{T}\left[\left(\frac{\partial L_2}{\partial P_1}\bigg|_u+\theta\frac{\partial L_2}{\partial P_2}\bigg|_u\right)+(\theta NT-L_1-\theta L_2)\frac{\partial L_2}{\partial F}\right]$$

$$=\frac{\partial K}{\partial W}\bigg|_u+A\cdot\frac{\partial K}{\partial Y}\qquad\qquad(3.22)$$

using equations 3.7 and 3.10; and

$$\frac{\partial A}{\partial W}=-\frac{\partial L}{\partial W}\bigg|_u-(\theta NT-L)\frac{\partial L}{\partial F}=\frac{\partial A}{\partial W}\bigg|_u+A\cdot\frac{\partial A}{\partial Y}$$

using equations 3.18 and 3.19i.

An intuitive explanation of this result is as follows: For compensated variations, the marginal compensation for varying W at the optimum, in terms of annual income, is always equal to annual hours A, whether

---

[17] See Slutsky (1915), Samuelson (1947).

it is the weeks or the hours supply equation, since

$$\frac{\partial X}{\partial W}\bigg|_{Y,A} = \frac{\partial}{\partial W}(Y + WA) = A.$$

The effects on both supplies and on the reservation wage of variations in time costs may be analyzed similarly by changing the cost
parameter θ. Figure 3.3 illustrates these effects. Comparing the curves
for $\theta = 0.9$ and $\theta = 0.8$ in the figure shows that, as time costs increase
(θ decreases), the reservation wage necessarily increases (Figure 3.2)
and the supply curves for workers (at $W > W_0$) shift to the left. (These
are general results under normality of the three commodities.)[18]

For some analytical purposes, it is useful to draw on results known
from duality theory of demand, employing the indirect utility function
and the expenditure function as alternative complete specifications of
preferences and convenient tools of analysis.

The indirect utility function V is derived by substituting the demand
functions, which are the solutions to equation 3.9, into the three-
commodity utility function:

$$u^* = U[X(\mathbf{P}, F), L_1(\mathbf{P}, F), L_2(\mathbf{P}, F)] = V(P_X, P_1, P_2, F). \quad (3.23)$$

Maximum utility level u^* is thus expressed by V as a function of prices
and full income. By duality theory, V satisfies the following conditions:
V is increasing in F, decreasing and quasiconvex in prices $\mathbf{P}$, and
homogeneous of degree zero in $(\mathbf{P}, F)$. In addition, it contains all the
information about the direct utility function $U(X, L_1, L_2)$, being uniquely related to it by duality. A specification of V, rather than U, thus
completely specifies the model. (Both U and V are ordinal; namely,
they yield the same model under any arbitrary, positively monotone
transformation $f(u^*)$, with $f' > 0$.) For some preferences, the function
V may be expressed in closed form, whereas its dual function U may
not. The major advantage of using V, however, is its feature known as
Roy's identity.[19] The demand functions are simply related to the partial
derivatives of V as follows:

$$X = \frac{-\partial V}{\partial P_x}\bigg/\frac{\partial V}{\partial F}; \qquad L_1 = \frac{-\partial V}{\partial P_1}\bigg/\frac{\partial V}{\partial F}; \qquad L_2 = \frac{-\partial V}{\partial P_2}\bigg/\frac{\partial V}{\partial F}; \quad (3.24)$$

---

[18] The net effects on the minimum quantities A_0 and K_0 are generally indeterminate,
although both increase with costs in this particular example.

[19] See Roy (1947), Diewert (1975).

and, also,

$$\frac{-\partial V}{\partial F} = P_X \frac{\partial V}{\partial P_X} + P_1 \frac{\partial V}{\partial P_1} + P_2 \frac{\partial V}{\partial P_2}. \tag{3.25}$$

A valid specification of the functional form of V therefore implies immediately a complete, internally consistent specification of functional forms for the three demand functions—requiring only partial differentiation. (Note also that, if the demands are single-valued functions, V is differentiable even if its dual function U is not.) Expressing the variables $(L_1, L_2, \mathbf{P}, F)$ in terms of the labor supply variables (A, K, W, Y) of this model (equations 3.5, 3.7, 3.8) thus gives an easy derivation of the supply equations from the indirect utility function V.

Another equivalent specification of the model implied by duality uses the *expenditure function* (analogous to the cost function of production theory). Regarding equation 3.23 as an identity that implicitly defines F as a function of prices $\mathbf{P}$ and the utility level u^*, the expenditure function is

$$F = E(P_X, P_1, P_2, u^*). \tag{3.26}$$

The function E satisfies the following general restrictions:[20] E is increasing in all the arguments, positive, and linear-homogeneous and concave in the prices $\mathbf{P}$.

Again, a specification of $E(\ )$ uniquely determines the utility function $U(\ )$ or the indirect utility function $V(\ )$, and thus completely specifies the model. It is convenient because the *compensated* demand functions are given simply by the partial derivatives of E with respect to the corresponding prices:[21]

$$X(\mathbf{P}, u^*) = \frac{\partial E}{\partial P_X}; \qquad L_1(\mathbf{P}, u^*) = \frac{\partial E}{\partial P_1}; \qquad L_2(\mathbf{P}, u^*) = \frac{\partial E}{\partial P_2}. \tag{3.27}$$

The derivative with respect to u^* is the reciprocal of marginal utility of full income; i.e., $\partial E/\partial u^* = 1/(\partial V/\partial F)$. As shown below, the use of the

[20] See Diewert (1975).

[21] This is known in production theory as Shephard's Lemma, but was previously stated or proved by Hotelling, Hicks, Samuelson, and others. See references in Diewert (1975).

expenditure function facilitates the integration of preferences from a given specification of the supply equations.

Returning to the labor supply model, substitute first the prices $\mathbf{P} = (1, W, \theta W)$ in V of equation 3.23 (retaining F as a variable):

$$u^* = V(1, W, \theta W, F) = V^*(W, F). \tag{3.28}$$

The function V^* in equation 3.28 is the reduced indirect utility function dual to the *reduced* utility function U^* of equation 3.14 or 3.16, which is a function of X and composite leisure L. The first-stage optimization is thus easily performed in the analysis by using the dual indirect function. The reduced expenditure function $F = E^*(W, u^*)$ is also defined by 3.28, viewed as an identity.

Another indirect function, $\bar{V}(W, Y)$, is obtained as a function of the exogenous labor supply variables by substituting $F = Y + \theta WNT$ in 3.28:

$$u^* = V^*(W, Y + \theta WNT) = \bar{V}(W, Y). \tag{3.29}$$

The demand for composite leisure L may now be derived from each of the indirect utility functions by differentiation:

$$L = L_1 + \theta L_2 = -\frac{\partial V/\partial P_1}{\partial V/\partial F} - \theta \frac{\partial V/\partial P_2}{\partial V/\partial F} = -\frac{\partial V^*/\partial W}{\partial V^*/\partial F} = \theta NT - \frac{\partial \bar{V}/\partial W}{\partial \bar{V}/\partial Y}, \tag{3.30}$$

since $\partial \bar{V}/\partial Y = \partial V^*/\partial F$ and $\partial \bar{V}/\partial W = \partial V^*/\partial W + \theta NT(\partial V^*/\partial F)$. The compensated demand is derived from the expenditure functions by

$$L = \frac{\partial E}{\partial P_1} + \theta \frac{\partial E}{\partial P_2} = \frac{\partial E^*}{\partial W}. \tag{3.31}$$

Using the last equality in equation 3.30, the supply of annual hours is simply derived from $\bar{V}$:

$$A = \theta NT - L = \frac{\partial \bar{V}/\partial W}{\partial \bar{V}/\partial Y}. \tag{3.32}$$

On the other hand, if a form of the hours supply function $A(W, Y)$ is given, the expenditure function $E^*(W, u)$ may be found by solving the following first-order partial differential equation:

$$\theta NT - \frac{\partial E^*}{\partial W} - A(W, E^* - \theta WNT) = 0, \tag{3.33}$$

where equation 3.33 is derived by using equation 3.31 and the relations $Y = F - \theta WNT$ and $L = \theta NT - A$.

The supply of weeks $K = N - (1/T)L_2$ is related to the unreduced functions V and E by similar relations, but may not be expressed in terms of the reduced functions V^*, $\bar{V}$, or E^*. Therefore, the integration of the unreduced functions E or V from the pair of supply equations for A and K is not as simple, involving a simultaneous solution to *two* partial differential equations.

Finally, whereas both A and K, viewed as functions of W and Y (or W and F), behave qualitatively as the labor supply function of the naive model with one leisure, the magnitude H, *weekly hours* of work, is not of this nature. It is expressed as a *ratio* of the two supply functions, and is not related linearly to the underlying demand functions L_1 and L_2, since $L_2(\mathbf{P}, F)$ appears in both the numerator and the denominator:

$$H = \frac{A(W, Y)}{K(W, Y)} = \frac{\theta NT - L_2 - L_1}{N - (1/T)L_2}.$$

Therefore, one cannot expect $H(W, Y)$ to manifest behavior similar to that of the labor supply function of the naive model, or to that of annual hours A or annual weeks K. Caution should thus be exercised in analyzing and interpreting equations estimated with H as the dependent variable, and the annual magnitudes A and K should be used as the labor supply variables in the specification of new models.

III. RESTRICTED AND CORNER SOLUTIONS

The preceding discussion must be modified, however, if the individual is a full-time worker in terms of annual weeks. If the relevant demand for his labor services confronts him with an all-or-nothing choice in terms of weeks—i.e., to work $\bar{K}$ weeks (where $\bar{K}$ may be less than N, owing to exogenously determined vacation time, or seasonal and other involuntary layoffs) or not to work at all—then L_2 is no longer a choice variable and the model is again equivalent to the one-dimensional leisure model. The consumer's utility function (assuming he is still free to vary hours of work H) in this case is

$$U(X_1, L_1; \bar{L}_2) = U[Y + W(\bar{K}H), \theta\bar{K}T - (\bar{K}H); (N - \bar{K})T],$$

where $\bar{K}H$ is the only endogenous variable in the model and plays a role perfectly analogous to labor supply in a single-leisure model.

The same result is obtained when $\bar{K}$ is equal to N, not because $\bar{K}$ is given exogenously, but because weeks labor supply reaches a corner solution. (In terms of Figure 3.1, the extended expansion locus $\ell \mid \ell_0$ intersects the horizontal L_1-axis at a point where $L_2 = 0$, i.e., $K = N$, and $L_1 = N(\theta T - H) > 0$.) Presumably, this corner solution is much more probable than full-time work in terms of hours ($H = \theta T$), unless maximum hours $\bar{H} < \theta T$ are exogenously determined as well. Judging by the large numbers of individuals working 50 to 52 weeks per year, particularly among adult males but also among all other groups,[22] this corner solution is common. If it is recognized, the estimation equation for weeks supply must be treated as applying to a distribution of weeks truncated at both ends: the lower end at a point corresponding to the reservation wage, and the upper end corresponding to the corner-solution wage with full-year participation.

Within groups (such as adult married males) in which this corner solution is the rule with very few exceptions, labor supply may validly be specified in terms of weekly hours H (equivalent to $\bar{K}H$, NH, or $52H$) and may be expected to behave as annual hours A, or as total hours in the single-leisure labor supply model.

Another corner-like situation (which may characterize some actual labor markets) occurs when weekly (and daily) hours are determined exogenously by employers (at $\bar{H}$), but individuals can still choose their number of weeks worked K—for example, substitute teachers.

The individual's optimization involves only the choice of $K\bar{H}$ (annual hours) in maximizing his utility:

$$U(X, L_1, L_2) = \left[Y + W(K\bar{H}), \left(\frac{\theta T - \bar{H}}{\bar{H}}\right)(K\bar{H}), NT - \frac{T}{\bar{H}}(K\bar{H}) \right]$$
$$= \bar{U}[Y + W(K\bar{H}), (K\bar{H})],$$

by satisfying the first-order condition

$$W\frac{\partial U}{\partial X} + \left(\frac{\theta T - \bar{H}}{\bar{H}}\right)\frac{\partial U}{\partial L_1} - \frac{T}{\bar{H}} \cdot \frac{\partial U}{\partial L_2} = W\bar{U}_1 + \bar{U}_2 = 0,$$

which gives a solution for $K\bar{H}$ in terms of W and Y.

[22] For example, in the SEO sample of married couples (see note 8 above), these proportions are 87.9 percent for white husbands and 20.0 percent for white wives; 81.3 percent and 29.4 percent, respectively, for blacks.

However, since K (or $K\bar{H}$) appears in both L_1 and L_2 (with different coefficients), the simple one-leisure model and the usual two-commodity demand model are no longer analogous to this case. Although the budget constraint equation (3.8) still holds, the analogy with the three-commodity (X, L_1, L_2) demand model breaks down as well, since L_1 and L_2 can no longer be varied independently, being subject to the constraint of equation 3.17.

The effective reservation wage under partially restricted supply situations cannot be lower than in the unrestricted case, as proved by

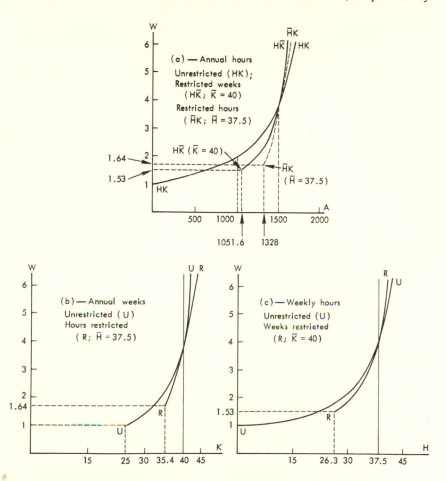

FIGURE 3.4 Effects of restrictions on hours and weeks on labor supply (simulated Cobb–Douglas utility function; $a = b = 0.1$; $T = N = 50$; $Y = 10,000$; $\theta = 1$)

the following argument. The maximum unrestricted utility at the reservation wage $\bar{W}_0$ is exactly equal to the reduced utility $U^*(Y, NT)$ (equation 3.16) corresponding to nonparticipation, by definition. Since at $\bar{W}_0$ the maximized restricted utility cannot exceed the unrestricted maximum (and is lower if the restriction is effective), and since utility increases with the wage rate, a higher reservation wage $W_0 \geq \bar{W}_0$ is required to equate the restricted utility level to $U^*(Y, NT)$. This higher wage will generally make the restricted supply curve for annual hours discontinuous at W_0, even if time costs are zero ($\theta = 1$)—since, if $W_0 > \bar{W}_0$, the hours supplied at W_0 are positive. Similarly, the weeks supply discontinuity is expected to be larger in magnitude in the restricted cases if the restricted supply of weeks is positively sloped between $\bar{W}_0$ and W_0.

These effects are demonstrated in Figure 3.4, which extends the example of Figure 3.3 to cases where either K or H are restricted exogenously. (The levels of $\bar{K}$ and $\bar{H}$ are chosen as equal, in each case, to the unrestricted level corresponding to $W = 4$.) As expected generally, the reservation wage increases as a result of the partial restrictions (by 53 percent and 64 percent, in these examples), leading to discontinuities of the annual hours supply curves (Figure 3.4a) and the weekly hours supply (when $K = \bar{K}$—Figure 3.4c), and to an increase in .the discontinuity of the weeks supply (when $H = \bar{H}$—Figure 3.4b)— even when no time costs are assumed ($\theta = 1$). In addition, the elasticity of supply (for workers) is smaller in the restricted case than in the unrestricted case.[23]

IV. Generalization of the Model to Family Context

The model and the examples of the previous sections are now generalized to apply to a two-earner family (say husband and wife), where decisions about family consumption and each member's labor supply are made jointly and consistently, under one common family budget constraint (given the family's nonwage income $\hat{Y}$) but separate time constraints for each member. As before, two types of leisure are distinguished for each member: leisure during workweeks (L_1 and $\hat{L}_1$, where the notation $\hat{Z}$ for the husband's variable Z is used throughout), and leisure during nonworkweeks (L_2 and $\hat{L}_2$).

[23] This is a special case of the general Le Chatelier principle, as explained in Samuelson.

The time constraints and the definitions of L_1 and $\hat{L}_1$ are similar to equations 3.1 and 3.2:

$$L_1 = K(\theta T - H), \qquad L_2 = (N - K)T,$$

$$K \leq N \leq 52, \qquad H \leq \theta T \leq T \leq 168;$$

and

$$\hat{L}_1 = \hat{K}(\hat{\theta}\hat{T} - \hat{H}), \qquad \hat{L}_2 = (\hat{N} - \hat{K})\hat{T},$$

$$\hat{K} \leq \hat{N} \leq 52, \qquad \hat{H} \leq \hat{\theta}\hat{T} \leq \hat{T} \leq 168, \tag{3.34}$$

where the various time parameters (i.e., θ, T, and N) are allowed to differ between members.

The family consumption is limited by the total budget constraint

$$X = \hat{Y} + WKH + \hat{W}\hat{K}\hat{H}, \tag{3.35}$$

which generalizes equation 3.30. The family utility function is assumed to be

$$u = U(X, L_1, L_2, \hat{L}_1, \hat{L}_2), \tag{3.36}$$

with the usual properties with respect to all five goods. The model is identical to that of Section II if, for example, the husband's labor supply variables $\hat{H}$ and $\hat{K}$ are determined exogenously and are therefore not subject to family decisions (or if $\hat{K}$ is at a corner solution $\hat{K} = \hat{N}$ at the relevant range and $\hat{H}_0$ is given, as are all the other variables except the wife's H and K, or L_1 and L_2). In this case, one must redefine the exogenous nonwage income to be $Y = \hat{Y} + \hat{W}\hat{K}\hat{H}$ and omit the given magnitudes $\hat{L}_1$ and $\hat{L}_2$ from the definition of U in equation 3.26 to obtain the optimization problem of equation 3.4.

However, if both wage earners can vary their weeks and hours labor supplies (under given hourly wage rates), the maximization of equation 3.36 subject to 3.34 and 3.35 leads to a truly generalized model, with many new variations arising from the possibility of substitution between the two partners of their two types of leisure, in conjunction with the assumed perfect substitutability of their consumptions. As in the individual case, the family's total budget constraint may be put in the usual demand-analysis form. Substituting equation 3.34 into 3.35 and regrouping gives

$$X + WL_1 + \theta WL_2 + \hat{W}\hat{L}_1 + \hat{\theta}\hat{W}\hat{L}_2 = F = \hat{Y} + W\theta NT + \hat{W}\hat{\theta}\hat{N}\hat{T}, \tag{3.37}$$

where the family's full income F corresponds to maximum potential family income, which is subject to allocation by the family among the five commodities.

Defining the prices $= (1, W, \theta W, \hat{W}, \hat{\theta}\hat{W}) = (P_X, P_1, P_2, \hat{P}_1, \hat{P}_2) = \mathbf{P}$, the problem of maximizing U under equation 3.37 is identical to the usual demand analysis with five goods. The demand functions are each a function of $(\mathbf{P}, F)$, and may be analyzed in these terms to characterize the family's preferences.

As in the one-earner model, however, there are additional implications due to the constant relative price of each member's two leisures: $P_2/P_1 = \theta$ and $\hat{P}_2/\hat{P}_1 = \hat{\theta}$. Further analysis is needed to relate these leisure demands to the labor supplies. In analogy to equations 3.6 and 3.7, the supplies of annual hours A and $\hat{A}$, and of annual weeks K and $\hat{K}$, are linear functions of the members' leisure demands:

$$K = N - (1/T)L_2, \qquad \hat{K} = \hat{N} - (1/\hat{T})\hat{L}_2;$$

and   (3.38)

$$A = \theta NT - \theta L_2 - L_1, \qquad \hat{A} = \hat{\theta}\hat{N}\hat{T} - \hat{\theta}\hat{L}_2 - \hat{L}_1,$$

where $A = KH$ and $\hat{A} = \hat{K}\hat{H}$.

Again, the weeks supply depends only on demand for own type-2 leisure. However, since each of these demands is in general a function of *all prices*, it depends on spouse's wage rate as well—and so do the supply functions, such as $K = K(W, \hat{W}, \hat{Y})$ and $\hat{K} = \hat{K}(W, \hat{W}, \hat{Y})$. The partial effects of the three exogenous variables on each of the four labor supplies may be derived in analogy to equations 3.10, 3.11, and 3.20. To use just two examples here, consider own-wage and husband's-wage effects on the wife's supply of annual weeks:

$$\frac{\partial K}{\partial W} = -\frac{1}{T} \cdot \frac{\partial L_2}{\partial W}\bigg|_{W,Y} = -\frac{1}{T}\left(\frac{\partial L_2}{\partial P_1} + \theta\frac{\partial L_2}{\partial P_2} + \theta NT\frac{\partial L_2}{\partial F}\right),$$

as in equation 3.11. Also,

$$\frac{\partial K}{\partial \hat{W}} = -\left(\frac{\partial L_2}{\partial \hat{P}_1} + \hat{\theta}\frac{\partial L_2}{\partial \hat{P}_2} + \hat{\theta}\hat{N}\hat{T}\frac{\partial L_2}{\partial F}\right), \qquad (3.39)$$

where the signs of the first two terms in equation 3.39 depend on whether the husband's two types of leisure are gross substitutes for or complements to the time spent by the wife "at home" (away from the market) in weeks in which she is not working (L_2). A variety of hypotheses may be formulated in this framework to account for various interpretations of casual observations or logical conjectures. For example, L_2 and $\hat{L}_2$ should be somewhat complementary, owing to both spouses' preference for joint vacations (or the converse, under other lifestyles). It is hoped that a full estimation of a joint labor supply model can identify all these own- and cross-effects (12 effects in all), and verify such conjectured modes of behavior.

Continuing the analogy to the one-individual model, if both members work, each member's two leisures may be combined to one composite good, owing to their constant relative price. The derivation of the annual hours supplies is facilitated by the conceptual framework of two-stage maximization. The second stage maximizes the reduced utility function, which is now a function of three variables—consumption X and two composite leisures L and $\hat{L}$. That is,

$$L = L_1 + \theta L_2 = \theta NT - A, \qquad \hat{L} = \hat{L}_1 + \hat{\theta}\hat{L}_2 = \hat{\theta}\hat{N}\hat{T} - \hat{A},$$

(see 3.12); and

$$u^* = U^*(X, L, \hat{L}). \tag{3.40}$$

U^* is maximized under the collapsed budget constraint

$$X + WL + \hat{W}\hat{L} = F. \tag{3.41}$$

The first stage, optimizing the allocation of L (or $\hat{L}$) between its components L_1 and L_2, is formally similar to the analysis in Section I and Figure 3.1 except that both $\hat{L}$ and X are now taken as fixed for finding the optimal allocation of any given L. However, if each partner's leisures are weakly separable in the utility function, namely,

$$u = U[X, \phi(L_1, L_2), \hat{\phi}(\hat{L}_1, \hat{L}_2)],$$

then rates of substitution between own two leisures are independent of X and of the spouse's two leisures, and the allocation of L between L_1 and L_2 depends on the level of L only (the expansion path in Fig. 3.1 is fixed), and similarly for $\hat{L}_i(\hat{L})$.

The preceding analysis applies only when both earners' hours and weeks are freely determined, and as long as no corner solutions are obtained, including *nonparticipation*, which is a corner solution obtained when one member's wage rate is below the reservation wage. However, the wife's reservation wage now depends on the husband's wage rate (and not merely on his total earnings), and vice versa.

Suppose, first, that no time costs are involved in the wife's participation in the labor force: $\theta = 1$. Her hours labor supply $A = NT - L$ depends on $(W, \hat{W}, \hat{Y})$, and her reservation wage $\hat{W}_0$ is given by the equation $A(\bar{W}_0, \hat{W}, \hat{Y}) = 0$, so that $\bar{W}_0 = \bar{W}_0(\hat{W}, \hat{Y})$. Analogy to Figure 3.1 shows that $K(\bar{W}_0, \hat{W}, \hat{Y})$ is generally positive. That is, participation at wages slightly above $\bar{W}_0$ starts with a minimum positive number of weeks, and the wife's supply curve for weeks is discontinuous at $\bar{W}_0$. Once $W < \bar{W}_0$, the wife leaves the labor market and the husband's labor supplies are again the same as in the one-individual model, with both supplies determined by $(\hat{W}, \hat{Y})$ but independent of the wife's rejected wage offers W. Since the wife's supply of hours A is generally continuous at $\bar{W}_0$ (if $\theta = 1$), the husband's supply of hours $\hat{A}$ should not show any discontinuity with respect to variations of the wife's wage W around her reservation wage $\bar{W}_0$. However, because substitution possibilities between the marketed times of the two spouses are eliminated if the wife does not work, the slopes of $\hat{A}$ may be different for the working-wife case, with $\hat{A} = \hat{A}(\hat{W}, W, \hat{Y})$ and $W > \bar{W}_0$; and for the nonworking-wife case, with $\hat{A}_0 = \hat{A}_0(\hat{W}, \hat{Y})$ and $W < \bar{W}_0$. Since the wife's weeks supply is discontinuous, the husband's $\hat{K}$ may also jump at $W = \bar{W}_0$, reflecting a change in substitution possibilities between L_2 and $\hat{L}_2$, the nonworkweek leisures of the two partners. (However, if the pair $(\hat{L}_1, \hat{L}_2)$ is separable in the family utility function, then $\hat{L}_2$ (and $\hat{K}$) is a function of $\hat{L} = \theta \hat{N} \hat{T} - \hat{A}$ only, and will therefore be continuous if $\hat{A}$ is continuous.)

Suppose, second, that the wife's participation in the labor force requires time costs: $\theta < 1$. The effective reservation wage W_0 will be higher than $\bar{W}_0$, and both spouses' hours and weeks supplies will be discontinuous at W_0, which is obtained by equating U^* under the two alternatives:

$$U^*(\hat{Y} + \hat{W}\hat{A}_0, NT, \theta \hat{N} \hat{T} - \hat{A}_0)$$
$$= U^*(\hat{Y} + \hat{W}\hat{A}_1 + W_0 A_0, \theta NT - A_0, \theta \hat{N} \hat{T} - \hat{A}_1). \quad (3.42)$$

The left side corresponds to nonparticipation of the wife, with the husband working $\hat{A}_0 = \hat{A}_0(\hat{W}, \hat{Y})$ hours; and the right side corresponds to the wife working $A_0 = A(W_0, \hat{W}, \hat{Y}; \theta)$ hours, and the husband working $\hat{A}_1 = \hat{A}(\hat{W}, W_0, \hat{Y}; \theta)$ hours. In general, $\hat{A}_0 \neq \hat{A}_1$, since the wife's earnings and leisures are discontinuous at W_0. *Therefore, in the general case, both hours and weeks supply functions of the husband will*

TABLE 3.1: Example of Family Labor Supplies

$$(u = X^{0.6}L_1^{0.1}L_2^{0.1}\hat{L}_1^{0.1}\hat{L}_2^{0.1}; \ N = \hat{N} = T = \hat{T} = 50; \ \theta = \hat{\theta} = 1; \ \hat{Y} = 2000)$$

Variable	Symbol	Husband's Wage $\hat{W}$	$\bar{W}_0$	Wife's Wage W 2.	4.	6.
Husband						
Annual hours	$\hat{A}$	4.	1750	1650	1400	1150
		6.	1792	1767	1600	1433
Annual weeks	$\hat{K}$	4.	42.5	41.5	39.0	36.5
		6.	42.9	42.7	41.0	39.3
Weekly hours	$\hat{H}$	4.	41.2	39.8	35.9	31.5
	$(=\hat{A}/\hat{K})$	6.	41.8	41.4	39.0	36.4
Wife						
Annual hours	A	4.	0	800	1400	1600
		6.	0	300	1150	1433
Annual weeks	K	4.	25.0	33.0	39.0	41.0
		6.	25.0	28.0	36.5	39.3
Weekly hours	H	4.	0	24.2	35.9	39.0
	$(=A/K)$	6.	0	10.7	31.5	36.4
Reservation wage	$\bar{W}_0$	4.	1.2	—	—	—
		6.	1.7	—	—	—

shift discontinuously as the wife enters or leaves the labor market. This situation has implications, of course, with regard to estimation of labor supply functions for married men, requiring a specification that allows shifts in all parameters between men with working wives ($K > 0$) and men with nonworking wives ($K = 0$).[24] (The converse analysis is analogous, of course, if the husband is the first to leave the labor force.)

To illustrate these relations, the example of Figure 3.3 is extended to a five-good family utility function. The results are summarized in Tables 3.1 and 3.2 and Figures 3.5(a) and 3.5(b), and detailed in the appendix. The parameters selected are symmetric with respect to the

---

[24] As in Ashenfelter and Heckman, who restricted their sample to husbands with nonworking wives. This restriction should be made with caution, however, since classifying the sample by *measured* positive K, which includes a transitory component (see note 11), introduces a selectivity bias. A possible consistent selection is by *predicted* positive K. See Hanoch, Chapter 6.

TABLE 3.2: Example of Effect of Wife's Time Costs on
Family Labor Supplies

$$(u = X^{0.6} L_1^{0.1} L_2^{0.1} \hat{L}_1^{0.1} \hat{L}_2^{0.1}; \ N = \hat{N} = T = \hat{T} = 50; \ \hat{\theta} = 1; \ \hat{Y} = 2000; \ \theta = 1$$
$$\text{or } 0.8; \ \hat{W} = 4)$$

Variable	Symbol	θ	$W < W_0$	Wife's Wage W $W = W_0$	3.	4.	6.
Husband							
Annual hours	$\hat{A}$	1.	1750	1750	1525	1400	1150
		0.8	1750	1652	1600	1500	1300
Annual weeks	$\hat{K}$	1.	42.5	42.5	40.25	39.0	36.5
		0.8	42.5	41.5	41.0	40.0	38.0
Weekly hours	$\hat{H}$	1.	41.2	41.2	37.9	35.9	31.5
		0.8	41.2	39.8	39.0	37.5	34.2
Wife							
Annual hours	A	1.	0	0	1200	1400	1600
		0.8	0	632	800	1000	1200
Annual weeks	K	1.	0	25.0	37.0	39.0	41.0
		0.8	0	32.9	35.0	37.5	40.0
Weekly hours	H	1.	0	0	32.4	35.9	39.0
		0.8	0	19.2	22.9	26.7	30.0
Reservation wage	W_0	1.	—	1.2	—	—	—
		0.8	—	2.48	—	—	—

two partners so as to focus attention on the effects of market wage
differences, rather than tastes or household technology, in determining
differences in their behavior.

Figure 3.5(a) demonstrates the effects of variations in the wife's
wage rate on the husband's hours and weeks (along each curve), as
well as the effect of a change in the husband's wage rate (from $\hat{W} = 4$
to $\hat{W} = 6$) on his own supplies (shifts in the curves $\hat{A}(W)$ and $\hat{K}(W)$)
and on the wife's reservation wage $\bar{W}_0$ (corresponding to the point of
change in slope). Figure 3.5(b) illustrates the effect of the wife's time
costs ($\theta = 0.8$ compared with no cost, $\theta = 1$), which tend to increase her
reservation wage and to shift the husband's supplies discontinuously at
W_0 (for fixed husband's wage rate $\hat{W} = 4$, and assuming $\hat{\theta} = 1$, i.e., no
time costs for husband).

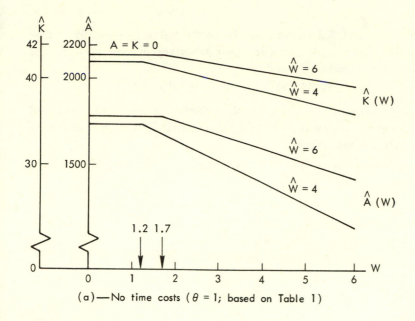

(a)—No time costs (θ = 1; based on Table 1)

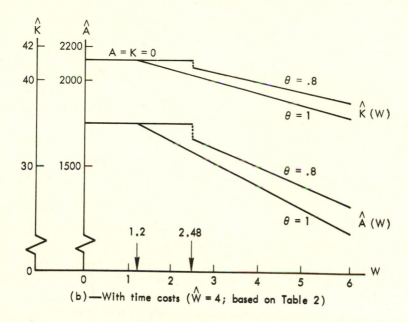

(b)—With time costs ($\hat{W}$ = 4; based on Table 2)

FIGURE 3.5 Effects of wife's wage on husband's labor supply

Tables 3.1 and 3.2 summarize the numerical values for these diagrams, and also include the wife's own labor supply variables and the weekly hours variables H and $\hat{H}$.

These examples verify the following general features:

1. A large disparity in labor supply behavior between husband and wife may occur, even if tastes are symmetric—owing to a disparity in market wage offers.

2. Both spouse's wage rate and own time costs tend to increase the reservation wage.

3. Under no time costs, husband's supplies and wife's annual hours are continuous with respect to wife's wage offers W, but the marginal effects as well as the level of own weeks supplied K change discontinuously as the wife enters the labor force.

4. If wife's time costs exist, levels as well as slopes of all supply variables change discontinuously at the wife's reservation wage W_0.

These examples may be extended to the restricted case mentioned above, in which husband's labor variables $\hat{K}_0$ and $\hat{H}_0$ (and thus $\hat{L}_{10}$, $\hat{L}_{20}$, and thus also $\hat{L}_0$ and $\hat{A}_0$)[25] are fixed exogenously. It may be shown that each type of wife's leisure demand is larger than the corresponding unrestricted demand in this restricted case, if $\hat{L} < \hat{L}_0$— that is, if the husband's leisure is restricted to less than his desired level, and vice versa. Corresponding relations apply to labor supplies. For example, if the husband is restricted to work less than he desires, the family will compensate by having the wife work more.

Similarly, if the husband is restricted to work less than he would freely desire in the nonworking-wife case, the wife's reservation wage decreases. That is, she enters the labor force at a lower wage, to compensate for the loss of income due to the restriction. Conversely, if the husband works more than desired, his extra income compensates the family and causes an increase in the wife's reservation wage, reducing the probability of her participation in the labor force.

The cases of partial restrictions on the husband's labor, where only his weeks $\hat{K}$ or his hours $\hat{H}$ are restricted, may be analyzed similarly. As expected, the effects on the wife's labor generally tend to be intermediary between the two extremes of fully restricted and unrestricted husband labor supply.

[25] $\hat{L}_{10}$ and $\hat{L}_{20}$ refer to fixed levels of leisure of type 1 and type 2.

V. WEEKLY MONEY COSTS OF PARTICIPATION

If going to work involves, in addition to time costs, weekly (or daily) money costs[26] (e.g., for transportation, meals) that are not covered by the employer and are independent of weekly hours worked, then the model loses some of its simple properties. However, the analysis is still similar, since both leisure prices remain *linear functions of the wage rate*, as shown below.

Let m be the fixed money costs per week worked. The budget constraint, for individuals and with no tax, is $X = Y + WKH - mK$. Substituting in this constraint equations 3.2 and 3.7 gives the modified budget constraint

$$X + WL_1 + (\theta W - m/T)L_2 = \bar{F} = Y + \theta WNT - mN. \qquad (3.43)$$

Equation 3.43 shows that the price $P_2 = \theta W - m/T$ of type-2 leisure is no longer proportional to $P_1 = W$, but is a linear function of W (where both time and money costs reduce it relative to W, which remains the shadow price of type-1 leisure). Full income F is reduced by the full-year equivalent (mN) of these money costs.

However, since both P_1 and P_2 remain single-valued functions of the wage rate W, the two-stage maximization procedure may be extended to cover this case. Recalling that Figure 3.1 gives a unique expansion path with regard to L_1 and L_2, for variation in W (fixed Y) the following "pseudo-composite good" may be defined: $L = L_1 + (\theta - m/WT)L_2$ (however, L is no longer independent of W as in the case $m = 0$). For fixed W, the fixed-L budget line in $L_1 \mid L_2$ space is a straight line with a slope: $WT/(\theta WT - m) > 1$. For given X, a unique optimal point exists on the given budget line (corresponding to tangency with an $L_1 \mid L_2$ indifference curve), which allocates L between L_1 and L_2. Again, if $U(X, L_1, L_2)$ is *separable*, i.e., $U[X, \psi(L_1, L_2)]$, then the indifference map is independent of X, and the point of optimum depends only on L (and W): $L_1 = L_1[L(W)]$ and $L_2 = L_2[L(W)]$. Connecting these points for different values of W gives a unique expansion path, corresponding to the functions $L_1(L, X)$ and $L_2(L, X)$ in the general nonseparable case. A reduced utility function may thus be defined for variations in W, although in this case it is

---

[26] Fixed annual money costs are not discussed here. They produce the same effect as a reduction in nonwage income Y, conditional on participation. They thus cause the supply curve for workers to shift to the right, and the reservation wage to increase (as with fixed annual time costs).

different for variations in Y: $u^* = U^*(X, L) = U[X, L_1(L, X),$ $L_2(L, X)]$. The *first-stage* maximization consists of maximizing U^* under the budget constraint $X + WL(W) = \bar{F} = Y + \theta WNT - mN$.

The resulting demands $X^*(W, \bar{F})$ and $L^*(W, \bar{F})$ uniquely determine the demands for the two leisures $L_i[L(W, \bar{F}), X(W, \bar{F})] = L_i(W, \bar{F})$, $(i = 1, 2)$. The labor supply variables A, K, and H are thus determined as functions of $(W, \bar{F})$ or of $(W, Y; \theta, m)$.

The analysis is simplified if the indirect utility function is used. Maximizing $U(X, L_1, L_2)$ under the budget constraint $X + P_1 L_1 + P_2 L_2 = \bar{F}$ gives the three demands $X(\mathbf{P}, \bar{F})$, $L_i(\mathbf{P}, \bar{F})$, as in the no-cost case. Substitution into U gives the indirect utility $V(1, P_1, P_2, \bar{F})$ as before (equation 3.23), where the relations 3.24 and 3.25 still hold. Expressing the prices in terms of W gives the reduced indirect utility (analogous to 3.28)

$$u^* = V(1, W, \theta W - m/T, \bar{F}) = V^*(W, \bar{F}). \qquad (3.44)$$

Substitution of $\bar{F}$ from equation 3.43 gives

$$u^* = V^*(W, Y + \theta WNT - mN) = \bar{V}(W, Y), \qquad (3.45)$$

where both V^* and $\bar{V}$ depend also on θ and m. The derivatives of V^* or $\bar{V}$ with respect to W and Y are related to the derivatives of V exactly as in equations 3.28 and 3.29, however, since $\partial P_1/\partial W = 1$; $\partial P_2/\partial W = 0$; $\partial \bar{F}/\partial W = \theta NT$; and $\partial \bar{F}/\partial Y = 1$. That is, $\mathbf{P}$ and $\bar{F}$ are linear in W, with the same coefficients as under $m = 0$.

The derivation of the labor supplies is thus formally identical to equations 3.24, 3.30, and 3.32: and

$$K = N + \frac{1}{T} \cdot \frac{\partial V/\partial P_2}{\partial V/\partial \bar{F}} \, ;$$

and   (3.46)

$$A = \theta NT + \frac{1}{\partial V/\partial \bar{F}} \left(\frac{\partial V}{\partial P_1} + \theta \cdot \frac{\partial V}{\partial P_2} \right) = \theta NT + \frac{\partial V^*/\partial W}{\partial V^*/\partial \bar{F}} = \frac{\partial \bar{V}/\partial W}{\partial \bar{V}/\partial Y} \, ,$$

where both K and A may be expressed as functions of $(W, Y; \theta, m)$ by substitution from equation 3.43.

As a result of this formal identity, if preferences are specified in terms of the indirect utility V (which is an equivalent specification to that of the direct utility U), the derivation of the supply functions by differentiation is formally identical and is straightforward (thus demonstrating that use of duality relations may be extremely convenient).

The analysis of the two-workers family model proceeds analogously, with full income given by $F = Y + \theta WNT + \hat{\theta}\hat{W}\hat{N}\hat{T} - mN - \hat{m}\hat{N}$, and so on.

Although the analytical derivation of the labor supplies is easily performed, the simplicity of the equations under various simple specifications is lost, and the estimation procedures may become more demanding. To illustrate this, consider the simple individual Cobb–Douglas function, where the indirect utility function is given by $V = DP_1^{-a}P_2^{-b}\bar{F}$.[27] Applying equation 3.46 to derive the weeks labor supply gives (substituting from 3.43):

$$K = N - \frac{b}{TP_2}\bar{F} = N(1-b) - b\frac{Y}{\theta WT - m}$$

$$= N(1-b) - \frac{b}{\theta T}\left(\frac{Y}{W}\right)\left(1 + \frac{m}{WT - m}\right).$$

The reduced function $\bar{V}$ is given by

$$\bar{V} = D(Y + \theta WNT - mN)W^{-a}(\theta WT - m)^{-b}T^b,$$

and the annual hours supply equation is derived, using 3.46, as

$$A = \theta NT(1 - a - b) - (a + b)\frac{Y}{W} - bm\frac{Y}{W(W\theta T - m)} + amN\frac{1}{W}.$$

These should be contrasted with the simple forms (linear in Y/W) obtained under $m = 0$.

One specification that retains its simplicity in the presence of weekly money costs is the linear specification of demands for both leisures, which yields supply equations linear in W and Y.[28] Suppose

$$L_1 = \alpha_0 + \alpha_1 P_1 + \alpha_2 P_2 + \alpha_3 \bar{F}$$

[27] D is a constant: $D = (1 - a - b)^{1-a-b}a^a b^b$. This form is derived by substituting equation A.2 into equation A.1 in the appendix.

[28] One specification of the indirect utility function that gives linear equations as in equation 3.47 is

$$V = [F - a_1 P_1 - a_2 P_2 - b]e^{-c_1 P_1 - c_2 P_2},$$

as may be verified by differentiation, using equation 3.24. However, this formulation implies the following additional restrictions in 3.47:

$$\frac{\alpha_1}{\beta_1} = \frac{\alpha_2}{\beta_2} = \frac{\alpha_3}{\beta_3} = \frac{c_1}{c_2}.$$

I am not certain whether an unrestricted specification exists.

and

$$L_2 = \beta_0 + \beta_1 P_1 + \beta_2 P_2 + \beta_3 \bar{F}, \tag{3.47}$$

with restrictions on α and β as implied by the theory. Substituting $P_1 = W$, $P_2 = \theta W - m/T$ and $\bar{F} = Y + \theta WNT - mN$ from 3.43 into 3.47 gives, after regrouping,

$$L_1 = \alpha_0 + (\alpha_1 + \theta\alpha_2 + \theta NT\alpha_3)W + \alpha_3 Y - \left(\frac{\alpha_2}{T} + \alpha_3 N\right)m$$

and   (3.48)

$$L_2 = \beta_0 + (\beta_1 + \theta\beta_2 + \theta NT\beta_3)W + \beta_3 Y - \left(\frac{\beta_2}{T} + \beta_3 N\right)m.$$

By equations 3.6 and 3.7, the weeks and annual hours supplies are linear in L_1 and L_2, and hence (by 3.48) also linear in the variables W, Y, and m in this model. If m varies among individuals but is not observed, the terms in m in the supply equations may be regarded as embedded in the additive error terms of the estimation equations. If some measurements on m (or on variables affecting m or proxies for m) are available, equations linear in Y, W, and m (or its substitutes) may be conveniently estimated without interaction terms between m and W or Y.[29] However, the effect of $m > 0$ on participation, through the reservation wage, complicates matters considerably—even in this simple model.

VI. OTHER TIME DIMENSIONS OF LABOR SUPPLY

The present interpretation of the model and its extensions in terms of hours and weeks is not necessarily the only one.

No modifications are required in the formal model if the variables H and K, their product $A = HK$, and their limits T, θT, and N, are interpreted with respect to another pair of time dimensions. For example, H may stand for daily hours of work, and K for monthly days of work (correspondingly, X is monthly consumption); or H may be weekly days of work (assuming that daily hours are exogenously fixed), and K, annual weeks as before. The corresponding leisure

[29] If, however, there exist weekly time costs ($\theta < 1$), then θ interacts with all variables of the supply equations, including m, under this specification. For example, substituting equation 3.48 into $A = NT - L_1 - \theta L_2$ yields the coefficient of m as

$$\left[\frac{\alpha_2 + \theta\beta_2}{T} + N(\alpha_3 + \theta\beta_3)\right].$$

variables are reinterpreted accordingly. For example, in the last formulation, $L_1 = K(\theta T - H)$ is the number of weekly nonworkdays, and $L_2 = (N - K)T$, the number of *days* in weeks of nonwork (modifying, of course, the upper limit $T \leq 7$). The utility function also must be reinterpreted in terms of these new time dimensions, but needs no formal modification.

The choice among alternative specifications of this nature depends on the type of data available, as well as on assumptions regarding choice of time variables. For example, if the length of the workday is not subject to choice, but the number of days per week is, then the preceding interpretation is useful provided the consumer is not assumed to regard weekend-days-off as perfect substitutes for days off during nonworkweeks, and provided data on days per week and on daily wages are available.

But suppose, now, that more than two time dimensions are involved in the labor/leisure choice. For example, the worker may be free to choose H hours daily, D days weekly, as well as K weeks annually, and he does not regard the corresponding leisures as perfect substitutes. In this case, the model may be extended along similar lines to apply to three time dimensions. This extension is outlined below and may be applied to any other three-dimensional structure of time for labor supply. Suppose the limits are $H \leq \theta T \leq T(\leq 24)$, $D \leq S(\leq 7)$, and $K \leq N(\leq 52)$, where $(1 - \theta)T$ are the daily time costs of going to work. The three annual leisures are

$L_1 = (\theta T - H)DK$ (leisure during workdays),

$L_2 = T(S - D)K$ (leisure on weekends during workweeks),

$L_3 = TS(N - K)$ (leisure during nonworkweeks),

and the annual individual utility function has four arguments—$U(X, L_1, L_2, L_3)$. Total annual workhours are given by

$$A = HDK = \theta TSN - \theta L_3 - \theta L_2 - L,$$

as can be verified by substitution. Therefore, the budget constraint $X = Y + WA$ may be written as

$$X + WL_1 + \theta WL_2 + \theta WL_3 = F = Y + \theta WTSN,$$

which is analogous to equation 3.8. (The shadow prices of L_2 and L_3 are equal, since no additional time costs were assumed on weekend days during workweeks, compared with days in nonworkweeks.) Thus, $L_2 + L_3$ may be defined as one composite good $\tilde{L}_2$, and the present model in terms of L_1 and $\tilde{L}_2$ will be identical to the previous model for determining annual hours A and weeks K (where TS is substituted for T). The composite good $L = \theta TSN - A$ is defined similarly, since the relative price of $\tilde{L}_2$ to L_1 is constant: $P_3/P_1 = P_2/P_1 = \theta$. However, another dimension exists, and thus another equation should be added to this model, for determining days per week D. Deriving the three leisure demands $L_i(\mathbf{P}, F)$, $(i = 1, 2, 3)$, and substituting in the utility function U gives the indirect utility $V(P_X, P_1, P_2, P_3, F)$ in the general case, and the reduced function $\bar{V}(Y, W)$ (identical to equation 3.29) for this particular case. An intermediary function $\tilde{V}$, analogous to equation 3.23, can be defined for the goods X, L_1, and $\tilde{L}_2$, where the shadow price of $\tilde{L}_2$ is $\tilde{P}_2 = P_2 = P_3$:

$$\tilde{V}(P_X, P_1, \tilde{P}_2, F) = V(P_X, P_1, P_2, P_2, F).$$

The supply variable that is a mirror image of the demand for the composite good $\tilde{L}_2$ may be defined as $B = DK$, the number of annual working *days*, since $DK = SN - \tilde{L}_2 T$. Therefore, the three labor supply equations that are linear in the corresponding leisure demands L_1, L_2, and L_3 are

$$
\begin{aligned}
A &= HDK = \theta TSN - L_1 - \theta L_2 - \theta L_3 = \theta(TSN) - L & \text{(annual hours),} \\
B &= DK = SN - (1/T)L_2 - (1/T)L_3 = (SN) - (1/T)\tilde{L}_2 & \text{(annual days),} \\
K &= N - (1/TS)L_3 & \text{(annual weeks).}
\end{aligned}
$$

Each of the variables A, B, and K will thus exhibit the usual properties of the one-dimensional labor supply model, with respect to the exogenous variables W and Y.

The other variables of interest—namely, daily hours H, and weekly days D—do not have these properties, since $H = A/B$ and $D = B/K$. In other words, each is a *ratio* of linear combinations of demands (as is H in the two-dimensional model).

Other properties of the two-dimensional model may be extended analogously. For example, the effective reservation wage $\bar{W}_0$ is generally given by the equation for annual hours A, whereas both B and K supply curves are discontinuous at $\bar{W}_0$, implying that both $D(\bar{W}_0)$ and $K(\bar{W}_0)$ are positive but $H(\bar{W}_0) = 0$ (if $\theta = 1$). Similarly, in the normal case, the supplies are ranked by their slopes with respect to W in the order A, B, K—since they mirror-image the sum of three, two, and one leisure demands, respectively. The extension to a six-equation family model is straightforward.

Inspection of this case should also clarify the direction of generalization to more than three dimensions. For example, a fourth dimension may be years over a period of the life cycle (such as the period after small children are no longer present in the home and before retirement). The present model should not be extended mechanically, however. It could not reasonably be expected to apply to the entire life cycle or working period, because (abstracting from problems of uncertainty) it assumes utility to depend on *total* consumption X for the whole period. A reasonable life-cycle model should permit variations in consumption between work and nonwork periods (or variations with respect to intensity of work). It should also let the utility function reflect these variations, so that utility depends on *timing* (or age) of work and nonwork years, as well as on timing of consumption, and not merely on their total sum over the entire period.[30]

As mentioned in the introduction, the model as specified does not resolve the question of timing even over a shorter period, such as one year, where consumption averaging may reasonably be assumed. Determining average weekly hours H does not imply the timing of workhours. Similarly, determination of K, or the number of vacation weeks (or weeks off the labor market in general), $N - K$, does not imply a determinate timing or clustering. This lack of determination is, of course, due to the assumption that alternative vacation weeks are perfect substitutes in utility. In reality, however, many exogenous factors may cumulatively determine timing, such as variations over the year in wage offers, school vacations, and weather. Many such factors tend to induce clustering—i.e., a longer continuous vacation period, rather than scattered weeks or days throughout the year; a continuous daily work period; and a continuous weekend. Of course, preferences may also be influenced by timing. For many purposes of analysis, however, the question of timing may be ignored in a first-order approximation, without essentially affecting the theory or its applications.

---

[30] In most life-cycle models, utility is assumed to be additively separable over time, of the form

$$u = \int U(X_t, L_t)e^{-rt}\, dt,$$

where U is stable over time but varies with current consumption X_t. See Smith (1973, 1975), Blinder and Weiss (1975), and Weiss (1972).

DERIVATION AND COMPUTATION OF EXAMPLES BASED ON A COBB–DOUGLAS UTILITY FUNCTION

THE INDIVIDUAL CASE (Figure 3.3)

Let the utility function be

$$u = U(X, L_1, L_2) = X^{1-a-b}L_1^a L_2^b. \tag{A.1}$$

Maximizing u subject to the budget constraint in equation 3.9 gives

$$L_1 = a\frac{F}{P_1},$$

$$L_2 = b\frac{F}{P_2}, \tag{A.2}$$

$$X = F - P_1 L_1 - P_2 L_2 = (1-a-b)F.$$

Substituting $(\mathbf{P}, F) = (1, W, \theta W, Y + \theta WNT)$, as in equation 3.8, into equation A.2 gives

$$L_1 = a\theta NT + a\frac{Y}{W},$$

$$L_2 = bNT + \theta b\frac{Y}{W}. \tag{A.3}$$

Now equation A.3 is substituted into 3.5 and 3.6 to yield the supplies

$$K(W, Y) = N(1-b) - \frac{b}{\theta T} \cdot \frac{Y}{W},$$

$$A(W, Y) = \theta NT(1-a-b) - (a+b)\frac{Y}{W}. \tag{A.4}$$

If no time costs are involved, $\theta = 1$ and the reservation wage $\bar{W}_0$ is derived by equating A to 0 in A.4:

$$\bar{W}_0 = \frac{(a+b)Y}{NT(1-a-b)}. \qquad (A.5)$$

At this reservation wage, $\bar{K}_0$ is positive, as seen by substituting A.5 into $K(W, Y)$ of A.4:

$$K(\bar{W}_0, Y) = \frac{aN}{a+b} > 0.$$

If $\theta < 1$, the effective reservation wage is derived by using the reduced utility function $U^*(X, L)$ of equation 3.16. Solving the problem of 3.15 for this model gives the first-order conditions

$$L_1 + \theta L_2 = L$$

and

$$\frac{\partial U/\partial L_2}{\partial U/\partial L_1} = \frac{bL_1}{aL_2} = \theta,$$

which give the first-stage solutions

$$L_1 = \frac{a}{a+b} L$$

and

$$L_2 = \frac{1}{\theta} \cdot \frac{b}{a+b} L.$$

L_i are independent of X, since u is separable. Substitution into equation A.1 gives the reduced function

$$U^*(X, L) = \frac{a^a b^b}{(a+b)^{a+b} \theta^b} X^{1-a-b} L^{a+b} = B \frac{1}{\theta^b} X^{1-c} L^c, \qquad (A.6)$$

where B is constant and $c = a + b$. U^* is again of the Cobb–Douglas form in two commodities. The solution L that maximizes A.6 under the constraint equation (3.13) gives the hours supply in A.4 by putting $A = \theta NT - L$. The reservation wage W_0 and the corresponding minimum hours of work A_0 are derived as follows. Under the nonparticipation alternative, $L = L_2 = NT$, $X = Y$, and time costs have no effect on utility; hence, $\theta = 1$ is substituted into A.6 to obtain

$$u_0^* = BY^{1-c}(NT)^c. \qquad (A.7)$$

With participation, time costs are effective ($\theta < 1$), and the minimum participation point is $L_0 = \theta NT - A_0$ and $X_0 = Y + W_0 A_0$. If the utility level equals u_0^*, we get

$$\frac{1}{\theta^b} (Y + W_0 A_0)^{1-c} (\theta NT - A_0)^c = Y^{1-c} (NT)^c. \qquad (A.8)$$

In addition, W_0 equals the marginal rate of substitution at (X_0, L_0) and is derived as a function of A_0 from equation A.4:

$$W_0 = \frac{cY}{(1-c)\theta NT - A_0}. \qquad (A.9)$$

Substitution of A.9 into A.8 and some manipulations give

$$(\theta NT - A_0) = \theta^b (NT)^c \left(\theta NT - \frac{A_0}{1-c} \right)^{1-c}, \qquad (A.10)$$

which may be solved numerically to obtain A_0, and, by A.9, the reservation wage W_0. Note that $A_0 = 0$ is a solution to A.10 if $\theta = 1$, and that $W_0 > \bar{W}_0$ if $A_0 > 0$ (by A.9). If $W < W_0$, the preferred solution is $A = K = 0$. If $W > W_0$, then $A > A_0 > 0$ and $K > K_0 > \bar{K}_0 > 0$.

Figure 3.3 is computed with the parameter values $a = b = 0.1$; $Y = 10,000$; $T = N = 50$; and $\theta = 1$, 0.9, or 0.8. The numerical results give $\bar{W}_0 = 1$, $W_0 = 1.58$ for $\theta = 0.9$ (i.e., time costs of $(1-\theta)T = 5$ hr/wk), and $W_0 = 2.07$ for $\theta = 0.8$ (10 hr/wk). The corresponding minimum quantities (the solutions to equation A.10) are $A_0(\theta = 0.9) = 533$ and $A_0(\theta = 0.8) = 633$. The minimum weeks are 25, 30.9, and 32.9, for $\theta = 1$, 0.9, and 0.8, respectively.

THE INDIVIDUAL CASE WITH PARTIAL RESTRICTIONS (Figure 3.4)

First, if $K = \bar{K}$ is given, and $W > W_0$, the utility function in this case is derived by applying equation 3.2 to the specification equation A.1:

$$u = [Y + W(\bar{K}H)^{1-a-b}(K\theta T - \bar{K}H)^a [(N - \bar{K})T]^b. \qquad (A.11)$$

Denoting $\bar{A} = \bar{K}H$, $\bar{a} = a/(1-b)$, and $C = [(N - \bar{K})T]^b$ (a constant), the following transformation may be applied to u without loss of generality (since preferences are ordinal):

$$\bar{u} = \left(\frac{u}{c} \right)^{1/(1-b)} = (Y + W\bar{A})^{1-a}(K\theta T - \bar{A})^{\bar{a}}. \qquad (A.12)$$

Since equation A.12 is completely analogous to the one-leisure Cobb–Douglas model, the supply equation for $\bar{A}$ may be derived analogously to yield

$$\bar{A} = \bar{K}\theta T(1 - \bar{a}) - \bar{a}\frac{Y}{W}. \tag{A.13}$$

Comparing this with the unrestricted (desired) supply gives

$$\bar{A} - A = \theta T(1 - a - b)(1 - b)\left[\bar{K} - \left(N(1 - b) - \frac{b}{\theta T} \cdot \frac{Y}{W}\right)\right],$$

where the last term inside the brackets equals the desired K, by equation A.4. Thus, $\bar{A} > A$ if and only if $\bar{K} > K$.

Second, if weekly hours are restricted, $H = \bar{H}$ is given for participants, and utility is expressed, substituting into equations 3.1, 3.2, and A.1, as

$$u = D(Y + W\tilde{A})^{1-a-b}\tilde{A}^a\left(N - \frac{1}{\bar{H}}\tilde{A}\right)^b, \tag{A.14}$$

where $D = (\theta T - \bar{H}/\bar{H})^a T^b$, a constant; and $\tilde{A} = K\bar{H}$.

The first-order conditions are derived by differentiation of equation A.14:

$$\frac{1}{u} \cdot \frac{\partial u}{\partial \tilde{A}} = \frac{(1 - a - b)W}{Y + W\tilde{A}} + \frac{a}{\tilde{A}} - \frac{b}{N\bar{H} - \tilde{A}} = 0.$$

This formulation yields a quadratic equation for $\tilde{A}$:

$$\tilde{A}^2 - \left[(1 - b)N\bar{H} - (a + b)\frac{Y}{W}\right]\tilde{A} - aN\bar{H}\frac{Y}{W} = 0. \tag{A.15}$$

Taking the positive root, the solution $\tilde{A}$ is a function of Y/W, as in the previous cases, but a nonlinear function now. The corresponding supply of weeks is derived by $\tilde{A}/\bar{H} = \tilde{K}(Y, W, \bar{H})$. Again, it can be shown that if $\bar{H} < H(Y, W)$—that is, if weekly hours are restricted below the desired level—then $\tilde{A}$ is less than $A(Y, W)$. However, $\tilde{K}$ increases, relative to K, for $\bar{H}$ above as well as below the desired level, as Figure 3.4(b) shows. Moreover, A and K are independent of θ in this case, since variations in $\bar{H}$ are impossible.

Third, the reservation wages W_0 for these restricted cases (assuming $\theta = 1$) are computed as follows. The nonparticipation alternative yields the utility level u_0^* of equation A.7 in both cases. Substituting the restricted supply equation (A.13) into the utility function equation (A.11), corresponding to the restriction $K = \bar{K}$, gives for $W = W_0$ (after regrouping) the utility level

$$u = \frac{(1-a-b)^{1-a-b}a^a}{(1-b)^{1-b}}[(N-\bar{K})T]^b[W_0\bar{K}T+Y]^{1-b}W_0^{-a}. \quad (A.16)$$

Equating A.16 to A.7 gives an implicit nonlinear equation for the reservation wage W_0, which is solved numerically. The case chosen for Figure 3.4 ($\bar{K} = 40$) gives $W_0 = 1.53$ (compared with $\bar{W}_0 = 1$ for K unrestricted). The corresponding minimum hours are $A_0 = 1051.56$ yearly, or $H_0 = 26.3$ weekly.

A similar analysis applies for the restricted-hours case $H = \bar{H}$. Substitution of the supply equation (the solution to A.15) into A.14 gives utility as a function of Y and W_0, and W_0 is computed by equating this to equation A.7. Using the same example and fixing $\bar{H}$ at 37.5 (both $\bar{K}$ and $\bar{H}$ are optimal for $W = 4$), the reservation wage W_0 is computed to be 1.64, with $A_0 = 1328.5$ and $K_0 = 35.4$ (compared with 0 and 25, respectively), under this restriction.

Introduction of time costs ($\theta < 1$) will certainly increase the reservation wage further in this case.

EXTENSION OF EXAMPLE TO TWO-MEMBER FAMILY MODEL (Tables 3.1 and 3.2; Figure 3.5)

If both family members are working, the extended five-commodity utility function is

$$u = X^d L_1^a L_2^b \hat{L}_1^{\hat{a}} \hat{L}_2^{\hat{b}}. \quad (A.17)$$

Proceeding analogously to the three-commodity case, the corresponding supply curves are derived as follows (using the budget constraint equation 3.37):

$$K = N - \frac{1}{T}L_2 = N - \frac{1}{T}\cdot\frac{bF}{P_2} = N(1-b) - \frac{b}{\theta T}\cdot\frac{\hat{Y}}{W} - \frac{b\hat{\theta}\hat{N}\hat{T}}{\theta T}\cdot\frac{\hat{W}}{W}$$

$$(A.18)$$

and

$$A = \theta NT - L_1 - \theta L_2 = \theta NT - \frac{aF}{P_1} - \frac{bF}{P_2}$$

$$= \theta NT(1-a-b) - (a+b)\frac{\hat{Y}}{W} - (a+b)\hat{\theta}\hat{N}\hat{T}\frac{\hat{W}}{W}. \quad (A.19)$$

The equations for the husband's supplies $\hat{A}$ and $\hat{K}$ are completely analogous, interchanging Z with $\hat{Z}$ for each parameter and variable. Strikingly, both equations are now linear in the pair of variables Y/W and $\hat{W}/W$ (compared with Y/W in the individual case).

Turning to analyze the wife's reservation wage, assume first that $\theta = 1$. Solving for $\bar{W}_0$ by equating $A(\bar{W}_0, \hat{W}, \hat{Y})$ of equation A.19 to zero,

$$\bar{W}_0 = \frac{(a+b)(\hat{Y} + \hat{\theta}\hat{W}\hat{N}\hat{T})}{NT(1-a-b)}, \tag{A.20}$$

with $\bar{W}_0$ increasing in $\hat{Y}$, $\hat{W}$, and $\hat{\theta}$. If $\theta < 1$, the effective reservation wage W_0 is computed by substitution of the hours supplies of this model in equation 3.42, yielding a numerical solution for $W_0(\hat{W}, \hat{Y}, \theta)$. If the wife is out of the labor market ($W < W_0$), the husband's supply equations are analogous to the individual case above, and are given by (denoting $a+b$ by c)

$$\hat{K}_0 = \hat{N}\left(1 - \frac{\hat{b}}{\hat{a}+\hat{b}+c}\right) - \frac{b}{\hat{a}+\hat{b}+c} \cdot \frac{1}{\hat{\theta}\hat{T}} \cdot \frac{\hat{Y}}{\hat{W}}$$

and $\tag{A.21}$

$$\hat{A}_0 = \hat{\theta}\hat{N}\hat{T}\left(1 - \frac{\hat{a}+\hat{b}}{\hat{a}+\hat{b}+c}\right) - \frac{\hat{a}+\hat{b}}{\hat{a}+\hat{b}+c} \cdot \frac{\hat{Y}}{\hat{W}}.$$

This formulation may be compared to equation A.4, substituting $a = \hat{a}/(\hat{a}+\hat{b}+c)$, and so on. The wife's (rejected) wage offer W does not appear in equations A.21, but one can verify that, if $\theta = 1$, then $\hat{A}_0(\hat{W}, \hat{Y}) = \hat{A}(\hat{W}, \hat{W}_0, \hat{Y})$ and $\hat{K}_0(\hat{W}, \hat{Y}) = \hat{K}(\hat{W}, \hat{W}_0, \hat{Y})$, where $\hat{A}$ and $\hat{K}$ are computed as in A.18 and A.19. Thus, if no time costs exist, the supplies are continuous in W at W_0, as Figure 3.5 shows.

The reduced utility function used for computing the reservation wage (if $\theta < 1$) is given, in terms of composite leisures, as follows:

$$U^* = B^* \cdot \frac{1}{\theta^b} \cdot \frac{1}{\hat{\theta}^{\hat{b}}} X^{1-c-\hat{c}}L^c\hat{L}^{\hat{c}}, \tag{A.22}$$

where B^* is a constant, $c = a + b$, and $\hat{c} = \hat{a} + \hat{b}$, in complete analogy to equation A.6. For the nonworking-wife case, $\theta = 1$ is put in equation A.22, or in the left side of equation 3.42.

Results of these computations for the chosen parameter values are summarized in Tables 3.1 and 3.2.

CHAPTER 4

ASSETS AND LABOR SUPPLY

JAMES P. SMITH

THE RAND CORPORATION

> Knowledge of the variation in consumption as between different households having different asset holdings would give little information as to how a household would react if its assets were increased unexpectedly by a given amount. ... this failing occurs because the observed asset holdings do not just happen to be there; instead they reflect the life plan of the individual.
> —Richard Brumberg and Franco Modigliani (1962), pp. 425–426.

I. Introduction

This paper examines the role of assets in labor supply functions. In recent work, variables measuring assets have been used with increasing frequency to measure the response of hours worked to nonwage-related income.[1] Empirical labor supply studies have previously used an aggregate of all current period nonearnings income to estimate pure income effects.[2] The estimated income slopes were disappointing because the income variable either had the wrong sign (positive), implying that leisure was an inferior good, or it was sufficiently small so that compensated own-wage slopes in the labor supply equation remained negative. In addition, the estimated income response exhibited considerable instability from study to study.

Many reasons have been suggested to explain these failures. First, the income variable was often characterized by severe underreporting, leading, on standard errors in variables grounds, to biased income coefficients. Second, nonemployment income contained income that did not correspond to the theoretical construct. Unemployment compensation, disability insurance, and pension income, for example, are

---

[1] See Greenberg and Kosters (1970); Fleisher, Parsons, and Porter (1973); DaVanzo, De Tray, and Greenberg (1973); Heckman (Chapter 5); and Cogan (Chapters 2 and 7).

[2] Such studies are too numerous to list. One example is Greenberg and Kosters (1970).

usually contingent upon the absence of market work. Since these were often included in total income, a spurious negative correlation between work and income was introduced. Third, data on assets and liabilities were unavailable. Inputed income flows from such assets are quite large for many individuals. A more detailed questioning of sources of income has been undertaken in recent microdata files, and in some surveys attempts were made to measure the market value of a variety of assets and liabilities.[3] Many estimates of the income response of hours worked are available, using these new data sources and their asset information, but it is apparent that there is still little tendency for convergence across different studies. A listing of the income effects estimated in other chapters of this book would alone indicate the extent of the problem. Cogan and Heckman use a measure of aggregate net worth to estimate income effects. While rarely statistically significant, the asset variable consistently has a positive effect in their labor supply equations. In Chapter 1, Shultz employs the more standard nonearnings income variable. His estimates vacillate in sign and statistical significance. Moreover, they vary with the age sample considered, with negative effects (consistent with the wealth interpretation) only evident in the older samples.

A number of theoretical arguments have been offered to explain these empirical findings. Greenberg and Kosters (1972) assert that taste variation regarding the process of asset accumulation is a serious source of bias. They argue that some individuals prefer to acquire assets because of their conservative or risk-averse nature, and that to achieve their desired asset levels, such individuals will tend to work longer hours. Greenberg and Kosters contend that it is necessary to purge assets of this taste factor before using them to estimate wealth effects. In their study, they develop statistical techniques that they hope will do precisely that. Fleisher, Parsons, and Porter (1973) take a different approach. In their model, individuals can be temporarily out of equilibrium with more or fewer assets than they prefer. A person with excess assets will try to restore his position by working less, and one with deficient assets, by working more. Like Greenberg and

---

[3] Three of the more prominent new data sets—The Survey of Economic Opportunity, The Income Dynamics Panel, and the National Longitudinal Survey—contain information on assets. For a complete list of the asset information available in all three, see Greenberg (1972).

Kosters, they attempt to control statistically for this secondary relation between assets and hours worked before using assets for their primary purpose—wealth effects.

While there may be truth in both of these views, much of the discussion concerning assets and labor supply appears to have concentrated on second-order effects, involving taste variation or disequilibrium analysis. Moreover, it is interesting to note that while the Greenberg and Kosters and Fleisher, Parsons, and Porter arguments predict diametrically opposite relations between assets and labor supply, both studies find empirical support for their contentions. Theoretical treatment of the relation between assets and hours worked at a more elementary but fundamental level may offer greater insight into the causes of the empirical anomalies. To a large extent, this represents, as the quote from Brumberg and Modigliani suggests, relearning many of the lessons from the older consumption-function literature and applying them to a new problem.

The principal deficiency in the current use of assets is the neglect or lack of emphasis on the life-cycle dimension. To understand the relationship between assets and hours of work, an adequate theory of asset accumulation and savings is required. Assets have too often been forced into the confines of a one-period model, but it is only when one considers the multiperiod problem that it makes sense to speak of the asset and savings behavior of individuals. In this paper, a simple life-cycle theory is used to explore the relationships that one might expect to find between working hours and assets. This approach shows that both are simultaneously determined by similar economic forces, and that the correlation between them should not be accepted as evidence of a causal sequence from assets to market work.

The life-cycle model is derived in Section II. The resulting asset profile will be examined in four separate examples, each being a special case of a more general model and each highlighting one of the economic forces determining assets and market hours. Within each example, a statistical relation between net assets and labor supply results, but this association is independent of any wealth effect running from assets to the amount of labor supplied.

In Section III, some empirical applications are made using data from the 1967 Survey of Economic Opportunity (SEO). First, the net worth age profiles derived from the SEO data are examined. The characteristics of these profiles tend to support the life-cycle view taken in this analysis. The most direct test of the model consists in estimating a life-cycle savings function. Although the SEO savings data are not ideal, the signs of coefficients seem generally consistent with the implications of the life-cycle approach.

II. THE LIFE CYCLE MODEL

When viewed in a lifetime perspective, savings depends entirely on lifetime consumption and income profiles.[4] If the optimal levels of consumption and income are not coincident, savings allows them to differ by the transfer of funds between time periods. In order to determine the optimal amount of savings, it is convenient first to derive the consumption and income profiles. The income profile, in turn, depends on the paths of market hours and wage rates. Ghez and Becker (1975), in an important work, developed a model that dealt with the life-cycle consumption and hours profiles. In a previous paper (Smith, 1972), I extended their approach to deal with the family context.

A model is developed in the appendix from which derived demand equations are obtained giving the amount of time and goods required in home production at every age. This model allows the intensity of market participation to vary with age, due to temporal variations in wages and other variables that elicit timing responses about the long-run desired levels. In deciding on the number of hours to supply to the market, an individual is actually confronted with two problems. Given his long-run or permanent values of wealth and his wages, he must determine the lifetime levels of market time and consumption of market goods. In addition, since he is faced with temporal variation in wages and other variables, he must decide on an optimal timing of hours and consumption. The intensity of market participation is not constant over the cycle, because factors are present that change the demand for commodities and the marginal costs of household production.

---

[4] Several potential motivations for savings are not included in this model. The miser's motive in which assets provide utility directly, the precautionary motive in which attitudes toward risk must be considered explicitly, and the complications that arise because of durable goods are all heroically ignored. This does not reflect any assessment concerning the relative importance of these motives, but rather that the arguments made in this chapter can be illustrated in a simpler world.

The demand equations for home time (M_t) and market goods consumption derived in the appendix are[5,6]

$$\frac{dM_t}{M_t} = -(s_{mt}\sigma_c + s_{xt}\sigma_{MX})\frac{dw_{mt}}{w_{mt}} + \sigma_c(r-\alpha),$$ (4.1)

$$\frac{dX_t}{X_t} = s_{mt}(\sigma_{MX} - \sigma_c)\frac{dw_{mt}}{w_{mt}} + \sigma_c(r-\alpha).$$ (4.2)

Equations 4.1 and 4.2 indicate that work time and market goods consumption, given the parameters of the utility and household production function, are determined by variations in the price of time (w_{mt}), the rate of interest, and the rate of time preference.[7] To illustrate: As an individual's real wage increases over the life cycle, the amount of his time spent in the nonmarket sector will decline for two reasons. Because the price of one of the inputs is rising, the relative price of future commodities rises. The resulting decline in future consumption will, due to this scale effect, reduce the demand for home time. The magnitude of this effect (represented by $s_{mt}\sigma_c$) depends on the possibilities for intertemporal substitution (i.e., the larger σ_c, the more elastic is the demand curve for commodities) and the share of time in total costs of nonmarket production.

In addition to this intertemporal substitution between commodities, there exists the possibility of substitution in the production process. As w_{mt} increases, market goods will be substituted for time. This effect $(s_{mt}\sigma_{MX})$ will also lead to a decline in the use of time as the real wage rises. It follows, then, that in those periods when the real wage is high, the model predicts, *ceteris paribus*, that hours of market work will also be high. Note that in contrast to the traditional one-period labor-leisure choice, the sign of this effect is unambiguous. Since full wealth is fixed in this analysis, there are no income effects. It is, of course, the existence of income effects in the static theory that gives rise to the possibility of a negatively sloped curve of hours.

---

[5] All symbols are defined in the Glossary of Symbols.

[6] For expositional simplicity, the model at this point is confined to a single-person family. This assumption is relaxed in Section III.

[7] The language of the household production model developed by Becker is used in the exposition. Households are viewed in each period as producing their basic wants (commodities) using purchased market goods and their own time. The language is not essential to any of the arguments made, since exactly the same results are obtained if we take the traditional view where leisure and market goods directly enter the utility function.

The roles of a positive interest rate and the rate of time preference are the standard Fisherian ones. By lowering the relative price of future commodities, a positive interest rate will raise future consumption levels for both market goods and nonmarket time. Time preference for the future ($\alpha < 0$) will obviously have the same effect of increasing the desired levels of consumption in the future.

ASSETS, SAVINGS, AND LABOR SUPPLY

Equations 4.1 and 4.2 describe the age profiles of market goods consumption and hours of market work. If an exogenous wage pattern is assumed, the life-cycle pattern of earnings is also given.[8] These earnings and consumption profiles define the savings behavior of the individual at each age, and, by appropriate accumulation of savings, the asset position at each point in the life cycle is determined.

Savings is defined in the conventional manner as the difference between current income and current market-goods consumption. Thus

$$S_t = E_t - X_t + rA_t, \tag{4.3}$$

while net assets at any age t equal

$$A_t = A_0 + \int_0^t S_t \, dt. \tag{4.4}$$

CASE 1—THE FISHERIAN APPROACH

Since Irving Fisher's work (1965), economists have recognized that one factor determining the time pattern of consumption is a divergence between the rate of interest and the rate of time preference. In Case 1, it is the only factor allowed to influence the income, consumption, and savings profiles. The impact of other factors can be eliminated with two assumptions: (1) the wage level is constant over the cycle and the same for all individuals; and (2) initial and desired terminal assets (A_n) are zero.[9] Since all individuals have the same real wealth, the life-cycle demand equations for goods and time simplify to

$$\frac{dM_t}{M_t} = \frac{dX_t}{X_t} = \sigma_c(r - \alpha). \tag{4.5}$$

---

[8] This assumption is discussed in Section IV.

[9] Throughout, I am also assuming that r is constant. It is well within the spirit of Fisher's work to allow r to be a function of the amount borrowed, but this complication is ignored.

Consumption and earnings are equal and age-invariant and savings and net assets are identically zero when the interest rate equals the subjective rate of time preference. If r and α differ, the time paths of consumption and income are no longer coincident. For example, consider a more optimistic individual who does not discount the future as severely (Figure 4.1). Compared with an individual whose preference for the present offsets the positive interest rate, this optimist will consume commodities (Z_t) in relatively greater proportions in the latter stages of the cycle. The derived demands for market goods and home

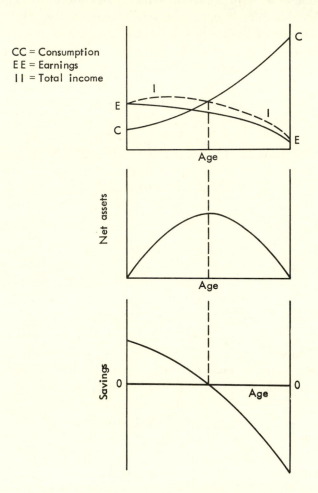

FIGURE 4.1   The Fisherian model

time are also larger during the later ages, imparting a positive slope to the age profiles of consumption and household hours. Since wages are constant, the age earnings profile is determined exclusively by the hours profile, and market earnings will decline monotonically with age. The change in savings with age[10] is

$$dS_t = -\pi_t Z_t \sigma_c (r - \alpha) + r \, dA_t. \tag{4.6}$$

In the early stages of the life cycle, earnings exceed consumption, and the savings generated become positive net assets. In succeeding periods, these assets produce income flows augmenting earnings. Net assets will continue to grow until the income and consumption profiles cross and savings are zero. After this age, the individual dissaves and the rate of his dissavings increases until net assets are once again zero at the end of the life cycle.

In this Fisherian world, the empirical association between assets and labor supply depends on the life-cycle stage. At younger ages, there exists, holding age constant, a positive correlation between assets and market work, but the sign of the correlation reverses for the older age groups. Those individuals with a stronger future-time preference have larger assets at every age, but they work more only during the younger ages. Even if we confine ourselves to periods in which the relation between nonearnings income and market work remains positive, the size of an estimated income elasticity is a negative function of age.[11] More importantly, the empirical relation between assets and work does not reflect a wealth effect at all, for the wealth of all individuals is identical by assumption. Taste variation among individuals in their respective rates of time preferences will determine the extent of the observed relation between assets and market work.

---

[10] Using equation 4.5 we have

$$dS_t = -M_t w_{mt} \frac{dM_t}{M_t} - X_t \frac{dX_t}{X_t} + r \, dA_t,$$

$$dS_t = -(M_t w_{mt} + X_t) \sigma_c (r - \alpha) + r \, dA_t.$$

[11] For individuals whose rate of present time preference exceeds the rate of interest, earnings will be relatively high and consumption low at the older ages. Net assets will always be negative, and once again assets and market hours are both low during the younger ages. In the text, I always consider the case where r exceeds α because that appears to be true empirically.

CASE 2—THE PRICE OF TIME

Ghez and Becker, in their work on life-cycle consumption, introduced another factor accounting for a nonconstant consumption age profile. Becker, and especially Ghez, demonstrated that age variation in the price of time may also affect the time path of market consumption. We can isolate the pure life-cycle price-of-time effect with the following simplifying assumptions: (1) the rate of interest, the rate of time preference, and initial and terminal assets are all zero; and (2), across all individuals, full wealth is constant. The second assumption follows if the arithmetic sum of life-cycle wages is the same for all individuals. However, the age pattern of wage rates is allowed to vary among individuals. In this second case, savings are[12]

$$S_t = E_t - X_t,$$

$$dS_t = [w_{mt}N_{mt} + \sigma_c w_{mt}M_t]\frac{dw_{mt}}{w_{mt}}. \tag{4.7}$$

Note that the savings profile is independent of the production elasticity of substitution (σ_{MX}). The increased consumption caused by the substitution of goods for time is matched dollar for dollar by additional earnings. This result holds because the elasticity of factor demand, the production effect only, is proportional to the share of the other factor, whereas the effect of this increased factor demand on savings is proportional to the share of the factor itself.[13]

[12] Taking the differential of the saving equation gives

$$dS_t = w_{mt}N_{mt}\frac{dw_{mt}}{w_{mt}} - w_{mt}M_t\frac{dM_t}{M_t} - \frac{dX_t}{X_t}X_t.$$

If we substitute the life-cycle demand for time and goods,

$$\frac{dM_t}{M_t} = -(\sigma_{MX}s_{xt} + \sigma_c s_{mt})\frac{dw_{mt}}{w_{mt}},$$

$$\frac{dX_t}{X_t} = s_{mt}(\sigma_{MX} - \sigma_c)\frac{dw_{mt}}{w_{mt}},$$

$$dS_t = [w_{mt}N_{mt} + (\sigma_{MX}s_{xt} + s_{mt}\sigma_c)w_{mt}M_t - X_t(\sigma_{MX} - \sigma_c)s_{mt}]\frac{dw_{mt}}{w_{mt}},$$

$$dS_t = [w_{mt}N_{mt} + s_{mt}\sigma_c(M_t w_{mt} + X_t)]\frac{dw_{mt}}{w_{mt}}.$$

[13] An interesting special case of this model is when the intertemporal utility function is Cobb Douglas. In that case, a dollar per hour increase in the wage leads to a dollar per hour increase in savings.

In this second case, consumption and earnings are equal and stationary for individuals with flat wage profiles. An individual who faces a rising wage profile has an incentive to concentrate his market time in the future, giving his earnings profile a positive slope. Since the rising wage trend will also increase the relative price of future commodities, the consumption of future commodities will fall. Due to the scale effect, this will reduce the demand for future market-goods consumption. In addition, a higher wage provides an incentive to substitute market goods for time. If intertemporal commodity substitution outweighs production substitution, the market-goods age profile will have a negative slope.

The profiles of such an individual are drawn in Figure 4.2. Initially, consumption exceeds earnings, and this individual dissaves. Net assets become negative and decline further until savings are zero. In the later stages of the life cycle, positive savings occur as this individual finances his earlier consumption. At young ages, those with the steepest wage profile will have the lowest levels of net assets and market work. Once again, the sign of this correlation reverses for older groups where individuals now observed working more have fewer net assets.

These conclusions will not change if we consider the case in which production substitution is stronger than the ability to substitute between commodities over time. Although both consumption and earnings will now increase with age, earnings must rise at a more rapid rate than market-goods consumption. This follows because sufficient earnings are generated to finance the additional consumption due to the production effect alone. The scale effect will further increase earnings, but will lower consumption.

In this example the sign and the magnitude of the relation between assets and market work also change as one moves through the life cycle. As was true in the Fisherian model, the strongest positive (negative) correlation occurs at the youngest (oldest) ages. This expected age pattern may explain the results reported by Schultz in Chapter 1. Schultz's estimates indicated a systematic pattern to the income effects, with a tendency for positive effects early in the life cycle and negative ones for older groups. Moreover, the Cogan and Heckman studies reporting positive asset coefficients were estimated with relatively young samples. It is not surprising, in view of my analysis, that the income effects are so unstable across different studies where the samples differ in the age groupings included.

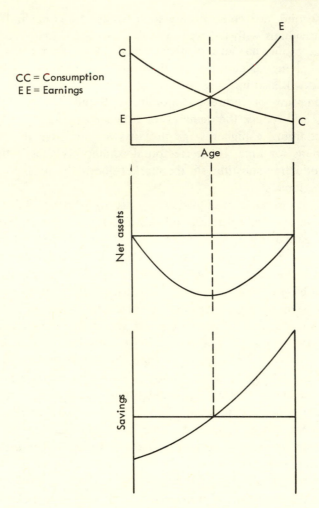

CC = Consumption
E E = Earnings

FIGURE 4.2   Life-cycle wage variation

In terms of the model specification, it would be inappropriate to include current wages and net assets as regressors in the labor supply equation. The net asset term would most likely capture (holding current wages constant) the effects of the past and future wage streams. One should certainly not interpret the asset term as measuring wealth effects.

CASE 3—HUMAN CAPITAL VARIATION

The first two cases investigated the timing of work and expenditures induced by differential costs of economic activity at different ages. In those examples, we were attempting to follow individuals over their life cycles. In this third case, and the one that follows, the emphasis shifts to factors that represent permanent differences across individuals. Case 3 concerns human capital wealth variation and Case 4, nonhuman capital wealth variation.[14]

In the previous example, all wage variation was a life-cycle phenomenon. More realistically, some of the wage differences among individuals represent dispersion in wage levels and wealth (initial human capital). In Case 3, the savings behavior generated by non-life-cycle wage variation is examined. To isolate the variation in initial human capital, I shall employ the age neutrality assumption; i.e., if individual j's wage at t exceeds individual i's by λ percent, j's wages exceed i's by λ percent at all ages.

Since we want to examine variation in the demand for time and goods across individuals at a particular age, the one-period model is appropriate.[15] The change in savings induced by an increase in the initial human capital stock is

$$dS_t = [w_{mt}N_{mt} - X_t\eta_t]\frac{dw_{mt}}{w_{mt}}. \tag{4.8}$$

---

[14] In this section and the one that follows, I ignore complexities that result from the effects of initial human and nonhuman wealth on the human capital investment profiles. Apparently, little can be said unambiguously about these effects. For a treatment of such issues, see Heckman (1974c).

[15] Using equation A.19 in the Appendix, and assuming zero initial and terminal assets and that the household production function is homogenous of degree one, we may write the demand for time and goods as

$$\frac{dM_t}{M_t} = (s_{xt}\eta_t - s_{xt}\sigma_{MX})\frac{dw_{mt}}{w_{mt}},$$

$$\frac{dX_t}{X_t} = (\eta_t s_{xt} + s_{mt}\sigma_{MX})\frac{dw_{mt}}{w_{mt}},$$

$$dS_t = w_{mt}N_{mt}\frac{dw_{mt}}{w_{mt}} - M_t w_{mt}\frac{dM_t}{M_t} - \frac{dX_t}{X_t}X_t,$$

$$dS_t = [w_{mt}N_{mt} - M_t w_{mt}(\eta_t - \sigma_{MX})s_X - X_t(\eta_t s_{xt} + s_{mt}\sigma_{MX})]\frac{dw_{mt}}{w_{mt}},$$

$$dS_t = [w_{mt}N_{mt} - M_t w_{mt}s_{xt}\eta_t - X_t s_{xt}\eta_t]\frac{dw_{mt}}{w_{mt}}.$$

Note that savings at any age is independent of the consumption and production elasticities of substitution. The consumption term is eliminated, since we are going across profiles at the same point in the cycle. The production term does not appear because the increased market hours due to the production effect are sufficient to finance the increased market goods induced by the substitution in production.

Generally, if wealth elasticities are unity, the additional (dis)savings generated by a 100 percent increase in wage rates at every age equals the original level of (dis)savings. When individual period-consumption wealth elasticities differ from unity, the correlation between these elasticities and the original savings position must be considered. If wealth elasticities are higher in those periods when savings would have occurred, the additional savings induced will be smaller than the unit elastic case. If the wealth effect exceeds the substitution effect, individual j will work less than individual i and we will observe a negative correlation between hours and net assets. The association between assets and market work depends on the familiar conflict between the income and substitution effects, with a positive correlation implied if the substitution effect exceeds the income effect. Time-series evidence indicates that for men the income effect may dominate, but for women, the substitution effect appears stronger.[16] Hence, it is not inconsistent with economic theory to find a negative empirical relation between assets and market work for men and a positive one for women.

This case may best be illustrated with an example: Two individuals have age invariant wages, but individual i's wage is higher than j's. If the rate of time preference equals the interest rate for individual i, consumption and earnings will be identical and savings and net assets will be zero. For individual j, if the wealth elasticity of consumption is the same in every period (and, hence, equal to unity), his savings will also be zero:

$$dS = w_{mt}N_{mt} - X_t = 0. \qquad (4.9)$$

However, if the wealth elasticity for future consumption exceeds that of present consumption (and therefore is greater than unity),[17] positive savings results at young ages and dissavings during older ages. This would lead to a positive asset level at every point in the cycle. The

[16] See Mincer (1962).
[17] This is equivalent to allowing the rate of time preference to depend on the level of wealth.

savings and asset positions of individuals reflect only their wage levels and profiles and supply no information that would enable us to measure the wealth elasticity for leisure.

CASE 4—NONHUMAN WEALTH VARIATION

In all cases discussed thus far, initial and desired terminal assets were zero by assumption. In the final example, individuals are allowed to differ in their initial asset holdings. Differences among individuals in their initial nonhuman wealth presumably correspond most closely to the appropriate theoretical variable. However, empirical and theoretical problems are encountered before one may use these exogenous assets to estimate wealth effects in labor supply equations. Because it is difficult to identify assets that are completely exogenous and independent of life-cycle behavior, such assets are likely to be of little use empirically. Conceptually, A_0 corresponds to the discounted value at the beginning of the horizon (working life) of the entire stream of exogenous assets that one receives over a lifetime. Exogenous assets certainly should not be equated with assets actually held at the beginning of the horizon. Inheritances, which presumably qualify as part of A_0, are typically not received at young ages—indeed the actual receipt may occur a good deal later. To the extent that such future receipts are anticipated, their discounted value should be part of the asset variable. Clearly, reported net asset figures in most data sets omit most of these expected future receipts.

Even if adequate data on exogenous assets existed, interpreting their effects on labor supply is not straightforward. Although assets are usually received in a single year or over a relatively few time periods, their receipt will set in motion consumption and earnings patterns in all future years that will alter expected savings. The effect on savings of an increase in A_0 is[18]

$$dS_t = -k_t \eta_t \, dA_0 + r \, dA_t. \tag{4.10}$$

[18] Once again, taking total differentials of the savings identity gives

$$dS = w_{mt} M_t \frac{dM_t}{M_t} - \frac{dX_t}{X_t} X_t + r \, dA_t,$$

where

$$\frac{dM_t}{M_t} = \frac{dX_t}{X_t} = \eta_t \frac{dA}{A} \frac{A}{R},$$

so

$$dS_t = -(s_{mt} M_t + X_t) \left(\eta_t \frac{dA}{A} \frac{A}{R} \right) + r \, dA_t,$$

$$dS = -\pi_t Z_t \eta_t \frac{dA_0}{R} + r \, dA_t.$$

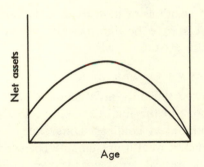

FIGURE 4.3   Nonhuman wealth variation

The savings behavior generated in the first period is

$$dS = (r - k_t \eta_t) \, dA_0. \tag{4.11}$$

Savings will increase if the rate of return on assets exceeds the share of commodity consumption in the initial period times the wealth elasticity of consumption. In the initial period, if η_t is in the vicinity of unity, r is likely to exceed k_t and savings will increase; but in later periods, savings must decrease in order to bring assets back to their terminal state. The profiles of two individuals with different initial assets are illustrated in Figure 4.3. The reduction in labor supply that results from the increase in A_0 will be the same in all periods if η_t is unity. Because future savings behavior of an individual is altered by the higher initial assets, the difference in nonlabor income (rA_t) between any two people with different initial assets will change over the life cycle. Even in this model, the estimated wealth elasticity of leisure depends on the life-cycle stage. No unique estimate of this wealth elasticity is possible if current assets are used.

III. Some Extensions and Qualifications

The basic determinants of savings have been presented. Before the model can be tested empirically, it is necessary to consider a few

---

It is the difference between A_0 and $A_n e^{-rt}$ that is really important. If a dollar increase in A_0 increased transfers to future generations by $A_n e^{-rt}$, then the consumption, hours, and earnings profiles would be unaffected. The example discussed in the text corresponds to situations in which an additional dollar of inheritance is not affected completely by the discounted value of bequests.

additional problems. Although these will not invalidate the arguments made above, they are important in designing and interpreting empirical work.

THE FAMILY CONTEXT

At one level, extending the model to the family context is straightforward. If there are two working members in the family (the husband and wife), savings is redefined as

$$S_t = w_{mt}N_{mt} + w_{ft}N_{ft} - X_t + rA_t. \tag{4.12}$$

Using the life-cycle demand equations for male time, female time, and market goods, the change in savings is[19]

$$dS_t = [w_{mt}N_{mt} + w_{mt}M_t\sigma_c]\frac{dw_{mt}}{w_{mt}}$$

$$+ [(w_{ft}N_{ft} + w_{ft}F_t\sigma_c)]\frac{dw_{ft}}{w_{ft}} - \pi_t Z_t \sigma_c(r-\alpha). \tag{4.13}$$

The wife's wage coefficient is identical to the husband's, with the appropriate relabeling of subscripts. The absolute magnitude of a dollar change in male wage should exceed that of a dollar change in a female wage. The male wage effect is larger, because of the relative home specialization of females, as long as the elasticity of substitution between time periods is not large. The female coefficient would exceed that of the male only if $\sigma_c > (N_{mt} - N_{ft})/(F_t - M_t) = 1$. Empirical evidence suggests that σ_c is less than one, so the male wage coefficient should be larger than that of the female.[20]

---

[19] Using the life-cycle demand equations for male time, female time, and market goods,

$$\frac{dM_t}{M_t} = s_{mt}(\sigma_{MM} - \sigma_c)\frac{dw_{mt}}{w_{mt}} + s_{ft}(\sigma_{MF} - \sigma_c)\frac{dw_{ft}}{w_{ft}} + \sigma_c(r-\alpha),$$

$$\frac{dF_t}{F_t} = s_{mt}(\sigma_{MF} - \sigma_c)\frac{dw_{mt}}{w_{mt}} + s_{ft}(\sigma_{FF} - \sigma_c)\frac{dw_{ft}}{w_{ft}} + \sigma_c(r-\alpha),$$

$$\frac{dX_t}{X_t} = s_{mt}(\sigma_{XM} - \sigma_c)\frac{dw_{mt}}{w_{mt}} + s_{ft}(\sigma_{XF} - \sigma_c)\frac{dw_{ft}}{w_{ft}} + \sigma_c(r-\alpha).$$

Concentrating on the husband's wage term, we have

$$dS_t = [w_{mt}N_{mt} + S_{M_t}\sigma_c(N_{mt}w_{mt} + N_{ft}w_{ft} + X_t)$$

$$- s_{mt}(\sigma_{MM}M_t w_{mt} + \sigma_{MX}X_t + \sigma_{MF}M_t w_{mt}]\frac{dw_{mt}}{w_{mt}} + \cdots,$$

$$dS_t = [w_{mt}N_{mt} + w_{mt}M_t\sigma_c]\frac{dw_{mt}}{w_{mt}} + \cdots.$$

[20] For an attempt to estimate σ_c, see Ghez and Becker (1975).

The importance of the family context for understanding motives for asset accumulation is certainly not captured by this simple extension. One obvious neglected factor is the influence of children on a family's savings behavior. Although a life-cycle theory that includes the optimal timing and spacing pattern of children is outside the scope of this paper, I will sketch some of the issues involved and present some empirical findings in Section IV.

SECULAR CHANGES

In the derivation of the purely life-cycle motivation for savings (Cases 1 and 2), it was assumed that lifetime full wealth did not change from one age to the next. Because the model will be tested using simulated cohorts derived from cross-sectional data, this assumption must be relaxed. The negative correlation between age and savings implied by the life-cycle argument could be negated if the dissimilarities among cohorts are large. In any cross-sectional survey, two individuals who differ in age are not only observed at alternative points in their progress through the life-cycle experience, but they are also members of distinct cohorts. The measured age difference captures both a movement along a life-cycle hours path and across the profiles of different cohorts; age becomes, in part, a cohort index.

Perhaps the most systematic cohort bias results from secular trends in wages and real wealth that make younger cohorts in any cross section wealthier than their predecessors. If wages increase over time by λ percent,[21] nominal wealth (R) will decline by λ percent as we move toward older ages in a cross section (or equivalently from younger to older cohorts).[22] Real wealth will decline by less than λ percent, since the higher wages of the younger cohorts increase the

---

[21] The point made in the text does not depend on the assumption that the secular rises in male and female wage rates are identical. Although the rates of growth of male and female wages can differ, it is only essential that these secular growth rates be constant. I am also assuming that all initial wealth is in the form of human capital.

[22] Full wealth is defined as

$$R = T \int_0^N w_{mt} e^{-rt} \, dt,$$

$$\frac{dR}{R} = \frac{T}{R} \frac{dw_{mt}}{w_{mt}} \int_0^N w_{mt} e^{-rt} \, dt,$$

$$\frac{dR}{R} = -\lambda.$$

cost to them of producing a given amount of household commodities. For each new cohort, household production costs (P) rise by $s_{mt}\lambda$ percent.[23] To illustrate: If time accounts for 75 percent of the cost of household production, and if wages rise over time by 4 percent per year, real wealth will increase at an annual rate of 1 percent.

Including the secular rise in real wages, the savings function can be rewritten as[24]

$$dS_t = \frac{dw_{mt}}{w_{mt}}[w_{mt}N_{mt} + \sigma_c w_{mt}M_t]$$
$$- \pi_t Z_t[\sigma_c(r-\alpha) - \lambda(s_{xt} + s_{mt}\sigma_c)] + r\,dA_t. \qquad (4.14)$$

Secular increases in real wealth will move the age term toward positive values ($[s_{xt} + s_{mt}\sigma_c]$ is necessarily positive).[25] If this bias offsets the life-cycle effect, the age coefficient in a savings function need not be negative. There are two reasons for this bias. As we increase age, real wealth now decreases by $s_{xt}\lambda$ percent, depressing consumption and increasing saving. In addition, the lifetime price index falls by $s_{mt}\lambda$ percent. Holding π_t constant, as we do in equation 4.14, this increases the relative cost of consuming as we increment age by a year, reducing

[23] For a change in price in any single period, we have

$$\frac{dP}{P} = P^{\sigma_c - 1} e^{\alpha^\sigma c}(\pi_t e^{-rt})^{1-\sigma_c} \frac{d\pi_t}{\pi_t};$$

and summing across all ages

$$\frac{dP}{P} = P^{\sigma_c - 1} \frac{dw_{mt}}{w_{mt}}\left(\int_0^N e^{\alpha^\sigma c}[\pi_t]^{1-\sigma_c} s_{mt} e^{-rt}\,dt\right),$$

$$\frac{dP}{P} = \frac{dw_{mt}}{w_{mt}}\int_0^N k_t s_{mt}\,dt,$$

$$\frac{dP}{P} = \frac{dw_{mt}}{w_{mt}} s_{mt}.$$

[24] Rewriting the consumption demand equation, we obtain

$$Z_t = RP(\sigma_c - 1)\pi_t - \sigma_c e^{(r-\alpha)}\sigma_c,$$

$$\frac{dZ_t}{Z_t} = -\lambda + (1-\sigma_c)s_{mt}\lambda + \sigma_c(r-\alpha) - \sigma_c s_{mt}\frac{dw_{mt}}{w_{mt}},$$

$$\frac{dZ_t}{Z_t} = -\sigma_c s_{mt}\frac{dw_{mt}}{w_{mt}} + \sigma_c(r-\alpha) - \lambda[s_{xt} + s_{mt}\sigma_c].$$

[25] An age term is included in the regression because we first integrate equation 4.14 before estimate. The term $-\pi_t Z_t[\sigma_c(r-\alpha) - \lambda(s_{xt} + s_{mt}\sigma_c)]$ became the coefficient of the age term.

consumption and increasing saving. Note, however, that the wage coefficient in equation 4.14 is not affected by the presence of secular growth.

It is also of interest to investigate the impact of secular growth on observed cross-sectional savings-age profiles. To do so, it is necessary to calculate the total effect of the wage change, which is[26]

$$dS_t = -S_t\lambda. \tag{4.15}$$

As a new cohort enters with proportionately higher wages at every age, their savings will be proportionate to the level of the previous cohort.[27]

The change in savings with age will be more negatively sloped when savings were originally positive, and more positively sloped at ages when dissavings occur. This is illustrated in Figure 4.4, where the savings profiles of two consecutive cohorts are drawn. Figure 4.4 illustrates the savings profiles of Cases 1 and 2. At those ages with positive savings, observed savings will decrease more rapidly (or increase less rapidly) than the true life-cycle age effect. Correspondingly, when dissavings occur, dissaving will increase less rapidly (or decrease more rapidly) than the true life-cycle profile.

RETIREMENT

An important motive for saving is that one's consumption horizon usually exceeds one's working horizon. In order to consume during retirement, it is necessary to consume at a rate less than earnings during the working period. The existence and size of pension funds suggests that savings for retirement is of great practical importance. Indeed, this motive for savings was the only one present in the original Brumberg-Modigliani life-cycle model. In their framework, leisure was not an object of choice, there were no inheritances or bequests, and the interest rate and rate of time preference were zero. Under these

[26] Taking differentials of the savings function,

$$dS_t = -\lambda w_{mt} - \pi_t Z_t[-s_{mt} - s_{xt} - \sigma_c s_{mt} + \sigma_c s_{mt}]\lambda + r\,dA_t,$$
$$dS_t = -\lambda w + \pi_t Z_t[s_{mt} + s_{xt}]\lambda + r\,dA_t,$$
$$dS_t = X_t - w_{mt}N + r\,dA_t.$$

[27] The difference between this exercise and the previous one is that in the regression, if the true life-cycle wage change is dw_{mt}/w_{mt}, the observed change in a cross section will be $dw_{mt}/w_{mt} - \lambda$. This is the measured wage change with age and is captured in the wage coefficient in the regression. To get the total effect on the savings profiles, we must add the wage coefficient to the secular change in wages.

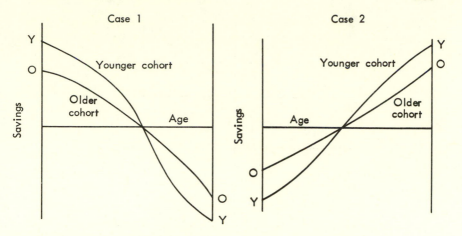

FIGURE 4.4   Savings profiles of two consecutive cohorts

assumptions, the following consumption, saving, and asset functions result (if the earnings stream is constant):

Before retirement
$$\begin{cases} X_t = \dfrac{V}{N} E_{mt}, \\[2mm] S_t = \dfrac{N-V}{N} E_{mt}, \\[2mm] A_t = \dfrac{t(N-V)}{N} E_{mt}, \end{cases}$$

After retirement
$$\begin{cases} X_t = \dfrac{V}{N} E_{mt}, \\[2mm] S_t = \dfrac{V}{N} E_{mt}, \\[2mm] A_t = \dfrac{V(N+1-t)}{N} E_{mt}, \end{cases}$$

where V is the number of working years, N is the number of consuming years, and E_{mt} is earnings in a given year. The profiles resulting from this model are illustrated in Figure 4.5. The constant rate by which assets grow during the working period depends on the proportion of the horizon in which one works. These assets are then drawn down during the retirement period.

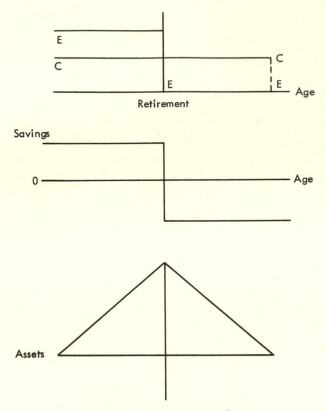

FIGURE 4.5   Retirement profiles

Generalizing the simple Brumberg-Modigliani model to include leisure, interest rates, time preferences, and wage rates becomes complicated. Because wage rates no longer measure time values during the retirement period, it is difficult to obtain explicit equations and one must rely on heuristic discussion of the implications. For simplicity, I will assume that retirement decision is exogenous—i.e., that an individual is constrained by fiat to work zero hours at all ages after 65.[28] Given the weakly separable utility function (CES), the retirement and preretirement periods can be separated, because the ratio of marginal utilities between any two periods during the working interval depends only on consumption in those two periods and is independent of

[28] A complete model should predict the optimal length of working life as a function of institutional factors (social security) and of the factors emphasized in my model—interest rate, time preference, and wage rates.

consumption during the retirement period.[29] As long as prices in the
working interval are unchanged, rates of growth of consumption and
leisure during the preretirement periods remain unaltered. Because the
income transfer from the retirement period is reduced, the levels of
consumption of goods and leisure will decline by the same proportionate amount, increasing earnings at every age during the working life.
With the separability assumption, the analysis for the working period is
equivalent to that of an increase in bequests at the end of working life.
In addition, the lower value of time during retirement shifts consumption of goods and leisure from the preretirement to the retirement
segment of the life cycle. Savings during working life will then rise at
each age, with the largest increases occurring at those ages where the
consumption of goods and leisure is greatest. The change in savings
during the working life is

$$dS = \pi_t Z_t \frac{d\lambda}{\lambda} + r\, dA_t,$$

where $d\lambda/\lambda$ is the proportion of full lifetime income that must be
transferred from the working period to the retirement period.

The profiles of consumption of goods and leisure during the retirement period are affected. Since wage rates no longer measure the value
of time, prices become endogenous. The profiles of consumption of
market goods will be flatter than if one were free to choose one's
working hours. For example, if the consumption of goods were rising,
this rise would be partly offset as the rising ratio of goods to time
reduced the value placed on consumption. Similarly, if goods consumption were falling, the decline in consumption would be mitigated by the
rising value placed on goods. If the weakly separable assumption is a
reasonable approximation, empirical problems will be reduced if the
analysis is confined to the preretirement period. In my empirical work,
regressions are run using observations that never extend beyond age
65.[30]

[29] The assumption of weak separability can easily be questioned. It seems plausible
that the years close to retirement would be affected more.

[30] In addition to the direct impact of retirement, considerable literature has emerged
in the last few years concerning the effect of the social security system on savings (see
Feldstein, 1974, and Munnell, 1974). Feldstein has argued that social security has
replaced private savings and led to a substantial reduction in the capital stock. However,
the theoretical arguments are not unambiguous. Burkhauser and Turner (1978) have
suggested that social security may have increased savings because the tax on earnings
during retirement provides individuals with an incentive to work more before retirement.
The empirical evidence seems to be somewhat mixed at best. This issue will not be
confronted in the empirical work in this chapter.

IV. Empirical Tests

Because of the demands it places on currently available data, the
life-cycle model (Cases 1 and 2) is difficult to test empirically. Since it
deals with the timing of participation and expenditures, we must be
able to follow people through at least part of their lifetime experience.
Moreover, the data source should contain information on assets,
savings, labor force participation, and wage rates. Obviously no existing data set meets all of these criteria, and some concessions and
simplifications are necessary. The ideal data to use would be observations on the same individuals over a number of years. But the absence
of extensive panel data for large segments of the life-cycle forces us to
simulate data with the more available cross-sectional information.
Essentially this involves creating a synthetic cohort from the cross
section. First, the sample is stratified by age of the family unit.[31] Then,
within every age group, mean values of all variables are calculated. In
the absence of secular growth, the observed variation between these
age cells corresponds to the expected life-cycle variation for any cohort
if a cohort's expectation is unbiased on average. Using the first two
cases as the life-cycle model, and aggregating over all families, we
have[32]

$$dS = a_1 \frac{dw_{mt}}{w_{mt}} + a_2 \frac{dw_{ft}}{w_{ft}} + a_3.$$

Upon integrating,

$$S = a_1 \log w_{mt} + a_2 \log w_{ft} + a_3 \text{ age},$$

where a_1 and a_2 are the male and female wage coefficients derived
above, and a_3 is the age coefficient that captures the interplay of
interest rates and time preferences. If $r > \alpha$, a_3 will be negative. The
wage terms should both be positive, with the male wage coefficient
exceeding that of the female.

The 1967 Survey of Economic Opportunity (SEO) sample was
selected because it contains data on the asset and debt positions of
families. Age, sex, race, educational attainment, and family relationship data are given for each individual in the family. Adult members

---

[31] In my empirical work, the sample is stratified by age of the husband.

[32] A number of difficulties are encountered in this step. First, the aggregation
problems are well known. Second, in the integration, we are implicitly assuming that the
coefficients are locally constant.

were questioned about their earnings, health, and labor force behavior.[33] Another advantage of the SEO data is that it is possible to
analyze at one time the savings, consumption, and leisure decisions.
Because of the identity linking the three, family consumption can be
computed as a residual from the savings and income data.

LIFE-CYCLE PROFILES

The life-cycle profiles of assets and debts obtained from the SEO seem
consistent with the implications of the model.[34] Graphs (a) and (b) of
Figure 4.6 show the mean net worth[35] holdings of families, stratified by
husband's age.[36] For the all-white sample, asset accumulation continues into the mid-fifties. Although the profile becomes quite erratic
after this point, there is apparently some tendency for the net worth
position to decline slightly after retirement. The peak in the net worth

[33] More recently, other data sets, such as the National Longitudinal Survey ("Parnes"
data) and the Income Dynamics Panel, have included information on assets.

[34] The general picture emerging from the SEO does not conflict with data from those
surveys whose primary purpose was to collect accurate asset and savings information for
families. The following table gives the net worth-age relationship from the Survey of
Consumer Finances. The age trend is similar to the SEO profiles.

Net Worth-Age, December 31, 1962

Age of Household Head (yr)	Net Worth ($)
Less than 25	557
25–34	4,831
35–44	14,792
45–54	22,237
55–64	32,511
65 and over	30,124

Source: Dorothy S. Projector, *Survey of Changes in Family Finances*, Board of Governors of the Federal Reserve System, 1968.

[35] Net worth consists of the sum of assets held in the form of business, land, home, car,
bank accounts, government bonds, stocks, personal loans, and other assets minus debts
in the form of business, home, land, car, clothing, fuel, medical, bank, and other debts.
The other assets are boats, royalties, and commodity contracts. Not included as assets
are household furnishings, clothing, many consumer durables (refrigerators, televisions,
etc.), cash, pension benefits, inheritances, life insurance policies, and human capital
investments.

[36] The sample consisted of white and black nonfarm, married, spouse-present families.
The asset variables in these graphs are 3-year moving averages. Since the probability of
being included in the original tape was not identical across families, these means were
constructed using the probability of sample inclusion as the weight for the family.

profiles certainly occurs at a later point in the life cycle than the peak in the earnings profiles.[37] The obvious life-cycle asset accumulation evident in these graphs is consistent with the motivations stressed in this report, namely, that the wealth owned at any point is the consequence of past savings behavior. The model highlighted two factors that underlie life-cycle savings: (1) age-related wage increases that increased the amount saved and (2) a pure age term that implied reductions in savings with age.[38] These profiles suggest that the wage effect initially dominates the age term so that savings and net worth rise initially with age. As an individual ages, the increases in wages diminish and the age effect begins to rival and eventually dominate the wage term as savings and net worth both decline. One characteristic of these profiles that is not consistent with the purely life-cycle perspective is the substantial level of assets held by older families. Obviously, the bequest motive is also an important determinant of individual savings.

Graphs (c) and (d) of Figure 4.6 show the age pattern and form in which assets are held.[39] Automobiles are the most popular type of savings for the young, and dominate other assets for the first few years. Automobile net worth is relatively age invariant, and it quickly becomes a minor component of wealth. Another characteristic of young households is the relative abundance of debts. Car, clothing, fuel, and bank debt do not increase much over the cycle, so for the young these debts are large in relation to total wealth. Consumer durable purchases are also concentrated among younger families. Quite often these purchases are the initial form in which savings takes place, and we

[37] The life-cycle model predicts the following order to peaks in profiles: working hours, earnings, wage rates, consumption.

[38] It was proved that

$$dS_t = \frac{dw_{mt}}{w_{mt}}[w_{mt}N_{mt} + \sigma_c w_{mt}M_t] - \pi_t Z_t \sigma_c (r - \alpha).$$

I am assuming throughout that $r > \alpha$, based on the empirical evidence that follows.

[39] Because it concentrated on the aggregate savings rate and not on the savings portfolio, the life-cycle model offers no insights concerning the composition of assets. Essentially, I viewed the family as solving its savings problem by a two-stage maximization procedure. In the first stage, the family selects its optimal level of savings and the implied pattern of asset accumulation. The determinants of saving in this first stage are the factors emphasized in this chapter. In the second stage, such factors as liquidity, capital transactions costs, and consumer durable purchases become important ingredients of the theory. I am assuming that these factors can be safely ignored in the first stage.

know from other data sources that they tend to decline with age.[40] During the middle years of the life cycle, housing and land dominate the asset portfolio. Both gross housing assets and mortgage debt rise with age, with mortgage debt peaking at an earlier age (40) than gross assets (53). At this stage, asset holdings become more diverse as families begin to accumulate assets that are financial and liquid in nature (stocks, bonds, etc.). These financial assets also have a considerable age trend and are most important during the older ages. Among older families, automobile wealth declines as ownership becomes less frequent. After retirement, business assets are generally converted into financial assets and these financial assets rival in magnitude home and land wealth.

The graphs of Figure 4.6 provide useful comparisons between racial groups.[41] White-black differences in economic well-being are typically analyzed using income as the index of economic position. But the relative disadvantage of black families, using net worth as the welfare indicator, far exceeds that shown when income is used; the average net worth of white families is approximately four times that of black families. Net worth is also more unevenly distributed between groups than is income.[42]

Homeownership comprises a larger share of net worth for the less-educated and black families. The most striking contrast between

---

[40] In the *1970 Survey of Consumer Finances*, the proportion of families having expenditures on household durables in 1969 are, by age of head,

Age (yr)	Proportion of Families with Household Durable Expenditures
25–34	57
35–44	53
45–54	47
55–64	39
65 and over	25

Household durable expenditures include televisions, washing machines, cooking ranges, refrigerators, dryers, dishwashers, air conditioners, furniture, sewing machines, stereos, radios, and tape recorders. (See *1970 Survey of Consumer Finances*, p. 73.)

[41] Separate regressions were not run for blacks because of the quality of the data.

[42] Projector (1968) reports that the Gini coefficient for assets was .67; for the same group, the Gini coefficient for income was .45 (see the *1970 Survey of Consumer Finances*). The erratic nature of the black profile may be attributed to the greater sampling variability caused by smaller sample sizes.

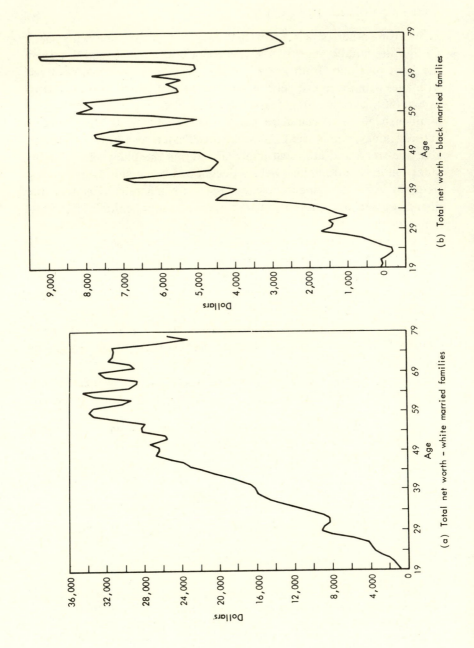

(a) Total net worth – white married families

(b) Total net worth – black married families

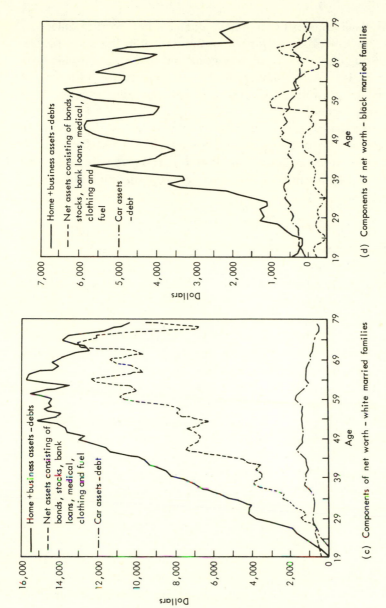

(c) Components of net worth – white married families

(d) Components of net worth – black married families

FIGURE 4.6 Net worth and components of net worth of white and black families

white and black families occurs in the financial net worth profile. The increases with age observed for whites are absent in the black profile. Indeed, throughout much of the life cycle, net assets held in this form are negative for black families. The consequences of this lack of liquidity in the portfolio of blacks have, unfortunately, received little attention from economists.

Clearly, the age pattern of individual components of net worth can differ drastically from the aggregate relationships, and limiting the empirical work to some subset of total savings can give very misleading results. In the empirical work, the most aggregate definition of savings available is used.

REGRESSION ANALYSIS

Although suggestive, these asset profiles provide no real test of the life-cycle savings model. To obtain a stronger test, regressions were run using as regressors wage rates of family members, age, and the number of children under 7 years. Actual savings measures did not exist in the SEO, so they were constructed by taking first differences of the asset series. Because assets contained considerable measurement error, I smoothed the asset profiles by taking 3 and 4 year moving averages, and then first-differenced the moving average series. To compute savings, we are essentially taking linear approximations 3 or 4 years apart in the asset age profile.[43] Since assets will reappear in the savings computation 3 or 4 years later, some (negative) serial correlation is present. As is well known, standard errors must therefore be treated with more than the usual skepticism.

An examination of the residuals clearly indicated that they tended to fan out as age increased. The sample was divided into two equal age groups, and separate regressions were run for ages 19–42 and 43–65. An F-test on the ratio of the sum of squared residuals from the two regressions was performed, and the hypothesis of constant variances was rejected at the 5 percent confidence limit.[44] The presence of heteroskedastic residuals is not surprising because the savings measures are computed from assets, and the error in assets appears proportional to the level of assets.[45] In the regressions reported in this

[43] Using 3-year moving averages, savings at age $t = (A_{t+2} - A_{t-1})/3$.

[44] The F-value for (18, 18) degrees of freedom is 2.25. The computed F was 3.06.

[45] An alternative would have been to use log savings as the dependent variable. The negative values for savings precluded such use.

chapter all observations were weighted by the inverse of assets.[46] The savings functions are reported in Table 4.1.

In previous work, I analyzed the leisure hours profiles of both men and women.[47] Regressions of family consumption and home hours of males and females are reported in Tables 4.2 and 4.3. One could easily argue that the principal explanatory variables, wage rates and children, are themselves endogenous and part of the life-cycle decisionmaking process of the family. For example, the pattern of observed wages reflects human capital accumulation over a lifetime. However, one can show that the predictions regarding the hours and consumption profiles are not substantially affected by including human capital investment.[48] Because investment time will fall as the wage rate rises, the predictions of the model without human capital are reinforced by the decline in the investment time. However, the omission of human capital investment leads to underreporting of savings among young families, and the overall savings-age relationship is distorted. Since savings used to finance human capital are large at the youngest ages, my savings profiles, which exclude human capital investments, will overstate the decrease in savings with age.

The severe measurement problem connected with the savings data is evident in the low R^2 and in the lack of significance for some of the variables. Still, the empirical estimates basically support the life-cycle model. In the savings function, all variables have the theoretically expected sign except the female wage variable, which has an insignificant coefficient. The male wage variable has the predicted positive sign in the savings function.[49] In addition, the male wage coefficient has the correct negative (positive) effect in the male home hours (consumption) equations.[50]

I anticipated difficulty in estimating an independent effect for female wages. The true life-cycle variation in female wages is small compared with that of male wages, so it should play a smaller role in explaining

[46] Other weights (the reciprocal of log male hourly wage or log male earnings) were used as well. The results were similar to those reported in the text.

[47] See Smith (1972).

[48] See Ghez and Becker (1975).

[49] Variation in nonmarket productivity biases the savings-function wage coefficient upward. If λ is the percentage increase in nonmarket productivity, $dS = (1 - \sigma_c)\pi_t F_t \lambda$. Empirical estimates suggest that $\sigma_c < 1$. (See Ghez and Becker, 1975.)

[50] The absolute magnitude of the male wage coefficient in the consumption function is approximately the same size as Ghez and Becker's estimates.

TABLE 4.1: Family Savings
Independent Variables[a]

Equation	Husband's Earnings	Husband's Hourly Wage	Wife's Hourly Wage	Age	Children under 7 years	Constant	R^2
4.1	2976[b] (2.00)	—	−879.1[b] (.32)	−73.09 (2.02)	−743.5 (1.40)	−23090 (2.07)	.13
4.2	—	2998[b] (1.53)	739.4[b] (.29)	−47.63 (1.55)	−366.7 (.77)	−236.7 (1.40)	.10
4.3	3216[b] (2.87)	—	−2016.0[b] (.93)	−65.25 (2.40)	−483.6 (1.21)	−247.0 (28.9)	.22
4.4	.4553 (2.74)	—	793.0 (.82)	−55.91 (2.19)	−296.5 (.80)	−344.4 (.27)	.21
4.5	—	4664[b] (2.42)	−2255.0 (.68)	−62.07 (2.42)	−377.4 (.70)	−1724 (.95)	.20
4.6	—	1573 (2.17)	617.1 (.61)	−37.96 (1.63)	−315.6 (.08)	−902.5 (.58)	.15

Note: The first two equations used 3-year moving averages of the asset data, and the last four equations used 4-year averages.

[a] *t*-values are indicated in parentheses.

[b] Variables entered in log form.

TABLE 4.2: Family Consumption
Independent Variables[a]

Dependent Variable	Log Husband's Hourly Wage	Log Wife's Hourly Wage	Age	Children under 7 Years	Constant	R^2	D.W.
Log consumption 1	.7192 (2.68)	.0929 (.22)	.0080 (2.30)	.0193 (.30)	7.89 (30.7)	.68	2.18
Log consumption 2	.7832 (3.05)	.0452 (.11)	.0105 (3.15)	.0151 (.24)	7.87 (32.05)	.78	2.10

Note: Consumption 1 is defined as the difference between family income minus savings. Savings was defined as net worth at age *t* minus net worth at age *t* minus 1. Family income equals male earnings plus female earnings plus all nonlabor income flows received in that period. Consumption 2 equals consumption 1 plus an imputed income return to the net worth held in the previous period. An interest rate of 5 percent was used.

[a] *t*-values are indicated in parentheses.

TABLE 4.3: Home Hours of Men and Women
Independent Variables[a]

Dependent Variable	Log Husband's Hourly Wage	Log Wife's Weekly Wage	Age	Children under 7 Years	Asset/Debt Ratio	Log Net Worth	Constant	R^2
Log husband's home hours	-.1040 (6.88)	.0202 (.82)	.00014 (.67)	-.0177 (4.60)	—	—	8.92 (524.5)	.75
Log wife's home hours	.0444 (2.74)	-.0396 (1.50)	.00057 (2.54)	.0358 (3.68)	—	—	8.95 (491.7)	.82
Log husband's home hours	-.0281 (.97)	-.003 (.13)	.0095 (2.83)	-.0209 (4.52)	—	-.0213 (2.94)	9.02 (233.0)	.80
Log wife's home hours	.1023 (3.10)	-.0574 (2.13)	.0012 (3.14)	.0367 (9.18)	—	-.0164 (1.99)	9.03 (2.06)	.83
Log husband's home hours	-.0792 (4.37)	.034 (1.41)	-.0008 (1.75)	-.0236 (5.25)	.00127 (2.26)	—	8.89 (457.0)	.81
Log wife's home hours	.0692 (3.53)	-.0258 (.99)	-.0004 (.77)	.0230 (6.15)	.00126 (2.07)	—	8.93 (424.3)	.84

[a] t-values are indicated in parentheses.

the timing of expenditures, market participation, and savings. Also, the value of time (shadow home wage) of nonworking women is not necessarily equal to the observed wage of workers. As Gronau demonstrates, observed wage can change, due to a selectivity bias, without any alterations in the wages offered by firms. For example, in time periods when there are young children in the family, the implicit home wage increases, and many women will leave the labor force. Indeed, it is only the women receiving the highest wage offers in the distribution who will remain in the labor force. Therefore, only part of the observed life-cycle variation in female wages reflects any real change in their market opportunities. In both the savings and consumption functions, female wages had no discernible effect. The female own wage coefficient in the female hours equation is negative—a result consistent with the model. The positive female wage coefficient in the male function suggests that male time and female time are substitutes.

Age has the predicted negative sign in the savings function. A year increase in age reduces savings by approximately $60. As pointed out above, secular growth in real wages biases the age term toward positive values, and so to obtain the negative age term is encouraging. The age coefficients in the consumption and home hours equations are consistent with the savings function. An interest rate larger than the rate of time preference leads to a positive coefficient in the consumption and home hours equations and a negative coefficient in the savings equations. The consistency in the estimates across the savings consumption and leisure regressions lends considerable support to the life-cycle model.

The effect of children under 7 years of age on savings is negative, although the t-values are not very high. One problem with this variable is that children are concentrated in a relatively small part of the life cycle. Notice that as we go from a 3 to a 4 year moving average, the children's variable becomes smaller in absolute size. The smoothing process tends to dampen this variable, since we are approximating the savings function over a wide enough age range that we are soon outside the ages of concentrated childbearing.

The presence of children in the household may affect savings by altering consumption expenditures or money income. Preschool children apparently have a depressing effect on the market participation of females, but have the opposite effect of increasing male working hours (Table 4.3). Evaluating at the mean market hours and wages for males

Table 4.4: Effect of Children's Age on Working Time
of Their Mothers

Sample Group	Child Groups, by Age (years)						
	<6	<6, 6–13	<6, >13	<6, 6–13, >13	6–13	>13	6–13, >13
All whites	−	−	?	?	+	+	−
All blacks	?	?	+	?	+	?	?
College whites	−	−	?	?	?	+	−
High school whites	−	−	−	−	?	+	?
Elementary school whites	?	−	?	−	+	?	?

Note: + indicates effect is to increase hours of work.
− indicates effect is to decrease hours of work.
? indicates t-value less than 1.

and females, I find an increase of 116 male market hours and $405 in male earnings and a decrease of 294 female market hours and $636 in female market earnings[51]—a net decrease of approximately $231, implying a reduction in savings through reduced family income.

A simple count of the number of young children at home cannot be expected to measure many changes that occur during the life cycle in those characteristics of family structure that determine a family member's labor market behavior. Therefore, I defined a group of variables measuring the fraction of women at each age with children at home in a set of mutually exclusive child-age categories (Table 4.4). For males, the presence of children in any age category tended to increase their market work, but for females it appears that the factor intensity of children might well switch as the child proceeds through his aging process. Although parents with preschool children are consuming a relatively (wife) time-intensive commodity, children become less time-intensive as they age, so that the presence of an older child makes household consumption more goods-intensive than consumption in childless families. Through the mechanism of changes in earnings, the

[51] The mean male and female hourly wages are 3.47 and 2.17. The mean male and female hour times are 6,604 and 8,201.

presence of children may produce smaller savings at younger ages and larger savings at older ones.

The relationship between family size and household savings has long been a popular subject in the demographic and development literature, and the postulated negative correlation is thought to be a contributing factor in limiting capital formation and growth. But the theoretical grounds for this hypothesis are not particularly convincing.[52] The models employed by economic demographers were couched in a one-period framework, and children were assumed to increase the consumption "needs" of the family. But if savings results from a divergence between the desired expenditure and income profiles, the effect of children on the absolute level of lifetime consumption is far less critical than their impact on the timing of consumption over the life cycle. Children undeniably have a large impact on the amount and type of goods consumed, increasing the consumption of food and housing and reducing the consumption of stereos and travel. Their effect on total consumption expenditures is far less clear. The relative market goods intensity of the commodity of child services, compared with all other household commodities, is basically an empirical issue in the same way that the relative wife and husband time intensity of children is an empirical issue. As we find for female time, the relative goods intensity of children may well be a function of the age of children. My empirical results (Table 4.2) show an insignificant positive effect of the number of children under 7 years on family consumption.[53] Apparently the main avenue through which children influence

[52] Indeed, Irving Fisher, to whom we owe much of our existing theory of capital and savings, hypothesized that increasing family size would increase savings. "Not only does regard for one's offspring lower impatience, but the increase of offspring has in part the same effect. So far as it adds to future needs rather than to immediate needs, it operates, like a descending income stream, to diminish impatience. Parents whose families are increasing often feel the importance of providing for future years far more than parents in similar circumstances but with small families. Consequently, an increase in family size, other things being equal, will reduce the rate of interest" (Fisher, 1965).

[53] Two studies dealing with this empirical issue were those of Ghez and Becker (1975) and Landsberger (1973). Ghez and Becker estimate that doubling family size would increase consumption by 25 percent. Landsberger took into account the age structure of children and reported a reduction in consumption if the number of young children under 6 years increased, but an increase in consumption when the number of children older than 13 years increased. Unfortunately, both studies have serious defects; Ghez ignored the age structure of children, and Landsberger did not include household age as an explanatory variable. Landsberger's finding could simply reflect the positive consumption-age relationship implied by the life-cycle theory.

savings is through the labor supply side[54] rather than the consumption expenditure side.[55]

Although I have argued that it is inappropriate to introduce assets in labor supply regressions, I included them in the male and female home hours regressions in column 6 of Table 4.3. Notice that contrary to the view that assets serve as a measure of wealth and should have a positive sign in the home-hours regressions, increasing assets increase market work. As argued earlier, this probably reflects the positive serial correlation of work time with past work, producing the current assets. Note also that including assets reduces the male wage coefficient in the male home-hours equation. The total male wage effect should include the male wage coefficient plus the asset coefficient times the change in assets induced by the higher wage.[56]

CONCLUSION

In this chapter the role of assets in labor supply functions was examined. Based on a simple life-cycle model, a strong case was made that the standard practice of using assets to measure wealth effects on the demand for leisure is theoretically inappropriate. The relationship between currently held assets and labor supply conveys information mainly on the unfolding lifetime patterns of desired consumption and earnings. Any attempt to separate out these life-cycle considerations to obtain wealth elasticities seems beyond the capacity of available data.

[54] Children may also affect earnings profiles by changing the wages received by men and women. One determinant of the incentives to invest in market-oriented activities is the amount of expected future market work. Moreover, the rate at which one's human capital depreciates may, in part, be a function of the duration and continuity of one's market participation. We might anticipate that the presence of children may indirectly increase male market wages because of the added incentives for men to invest. Mincer and Polachek (1974) estimated that the net depreciation of female human capital caused by the birth of a first child is 1.5 percent. They also found that the depreciation increased with the level of female education. Although their results cannot yet be regarded as conclusive, this potential avenue of causation from children to future wages, earnings, and savings should be more carefully explored.

[55] Attempts at including variables that measured the number of children in other age groups produced so much multicollinearity that no useful results were obtained.

[56] Another problem is that male wages and assets are so collinear that the significance of the male wage is substantially reduced.

APPENDIX

MATHEMATICAL MODEL

Let the family maximize lifetime utility

$$U = \left[\int_0^N Z_t^{(\sigma_c - 1)/\sigma_c} e^{-\alpha t} \, dt \right]^{\sigma_c/(\sigma_c - 1)} \tag{A.1}$$

with the production function, and subject to the following time and money expenditure constraints:

$$Z_t = f(X_t, M_t, F_t), \tag{A.2}$$

where t_0 is homogenous of degree 1,

$$M_t + N_{mt} = F_t + N_{ft} = T, \tag{A.3a}$$

$$\int_0^N X_t e^{-rt} \, dt = \int_0^N (w_{mt} N_{mt} + w_{ft} N_{ft}) e^{-rt} \, dt + A_0, \tag{A.3b}$$

$$R = \int_0^N \pi_t Z_t e^{-rt} \, dt = T \int_0^N (w_{mt} + w_{ft}) e^{-rt} \, dt + A_0. \tag{A.4}$$

When the family maximizes utility function A.1 subject to budget constraint A.4, the following must hold between consumption in period t and $t+j$:

$$\frac{-dZ_{t+j}}{Z_t} = \left(\frac{Z_{t+j}}{Z_t} \right)^{1/\sigma_c} e^{\alpha j} = \frac{\pi_t}{\pi_{t+j}} e^{rj}. \tag{A.5}$$

Therefore consumption in any period $t+j$ can be expressed as

$$Z_{t+j} = Z_t \left(e^{(r-\alpha)j} \frac{\pi_t}{\pi_{t+j}} \right)^{\sigma_c}; \tag{A.6}$$

and since

$$R = \int_0^N \pi_t Z_t e^{-rt} \, dt = \int_{-t}^{N-t} \pi_{t+j} Z_{t+j} e^{-r(t+j)} \, d_j, \tag{A.7}$$

we may substitute A.6 into A.7:

$$R = Z_t \pi_t^{\sigma_c} e^{(\alpha - r)t\sigma_c} \int_{-t}^{N-t} (\pi_{t+j} e^{-r(t+j)})^{1-\sigma_c} e^{-\alpha\sigma_c(t+j)} \, d_j \qquad (A.8)$$

or

$$R = Z_t \pi_t^{\sigma_c} e^{(\alpha - r)t\sigma_c} \int_0^N (\pi_t e^{-rt})^{1-\sigma_c} e^{-\alpha\sigma_c t} \, dt. \qquad (A.9)$$

Define the lifetime price index P as follows:

$$P = \left[\int_0^N (\pi_t e^{-rt})^{1-\sigma_c} e^{-\alpha t\sigma_c} \, dt \right] \frac{1}{1-\sigma_c}. \qquad (A.10)$$

Then

$$Z_t = \frac{R}{P} \left(\frac{\pi_t}{P} \right)^{-\sigma_c} e^{(r-\alpha)\sigma_c t},$$

which is equivalent to equation 4.5 in the text.

R and P are constant over the life cycle, so

$$\frac{dZ_t}{Z_t} = -\sigma_c \frac{d\pi_t}{\pi_t} + \sigma_c(r-\alpha) \qquad (A.11)$$

and

$$\frac{d\pi_t}{\pi_t} = s_{mt} \, dw_{mt} + s_{ft} \, dw_{ft}. \qquad (A.12)$$

The demand for male home time is

$$\frac{dM_t}{M_t} = \frac{dZ_t}{Z_t} - (s_{ft}\sigma_{MF} + s_{xt}\sigma_{MX}) \frac{dw_{mt}}{w_{mt}} + s_{ft}\sigma_{MF} \frac{dw_{ft}}{w_{ft}}. \qquad (A.13)$$

Finally, by substituting equation A.12 into A.11, and A.11 into A.13, we obtain the demand function for home time described in the text:

$$\frac{dM_t}{M_t} = -(s_{mt}\sigma_c + s_{ft}\sigma_{MF} + s_{xt}\sigma_{MX}) \frac{dw_{mt}}{w_{mt}}$$

$$+ s_{ft}(\sigma_{MF} - \sigma_c) \frac{dw_{ft}}{w_{ft}} + \sigma_c(r-\alpha), \qquad (A.14)$$

and the demand for goods is

$$\frac{dX_t}{X_t} = s_{mt}(\sigma_{MX} - \sigma_c)\frac{dw_{mt}}{w_{mt}} + s_{ft}(\sigma_{FX} - \sigma_c)\frac{dw_{ft}}{w_{ft}} + \sigma_c(r - \alpha). \quad (A.15)$$

The pure one-period model results when there are no interperiod price effects. Using the age neutrality assumption, the percentage difference in R among families is

$$\frac{dR}{R} = \left(\frac{T^*}{R}\right)\bar{w}_m\left(\frac{dw_{mt}}{w_{mt}}\right) + \left(\frac{T^*}{R}\right)\bar{w}_f\left(\frac{dw_{ft}}{w_{ft}}\right) + \left(\frac{dA_0}{A_0}\right)\left(\frac{A_0}{R}\right), \quad (A.16)$$

i.e., a weighted average of the percentage changes in male wages, female wages, and the initial assets of families. The weights are the shares in total full wealth of male human capital wealth, female human capital wealth, and all nonhuman forms of wealth. The percentage change in the lifetime price index may be expressed as

$$\frac{dP}{P} = \frac{dw_{mt}}{w_{mt}}\bar{S}_M + \frac{dw_{ft}}{w_{ft}}\bar{S}_F. \quad (A.17)$$

Thus,

$$\frac{dM_t}{M_t} = \frac{dA_0}{A_0}\frac{A_0}{R} + \left[\left(\frac{T^*w_{mt}}{R} - \bar{S}_M\right) + s_{mt}\sigma_{MM}\right]\frac{dw_{mt}}{w_{mt}}$$
$$+ \left[\left(\frac{T^*w_{ft}}{R} - \bar{S}_F\right) + s_{ft}\sigma_{MF}\right]\frac{dw_{ft}}{w_{ft}}$$

or

$$\frac{dM_t}{M_t} = \frac{dA_0}{A_0}\frac{A_0}{R} + \left(\frac{\bar{E}_m}{R} + s_{mt}\sigma_{MM}\right)\frac{dw_{mt}}{w_{mt}} + \left(\frac{\bar{E}_F}{R} + s_{ft}\sigma_{MF}\frac{dw_{ft}}{w_{ft}}\right).$$
$$(A.18)$$

If we drop the assumption of unitary income elasticities implied by the CES, this equation generalizes to

$$\frac{dM_t}{M_t} = \eta_t\frac{dA_0}{A_0}\frac{A_0}{R} + \left(\eta_t\frac{\bar{E}_m}{R} + s_{mt}\sigma_{MM}\right)\frac{dw_{mt}}{w_{mt}}$$
$$+ \left(\eta_t\frac{\bar{E}_F}{R} + s_{ft}\sigma_{MF}\right)\frac{dw_{ft}}{w_{ft}}, \quad (A.19)$$

which is the standard version of the one-period labor-supply model derived in a number of sources.

GLOSSARY OF SYMBOLS

A_t Assets in period t

A_0 Initial assets

E_{mt}, E_{ft} Total earnings in period t by husband and wife

k_t Share of full wealth accounted for by commodities consumed in period t

M_t, F_t Amount of male (husband's) time and female (wife's) time spent in home production in period t

N Number of periods in family's horizon (equal to life span)

N_{mt}, N_{ft} Amount of husband's time and wife's time spent at work in period t

P Lifetime price index index of commodities

R Family's level of full wealth

r Interest rate

S_t Savings in period t

s_{it} Share of total cost of commodities in period t accounted for by input $i (i = m, f,$ or $x)$

T Number of hours in time period

T^* Total time available over lifetime; equal to NT

U Family utility

V Number of working years in lifetime

$\bar{w}_m, \bar{w}_f$ Average discounted values of w_{mt} and w_{ft} over lifetime

w_{mt}, w_{ft} Husband's and wife's wage in period t

X_t Total quantity of market goods purchased in period t

Z_t Level of consumption of commodities in period t

α Index of time preference

η_t Wealth elasticity of consumption in period t

π_t Shadow price of commodities in period t

σ_c Elasticity of substitution in consumption between time periods

σ_{ij} Allen partial elasticity of substitution in home production between inputs i and j $(i, j = m, f,$ and $x)$

CHAPTER 5

SAMPLE SELECTION BIAS AS A SPECIFICATION ERROR WITH AN APPLICATION TO THE ESTIMATION OF LABOR SUPPLY FUNCTIONS

JAMES J. HECKMAN

UNIVERSITY OF CHICAGO AND NATIONAL BUREAU
OF ECONOMIC RESEARCH

In this chapter, the bias that results from using nonrandomly selected samples to estimate behavioral relationships is shown to arise because of a missing data problem. In contrast with the standard omitted variable problem in econometrics, in which certain explanatory variables of a regression model are lacking, the problem of sample selection bias arises because data are missing on the dependent variable of an analysis. Regressions estimated on the data available from the nonrandom sample will not, in general, enable the analyst to estimate parameters of direct interest to economists. Instead, such regression coefficients confound meaningful structural parameters with the parameters of the function determining the probability that an observation makes its way into the nonrandom sample.

Sample selection bias may arise for two distinct reasons. First, there may be self selection by the individuals being investigated. One observes market wages for certain women because their productivity in the market exceeds their productivity in the home.[1] Similarly, one observes wages for union members who found *their* nonunion alternative less desirable. Finally, the wages of migrants (or manpower trainees) do not, in general, afford an estimate of what nonmigrants (nontrainees) would have earned had they migrated (participated in training). In each of these cases, wage functions fit on the available

---

[1] Note that this does not imply that the more market productive women are the ones observed working.

data do not estimate the wage function that characterizes a *randomly* selected member of the general population subject to the "treatment" of work, unionism, migration, and manpower training programs, respectively. Moreover, in each case, if it were possible to obtain the missing wage data for either the treatment or nontreatment population, it would be possible to utilize simple regression techniques to estimate the parameters of population functions. Simple comparisons between pre and post treatment wages would yield unbiased estimates of the economic benefits of the treatment.

Sample selection bias may also arise as a direct consequence of actions taken by the analyst. In studies based on panel data, it is common to require that "intact" observations be employed for the analysis. For example, in analyses of the time series of the labor supply of married women, stability of the family unit is often required for an observation sequence to be analyzed. The effect of such criteria operates in precisely the same fashion as self selection: fitted functions confound behavioral functions with sample selection functions.

It is fair to say that most competent analysts have been aware of the possibility of both sources of selection bias. It is also fair to say that the accepted econometric practice has been to ignore the problem in making parameter estimates, but verbally to qualify the estimates in light of possible selection biases.

Recent work in econometrics has attempted to improve on previous studies by making specific assumptions about the source of selection bias. In particular, the present study assumes that both the missing data and the available data are drawn from a common probability distribution, typically assumed to be a normal law. Except for Amemiya (1973b) and Gronau (1974), the authors of earlier work rely on maximum likelihood estimators to produce parameter estimates free of selection bias.

In this chapter, I present a simple characterization of the sample selection bias problem that is also applicable to the conceptually distinct econometric problems that arise from truncated samples and from models with limited dependent variables.[2] The problem of sample selection bias is fit within the conventional specification error framework of Griliches and Theil. I also discuss a simple estimator that

[2] This relationship is spelled out in greater detail in a companion paper (Heckman, 1976).

enables analysts to utilize ordinary regression methods to estimate models free of selection bias.

The techniques discussed here are applied to reestimate and test a particular model of female labor supply (see Heckman, 1974b). In addition to providing an illustration of the methodology, this application is of interest in its own right for three reasons: (a) an important variable utilized in the previous analysis, the labor market experience of women, was incorrectly coded by the primary data source, (b) the simple estimators given here allow for much more extensive testing of the maintained hypotheses of the previous paper, and (c) the method shown here produces an initial consistent estimator for the likelihood equations of the previous paper. This last issue is important because the likelihood function proposed in the 1974 work is not globally concave, and hence the issue of selecting an initial starting value is a significant one, since local optima will not yield consistent estimators.

Four conclusions emerge from the empirical analysis of female labor supply that is conducted on the 1967 National Longitudinal Survey for women age 30–44. First, estimated coefficients of labor supply and wage functions are quite sensitive to alternative treatment of the labor market experience of the wife. Recent work (Heckman, 1977, 1978) suggests that unmeasured factors that determine participation also determine past work behavior. Treating the wife's labor force experience as an endogenous variable in participation probabilities, using standard instrumental variable estimation techniques, significantly alters the coefficients of estimated labor supply and wage functions. Second, in a model that treats the labor market experience of the wife as endogenous, there is evidence that selection bias is an important phenomenon in the estimates of labor supply functions, but there is little evidence of selection bias in estimates of the hourly wage function. Third, the empirical analysis casts some doubt on the validity of the simple model assumed in the 1974 paper. With a minor modification, the basic structure of the model remains intact and concordant with data. Fourth, conventional measures of labor supply overstate the amount of measured work, create the statistical illusion of a standard work week and work year, and considerably understate the true sample variation in labor supply.

This chapter is in three parts. In the first section, selection bias is presented within a specification error framework, and general distributional assumptions are maintained. In Section II, specific results are presented for the case of normal regression disturbances. Simple estimators are proposed and discussed. In Section III, empirical results are presented.

I. SAMPLE SELECTION BIAS AS A SPECIFICATION ERROR

To simplify the exposition, consider a two-equation model. Few new points arise in the multiple equation case, and the two-equation case has considerable pedagogical merit.

Consider a random sample of I observations. The equations for individual i may be written as

$$Y_{1i} = X_{1i}\beta_1 + U_{1i} \tag{5.1a}$$

$$Y_{2i} = X_{2i}\beta_2 + U_{2i}, \tag{5.1b}$$

where X_{ji} is a $1 \times K_j$ vector of exogenous regressors, β_j is a $K_j \times 1$ vector of parameters,

$$E(U_{ji}) = 0, \qquad E(U_{ji}U_{j'i}) = \sigma_{jj'}, \qquad j = 1, 2,$$
$$E(U_{ji}U_{j'i'}) = 0, \qquad i \neq i'. \tag{5.2}$$

The final assumption is an implication of a random sampling scheme. Denote the joint distribution of U_{1i}, U_{2i} by $h(U_{1i}, U_{2i})$, which may be a singular distribution. The regressor matrix is assumed to be of full rank so that if all data were available, unbiased estimators of the parameters of each equation could be achieved by least squares, and all parameters would be identified.

Suppose that one seeks estimates of equation 5.1a but that data are missing on Y_{1i} for certain observations. The crucial question is, "why are data missing for certain observations?"

No matter what the answer to this question, one can write the population regression function for equation 5.1a as

$$E(Y_{1i} \mid X_{1i}) = X_{1i}\beta_1, \qquad i = 1, \dots, I,$$

while the regression function for the subsample of available data is

$$E(Y_{1i} \mid X_{1i}, \text{ sample selection rule}) =$$
$$X_{1i}\beta_1 + E(U_{1i} \mid \text{sample selection rule}),$$

$i = 1, \dots, I_1$, where, for convenience, the i subscripts are labeled so that the first $I_1 < I$ observations have all data available. If the conditional expectation of U_{1i} is zero, the selected sample regression function is the same as the population regression function. In this case, least squares may be applied to the subsample of the available data to estimate the population regression function. The only cost of having an incomplete sample is a loss in efficiency.

In the general case, the sample selection rule that determines the available data has more serious consequences. Consider the following selection rule: data are available on Y_{1i} if

$$Y_{2i} \geq 0, \tag{5.3}$$

while if

$$Y_{2i} < 0$$

we do not obtain observations. Clearly the choice of zero as a threshold is an inessential normalization. Also, one could define a dummy variable d_i with the properties

$$\begin{aligned} d_i &= 1 \text{ iff } Y_{2i} \geq 0, \\ d_i &= 0 \text{ iff } Y_{2i} < 0, \end{aligned} \tag{5.4}$$

so that one could analyze the joint distribution of Y_{1i}, d_i dispensing with Y_{2i} altogether. The advantage in using the selection rule representation 5.3 is that it permits a unified summary of the existing literature. Utilizing this representation, we may write

$$E(U_{1i} \mid \text{sample selection rule}) = E(U_{1i} \mid Y_{2i} \geq 0)$$
$$= E(U_{1i} \mid U_{2i} \geq -X_{2i}\beta_2).$$

In the case of independence between U_{1i} and U_{2i}, so that the selection rule is independent of the behavioral function being estimated, the conditional mean of U_{1i} is zero.

In general, the conditional mean of the U_{1i} disturbance does not vanish. Accordingly, the selected sample regression function may be written as

$$E(Y_{1i} \mid X_{1i}, Y_{2i} > 0) = X_{1i}\beta_1 + E(U_{1i} \mid U_{2i} \geq -X_{2i}\beta_2). \tag{5.5}$$

The selected sample regression function depends on X_{1i} and X_{2i}. Regression estimators of equation 5.1a computed on the selected sample omit the final term of equation 5.5. Thus the problem of sample selection bias, initially viewed as a missing *dependent* variable problem, may be reformulated as an ordinary omitted explanatory variable problem.

Several special cases of this model are of interest. First assume that the only variable in the regressor vector X_{2i} is the constant "1." In this case, the probability that an observation is included in the sample is the same for all observations and is not a function of any explanatory variables. The conditional mean of U_{1i} is a constant. Ordinary least squares estimators of equation 5.1a yield unbiased estimators of slope coefficients, but a biased estimator for the intercept, and the population variance σ_{11}. The same analysis applies to a more general model with X_{2i} regressors, as long as the set of X_{1i} variables is uncorrelated with the conditional mean of U_{1i}. In particular, if X_{1i} and X_{2i} are independent random variables, this analysis continues to hold.

In the general case with nontrivial regressors included among the X_{2i} variables, it is unreasonable to expect that the regressors of equation 5.1a (i.e., X_{1i}) are uncorrelated with the conditional mean of U_{1i}. Accordingly, least squares estimators of the slope coefficients (β_1) are biased. Without further assumptions about the distribution of U_{1i}, it is not possible to sign the bias. If the conditional mean of the U_{1i} disturbance is well approximated by the linear terms of a Taylor's series expansion, this approximation may be substituted in equation 5.5 and an ordinary specification error analysis may be performed.

From equation 5.5, it is evident that a symptom of selection bias is that variables which do not belong in the true structural equation (e.g., elements of X_{2i} not in X_{1i}) may appear to be statistically significant determinants of Y_{1i} when regressions are fit on selected samples. For example, in Gronau's analysis of the selection bias that arises in using the wages of working women to estimate the potential wage of nonworking women, variables that affect the probability that a woman works, such as the presence of children, may appear to affect market wages when, in fact, no causal association exists. Thus, regression evidence that women with children earn lower wages is not necessarily evidence that there is discrimination against such women or that women with lower market experience—as proxied by children—earn lower wages. Indications that such extraneous variables "explain" wage rates may be interpreted as evidence in support of the selection hypothesis. However, even if no such extraneous variables appear in the selected sample regressions, estimates of the intercept and the population variance may be biased.

If one knew the conditional mean of U_{1i} or could estimate it, one could enter it as a regressor in equation 5.5 and use ordinary least squares to estimate the β_1 parameters. In the next section, I discuss a method of estimating the conditional mean for the case of jointly normal disturbances. Before turning to this discussion, it is helpful to relate the simple model presented here to previous work in the literature.

The justly celebrated model of Tobin (1958) may be fit within this framework. (See also Amemiya, 1973b.) In Tobin's model, data are missing on Y_{1i} if $Y_{1i} < 0$. Setting $Y_{1i} \equiv Y_{2i}$, $\beta_1 \equiv \beta_2$, $X_{1i} \equiv X_{2i}$, and $U_{1i} \equiv U_{2i}$, the "Tobit" model arises.[3] The bivariate density $h(U_{1i}, U_{2i})$ becomes degenerate, since $U_{1i} \equiv U_{2i}$. Since X_{1i} and X_{2i} are identical, the conditional mean of U_{1i} is not orthogonal to X_{1i}, and bias is guaranteed for the least squares estimators of equation 5.1a applied to selected samples.

Tobin's model was a major stimulus to later work. Its simplicity and elegance mask two important ideas that have been confused. Most economists have interpreted it as a prototype of a limited dependent variable model: the range of observed values of the random variable Y_{1i} cannot fall short of zero. Putting Tobin's model this way, it is less interesting. Many economists are willing to live with this type of truncation of the range of a variable, and simple transformations can eliminate it (e.g., use of logs).

The important feature of Tobin's model is that a selection rule ($Y_{1i} \gtreqless 0$) generates the sample of observed data. Both Cragg (1971) and Nelson (1974) note that the selection rule generating observations on Y_{1i} need not be as closely related to the population regression function as Tobin assumed. Their models may be fit within the schema of equations 5.1 and 5.3.

For example, consider Nelson's model. Y_{1i} is observed if

$$Y_{1i} \geq Z_{2i},$$

where Z_{2i} is a random variable. In terms of the notation of equation 5.1, his model becomes $Y_{2i} = Y_{1i} - Z_{2i}$, $\beta_2 = 0$. If $Y_{2i} \geq 0$, Y_{1i} is observed, while if $Y_{2i} < 0$, Y_{1i} is observed to be zero.[4]

Elsewhere, I present a model that can be fit within the sample selection framework (Heckman, 1974b). This model will be elaborated in Section III along with the closely related models of Gronau (1974) and Lewis (1974). I note, in passing, that multivariate extensions of the preceding models, while mathematically straightforward, may be of

---

[3] Tobin assumed a normal density of U_{1i}. The conceptual logic of his model does not rely on normality.

[4] Note, however, that Y_{1i} is not, strictly speaking, a limited dependent variable, since nothing prevents Y_{1i} from becoming negative.

considerable substantive interest. Two examples are offered. One concerns migrants choosing among K prospective regions. Each person can be viewed as possessing K distinct wage functions, one for each region. If the self selection rule is to choose that region with the highest income, both the selection rule and the subsample regression functions can be simply characterized by a direct $K+1$ variable extension of the previous analysis. The second example concerns the measurement of union-nonunion wage differentials. Each person in a hypothetical population can be viewed as possessing both a union and a nonunion wage function. One self selection rule, based on the assumption of freedom of entry into unionism, is to select the unionism status with the highest wage. Estimators of wage functions based on pooled union and nonunion samples yield biased estimates of the economic return to unionism if selection into unionism status is non-random.

Before concluding this section, it is useful to clarify three concepts that are frequently confused in the literature—the concept of a truncated variable, the concept of a truncated sample, and the concept of a censored sample.

A sample is said to be censored when it is possible to use sample evidence to estimate the probability that a hypothetical observation will be observed. This is the situation assumed in the model of equations 5.1 and 5.3. A truncated sample differs from a censored sample in that the probability of sample selection cannot be estimated from observed data. A random variable is said to be truncated when its range is limited. Clearly, random variables can be truncated in either censored or truncated samples. Also, quite clearly, the operational distinction between a censored and truncated sample vanishes if there is a priori information about the probability of sample selection for a hypothetical observation. These categories often overlap. Thus in Tobin's model the sample is censored but the random variable is truncated.

II. Simple Estimators for the Case of Normally Distributed U_{1i} and U_{2i}

In this section, the model of equations 5.1, 5.3 and 5.4 is derived for the specific case of joint normality for U_{1i} and U_{2i}. The normality assumption is used in the models surveyed in Section I and is a natural starting point for any analysis. A simple estimator for this normal model is derived and discussed.

The joint distribution of U_{1i}, U_{2i}, $h(U_{1i}, U_{2i})$ is a bivariate normal density fully characterized by the assumptions stated in equation 5.2. It is permitted to be singular as in Tobin's model. Using results well known in the literature (see Johnson and Kotz, 1972, pp. 112–113, Gronau, 1974, or Lewis, 1974),

$$E(U_{1i} \mid U_{2i} > -X_{2i}\beta_2) = \frac{\sigma_{12}}{(\sigma_{22})^{1/2}} \lambda_i,$$

$$E(U_{2i} \mid U_{2i} > -X_{2i}\beta_2) = \frac{\sigma_{22}}{(\sigma_{22})^{1/2}} \lambda_i,$$

$$\lambda_i = \frac{\phi(Z_i)}{1 - \Phi(Z_i)}$$

where ϕ and Φ are, respectively, the density and distribution function for the standard normal random variable and

$$Z_i = -\frac{X_{2i}\beta_2}{(\sigma_{22})^{1/2}}.$$

"λ_i" is the inverse of Mills' ratio, and is the ratio of the ordinate of a standard normal to the tail area of the distribution. There are several important features of λ_i: (1) its denominator is the probability that a population observation with characteristics X_{2i} is selected into the observed sample $(1 - \Phi(Z)) = \Phi(-Z)$; (2) $\lambda(Z)$ is a monotone increasing function of Z and hence is a monotone decreasing function of the probability of sample selection $(1 - \Phi(Z)) = \Phi(-Z)$. In particular,

$$\lim_{Z_i \to -\infty} \lambda_i = 0, \qquad \lim_{Z_i \to \infty} \lambda_i \to \infty, \quad \text{and} \quad \frac{\partial \lambda_i}{\partial Z_i} > 0.$$

Figure 5.1 displays the relationship between λ and Φ. In samples in which the sample selection rule guarantees that all population observations have an equal chance of being sampled, $\lambda(Z)$ is zero and the least squares estimator of equation 5.1a has optimal properties.

Using these results, equation 5.5 becomes

$$E(Y_{1i} \mid X_{1i}, T_{2i} \ge 0) = X_{1i}\beta_1 + \frac{\sigma_{12}}{(\sigma_{22})^{1/2}} \lambda(Z_i), \qquad (5.6a)$$

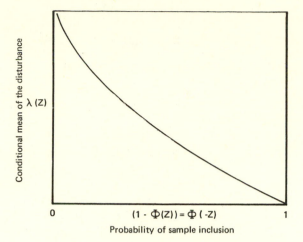

FIGURE 5.1   Probability of sample inclusion

while the comparable expression for Y_{2i} becomes

$$E(Y_{2i} \mid X_{2i}, Y_{2i} \geq 0) = X_{2i}\beta_2 + \frac{\sigma_{22}}{(\sigma_{22})^{1/2}} \lambda(Z_i). \qquad (5.6b)$$

If one could estimate Z_i and hence estimate λ_i, one could enter the latter variable as a regressor in equation 5.6a and estimate β_1 and $\sigma_{12}/(\sigma_{22})^{1/2}$ by least squares. Similarly, if one could measure Y_{2i} when $Y_{2i} \geq 0$, as in Tobin's model, knowledge of Y_{2i} and λ_i would permit direct estimation of β_2 and $(\sigma_{22})^{1/2}$. Representation 5.6a reveals that if $\sigma_{12} = 0$, so that the disturbances affecting sample selection are independent of the disturbances affecting the behavioral functions of interest, λ_i may be omitted as a regressor. Thus, if either λ or σ_{12} is zero, or both, least squares estimators of β_1 are unbiased.

The full statistical model of which equations 5.6a and 5.6b are expectations is now developed. One may write the model as

$$Y_{1i} = X_{1i}\beta_1 + \frac{\sigma_{12}}{(\sigma_{22})^{1/2}} \lambda_i + V_{1i}, \qquad (5.7a)$$

$$Y_{2i} = X_{2i}\beta_2 + \frac{\sigma_{22}}{(\sigma_{22})^{1/2}} \lambda_i + V_{2i}, \qquad (5.7b)$$

where

$$E(V_{1i} \mid X_{1i}, \lambda_i, U_{2i} \geq -X_{2i}\beta_2) = 0,$$
$$E(V_{2i} \mid X_{2i}, \lambda_i, U_{2i} \geq -X_{2i}\beta_2) = 0,$$

and

$$E(V_{ji}V_{ki'} \mid X_{1i}, X_{2i}, \lambda_i, U_{2i} \geq -X_{2i}\beta_2) = 0$$

for $i \neq i'$. It is straightforward to demonstrate that

$$E(V_{1i}^2 \mid X_{1i}, \lambda_i, U_{2i} \geq -X_{2i}\beta_2) = \sigma_{11}((1-\rho^2) + \rho^2(1 + Z_i\lambda_i - \lambda_i^2)),$$

$$(5.8a)$$

$$E(V_{1i}V_{2i} \mid X_{1i}, X_{2i}, \lambda_i, U_{2i} \geq -X_{2i}\beta_2) = \sigma_{12}(1 + Z_i\lambda_i - \lambda_i^2), \qquad (5.8b)$$

$$E(V_{2i}^2 \mid X_{2i}, \lambda_i, U_{2i} \geq -X_{2i}\beta_2) = \sigma_{22}(1 + Z_i\lambda_i - \lambda_i^2), \qquad (5.8c)$$

where

$$\rho^2 = \frac{\sigma_{12}^2}{\sigma_{11}\sigma_{22}}.$$

Moreover, one can readily verify that

$$0 \leq (1 + \lambda_i Z_i - \lambda_i^2) \leq 1. \qquad (5.9)$$

There are several important consequences of this inequality for the covariance structure of the disturbances of equations 5.7a,b. Suppose that one knows Z_i and λ_i, and enters λ_i as a regressor in equations 5.7a and 5.7b. Standard least squares estimators of the population variance of σ_{11} and σ_{22} are downward biased estimators of the appropriate parameters. Also, the standard estimator of the interequation covariance is downward biased in absolute value. Note further that if Z_i contains regressors (apart from "1"), the variances of the disturbances of equations 5.7a and 5.7b are heteroskedastic. Least squares estimators are not GLS estimators. The GLS estimators have an interesting interpretation. Unlikely observations (those with low probability of sample inclusion) receive greater weight than likely observations. This follows because the middle term in inequality 5.9 is a monotonically increasing function of the probability of sample inclusion, $1 - \Phi(Z)$.[5] Accordingly, less likely observations receive greater weight, and observations with zero probability of sample inclusion receive the greatest weight.

The GLS estimators based on known λ_i possess unusual properties, not fully developed here. In contrast with the usual case for GLS

---

[5] An elementary application of L'Hospital's rule reveals that in the limit, as $Z_i \rightarrow -\infty$, $\lambda_i \rightarrow \infty$, and $\lim E(V_{2i}^2) \rightarrow 0$. Similarly,

$$\lim_{Z_i \rightarrow -\infty} E(V_{1i}V_{2i}) = 0 \quad \text{and} \quad \lim_{Z_i \rightarrow -\infty} E(V_{1i}^2) = (1-\rho^2)\sigma_{11}.$$

estimators, parameters of the regression function enter the disturbance variance. This is seen most clearly in equations 5.7a and 5.8a. Using the definition of ρ presented below equations 5.8a–c, the coefficient on the λ_i variable in equation 5.7a may be rewritten as $\rho\sigma_{11}^{1/2}$ so that the dependence is explicit. The consequences of this dependence are interesting, although their full development is peripheral to this chapter. Nonetheless, a brief discussion of this point may be of some interest.

With known λ_i, one may use least squares to produce unbiased estimators of the regression parameters of equation 5.7a: β_1 and $\rho\sigma_{11}^{1/2}$. Using the least squares residuals from equation 5.7a, one may form a consistent estimator of σ_{11}.[6] Then, an approximate single equation GLS estimator that converges in distribution to the true single equation GLS estimator may be found by estimating equation 5.7a by weighted least squares with the estimated weights obtained from equation 5.8a. An important feature of this problem is that one round GLS estimators for equation 5.7a are not asymptotically efficient compared to the appropriate likelihood function estimator for this equation which is based on a truncated bivariate normal distribution with known points of truncation.[7]

The preceding analysis appears to be somewhat beside the point, since as a practical matter one does not know Z_i and λ_i and thus one cannot directly estimate equation 5.7a. But in the case of a censored sample, it is possible to compute the probability that an observation has missing data so that it is possible to use probit analysis to estimate Z_i and hence λ_i.

In the case of a truncated sample this is not so. However, if prior information is available on the probability that Y_{1i} is observed, it is

---

[6] Denote the residuals by $\hat{V}_{1i}$. Since λ_i and Z_i are known, and since $\rho\sigma_{11}^{1/2}$ is estimated, one can estimate

$$\sigma_{11} = \frac{\sum \hat{V}_{1i}^2}{T} - \frac{\rho^2\sigma_{11}}{T}\sum (\lambda_i Z_i - \lambda_i^2).$$

This yields a *consistent* estimate of the variance that is guaranteed to be positive. Note, however, that nothing in the procedure guarantees a value of $|\rho|$ inside the unit interval, although in large samples it must lie in that interval.

[7] This is so because ρ and σ_{11} appear in the regression coefficients and in the variance, so the information matrix is not block diagonal. An iterative likelihood estimator based on the initial consistent estimates previously discussed is asymptotically efficient. Also, note that the assumption that λ_i is known implies that $\beta_2/\sigma_{22}^{1/2}$ is known. Hence a "single equation" estimator is fully efficient.

possible to estimate Z_i and λ_i so that prior information on the probability of sample inclusion eliminates the distinction between censored and truncated samples.

In the censored case, the probit likelihood function is

$$\mathcal{L} = \prod_{i=1}^{I} [\Phi(Z_i)]^{d_i}[\Phi(-Z_i)]^{1-d_i}, \qquad (5.10)$$

where d_i denotes the event "observation of Y_{1i}." Under the standard conditions for identification in probit analysis (see Nerlove and Press, 1973), one may consistently estimate $\beta_2/\sigma_{22}^{1/2}$, and hence Z_i and λ_i. The estimated λ_i may be substituted for the actual λ_i in the preceding analysis.

In Appendix A, the asymptotic distribution is derived for the least squares estimator based on an estimated λ_i instead of the actual λ_i. The least squares estimators are consistent and asymptotically normally distributed. Moreover, in the important special case of the null hypothesis of no selection bias (e.g., $\sigma_{12} = 0$ in equation 5.7a), the standard least squares estimator of the variance-covariance matrix of the regression coefficients is the appropriate estimator. However, if $\sigma_{12} \neq 0$, the standard estimator is inappropriate and the formula A.2 in Appendix A should be used instead. In this Appendix it is also demonstrated that if $\sigma_{12} \neq 0$, the "standard" least squares variance-covariance matrix that treats λ_i as known *understates* the true standard errors for the estimated regression coefficients. Hence if $\sigma_{12} \neq 0$, "t" tests based on the "usual" variance-covariance matrix are upward biased.

As in the case of exact GLS estimators based on known values of λ_i, approximate GLS estimators are not asymptotically efficient, nor do they converge in distribution to GLS estimators based on known λ_i, except in the important special case of a null hypothesis of no selection bias. To achieve asymptotically efficient estimators, maximum likelihood estimators must be employed. Those suggested here provide initial consistent estimators for the likelihood equations so that a one-step iteration (Rothenberg and Leenders, 1964) yields estimates that are asymptotically efficient. Thus the task of computing efficient estimates is simplified, and the problem of locating a starting value for likelihood function iterations is resolved. Elsewhere (Heckman, 1976) it is shown that in a particular application the initial consistent estimators discussed here closely approximate the likelihood maximizing parameter estimators.

III. New Estimates of Female Labor Supply Functions and Wage Functions Free of Selection Bias: New Tests of an Old Model

A. THE MODEL

In this section, the techniques of Section II are applied to estimate the labor supply and wage functions of married women. In the absence of fixed costs of entering and leaving the labor market, and under the assumption that workers are free to choose their hours of work, two functions fully characterize the labor supply decision.

The first function is the market wage function for the woman, Y_{1i}, defined by equation 5.1a. The second function is the reservation wage that records the value that a woman places on her time if she does not work (W_i^*). If the market wage exceeds the reservation wage ($Y_{1i} > W_i^*$), a woman works and her hours of work adjust so that in equilibrium the marginal value of her time equals her market wage rate.

Under certain simplifying assumptions elaborated more fully elsewhere (Heckman, 1974b), hours of work, h_i, are proportional to the gap between market wages and reservation wages. Denoting this proportionality factor by $1/\gamma$, and letting $Y_{2i} = Y_{1i} - W_i^*$ be the gap, one is led to the following model:

$$E(Y_{1i} \mid X_{1i}, Y_{2i} > 0) = X_{1i}\beta_1 + E(U_{1i} \mid U_{2i} > -X_{2i}\beta_2), \qquad (5.11a)$$

$$E(h_i \mid X_{1i}, X_{2i}, Y_{2i} > 0) = \frac{1}{\gamma} E(Y_{2i} \mid X_{1i}, X_{2i}, Y_{2i} > 0)$$

$$= \frac{X_{2i}\beta_2}{\gamma} + \frac{1}{\gamma} E(U_{2i} \mid U_{2i} > -X_{2i}\beta_2),$$

$$(5.11b)$$

$$\gamma > 0. \qquad (5.11c)$$

This model differs from the sample selection model of equations 5.1a and 5.1b in one important respect. Unlike the case in equation 5.1b, there is information about Y_{2i} up to a factor proportionality $(1/\gamma)$ if a woman works ($Y_{2i} \geq 0$). The decision function that characterizes labor force entry, which is the sample selection rule for this model, is closely related to the hours of work equation. The model of Lewis (1974) and Gronau (1974) is exactly the model of equations 5.1a and 5.1b and does not utilize the potential source of information that closely links the participation decision and the labor supply function.

From inspection of equations 5.11a and 5.11b, it is clear that both wage and hours of work functions may be subject to selection bias. Least squares estimators of the wage and hours function fit for working women confound the parameters of the sample selection function with the parameters of the behavioral function of interest.

This is not to say that estimates of wage or labor supply functions fit on subsamples of working women are of no interest. A regression model that deletes the conditional expectation of the error terms approximates a function with a well-defined interpretation. Consider equation 5.11b. The same set of variables (X_2) appears in the regression function and in the conditional mean of U_2. If one deletes the conditional mean, to a first order approximation a regression equation estimates the vector

$$\frac{\hat{\beta}_2}{\gamma} = \frac{\beta_2}{\gamma} + \frac{1}{\gamma} \frac{\partial E(U_{2i} \mid U_{2i} > -X_{2i}\beta_2)}{\partial X_{2i}}.$$

Thus ordinary least squares coefficients estimate the effect of a variable moving along the behavioral function, the first term, and the effect of the variable in sorting people out in the taste distribution, the second term.

To clarify this decomposition, a concrete example may be helpful. Let vector X_{2i} consist of one variable—say, ability to perform market tasks. Ability is expected to increase the supply of hours to the market for a working woman $(\beta_2/\gamma > 0)$. Moreover, ability is expected to increase the probability that a woman works. But this means that as one samples across working women with greater ability, one is sampling women with progressively lower *average* tastes for work

$$\left(\frac{\partial E(U_{2i} \mid U_{2i} > -X_{2i}\beta_2)}{\partial X_{2i}} < 0\right).$$

Thus the regression coefficient on the ability variable is a downward biased estimator of β_2/γ.

Estimates of β_2/γ answer the question, "what is the *average* effect of an additional unit of ability on the labor supply of women already working?" Economic theory provides a guide to the sign and magnitude of this coefficient. Estimates of $\hat{\beta}_2/\gamma$ answer the question, "what is the change in the average labor supply of women when one moves across ability groups?" These estimates give the basic ingredients required to estimate the aggregate labor supply curve. Given a distribution of ability in the population, one can add up the average labor supply at each ability class to compute aggregate labor supply.[8] Typically, economic theory does not directly yield predictions about this parameter, which combines parameters describing movements along a given labor supply function with the parameters determining the entry of workers into the labor force.

The parameter $1/\gamma$ plays a crucial role in this analysis, and may be interpreted as the uncompensated effect of a change in wage rates on labor supply. From equation 5.11b it is not clear how this parameter may be estimated. Recall that Y_{2i} is defined as the difference between market wages and reservation wages ($Y_{1i} - W_i^*$). To demonstrate how γ can be estimated, one may introduce an explicit function for W_i^*,

$$W_i^* = N_i \psi + \varepsilon,$$

and note that

$$h_i = \frac{Y_{2i}}{\gamma} \equiv \frac{Y_{1i} - W_i^*}{\gamma} = \frac{X_{1i}\beta_1 - N_i\psi}{\gamma} + \frac{1}{\gamma}(U_{1i} - \varepsilon_i). \qquad (5.12)$$

It is clear that if one variable appears in X_{1i} that does not appear in N_i, such as the market human capital of the wife, then given estimates of equation 5.11a, one can estimate both γ and ψ. Note, too, that one can follow conventions in simultaneous equation theory to avoid the multiplicity of estimates of γ that arise in the overidentified case, if one inserts estimates of β_1 (obtained from 5.11a) to generate a predicted value of wage rates in 5.12, i.e., denoting such estimates by $\hat{\beta}_1$, estimating

$$\frac{Y_{2i}}{\gamma} = \frac{X_{1i}\hat{\beta}_1 - N_i\psi}{\gamma} + \frac{1}{\gamma}(U_{1i} - \varepsilon_i) + \frac{1}{\gamma}X_{1i}(\beta_1 - \hat{\beta}_1),$$

where the final term vanishes in large samples.

[8] More precisely, equation 5.11b multiplied by the probability that a woman works, yields an estimate of the average hours supplied to the market by women with traits X_{1i}, X_{2i}.

The crucial feature of labor supply function 5.12 is that the supply of labor is assumed to be a function of the gap between market wages and reservation wages. This gap, in turn, is a measure of the probability that a woman works. Thus a strong assumption of this formulation is that a woman more likely to work is also more likely to supply more labor when she works.

Over the empirically relevant range, the labor supply curve may become backward bending ($\gamma < 0$). Moreover, as noted by Cogan (Chapter 7) and Hanoch (Chapter 6), fixed costs of entry and exit may alter the simple relationship of equations 5.11b and 5.12, and may even result in opposite signs for the effect of certain variables on labor supply and participation.

As an example, consider the effect of money costs of child care. Holding everything else the same, the greater the number of preschool children, the greater the cost of child care, and hence the less likely is the event that a woman works. However, *given that a woman works*, greater expenditure on child care results in a reduction of income and hence an expansion in hours worked if leisure time is a normal good. Time indivisibilities in the availability of child care, and commutation costs tend to reinforce the work-increasing effect of child-care costs.[9]

It is straightforward to extend the model of equations 5.11a–c to allow for these effects. A more general model is the three-equation system,

$$Y_{1i} = X_{1i}\beta_1 + U_{1i} \tag{5.13a}$$

$$Y_{2i} = X_{2i}\beta_2 + U_{2i} \tag{5.13b}$$

$$h_i = Y_{3i} = X_{2i}\beta_3 + U_{3i}, \tag{5.13c}$$

$$E(U_{ji}) = 0, \qquad E(U_{ji}U_{j'i'}) = \sigma_{jj'} \qquad i = i'$$
$$= 0 \text{ otherwise.}$$

As before, a woman works and her hours are positive if and only if $Y_{2i} > 0$. A noteworthy feature of equations 5.13b and 5.13c is that the

---

[9] Obviously, *time* costs decrease leisure consumed but need not decrease hours of work. Writing the leisure demand function in terms of wage rates W and full income ($WT + A$) where A is asset income and T is total time available, $L = F(W, WT + A)$, $\partial L/\partial T = F_2 W$, $\partial h/\partial T = (1 - F_2 W)$. Since F_2 is positive, the sign of the derivative is ambiguous unless it is assumed that consumption is a normal good. If consumption is normal, $F_2 W < 1$, and $\partial h/\partial T > 0$. In this case, greater time costs result in a decrease in hours of work.

same set of variables determines the participation decision and the quantity of hours supplied. Under the null hypothesis that equation 5.11b is correct, β_2 and β_3 are equal up to a constant of proportionality $(\beta_2 = \beta_3/\gamma)$ and the joint distribution of the U_{ji} is a singular trivariate density. Assuming normality for the U_{ji} one can write

$$E(Y_{1i} \mid X_{2i}, Y_{2i} > 0) = X_{1i}\beta_1 + \frac{\sigma_{12}}{(\sigma_{22})^{1/2}} \lambda_i, \qquad (5.14a)$$

$$E(T_{3i} - h_i \mid X_{2i}, Y_{2i} > 0) = X_{2i}\beta_3 + \frac{\sigma_{23}}{(\sigma_{22})^{1/2}} \lambda_i \qquad (5.14b)$$

using the same definition of λ_i given before.[10]

B. MAIN EMPIRICAL RESULTS

The data utilized in the empirical analysis are a sample of 1,735 women taken from the 1967 National Longitudinal Survey of Work Experience of Women Age 30–44 (The "Parnes" data) who are white, married with spouse present with husbands working in the previous year (1966). A woman is classified as working if she worked for pay in 1966 and satisfied the other sample selection criteria. Using this definition, 812 of the women worked in 1966. The primary data source is described elsewhere in detail (Shea et al., 1970). A more complete description of the means of the data used here and the sources of sample attrition is provided in Appendix B.1.

Given current professional ignorance about the appropriate dimension of labor supply, a variety of measures could be utilized. In this study, a measure of annual labor supply is used that is obtained by dividing annual earnings in 1966 by a questionnaire wage asked in early 1967. A careful examination of the data suggests that this is the most reliable available measure. (See Hall, 1973, who also uses a similar measure in his work.) Another, more conventional, measure of annual labor supply could have been used: the product of "weeks worked in 1966" and "usual hours worked in a week." A defect of the

[10] Note that equation 5.13c is cast in terms of *Hours* of work. Technically speaking, hours should be treated as a limited dependent variable. In the empirical analysis presented below, I ignore that complication. Since hours of work distributions are concentrated far away from zero, it is possible to use log hours rather than hours in a more general formulation.

second measure vis-à-vis the first is that "weeks worked" includes vacation time and sick leave—two important margins of labor supply adjustment. Further, the second measure appears to exhibit too much bunching in standard intervals, as is suggested by inspection of the histograms of both "weeks worked" and "usual weekly hours" presented in Appendix C. (These histograms are computed only for working women.) The distribution of annual hours of work obtained by dividing reported earnings by the questionnaire wage rate (given in the third chart of Appendix C) exhibits much less bunching in standard intervals and bunching away from zero hours of work than the conventional measures of labor supply. It is precisely this bunching away from zero that has stimulated recent work that introduces fixed costs into the analysis of labor supply behavior (Cogan, Chapter 7; Hanoch, Chapter 6). Accordingly, it is not surprising to find the result reported below that with the measure of labor supply used in this paper, there is correspondingly less empirical evidence in favor of models with fixed costs of work.[11]

The specification of the economic relationships is conventional and requires little comment. Following Mincer (1974), the logarithm of wage rates is assumed to depend on schooling and market experience. Experience is defined as the number of years since leaving school that a woman has worked six months or longer. Following much previous research, female labor supply is postulated to depend on wage rates of the head and wife, the presence of children, family assets, and wife's education.

Recent work by the author (Heckman (1977, 1978)) presents evidence that the labor market experience of the wife cannot be treated

---

[11] It is important not to oversell the measure used here. First, as pointed out to me by Steve Sandell of Ohio State University, for many observations who report only annual earnings, the "questionnaire wage" is obtained by dividing annual earnings by the conventional measure of labor supply. For these observations, the measure of labor supply used in this study is *exactly* the same as the conventional measure. In the data used here, roughly 40 percent of the observations would have the same labor supply measured in either way, and thus, the measure I use is not entirely free of the bias discussed in the text. It is just less error-ridden. Second, one disadvantage of this choice of labor supply measure is that some women who worked in 1966 did not supply a questionnaire wage. However, only 5 percent of the sample is lost for this reason. Finally, it would be preferable to utilize the information on labor supply available from both measures and the nature of any systematic bias in each—information not at my disposal. Accordingly, I opt for what appears to be the better of the two available measures.

as an exogenous variable in the participation decision. (Evidence on this is offered below.) This variable records the wife's previous work history and is highly correlated with unmeasured determinants of current labor force participation. The empirical analysis that follows explicitly deals with the endogeneity issue; considerable support is found for endogeneity of experience in labor supply and participation equations, but little evidence is found in support of the notion of endogeneity of experience in wage functions. Estimates of labor supply functions that purge "experience" of its endogeneous component produce more plausible labor supply estimates.

The structure of the discussion of the empirical results is as follows. First, estimates of equation 5.13b are discussed. Then estimates of the labor supply and wage functions are presented. Finally, some tests of the simple model of equations 5.11a and 5.11b are performed in a separate section.

Table 5.1 records the estimates of the $(\sigma_{22}^{1/2})$ normalized coefficients of equation 5.13b which generates the probability that a woman works. The first column presents estimates based on the assumption that experience is exogenous. The second column presents estimates based on predicted experience. The instrumental variables used to predict experience are reported below the table.

As expected from a reading of the literature, the presence of small children and a higher husband's wage rate lower the probability that a randomly selected woman works. Women with greater education are more likely to work. For both sets of estimates, greater work experience raises the probability of participation, although both the size of the effect, and its statistical significance, are diminished when predicted experience is used in place of the actual variable in the estimation of the probit coefficients. A straightforward application of the Wu (1973) test rejects the null hypothesis that "experience" is uncorrelated with the error term in 5.13b.[12]

Following the methodology outlined in Section II, the probit coefficient estimates may be used consistently to estimate $\beta_2/\sigma_{22}^{1/2}$, Z_i, and hence $\lambda(Z_i)$. Hourly wage regressions with and without these estimated

---

[12] The Wu test as used here consists of entering both "experience" and the residual of "experience" from predicted "experience" in the probit function. If the coefficient on the residual is significantly different from zero, one rejects the null hypothesis of uncorrelatedness of experience with the error term. The test statistic for this model gave a "t" of 2.1.

TABLE 5.1: Probit Estimates of the Parameters Determining the Probability that a Woman Works (Equation 5.13b)
(Asymptotic normal statistics in parentheses)

| | $\beta_2/(\sigma_{22})^{1/2}$ | |
	(1) Estimates that Treat "Experience" as Exogenous	(2) Estimates that Treat "Experience" as Endogenous
Intercept	$-.817$ (4.7)	$-.412$ (1.56)
No. of children less than 6	$-.504$ (10)	$-.493$ (9.11)
Assets	$.436 \times 10^{-7}$ (.25)	$.619 \times 10^{-6}$ (.29)
Husband's hourly wage rate ($/hr.)	$-.177$ (8.0)	$-.167$ (7.81)
Wife's labor market experience (yrs.)	$.098$ (15.0)	$.046$ (1.81)
Wife's education	$.080$ (15.3)	$.074$ (5.3)
Log likelihood	-920.9	-1073.1
Observations	1735	1735

The probability that woman i works is given by the standard probability integral,

$$P(x) = \frac{1}{\sqrt{2\pi}} \int_{-\infty}^{x} e^{-t^2/2} \, dt,$$

where

$$x = X'_{2i}\beta_2(\sigma_{22})^{-1/2}$$

The instrumental variables used to predict experience are linear and squared terms for children less than six, 1967 assets, husband's age, husband's education, husband's hourly wage, wife's education, and interactions of all linear terms.

regressors are presented in Table 5.2, which also presents some evidence on the endogeneity of experience in the wage function. Column 1 gives the estimates of the traditional wage function. The estimates of the traditional equation corrected for censoring, but assuming experience to be exogenous, are presented in column 2. There is some indication of sample censoring, but it is not overwhelming. The test statistic on "λ" in column 2 is only marginal, and the wage coefficient estimates are essentially unchanged from column 1. Columns 3 and 4 record the results of an analysis that predicts

TABLE 5.2: Results for Hourly Wage Rates (Equation 5.13a)
(Asymptotic normal statistics in parentheses)

Variables	(1) Traditional Regression	(2) Traditional Regression Corrected for Censoring	(3)* Traditional Regression Corrected for Endogeneity	(4)* Traditional Regression Corrected for Endogeneity and Censoring
Wife's labor market experience (yrs.)	.0167 (7.85)	.0207 (5.99)	.003 (.33)	.0151 (1.2)
Wife's education (yrs.)	.0763 (13.6)	.0779 (13.7)	.074 (12.7)	.076 (12.8)
λ	· · ·	.0878 (1.48)	· · ·	.1002 (1.4)
Intercept	−.401	−.515	−.226	−.419
R^2	.230	.235	.168	.1709
Wu statistic†	· · ·	· · ·	.34 (t)	1.17 (F)

* The instrumental variables for experience are listed in Table 5.1.
† The Wu statistic is the "t" score on the residual of predicted experience from actual experience in column 3 and is the "F" score on this residual and the residual between predicted λ and actual λ (based on measured experience). Predicted λ is obtained from a regression of λ based on measured experience on polynomials in the instrumental variables.

experience and tests whether or not regression specifications based on predicted experience differ significantly from regression specifications with actual experience. Inspection of the Wu statistic on the bottom line of columns 3 and 4 suggests that the endogeneity of experience is not an important issue in the estimation of the coefficients of the wage function. In my judgment, there is little basis for preferring the estimates in column 1 over those in column 2. There is some evidence in favor of the hypothesis of selectivity bias in estimating female wage functions only for working women, but it is not strong. An appeal to simplicity would argue for preferring the wage estimates presented in column 1 over those presented in column 2. However, appeal to previous work (Gronau, 1974) suggests that selectivity is an important problem in estimating female wage functions, so that the estimates given in column 2 are preferred. Since I find this prior evidence compelling, I favor the estimates presented in column 2.

The story with respect to the estimates of the labor supply functions is different. There is strong evidence for both sample censoring and

TABLE 5.3: Annual Hours Worked Defined by Dividing Earnings by Wage Rates (Equation 5.13c)
(Asymptotic normal statistics in parentheses)

Variables	(1) Traditional Regression	(2) Traditional Regression Corrected for Censoring	(3) Traditional Regression w/Experience Treated as Endogenous	(4) Traditional Regression Corrected for Censoring w/ Exper. Treated as Endogenous	(5)† Marginal Effect of Variables from (4) Evaluated at Sample Mean
No. of children less than 6	-155.8 (3.73)	-94.1 (.93)	-141.04 (2.61)	-925.1 (2.75)	-207.2
Assets ($)	3.1×10^{-3} (.18)	3.2×10^{-3} (.191)	3.2×10^{-3} (.17)	3.1×10^{-3} (.17)	$+3.1 \times 10^{-3}$
Husband's hourly wage rate ($/hr.)	-33.1 (1.9)	-12.4 (.35)	-16.9 (.9)	-275.4 (2.5)	-32.9
Wife's experience (yrs.)	48.6 (12.1)	39.1 (2.66)	57.2 (2.55)	128.9 (3.4)	60.0
Wife's education (yrs.)	21.1 (1.89)	11.7 (.66)	10.9 (.89)	119.5 (2.5)	11.70
λ	$\cdots$	-201.8 (.67)	$\cdots$	2401 (2.36)	$\cdots$
Intercept	664.2	912.1	765.1	-1755	$\cdots$
R^2	.17	.176	.115	.121	$\cdots$
Wu statistic*	$\cdots$	$\cdots$	3.1 (t)	9.8 (F)	$\cdots$
Implied labor supply elasticity w/respect to hourly wage rates‡	1.81	1.45	2.12	4.83	2.23

* The Wu statistic is explained in Table 5.2.
† These estimates are obtained from the coefficients in column 4 added to the effect of the variable on the conditional mean of the disturbance, $(\partial \lambda / \partial X_{2i})$, multiplied by the coefficient on λ(2401).
‡ These estimates are obtained by dividing the experience coefficient in the wage function (from the second column of Table 5.2, i.e., .0207) into the experience coefficient in the labor supply function, and dividing by average labor supply (1289 hours) for working women.

endogeneity of experience. The estimates of the traditional regression specification are displayed in column 1 of Table 5.3. These estimates are in agreement with those in previous studies and need little comment. The regression estimates recorded in column 2 are unreasonable. There is little evidence of sample censoring, but the coefficients of the equation are not fit with much precision. Column 3 differs from column 1 in that experience is treated as an endogenous variable. The result of the Wu test applied to this equation strongly rejects the null hypothesis that experience is an exogenous or predetermined variable.

Column 4 displays the estimates of the labor supply function accounting for sample censoring and endogeneity of experience. The null hypothesis that experience is predetermined and the null hypothesis of no censoring are both rejected. Accordingly, the estimates in column 4 are offered as the best in this table.

A comparison of columns 3 and 4 reveals important differences. Except for insignificant coefficients, all of the slope coefficients in the labor supply equation presented in column 4 are larger in absolute value than the coefficients in column 3. The elasticity of labor supply in the column 3 estimates is high, but not too much outside the range of estimates presented by Schultz (Chapter 1). The elasticity of 4.8 derived from the specification in column 4 seems unduly large and requires some comment.

The important point to note is that traditional estimates of the coefficients of labor supply functions of working women confound two effects: movement along a given labor supply function for working women, and movement across taste distributions. Thus, for example, presence of an additional child under six has a dramatically negative effect on hours of work for a working woman (−925 hours reduction in supply). But *working* women with an additional child have a greater average taste for market work, since only the most work-prone women remain at work after the "imposition" of a child.

The two separate effects for each variable can be combined and evaluated at the sample mean. The result of such combination is displayed in column 5. By and large there is close agreement between the coefficients of column 3, which are estimates of the combined effect, and the coefficients in column 5. In particular, the estimates of the wage elasticities are in very close agreement.

The conclusion to be drawn from the labor supply analysis is that traditional methods of estimating labor supply functions on samples of working women give a downward biased (in absolute value) estimate of the true effect of economic variables. The estimates presented here reveal a strong behavioral response to wage changes which is not discordant with previous estimates, but which casts a new light on their interpretation.[13]

A final feature of the estimates presented in column 4 is worth noting. The coefficient on "λ" is large and positive.[14] This suggests that unmeasured factors that raise the probability of participation also tend to increase the volume of labor supplied to the market. The sign of the correlation is in accord with that predicted by the simple model of equations 5.11a and 5.11b.

[13] The estimated labor supply elasticity reported in column 3 is similar to an estimate of 2.3 reported by Harvey Rosen (1976), who uses the same data set. Rosen uses Tobit analysis to estimate his labor supply model. His elasticity is computed for hours of work defined as the expected hours of work for all women in the sample. Thus his labor supply elasticity is for the measure, while the elasticity reported in column 3 of Table 5.3,

$$E(h_i \mid X_{1i}, X_{2i}, Y_{2i} > 0) \, \text{Prob} \, (Y_{2i} > 0 \mid X_{1i}, X_{2i})$$

is taken with respect to the first term in the product, i.e., expected hours of work of *working women* (the second term in the product is the probability of participation). Neither elasticity is an estimate of a Hicks-Slutsky substitution effect. However, given that the probability of participation is positively related to wage rates, Rosen's estimated wage elasticity should overstate that obtained from the estimates reported in column 3 of Table 5.3, and it does.

[14] A number of people (especially Nick Kiefer and Jim Smith) have commented that the estimated coefficient on λ presented in column 4 of Table 5.3 is "too large." From equation 5.14b it is clear that the coefficient is $\rho_{23}\sigma_{33}^{1/2}$ where ρ_{23} is the correlation coefficient between the unobservables determining the *latent variable* that underlies the hours of work function, and the unobservables in the participation function, and where σ_{33} is the variance in the unobserved variables determining hours of work. Taken at face value, the estimated value of 2401 would seem to imply that the standard deviation in hours of work is at least 2401 hours, a large and apparently implausible number.

This interpretation is somewhat misleading since the standard deviation estimate is not for hours worked but for the residual determining the *latent variable* that generates hours of work. The latter variable could have (and indeed does have) a much greater variance than does the disturbance in an hours of work equation. Note also that the mean value of λ in the sample of working women is .642 (see Appendix B). Over the relevant range of the sample, large changes in values of the variables that determine λ (i.e., the Z) result in small changes in the value of λ. Thus the large value of the coefficient on λ does not imply that the estimated labor supply function is "unduly" sensitive to changes in Z variables that operate through λ, at least for the sort of variation observed in the sample used in this chapter.

C. TESTS OF THE SIMPLE MODEL OF EQUATIONS 5.11a AND 5.11b AND A
REVISED MODEL

In this section, some informal tests of the simple model of equations
5.11a and 5.11b are conducted.[15] Most, but not all, of the restrictions
predicted by the model are in accord with the data. An expanded
version of the simple model is offered that allows for the effect of
variation in the availability of informal day-care arrangements
(documented in Heckman, 1974a) as well as variation in the fixed costs
of work examined by Cogan (Chapter 7) and Hanoch (Chapter 6). The
structure of this section is as follows. First, informal tests are discussed.
Then, a revised model is offered.

As previously noted, one implication of the simple model of equations 5.11a and 5.11b is proportionality between the estimates of
$\beta_2/\sigma_{22}^{1/2}$ from the probit function and the parameters of the labor
supply function β_3, i.e.,

$$\beta_3 = \left(\frac{\sigma_{22}^{1/2}}{\gamma}\right)\beta_2/\sigma_{22}^{1/2}.$$

The constant of proportionality is predicted to be positive.

The ratios of the probit coefficient estimates (taken from column 2
of Table 5.1) to the hours of work coefficient estimates (presented in
column 4 of Table 5.3) are displayed in Table 5.4. Given the sampling
error in estimating these coefficients, the ratios are remarkably close to
each other. The agreement is closer yet if one examines only the ratios
of coefficients that are statistically significant in both equations. These
ratios are denoted by an asterisk.

A second test of the simple model is available. From equations 5.7b
and 5.11b, one can write the hours of work function as

$$h_i = \frac{\sigma_{22}^{1/2}}{\gamma}(-Z_i + \lambda_i) + \frac{1}{\gamma}V_{2i}.$$

[15] Several people have asked why I did not perform an exact likelihood ratio test of
the simple model (of equations 5.11a and 5.11b) against the more general model (of
equations 5.13a–c). Clearly one can use a likelihood ratio test to test the hypothesis that
$\beta_2 = \beta_3/\gamma$, provided that the covariance matrix of the three-equation system is left
unrestricted. But for equations 5.11a and 5.11b to hold strictly, the covariance matrix of
the three-equation system must become degenerate, i.e., the correlation between U_{3i}
and U_{2i} must be one. Thus a *full test* of the model is proportionality *and* singularity of
the covariance matrix. Testing the latter implication creates a problem. Since the
correlation coefficient cannot exceed one, the standard argument for application of a
likelihood ratio test or a Wald test is invalid, and so standard procedures are not
available. In this study, I opt for simple tests and defer more complete testing for
another occasion.

TABLE 5.4: Ratio of Probit Coefficients $(\beta_2/\sigma_{22}^{1/2})$ to Labor Supply Function Coefficients (β_3)

Intercept	No. of Children Less than 6	Assets	Husband's Hourly Wage Rate	Wife's Labor Market Experience	Wife's Education
$.23 \times 10^{-3}$	$.53 \times 10^{-3}$*	$.19 \times 10^{-3}$	$.61 \times 10^{-3}$*	$.36 \times 10^{-3}$	$.62 \times 10^{-3}$*

* Denotes a ratio of coefficients that are statistically significant at conventional levels in both relationships.

TABLE 5.5: Estimates of Equation 5.15

k (from regression coefficient)	Standard Error of Estimate (from regression residuals)
1424 (t stat. is 46)	1221

TABLE 5.6: Labor Supply Comparisons with the "Tobit" Model

	"Tobit" Estimates	Estimates from Table 5.3, Column 4
No. of children less than 6	−658.5 (9.5)	−925.1 (2.78)
Assets ($)	$.24 \times 10^{-2}$ (.9)	$.3 \times 10^{-2}$ (.2)
Husband's hourly wage rate ($/hr.)	−201.4 (7.6)	−275.4 (2.5)
Wife's experience* (yrs.)	87.02 (5.1)	128.9 (3.4)
Wife's education (yr.)	88.0 (5.1)	119.5 (2.5)
Intercept	−669 (2.0)	−1755
Estimated standard error of regression $(\sigma_{22}^{1/2}/\gamma)$	1409	$\cdots$
Ln likelihood	−7595.53	$\cdots$

* Predicted experience as defined in Table 5.1.

The variables in parentheses can be estimated from the probit coefficients. From equation 5.8c, the variance in the residual in the second term is given by

$$E(V_{2i}^2) = \left(\frac{\sigma_{22}^{1/2}}{\gamma}\right)^2 (1 + \lambda_i Z_i - \lambda_i^2).$$

Thus another test of the simple model can be conducted. Run the following weighted regression without intercept:

$$h_i w_i = k(-Z_i + \lambda_i) w_i + \varepsilon_i, \tag{5.15}$$

where $w_i = (1 + \lambda_i Z_i - \lambda_i^2)^{-1/2}$. The regression coefficient is a consistent estimator of $\sigma_{2y}^{1/2}/\gamma$, which is the square root of the residual variance in the estimated equation. A test of the simple model is to compare the square root of the estimated residual variance with the regression coefficient. This comparison is made in Table 5.5. The agreement between the two estimates is remarkably close. Moreover, as previously discussed in the first paragraph of this section, the constant of proportionality estimated in Table 5.4 is the inverse of $\sigma_{22}^{1/2}/\gamma$. Using $.6 \times 10^{-3}$ as an estimate of the average ratio, another estimate of $\sigma_{22}^{1/2}/\gamma$ is 1,666, again a number close to the regression coefficient estimate.

Other informal tests of the simple model are possible. If equation 5.11b is the labor supply function, the model of Tobin, discussed in Section I ("Tobit") is an appropriate description of it. Estimated Tobit coefficients are displayed in Table 5.6. "Tobit" *underestimates* (in absolute value) the coefficients of the labor supply function.[16] Except for the intercept term, each "Tobit" coefficient is about seven-tenths of the corresponding coefficient of the unrestricted labor supply estimates, reproduced in the second column of Table 5.6. Note, however, that the estimated standard error of the Tobit regression (1,409) is remarkably close to the previous estimate (1,424) obtained from equation 5.15.

At this point it may be helpful to take stock of what has been learned. The simple model is almost right. The "Tobit" estimates of the slope coefficients are smaller (in absolute value) than the initial consistent estimates, but by a constant of proportionality (.7). The only discordance in this pattern comes in the estimates of the intercept

---

[16] This understatement of Tobit coefficients suggests that the Schultz (Chapter 1) estimates of female labor supply elasticities, based on Tobit, are downward biased.

terms. The Tobit intercept is disproportionately larger than the unrestricted labor supply intercept—more so than the ratio of slope coefficients would suggest is appropriate.

The model of equations 5.11a–c and 5.12 may be modified slightly to rationalize this pattern. First it is useful to review the economics of the simple model. To focus ideas, suppose the wage function (corresponding to equation 5.11a) is

$$W = \alpha_0 + \alpha_1 E + U, \tag{5.16a}$$

while the reservation wage function (i.e., value of time) is

$$W^* = \gamma_0 + \gamma_1 h + \gamma_2 A + \varepsilon, \tag{5.16b}$$

where ε, U are disturbances, E is (exogenous) experience, A is asset income, and h is time not spent at home. The simple theory assumes that $\alpha_1 > 0$, $\gamma_1 > 0$, $\gamma_2 > 0$. A woman works if $W > W^*$ at zero hours of work, i.e.,

$$\alpha_0 + \alpha_1 E + U > \gamma_0 + \gamma_2 A + \varepsilon. \tag{5.17}$$

Her labor supply function is obtained by equating 5.16a and 5.16b when inequality 5.17 is met, i.e.,

$$h = \frac{1}{\gamma_1}(\alpha_0 + \alpha_1 E - \gamma_0 - \gamma_2 A) + \frac{U - \varepsilon}{\gamma}. \tag{5.18}$$

Suppose that there are work-related costs such as day care and other household expenses. Recent evidence (Heckman, 1974a) suggests that some women have access to limited quantities of low-cost day care and other household services from friends and neighbors. An analytically simple way to characterize such limited availability of low-cost substitutes is to view it as an augmentation of the woman's time budget that expands available time by less than one hour *for each hour worked* up to some given number of working hours. A consequence of the limited availability of low-cost substitutes is a discontinuity in the labor supply function at the given number of hours.

Figure 5.2 illustrates this case. The solid line AA' is the labor supply curve for a woman of given characteristics who uses market substitutes for her time. Market substitutes for the wife's household input are assumed to be available at fixed marginal prices. The reservation wage for such women is given by A.[17] The line, $BEFG$, illustrates a labor

[17] As discussed by Brumm (1976), no *unique* reservation wage is defined if there are such work-related costs. Nevertheless, the extension of the labor supply curve to A defines a wage that plays the same role as the reservation wage in a model with no work-related costs.

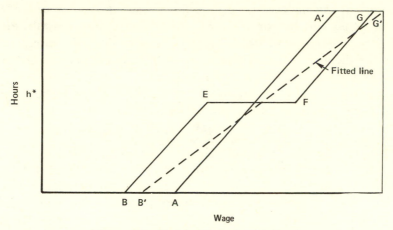

FIGURE 5.2   Model with work-related costs

supply curve for a woman who has access to informal sources that (imperfectly) replace her time at home up to h^* hours. Note that this woman has a lower reservation wage, B, than the other woman, but that beyond h^* hours, it takes a greater wage rate to induce her to work more hours. This is so because of the wealth effect that arises from her access to low-cost sources, and from the assumption that leisure is a normal good. The population of all women contains a mixture of women with the two types of labor supply functions.

In a general model it is plausible that both slopes and intercepts of labor supply functions are affected by the limited availability of low-cost substitutes for the woman's time. Before more elaborate models are explored, it is useful to examine more fully the implications of the simple model depicted in Figure 5.2.

Given a distribution of the two types of labor supply functions in the population, and given that some women with a "broken" labor supply function have hours of work in excess of h^*, the average reservation wage in the population (defined as the minimum acceptable wage required to induce the women to work) is *less* than the average of the estimated intercepts of the labor supply functions. In a model that ignores interpersonal variation in the cost of household substitutes, the two measures coincide so that the average of the intercepts is the average of the reservation wages. An important consequence of the inequality of reservation wages and intercepts is that if variation in costs of child care and domestic service of the sort considered here is important, any empirical procedure that constrains the intercept of the labor supply equation to be the reservation wage *understates* the effect of wages (and other variables) on labor supply. This point is important because the model of equations 5.11a–5.11b and the Tobit model both impose this constraint on the data.

To establish this result intuitively, note that by using equations 5.16a and 5.16b, equation 5.18 can be written as

$$h = \frac{1}{\gamma}(w - w^*)$$

so that the wage that just induces a woman to work a positive number of hours is the reservation wage w^*. In terms of the notation of Figure 5.2, $A = w^*$. If one constrains the intercept of the labor supply curve to be the reservation wage, then when the "broken line" function *BEFG* describes some or all of the data, one *underestimates* the response of hours to wage rates as well as the intercept in the labor supply equation. See the dashed line $B'G'$ in Figure 5.2. One can prove that "Tobit" and the model of equation 5.11b impose this constraint on the fitted function.

By way of contrast with these results, it is helpful to consider a model with fixed costs of work. For simplicity consider money costs of work. As both Cogan (Chapter 7) and Hanoch (Chapter 6) have shown, the effect of fixed costs of work on labor supply is that women who work at all must work a minimum number of hours, say $\hat{h}$, to recoup the fixed costs. The reservation wage is raised over a case without fixed costs. This model is depicted in Figure 5.3. Here the

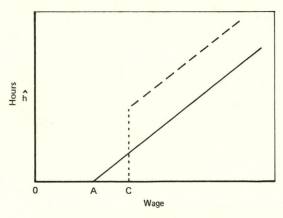

FIGURE 5.3   Model with fixed costs

standard labor supply function for a woman of given characteristics is indicated by a solid line, and the modified labor supply function is indicated by a dashed line. As before, "*A*" denotes the reservation wage in the standard case, while "*C*" denotes the reservation wage in the case of fixed costs of work. In the presence of fixed costs, the reservation wage is greater and the level of the supply function is *higher*, reflecting the assumption that leisure is a normal good, and the fact that fixed costs subtract from income. Unlike the situation in the previous case, the average of the reservation wages *exceeds* the average of the intercepts. Thus any model that constrains the intercept of the labor supply function to equal the average of the reservation wages *overstates* the effect of wages (and other variables) on labor supply.[18]

The empirical results reported in Tables 5.4 and 5.6 favor the model with differential access to low-cost substitutes for time in the home over a model with fixed costs in a dominant role. "Tobit" *underestimates* the response of labor supply to a change in economic variables, and the Tobit intercept is higher than the intercept of the unrestricted labor supply function, an implication of a model in which the true reservation wage is less than the estimated intercept of the labor supply equation. Finally, note that the only modification required to make equations 5.11a–5.11b consistent with data is relaxation of the interequation proportionality of *intercepts*. The corresponding interequation slope coefficients *are* related by a common factor of proportionality.[19]

It is important to note that the choice of the dependent variable crucially affects the outcome of such tests. In results not reported here, use of the conventional measure of labor supply defined as the product of "usual hours per week" and "usual weeks" leads to precisely opposite implications, i.e., one would accept a model of fixed costs. But as previously noted, the standard measures *induce* the illusion of

[18] This argument is made by both Cogan (Chapter 7) and Hanoch (Chapter 6). These effects would also arise if employers offered "tied" packages of wages and hours if each individual had his own "best" minimum hours offer in the market. In this case, the labor supply function for the tied case would coincide over the relevant range with the standard labor supply function, but the average of the intercepts would understate the reservation wage.

[19] Another implication of the modified model is that the correlation between the disturbances of the labor supply function and the participation equation need not be unity, because there is a source of variation in the labor supply function that does not affect the participation equation (maximum availability of close substitutes h^*).

fixed costs *via* reporting error that overstates the extent of labor supply and the frequency of occurrence of standard reporting intervals so that empirical analyses based on this measure of labor supply may yield misleading conclusions.

SUMMARY AND CONCLUSIONS

In this chapter the bias that results from using nonrandomly selected data is discussed within the specification error framework of Griliches and Theil. A computationally tractable technique is considered that enables economists to utilize simple regression techniques to estimate behavioral functions free of selection bias. Asymptotic properties of the estimator are developed.

A model of female labor supply and wage rates is estimated with this technique. The empirical results suggest that selection bias is an important problem in estimating labor supply functions, but is less important in estimating wage functions. Very high estimates of the elasticity of female labor supply are derived, but these are shown to be consistent with conventional estimates that ignore selection bias. The labor force experience of the wife is shown to be an endogenous variable in labor supply equations but not in wage functions.

Some informal tests of the model of Heckman (1974b) are presented. Many predictions of the model appear to be in accord with the data, but an expanded model that introduces the notion of limited household access to low-cost substitutes for the wife's time appears to fit the data better. With the measure of labor supply adopted here, the implications of a model with fixed costs of work in a dominant role are unsupported by the data.

ACKNOWLEDGMENTS

The research reported in this paper was supported by an HEW grant to the Rand Corporation and a U.S. Department of Labor grant to the National Bureau of Economic Research. A previous version circulated under the title "Shadow Prices, Market Wages, and Labor supply Revisited: Some Computational Simplifications and Revised Estimates," June 1975. I have greatly benefited from conversations with Paul Schultz and James Smith, and from detailed written comments of Mark Killingsworth on the first draft of this work. Takeshi Amemiya, John Cogan, Reuben Gronau, Ed Leamer, H. G. Lewis, and Bill Rodgers all made valuable comments on the second draft. Gary Becker, John Cogan, Tom MaCurdy, Nick Kiefer, Mark Killingsworth, James Smith, and Arnold Zellner made helpful suggestions at a later stage. Ralph Shnelvar performed the computations. I assume all responsibility for any remaining errors.

APPENDIX A[20]

THE ASYMPTOTIC DISTRIBUTION OF ESTIMATORS BASED ON AN ESTIMATED λ_i.

Equation 5.7a with an estimated value of λ_i used in place of the true value of λ_i may be written as

$$Y_{1i} = X_{1i}\beta_1 + C\hat{\lambda}_i + C(\lambda_i - \hat{\lambda}_i) + V_{1i} \qquad (A.1)$$

where $C = \sigma_{12}/\sigma_{22}^{1/2}$. The error term consists of the final *two* terms in the equation.

Since λ_i is estimated by $\beta_2/\sigma_{22}^{1/2}$ $(= \beta_2^*)$, which is estimated from the entire sample of I observations by a maximum likelihood probit analysis,[21] and since λ_i is a twice continuously differentiable function of β_2^*, $\sqrt{I}(\hat{\lambda}_i - \lambda_i)$ has a well-defined limiting normal distribution,

$$\sqrt{I}(\hat{\lambda}_i - \lambda_i) \sim N(0, \Sigma_i),$$

where Σ_i is the asymptotic variance-covariance matrix obtained from that of $\sqrt{I}(\beta_2^* - \beta_2)$ by the following equation:

$$\Sigma_i = \left(\frac{\partial \lambda_i}{\partial Z_i}\right)^2 X_{2i} \sum X'_{2i},$$

where $\partial \lambda_i/\partial Z_i$ is the derivative of λ_i with respect to Z_i, and Σ is the asymptotic variance-covariance matrix of β_2^*.

We seek the limiting distribution of

$$\sqrt{I_1}\begin{pmatrix}\hat{\beta}_1 - \beta_1 \\ \hat{C} - C\end{pmatrix} = I_1 \begin{pmatrix}\sum X'_{1i}X_{1i} & \sum X'_{1i}\hat{\lambda}_i \\ \sum X_{1i}\hat{\lambda}_i & \sum \hat{\lambda}_i^2\end{pmatrix}^{-1} \frac{1}{\sqrt{I_1}}\begin{pmatrix}\sum X'_{1i}(C(\lambda_i - \hat{\lambda}_i) + V_{1i}) \\ \sum \hat{\lambda}_i(C(\lambda_i - \hat{\lambda}_i) + V_{1i})\end{pmatrix}.$$

In the ensuing analysis, it is important to recall that the probit function is estimated on the entire sample of I observations, whereas the regression analysis is performed solely on the subsample of $I_1(<I)$

---

[20] Remarks by Takeshi Amemiya stimulated this section. Of course, he is not responsible for any errors in the analysis.

[21] The ensuing analysis can be modified in a straightforward fashion if Y_{2i} is observed and β_2^* is estimated by least squares.

observations where Y_{1i} is observed. Further, it is important to note that unlike the situation in the analysis of two-stage least squares procedures, the portion of the residual that arises from the use of an estimated value of λ_i in place of the actual value of λ_i *is not* orthogonal to the X_1 data vector.

Under general conditions for the regressors discussed extensively in Amemiya, 1973b,

$$\operatorname*{plim}_{I_1 \to \infty} I_1 \begin{pmatrix} \sum X'_{1i}X_{1i} & \sum X'_{1i}\hat{\lambda}_i \\ \sum X_{1i}\hat{\lambda}_i & \sum \hat{\lambda}_i^2 \end{pmatrix}^{-1} = \operatorname*{plim}_{I_1 \to \infty} I_1 \begin{pmatrix} \sum X'_{1i}X_{1i} & \sum X'_{1i}\lambda_i \\ \sum X_{1i}\lambda_i & \sum \lambda_i^2 \end{pmatrix}^{-1} = B,$$

where B is a finite positive definite matrix.[22] Under these assumptions,

$$\sqrt{I_1}\begin{pmatrix} \hat{\beta}_1 - \beta_1 \\ \hat{C} - C \end{pmatrix} \sim N(0, B\psi B'),\tag{A.2}$$

where

$$\psi = \operatorname*{plim}_{\substack{I_1 \to \infty \\ I \to \infty}} \left[\sigma_{11} \begin{pmatrix} \dfrac{\sum X'_{1i}X_{1i}\eta_i}{I_1} & \dfrac{\sum X'_{1i}\lambda_i\eta_i}{I_1} \\ \dfrac{\sum \lambda_i X_{1i}\eta_i}{I_1} & \dfrac{\sum \lambda_i^2 \eta_i}{I_1} \end{pmatrix} \right.$$

$$\left. + C^2\left(\dfrac{I_1}{I}\right) \begin{pmatrix} \displaystyle\sum_{i=1}^{I_1}\sum_{i'=1}^{I_1} \dfrac{X'_{1i}X_{1i'}\theta_{ii'}}{I_i^2} & \displaystyle\sum_{i=1}^{I_1}\sum_{i'=1}^{I_1} \dfrac{X'_{1i}\pi_{ii'}}{I_i^2} \\ \displaystyle\sum_{i'=1}^{I_1}\sum_{i=1}^{I_1} \dfrac{X_{1i}\pi_{ii'}}{I_i^2} & \displaystyle\sum_{i=1}^{I_1}\sum_{i'=1}^{I_1} \dfrac{\Omega_{ii'}}{I_1^2} \end{pmatrix} \right]$$

$$\operatorname*{plim}_{\substack{I \to \infty \\ I_1 \to \infty}} \dfrac{I_1}{I} = k,\ 0 < k < 1,$$

where

$$C = \sigma_{12}/\sigma_{22}^{1/2}$$

$$\eta_i = (1 + C^2(Z_i\lambda_i - \lambda_i^2)/\sigma_{11})$$

$$\pi_{ii'} = \left(\dfrac{\partial \lambda_i}{\partial Z_i}\right)\left(\dfrac{\partial \lambda_{i'}}{\partial Z_{i'}}\right)\lambda_i X_{2i} \sum X'_{2i'}$$

$$\theta_{ii'} = \left(\dfrac{\partial \lambda_i}{\partial Z_i}\right)\left(\dfrac{\partial \lambda_{i'}}{\partial Z_{i'}}\right)X_{2i} \sum Z'_{2i}$$

$$\Omega_{ii'} = (\lambda_i\lambda_{i'})\left(\dfrac{\partial \lambda_i}{\partial Z_i}\dfrac{\partial \lambda_{i'}}{\partial Z_{i'}}\right)X_{2i} \sum X'_{2i}$$

[22] Note that this requires that X_{2i} contains nontrivial regressors, or that there is no intercept in the equation, or both.

where $\partial \lambda_i / \partial Z_i$ is the derivative of λ_i with respect to Z_i,

$$\frac{\partial \lambda_i}{\partial Z_i} = \lambda_i^2 - Z_i \lambda_i.$$

In checking the algebra, it is helpful to note that $(\lambda_i - \hat{\lambda}_i)$ is independent of V_{1i} as a consequence of the fact that V_{1i} is defined to be independent of U_{2i}, and the sampling distribution of $\sqrt{I}(\lambda_i - \hat{\lambda}_i)$ is generated from the distribution of U_{2i}. Note that if $C = 0$, $B\psi B'$ collapses to the standard variance-covariance matrix for the least squares estimator. Note further that $B\psi B' = B + BJB'$ where J is the second matrix in ψ. J is positive semidefinite. Hence use of the standard least squares variance-covariance matrix when $\hat{\lambda}$ is estimated results in an *understatement* (more precisely, never leads to an overstatement) of the true standard errors of the estimated regression coefficients. Hence "t" statistics based on the usual variance-covariance matrix, which is the incorrect variance-covariance matrix if $C = 0$, *overstate* true significance levels. The "standard" least squares covariance matrix generates standard errors of regression coefficients that are systematically understated compared to the true values.

Under the Amemiya conditions previously cited, ψ is a bounded positive definite matrix. ψ and B can be simply estimated. Estimated values of λ_i, C, and σ_{11} can be used in place of actual values to obtain a consistent estimator of $B\psi B'$. Estimation of the variance-covariance matrix requires inversion of a $K_1 + 1 \times K_1 + 1$ matrix and so is computationally simple. A copy of a program that estimates the probit function coefficients β_2^* and the regression coefficients $\hat{\beta}_1$ and $\hat{C}$, and produces the correct asymptotic standard errors for the general case is available on request from the author.[23]

It is possible to develop a GLS procedure (see Heckman, 1977, pp. 45–47). This procedure is computationally more expensive, and since the GLS estimates are not asymptotically efficient, is not recommended.

---

[23] This offer expires two years after the publication of this book. The program will be provided at cost.

APPENDIX B

In the 1967 National Longitudinal Survey of the work experience of women age 30–44, 5,083 observations are available. The following sample selection criteria were imposed to reach a usable sample of 1,735 women, 812 of whom worked in 1966. The number of observations failing to meet a criterion is given in the column to the right of the rejection criterion. Observations may be rejected for any of the reasons listed, and a given observation may be rejected for several reasons.

(1)	Nonwhite	1,477
(2)	Married spouse present	1,019
(3)	Farmers	252
(4)	Missing husband's income	421
(5)	Missing annual hours of husband (including no work group)	336
(6)	Missing wife's experience	301
(7)	Missing wage data on women	126

Assets were assigned in 165 cases. An equation is fit on the available 1,570 observations. The equation is:

Assets (1967) = −6,891 + 73 (wife's experience)
+1,647 (wife's education) + 466.4 (number of children <6)
+806.8 (husband's education) + 2,040 (husband's age)
− 17.475 (husband's age squared).

TABLE 5.7: Sample Means of the Data Used in the Analysis
(From 1967 National Longitudinal Survey of the Work Experience of
Women 30–44)

	Workers	Total Sample
Number of observations	812	1735
Number of children less than 6	.312	.565
Assets ($)	11,711	11,974
Husband's 1966 hourly wage rate ($/hr.)	3.45	3.73
Wife's education (yrs.)	11.42	11.29
Labor force experience (yrs.)	10.63	7.80
Wife's annual hours worked	1289	· · ·
Wife's hourly wage rate	2.12	· · ·
λ	.6412	1.12

APPENDIX C

The histograms for reported weeks worked in 1966, reported annual hours worked, and estimated hours worked based on a division of 1966 earnings by a questionnaire wage rate, are displayed in that order. The ordinate gives the number of observations for the value of the variable displayed on the abscissa.

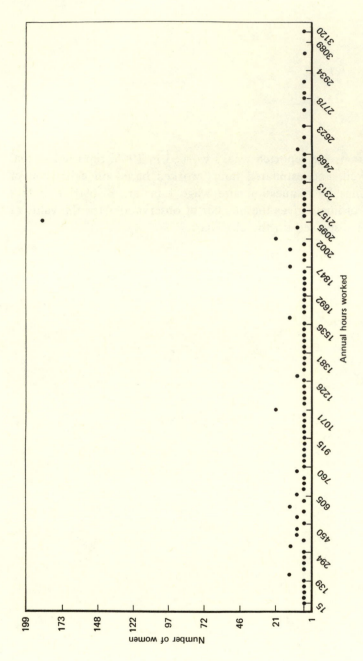

FIGURE 5.4 Annual hours worked defined as "usual hours worked per week" times "weeks worked in the year"

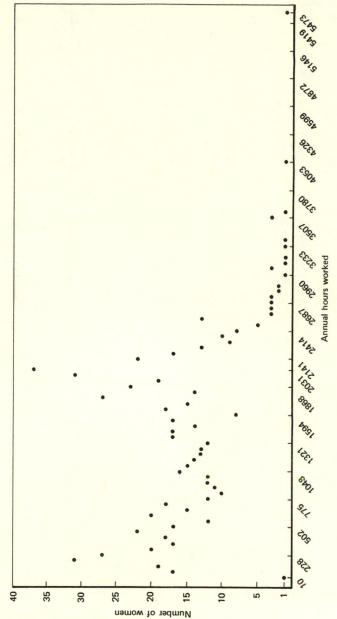

FIGURE 5.5   Annual hours defined as earnings divided by the questionnaire wage rates.

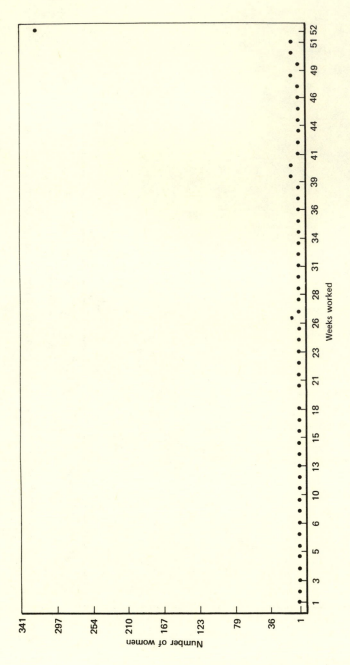

FIGURE 5.6 Weeks worked in the year

CHAPTER 6

A MULTIVARIATE MODEL OF
LABOR SUPPLY: METHODOLOGY
AND ESTIMATION

GIORA HANOCH

HEBREW UNIVERSITY, JERUSALEM

I. INTRODUCTION

Theoretical and empirical economists have spent much time and effort studying the individual labor supply function. But the more thoroughly they examined it, the less stable and more complex it seemed, with new conceptual and statistical problems surfacing at every stage. In Chapter 3 of this volume, I analyzed from a theoretical perspective several aspects of labor supply that were previously overlooked. The goal of this study is to provide a framework and a feasible method of estimation of the theory outlined in Chapter 3. Using this framework, the model is estimated with a sample of white married women in the 1967 Survey of Economic Opportunity (SEO). The econometric and theoretical issues considered are particularly significant with respect to women's labor supply. Men tend to participate in the labor force in much larger proportions, over more extended and uninterrupted periods, and to work full time when employed. Variations in male labor market quantities are thus smaller and determined more by labor demand conditions and restrictions than by individual supply, as compared especially to married women.[1]

---

[1] The theoretical study in Chapter 3 treated the problem of *family* labor supply, where substitution and complementarity of the husband's and wife's time may affect each family member's own labor supply behavior. For convenience of presentation, the present analysis applies the model to individual wives, ignoring the joint allocation of time in the family. But it could easily be extended to a family, with minor modifications, as shown in the theoretical study. For example, it allows husband's wages and earnings to affect the wife's supply of labor, but ignores, at this stage, the endogenous nature of these variables.

Of the theoretical and statistical problems peculiar to labor supply that the present model does recognize and resolve econometrically, the following six major elements may be cited. The first two have been examined empirically in other recent studies,[2] whereas the last four are related to theoretical issues discussed in Chapter 3, and are believed to be treated econometrically for the first time here.[3]

1. *The simultaneity bias in regression estimates of labor supply.* This bias occurs because the wage rate is an endogenous variable in cross-sectional data—that is, because some individual market productivity factors, unaccounted for by the included explanatory variables, tend to be correlated with the individual labor supply residuals, which in turn are associated with individual productivity of nonmarket time as well as individual preferences.

2. *The participation selectivity bias.* This bias occurs because market wage offers are measured only for workers (where they are assumed to equal the actual wage paid), but not for nonparticipants (who refuse these wage offers). Since the criterion for selecting the working sample is the wage-rate comparison with the individual's own reservation wage, this criterion is endogenous and induces a selectivity bias.

3. *The simultaneous joint determination of the supply of annual hours (A) and annual weeks (K) of work.* Individuals are not indifferent to variations in the allocation of any given total amount of time supplied among dimensions such as hours and weeks. As we have seen in Chapter 3, the hours and weeks dimensions correspond to the demand for two types of leisure—work-week leisure and nonwork-week leisure—which are jointly determined. Most previous empirical studies have treated hours and weeks of work as alternative measures of the same dependent supply variable, while theoretical discussions have usually regarded the two types of leisure associated with hours and weeks as perfect substitutes.

[2] The simultaneity bias was treated, for example, by Heckman (1974b) and Hall (1973). The selectivity bias was analyzed by Gronau (1974), Lewis (1974), and Heckman (1974b and Chapter 5).

[3] The essays by Heckman (Chapter 5) and Cogan (Chapter 7) in this book also treat one of these elements—namely, the discontinuity of supply due to fixed costs. Cogan also extends the analysis to include fixed costs as a choice variable, and to allow for its estimation.

4. *The discontinuity of supply at the reservation wage,* or the existence of minimum supply quantities. The theoretical model in Chapter 3 shows that, even in the absence of any fixed costs of participation, one of the variables A or K (and normally K) will be discontinuous, with minimum positive amounts supplied at the reservation wage. In addition, the presence of any fixed time or money costs associated with work induces a gap between the price of time at home (if not participating) and the reservation wage, and thus creates a discontinuity of supply of both annual hours and weeks worked at the reservation wage W_0. This discontinuity has been largely ignored in empirical models, tending to produce large positive biases in estimates of the wage elasticity of labor supply.[4]

5. *The corner solution in terms of full-year work.* The actual number of weeks worked in one year cannot exceed a physical limit, but the desired number of weeks, as determined by underlying preferences (defined and continuous for a domain exceeding available time) may exceed this limit. This restriction causes a corner solution at 52 in the supply of weeks worked. It may also cause the responses (slopes) of annual hours supplied to be discontinuous, through the effects of the corner solution in weeks on the total demand for composite leisure.[5] Quantitatively, about 40 percent of the women who participate in the labor force are full-year workers, so that the effect of this constraint on their labor supply may be quite significant.

6. *The survey-week selectivity bias.* In data sources such as the SEO and the Census, wage and hours information is available only for individuals who work during the week prior to their survey interviews. For individuals tending to work K weeks in the current year, the probability of working in a particular week is equal, on the average, to $K/52$. Since the selection probability is proportional to the endogenous variable K, a bias is introduced into labor supply estimates based on this type of data. The present analysis indicates the magnitude of this bias and suggests statistical methods to eliminate it.

A simple examination of the data shows the validity of this argument and its quantitative importance. For example, in our SEO

---

[4] For example, in Heckman (1974a and b). See also Hanoch (Chapter 3).
[5] See Hanoch, Chapter 3, Sec. III.

sample of white married women, out of 3,044 women participating
in the labor force during 1966 (i.e., with K positive), only 2,064
(67.8 percent) worked during the survey week (in March 1967).
Since the mean number of weeks worked by participants was 35.3,
the proportion working in a given week is predicted to be $35.3 \div 52$,
or 67.9 percent. On the other hand, the biased mean of K, as
measured for survey-week workers, is 41.6 weeks, compared with
the mean of 22.2 weeks for the excluded group (participants in
1966 who did not work in the survey week).

The methodology and the estimates presented are not aimed at
achieving maximum efficiency of estimation or at eliminating all
sources of specification and estimation biases; they are rather informal
and intuitive, preferring methods that are less costly to execute and
easier to understand. My empirical results generally indicate that all of
these considerations are important quantitatively, and that neglecting
any of them may cause serious biases and misinterpretations.

The model presented here abstracts from several potentially important determinants of labor supply. First, in choosing annual hours and
annual weeks as the time dimensions, and one year as the decision
period, the model ignores other time dimensions that may be
relevant—weekly days of work and daily hours of work—or a planning
horizon longer than one year (which could explain variations of labor
supply over the life cycle). Formally, one could extend the model to
additional dimensions and a longer horizon.[6] However, common limitations of data in large cross-sectional sources on individuals dictate
the present specification.

Second, the amount of daily hours may be related to variation in the
hourly wage rate as a function of hours, such as a lower wage for
part-time work or a higher wage for overtime. My model assumes that
the hourly wage rate is independent of the number of weekly hours of
work (as well as of weeks worked annually). In reality, employers may
have strong preferences regarding the length of the workday, because
of its effect on productivity and on work organization and scheduling.
The allocation of weekly hours of work among days is thus largely
determined by demand constraints. These effects are difficult to separate from pure supply effects related to preferences and productivity at
home. In view of this, the present specification dealing with weekly

[6] See Hanoch, Chapter 3, Sec. VI.

rather than daily hours seems preferable, since the dependence of wage offers on the weekly total hours is expected to be weaker than on daily hours.

Third, other equalizing differences in wages are also ignored. These may be connected with work conditions, opportunities for accumulation of human capital (on-the-job training), and nonpecuniary costs and benefits. Finally, the role of income taxes is not included. Clearly, if marginal and average tax rates differ among individuals, and if labor supply decisions depend on after-tax wages and incomes, an analysis based on gross (before-tax) wages and income is deficient. At present, data on effective rates of individual tax payments are scarce. In addition, the modifications required in the model to account for tax effects are complex, given the current structure of income taxes with their variable degree of progressivity, credits, deductions, and loopholes.

The remainder of this paper is organized as follows. Section II presents the basic model, which consists of a market wage equation, a reservation wage equation, and two supply equations for annual hours and weeks worked. From these are derived additional relations such as the probability-of-participation equation and its corresponding probit index, a "pseudo reservation wage equation" (in which the unobserved reservation wage is replaced by the market wage, in conjunction with the index of participation), and minimum-supply equations for hours and weeks.

Section III transforms the general model into an operational model, which is applicable to the working sample. The latter model contains only observable variables and equations modified to account for the two types of selectivity bias.

Section IV presents an iterative strategy for estimating the model. This section also discusses estimation problems in greater detail. The final stage of the proposed procedure applies a weighted three-stage least squares estimation to alternative simultaneous linear systems of modified equations.

Finally, Section V describes and discusses in detail the estimates obtained using the SEO sample. The contents of this section are outlined in subsection V.1, together with some introductory remarks.

Appendix A derives the magnitude of the survey-week bias, and the method of eliminating it by a weighting scheme. Appendix B details the definitions and the scope of the sample used, and Appendix C describes the method of calculating the approximate residual variance structure.

II. Types of Variables and Basic Model

The following definitions and assumptions are adopted:

Endogenous Variables

DP = A dichotomous dummy variable determining participation in the labor market: $DP = 1$ for participants and 0 for nonparticipants.

A = Annual hours of work by participants.

K = Annual weeks of work by participants—i.e., the number of weeks in which a positive number of hours were worked.

W = Market hourly wage rate. W is observed for workers, but not for nonparticipants.

w = ln W (natural logarithm).

W_0 = Reservation wage—i.e., the minimum hourly wage that induces participation. W_0 is unobserved.

w_0 = ln W_0.

It is assumed that decisions on DP, A, and K are made jointly and simultaneously, on a one-year basis. The condition for participation ($DP = 1$) is equivalent to the condition $W \geq W_0$, or $w \geq w_0$.

Exogenous Observable Variables

x = A set of variables that influence market wage offers—i.e., variables related to market productivity and labor demand conditions.

z = A set of variables that influence individual preferences between nonmarket time (leisure) and other consumption goods. These include personal tastes, productivity at home, and the availability of time and money in the family.

y = A set of variables that influence the reservation wage W_0. In general, y includes all z variables, as well as certain variables that may affect time and money costs of participation, but have a negligible effect on quantities of labor supplied by participants.

It is required for identification of the model that some x variables are not in z or y, and some z and y variables are not in x. By assumption, x and y (and therefore z) are observable for everyone, including nonparticipants.

Latent Unobserved (Random) Variables

The set $u^0 = (u_0, u_1, u_2, u_3, u_4)$ denotes additive latent components of the following five endogenous variables, respectively: $(w_0, w_0 - w, w, A, K)$. Thus $u_0 = u_1 + u_2$. The four random variables $u = (u_1, u_2, u_3, u_4)$ have a nondegenerate joint-normal distribution with zero means: $Eu = 0$; and a variance matrix $E uu' = \sum$ that is non-diagonal and nonsingular. Further, u is distributed independently of the exogenous variables (x, y), $(E[x, y]u' = 0)$, and is independent among individuals.[7] It is also assumed that $\sum$ is constant among individuals (homoskedasticity).[8] Denote also $\sum^0 = Eu^0 u^{0'} = \{\sigma_{ij}; i, j = 0, \ldots, 4\}$ and $\sigma_{ii} = \sigma_i^2$. Thus, $\sigma_0^2 = \sigma_1^2 + \sigma_2^2 + 2\sigma_{12}$.

The latent variables defined here combine different types of components that are not distinguished in a cross-sectional model like this, but are conceptually distinguishable: (1) permanent individual components, associated with various unobserved permanent exogenous variables, such as ability, personal tastes, motivation; (2) transitory components, which vary for a given individual from year to year (or from week to week if related to a variable measured on a weekly basis, such as the wage rate in the SEO sample); (3) measurement errors in observed endogenous variables (W, A, K, and DP); and (4) errors in specification of functional form, such as nonlinearity components, assumed either negligible or orthogonal to the right-side variables.

THE BASIC MODEL

The following four equations summarize the basic model, applicable to every individual, including nonparticipants, in terms of the variables defined above and the constant parameters α, β, γ_1, γ_2, δ_1, δ_2, and $\sum$.

Market wage equation:
$$w = \alpha' x + u_2. \tag{6.1}$$

Reservation wage equation:
$$w_0 = \beta' y + u_0. \tag{6.2}$$

---

[7] Similar assumptions apply to u^0, since $u_0 = u_1 + u_2$.

[8] It is not assumed, however, that $\sum$ is diagonal—i.e., that residuals are uncorrelated across equations. The homoskedasticity assumption is made as a convenient approximation only, and may be modified without greatly affecting the model. See equation 6.30.

Annual hours supply equation:

$$A = \begin{cases} \gamma_1' + \delta_1 w + u_3 & \text{if} \quad w \geq w_0 \\ 0 & \text{if} \quad w < w_0 \end{cases}$$

or

$$A = (\gamma_1' z + \delta_1 w + u_3) \cdot DP. \tag{6.3}$$

Annual weeks supply equation:

$$K = \begin{cases} \gamma_2' z + \delta_2 w + u_4 & \text{if} \quad w \geq w_0 \\ 0 & \text{if} \quad w < w_0 \end{cases}$$

or

$$K = (\gamma_2' z + \delta_2 w + u_4) \cdot DP. \tag{6.4}$$

Additional inequality constraints are imposed on the variables: $W > 0$, $W_0 > 0$, $A > 0$, and $0 < K \leq 52$, for participants. The positivity requirements on A and K are ignored here, assuming that the negative correlation between the reservation wage and the supply residuals is sufficiently high to make negligible the normal-distribution tail probabilities corresponding to negative supply quantities.[9]

The possibility of a corner solution corresponding to full-time work in terms of weeks (owing to the restriction $K \leq 52$) is important. To simplify the discussion, this restriction is ignored here, but is fully recognized and treated in Section IV below.

An equation determining the probability of participation p may be specified by combining equations 6.1 and 6.2. Denote the unit-normal cumulative probability by

$$P(\chi) = \frac{1}{\sqrt{2\pi}} \int_{-\infty}^{x} e^{-t^2/2} \, dt,$$

and define the *participation index* as the following exogenous variable:

$$I = \frac{1}{\sigma_1} (\alpha' x - \beta' y), \tag{6.5}$$

where σ_1^2 is the variance of u_1. Then the probability of participation is

$$\text{prob} \{w \geq w_0\} = \text{prob} \{u_0 - u_2 \leq \alpha' x - \beta' y\} = \text{prob} \{u_1 \leq \sigma_1 I\} = P(I),$$

---

[9] This problem could be eliminated if A and K were defined as logarithms of the corresponding quantities, but such definitions would seem to imply inferior functional-form specifications of the supply equations.

since (u_1/σ_1) is unit-normal. We thus get the

Probability-of-participation equation:

$$p = E(DP) = P(I) = P\left(\frac{1}{\sigma_1}\{\alpha'x - \beta'y\}\right). \tag{6.6}$$

Since the reservation wage is unobservable, a "pseudo reservation wage equation" may be specified in terms of the market wage and the participation index I by substituting from the identity equation (6.5) into equation 6.1.

Pseudo reservation wage equation:

$$w = \beta'y + \sigma_1 I + u_2. \tag{6.7}$$

Equation 6.2 of the basic model may thus be replaced by equations 6.6 or 6.7 by substituting the participation probability p or the participation index $I = P^{-1}(p)$, respectively, for the reservation wage variable w_0.

The minimum supply quantities for participants, A_0 and K_0 (assumed nonnegative), are derived by substituting w_0 from equation 6.2 into equations 6.3 and 6.4:

Minimum-supply equations:

$$A_0 = \gamma_1'z + \delta_1 w_0 + u_3 = \gamma_1'z + \delta_1\beta'y + (\delta_1 u_0 + u_3),$$
$$K_0 = \gamma_2'z + \delta_2 w_0 + u_4 = \gamma_2'z + \delta_2\beta'y + (\delta_2 u_0 + u_4). \tag{6.8}$$

If $\delta_1 > 0$ and $\delta_2 > 0$, the condition for participation ($DP = 1$, or $w \geq w_0$) is seen to be equivalent to each of the conditions $A \geq A_0$ and $K \geq K_0$ by comparing equations 6.3 and 6.4 with equation 6.8.

With no time or money costs of participation, either A_0 or K_0 is zero.[10] However, any fixed costs associated with market work (such as travel time to work and search costs) imply that A_0 and K_0 are both positive, manifesting discontinuity of both supply curves at the point of minimum participation. Simulations with various functional forms for the underlying utility function have shown that relatively small fixed costs tend to induce large magnitudes of A_0 and K_0.[11] The present model permits such discontinuities in the supply curves at W_0, thus

---

[10] As I showed in Chapter 3, K_0 is more likely to be nonzero if both types of leisure are normal goods.

[11] See Hanoch, Chapter 3, Fig. 3. See also Cogan, Chapter 7.

allowing for fixed costs of participation. These costs may constitute a
component of the latent random variables, or a component of the
effects of the observed variables y, and are therefore permitted to vary
among individuals.

This generalization should be contrasted with the model proposed
and estimated by Heckman[12] and others, which assumes (identically)
zero minimum hours, implying zero costs of participation and no
discontinuity of supply at the reservation wage. Translating Heckman's
model into the present notation, his restrictive assumptions are seen to
be

(i) y and z are identical,

(ii) $\beta = -\dfrac{1}{\delta_1}\,\gamma_1$,

(iii) $u_0 = -\dfrac{1}{\delta_1}\,u_3$, or $u_3 = -\delta_1(u_1 + u_2)$,

implying $A(\equiv K_0) \equiv 0$. In the present model, however, these assumptions may be tested after the model is estimated, but are not imposed
on the estimation.

III. Basic Model Corrected for Selectivity Biases

The model outlined in Section II applies to everyone, including non-participants. However, it is not operational in the given form, since in
general observed data do not include information about market wage
offers for nonparticipants. Wages are considered endogenous, including an unobserved individual component (u_2), which is correlated, in
the general case, with the other endogenous variables (DP, A, and K).
Therefore, the application of the model as specified to a sample of
participants (i.e., selecting the sample using $DP = 1$, which involves the
component u_1 as a criterion) implies a well-known *participation selectivity bias*.[13]

In addition, observations in some cross-sectional samples (such as in
census data and in the SEO) involve a selectivity bias of another type,
here termed the *survey-week selectivity bias*. In these surveys, information on hourly wage rates and on weekly hours worked H is available

[12] Heckman (1974a and b).
[13] See Gronau (1973a and 1974) and Heckman (1974b).

only for individuals working a positive number of hours during one particular week—namely, that prior to the survey interview; whereas information on number of weeks worked (during the previous year) and on x and y exists for all sample observations. If the survey week may be considered a random drawing from the current year's 52 weeks, then the probability of finding at work during the survey week an individual who decides to work K weeks in the survey year is simply $K/52$. The sample of workers during the survey week thus overrepresents individuals whose desired K exceeds the average, and underrepresents part-year workers whose K is below average. Since the probability of entry into the survey-week working sample is associated with the endogenous variable K, and since K (and its latent component u_4) is generally correlated with other endogenous variables (W and A, given $DP = 1$), a selectivity bias occurs if the model is applied as specified to the subsample of survey-week workers.

The present section indicates the magnitude of these biases and reformulates the model to eliminate them.

The following lemma will be useful for further discussion. First, some notation: Let u denote r joint-normal random variables with zero means and a variance matrix $\Sigma = \{\sigma_{jk}\} = Eu\, u'$. Denote $b_j = -(1/\sigma_1)\sigma_{ij}$, $j = 1, \ldots, r$, where $\sigma_1 = \sqrt{\sigma_{11}}$. Note that $b_1 = -\sigma_1$; in vector notation, $b = -(1/\sigma_1)\Sigma_1$, where Σ_1 is the $1st$ column of Σ. The function $f(x)$ denotes the unit-normal density:

$$f(x) = \left(\frac{1}{\sqrt{2\pi}}\right) e^{-x^2/2} = \frac{d}{dx} P(x),$$

where $P(x)$ denotes the probability (as in Section II). Define also $\lambda(x) = f(x)/P(x)$, and $\bar{\lambda}(x) = -f(x)/(1 - P(x)) = -\lambda p/(1-p)$. The magnitude $\lambda(x)$ is the conditional density of the truncated unit-normal variable x for an upper limit (left tail) truncation, whereas $(-\bar{\lambda})$ is the conditional density of x corresponding to a lower limit (right tail) truncation.[14]

Lemma: The u_1-truncated joint distributions (i.e., truncated with respect to u_1 only) of u have the following first and second moments

---

[14] As shown in equation 6.9 below, λ and $\bar{\lambda}$ are also (minus) the conditional means for upper or lower truncation, respectively, of the unit-normal truncated variable (substitute $\sigma_1 = 1$, and $j = 1$, and therefore $b_1 = -1$, in equation 6.9).

$(j, k = 1, \ldots, r)$:

$$E(u_j \mid u_1 \leq \sigma_1 I) = b_j \lambda(I),$$
$$E(u_j \mid u_1 \geq \sigma_1 I) = b_j \bar{\lambda}(I); \tag{6.9}$$

$$E(u_j u_k \mid u_1 \leq \sigma_1 I) = \sigma_{jk} - b_j b_k I \lambda(I),$$
$$E(u_j u_k \mid u_1 \geq \sigma_1 I) = \sigma_{jk} + b_j b_k I \bar{\lambda}(I); \tag{6.10}$$

$$\text{Cov}\,(u_j, u_k \mid u_1 \leq \sigma_1 I) = \sigma_{jk} - b_j b_k [\lambda(I)^2 + I\lambda(I)] = \sigma_{jk} - b_j b_k D(I),$$
$$\text{Cov}\,(u_j, u_k \mid u_1 \geq \sigma_1 I) = \sigma_{jk} - b_j b_k [\bar{\lambda}(I)^2 - I\bar{\lambda}(I)] = \sigma_{jk} - b_j b_k \bar{D}(I), \tag{6.11}$$

where $D = \lambda^2 + I\lambda$, and $\bar{D} = \bar{\lambda}^2 - I\bar{\lambda}$.

The proof is immediate, applying well-known formulas[15] corresponding to the general truncated-normal distribution in R^n to this particular case and notation.

We deal first with the case where wage-rate and hours data are available for all participants (as in Parnes's data),[16] and therefore only the first (participation) selectivity bias is present.[17]

CASE 1: WAGE AND HOURS DATA AVAILABLE FOR ALL PARTICIPANTS

Define participants as individuals working during at least one week in a given year $(K > 0)$. It is assumed here that data are given for a sample of N individuals, n of which are participants ($n < N$; and participants are ordered as the first n observations). The variables x_i, y_i, K_i, and A_i are observed for all N, whereas the hourly wage W_i is measured only for n participants (but not for $i = n + 1, \ldots, N$). The selectivity bias is manifested by the fact that the expected value of the variables $u = (u_1, u_2, u_3, u_4)$ within the sample of participants is given, using equation 6.9, by

$$E(u_i \mid u_{1i} \leq \sigma_1 I_i) = \lambda(I_i) b = \lambda_i b, \qquad (i = 1, \ldots, n)$$

since $DP_i = 1$ implies $u_{1i} \leq \sigma_1 I_i$, by equation 6.6, and σ_1 and b are independent of i (Σ is assumed constant among individuals). Define the

---

[15] For example, see Johnson and Kotz (1972), pp. 112–14.

[16] That is, the National Longitudinal Survey, 1967, described in Shea, Spitz, and Zeller, 1970. This is the data base used by Heckman (1974b).

[17] The magnitude of the selectivity bias was shown by Amemiya. A method essentially similar to the one presented here for correcting the selectivity bias was first proposed by Heckman, Chapter 5.

following random variables $v_i = (v_{1i}, v_{2i}, v_{3i}, v_{4i})$, $i = 1, \ldots, n$:

$$v_i = u_i - \lambda_i b. \tag{6.12}$$

Then the joint distribution of v_i (for $i \leq n$) has zero means, by equation 6.9; v_i are uncorrelated with the exogenous variables $E[v_i(x_i, y_i)'] = 0$, using equations 6.9 and 6.12; and v_i are independently distributed across individuals.

The joint distribution of v_i is not normal, however, and its variance matrix Σ_i^v depends on i (heteroskedastic) and is given, using equation 6.11 by

$$
\begin{aligned}
E(v_{ji}v_{ki}) &= \text{cov}\,(u_{ji}, u_{ki} \mid u_{1i} \leq \sigma_1 I_i) \\
&= \sigma_{jk} - b_j b_k D_i, \qquad (j, k = 1, \ldots, 4)
\end{aligned}
\tag{6.13}
$$

where $D_i = D[\lambda(I_i)] = \lambda_i^2 + I_i\lambda_i$, as above.

Equation 6.13 is expressed in matrix notation as follows:

$$\Sigma_i^v = \sum - bb'D_i = \sum - \frac{1}{\sigma_1^2}\Sigma_1 \cdot \Sigma_1' \cdot D_i. \tag{6.14}$$

Using these definitions and results, the model as applied to the working sample consists of the following equations (in addition to equation 6.6) in this case ($i = 1, \ldots, n$).

Market wage (modifying equation 6.1):

$$w_i = \alpha'x_1 + b_2\lambda_i + v_{2i}. \tag{6.15}$$

Annual hours supply (modifying equation 6.3):

$$A_i = \gamma_1'z_i + \delta_1 w_i + b_3\lambda_i + v_{3i}. \tag{6.16}$$

Weeks supply (modifying equation 6.4):

$$K_i = \gamma_2'z_i + \delta_2 w_i + b_4\lambda_i + v_{4i}. \tag{6.17}$$

The variables $v_i = (v_{1i}, v_{2i}, v_{3i}, v_{4i})$ satisfy $Ev_i = 0$; var v_i is given in equation 6.14, in particular, var $v_{1i} = \sigma_1^2(1 - D_i)$, since $b_1 = -\sigma_1$. Also v_i are uncorrelated with the exogenous variables, including λ_i.

Substitution from equation 6.5 into equation 6.15 gives the *modified pseudo reservation wage equation* (modifying equation 6.7):

$$w_i = \beta'y_i + \sigma_1 I_i + b_2\lambda_i + v_{2i}. \tag{6.18}$$

Denote by w_i^*, A_i^*, and K_i^* the expected values of the corresponding variables in the working sample (that is, conditional on $u_{1i} \leq \sigma_1 I_i$ or on $DP_i = 1$). Substitution of $w_i = w_i^* + v_{2i}$ into the supply equations gives

$$
\begin{aligned}
A_i &= \gamma_1' z_i + \delta_1 w_i^* + b_3 \lambda_i + (\delta_1 v_{2i} + v_{3i}) = A_i^* + (\delta_1 v_{2i} + v_{3i}), \\
K_i &= \gamma_2' z_i + \delta_2 w_i^* + b_4 \lambda_i + (\delta_1 v_{2i}) + v_{4i}) = K_i^* + (\delta_1 v_{2i} + v_{4i}).
\end{aligned}
\tag{6.19}
$$

Further substitution of w_i^* from equation 6.15 into equation 6.19 gives the *reduced-form supply equations:*

$$
\begin{aligned}
A_i &= \gamma_1' z_i + \delta_1 \alpha' x_i + (\delta_1 b_2 + b_3) \lambda_i + (\delta_1 v_{2i} + v_{3i}), \\
K_i &= \gamma_2' z_i + \delta_2 \alpha' x_i + (\delta_2 b_2 + b_4) \lambda_i + (\delta_2 v_{2i} + v_{4i}).
\end{aligned}
\tag{6.20}
$$

Equations 6.20 combined with 6.6 and 6.15 constitute, therefore, a complete *reduced-form model* for this case. The model specified above, which corrects for the participation bias, lends itself to known consistent estimation techniques, provided the participation index I_i (and hence $\lambda_i = \lambda(I_i)$) is given or measured with negligible errors and provided all other variables are measured for all participants.

The coefficients in equations 6.15 to 6.18 identify all the coefficients appearing in the original model, as well as the elements of the first column Σ_1 of the original variance matrix Σ. Additional elements of Σ (and Σ^0) are identifiable through the average variance matrix

$$
\bar{\Sigma}^v \left(= \frac{1}{n} \sum_i \hat{\Sigma}_i^v \right)
$$

of residuals in equations 6.15 to 6.17 or through moments of reduced-form residuals in 6.20 combined with 6.14.

CASE 2: WAGE AND HOURS DATA AVAILABLE
ONLY FOR SURVEY-WEEK WORKERS

Assume that m participants $(m < n)$ work during the survey week (ordered first among the n participants). An estimate of the hourly wage W_i (applicable to hours in the current survey year) is provided by the hourly wage rate measured for H_i hours worked in the survey week.[18] Annual hours are estimated by $A_i = H_i K_i$, where K_i corresponds to the number of weeks worked (assumed known) in the year preceding the survey.

---

[18] In surveys such as the SEO, workers are not asked directly about their hourly wage rates, but rather about their total weekly earnings E_i, with W_i computed as E_i/H_i. See Chapter 3 for a discussion of this definition as a source of error.

The residuals (random variables) u_2, u_3, and u_4 of equations 6.1, 6.3, and 6.4 now include additional error components, relative to Case 1: u_{2i} includes week-to-week variations in the mean hourly wage rate, u_{4i} includes year-to-year variations in weeks (for a given individual i), and u_{3i} compounds week-to-week variations in H_i with the year-to-year components in K_i (i.e., in u_{4i}). In addition, measurement-error components could be larger in this case. However, if all these components may be assumed transitory, such that the deterministic part of the model is identical to that of equations 6.1 to 6.4, and if these transitory components are also independent of the exogenous variables x and y, then the applicable underlying model is formally the same, except that the variance matrix Σ now incorporates these additional transitory error components. However, the probability of working during the survey week ($i \leq m$) is proportional to the endogenous variable K_i. Therefore, a survey-week bias is implied for equations 6.15 to 6.18, if applied to these workers only.

These biases and their magnitudes are derived explicitly in Appendix A. Equation A.3 shows that the expected values of v_i in the survey-week working sample (where $H_i > 0$) are generally not zero, and are given by

$$E(v_i \mid H_i > 0) = \frac{1}{K_i^*} E(\delta_2 v_{2i} + v_{4i})v_i$$

$$= \frac{1}{K_i^*}[(\delta_2 \Sigma_2 + \Sigma_4) - (\delta_2 b_2 + b_4)bD_i], \qquad (6.21)$$

where K_i^* is expected weeks (among participants, equation 6.19), and the bracketed term is the covariance between $(K_i - K_i^*)$ and v_i, as derived by equation 6.14.

Since this bias arises because the selection probability is proportional to the endogenous variable K_i, the bias is eliminated by transforming all the variables (including the constant) by the multiplicative factor $(K_i^*/K_i)^{1/2}$ for each individual i. Alternatively and equivalently, all the first and second moments may be weighted by the individual weights K_i^*/K_i in estimating equations 6.15 to 6.18 by linear methods. (See Appendix A.)

Since K_i^* is not observed, it may be estimated consistently from the weeks reduced-form equation in 6.20, which is estimable for the total sample of participants. Alternatively, K_i^* may be replaced by $E\hat{K}_i$, the expected value of K_i in a reduced-form estimate using Tobin,[19] which allows for the constraint $K_i \leq 52$.

If the individual residuals $(K_i - K_i^*)$ include no transitory components and are therefore constant in adjacent years, this method gives unbiased estimates even if K_i is measured in the year preceding the survey year. However, if a year-to-year transitory variation in K_i exists, the bias is only partially eliminated, since the selection probability is proportional to the desired K_i^t in the survey year t, whereas the weights use K_i^{t-1} measured in year $t-1$. In any case, the remaining bias is small relative to the bias in the unweighted case, since the permanent component in the weeks residuals accounts for most of the total residual variance in weeks.[20]

To summarize, the correction for the survey-week bias is performed by replacing each variable χ_i in the equations of Case 1 by its transform $\hat{\chi}_i = (\hat{K}_i^* / K_i)^{1/2} \chi_i$ and then applying the model to the transformed variables in the subsample of survey-week workers.

IV. Strategy for Estimating the Basic Model

GENERAL COMMENTS

In principle, the basic model (equations 6.1, 6.3, 6.4, and 6.6), subject to the modifications required because of insufficient information and to the weeks corner-solution truncation, could be estimated as a complete simultaneous model by a full-information maximum likelihood method. That is, the likelihood function corresponding to the sample in either Case 1 or 2 may be explicitly derived, and then maximized with respect to all the unknown parameters.

However, prohibitive complexity and costs preclude this method. The joint distribution of the random variables of the model involves a four-dimensional, multivariate, doubly truncated, normal distribution, where each of the variables is a function of many unknown parameters. Maximizing this likelihood seems infeasible in the present state of the art. In addition, it is doubtful that such full-information maximum likelihood estimates, which are asymptotically fully efficient if the model is specified perfectly, are sufficiently robust against various

---

[19] See Tobin, and also the discussion below in Sec. IV.
[20] See Appendix A and Hanoch (Chapter 3).

misspecifications of the model, such as variable exclusions, heteroskedasticity (of the underlying Σ), nonnormality, nonlinearities, and inhomogeneity of expected behavior among individuals.

The strategy proposed here for estimating the basic model is designed to handle all six types of problems unique to it, as outlined in the Introduction, and to yield approximately consistent estimates for all its parameters with relatively low computation and programming costs. Although these estimates are not fully efficient, they are satisfactory since they use efficient methods and the information contained in the total sample including nonparticipants.[21] In addition, the methods proposed seem robust against misspecification problems mentioned above, such as heteroskedasticity and nonnormality. More efficient estimates may be achieved, at some of the proposed steps in this scheme, by allowing for heteroskedasticity (as estimated from the residuals, in combination with that implied by the theory) and by iteratively repeating certain steps in the scheme. But these measures are more complex and therefore more costly, and yield unknown, possibly minor benefits.[22]

The discussion is aimed at estimating the model using a large (several thousands) cross-sectional sample, which falls under Case 2 in Section III—that is, a survey-type sample (census or SEO data) where hours of work and hourly wage rates are measured only for workers in the survey week. Since estimation of the model under Case 1 is similar but simpler, the more complex strategy could be modified to fit Case 1 by omitting the steps designed to eliminate the survey-week bias through the weighting scheme explained in the previous section.[23]

---

[21] The information is not used in each stage, however. For example, in the probit analysis, information on wages and hours of workers is ignored.

[22] The foregoing discussion of the proposed estimation scheme is mostly nonrigorous and intuitive, since a complete rigorous analysis of problems such as relative efficiency and robustness is extremely difficult. Intuition, like personal taste, varies among researchers, however. The expert econometrician who reads this might therefore choose to apply a different strategy to estimate the same model.

[23] Some sources, however, give panel-type data (e.g., the Income Dynamics sample), which combine cross-sectional with time-series information. Utilizing such data may considerably improve the estimates, as well as provide additional information and insights regarding the stability of the behavioral relations, the sizes of the transitory and permanent components, and the validity of various specifications. But the analysis of such data requires extension and completion of the model itself in addition to alternative estimation methods, and is outside the scope of this study.

ESTIMATING THE PROBABILITY OF PARTICIPATION: PROBIT ANALYSIS

In this first step, equation 6.6 is estimated by maximum likelihood (probit analysis), using data on x, y, and DP (participation) for the total sample, to get estimates of the unit-normal index I_i and to derive from it (using exact functional relations) estimates of λ_i, $D_i = \lambda_i(\lambda_i + I_i)$, and the participation probability p_i for each individual i.

The likelihood function is given by

$$L = \prod_{i=1}^{n} P(I_i) \prod_{i=n+1}^{N} [(1 - P(I_i)],\qquad (6.22)$$

where $I_i = (\alpha' x_i - \beta' y_i)/\sigma_1$, and $P(I)$ is the unit-normal probability function.

In following steps, the estimated I_i, λ_i, and D_i are substituted for their true values without distinguishing them in notation.[24] Since the method is maximum likelihood, it is asymptotically fully efficient relative to the information utilized—that is, the information on all exogenous variables for the total sample and on previous-year participation (ignoring at this stage the information pertaining to quantities supplied by participants and to measured wage rates).

Nevertheless, some estimation errors in λ_i and I_i exist, and are thus incorporated into the residuals in each equation that includes estimated λ_i or I_i. Since the estimated values are functions of the exogenous variables, λ_i and I_i are treated as exogenous variables (instruments) in these equations, thus providing a "two-stage" procedure, where the probit first stage is nonlinear (maximum likelihood).

Equation 6.6 is treated here as a reduced-form equation, not as a structural equation, in the procedure for estimating the simultaneous model. That is, the probit step is used for estimating the values of λ_i and I_i for each worker, but not for estimating directly the parameters $(\alpha, \beta)/\sigma_1$, since these are estimated directly at later steps using data on measured wage rates in equations 6.15 and 6.5 or 6.18. In principle, this step gives an estimate of the coefficient α_j/σ_1 for every variable x_j in x and not in y. Since α_j is estimated directly in the wage equation 6.15, this step provides multiple estimates of σ_1 (by taking ratios of coefficients for each such x_j) and of α_j (by multiplying the probit

---

[24] Except in the section below, where $\hat{I}$ denotes the estimate. The error in the actual participation equation—namely, $DP_i - E(DP_i) = DP_i - P(I_i)$—must not be confused with the relatively small errors of estimation—namely, $(I_i - EI_i)$ or $(\lambda_i - E\lambda_i)$.

coefficients by each alternative estimate of σ_1). This procedure can also estimate coefficients β_j, corresponding to variables y_j in y and not in x; and $(\alpha_k - \beta_k)$ for variables common to x and y, providing multiple indirect estimates of β_k for such variables (by using again the corresponding estimate of α_k from the wage equation). These possibilities thus indicate overidentification of parameters whenever there exists more than one variable x_j included in x and not in y.

In addition to sampling errors, however, the probit estimates of α_j (up to a factor of proportionately σ_1) may also differ conceptually from $\hat{\alpha}_j$ estimated in the wage equation. The "conceived" market wage rate influencing the individual's decision on participation in the labor force (which is associated with the probit coefficients) may be biased, relative to both actual wage offers and the wage rate conceived by workers in their decisions concerning quantities supplied. Since the latter is the focus of interest in this model, the estimated individual probit coefficients are ignored, except as they contribute to the linear combination index I_i. This index, in turn, is used for correcting the selectivity bias (through $\lambda(I_i)$), as well as for estimating the reservation wage coefficients, by introducing I as a variable in equation 6.5 or 6.18, together with y, and using as a dependent variable either the actual wage or the estimated expected wage.

Finally, experience with alternative models (such as linear probability or logit[25]) and alternative methods for estimating the probability of participation suggests that probit estimates are efficient and robust against nonnormality and heteroskedasticity,[26] although normality and homoskedasticity may appear to be crucial in formulating the likelihood function of equation 6.22. This observation seems to hold for a variety of problems and types of data.

PRELIMINARY REDUCED-FORM ESTIMATES OF WEIGHTING SCHEME
AND MARKET WAGE EQUATION

In order to apply the weighting scheme, which nearly eliminates the survey-week bias, an estimate of the weight K^*/K is required for each survey-week worker (denoted simply as "worker" in the following discussion, as distinguished from "participant"). Since information on

[25] See Berkson (1944 and 1955) regarding the logistic distribution (of u_{1i}, in this case). The binomial deviations $(DP_i - P_i)$ are heteroskedastic even if var u_{1i} is constant.

[26] That is, heteroskedasticity of the underlying normal distribution (of u_{1i}, in this case). The binomial deviations $(DP_i - E(DP_i)$ are heteroskedastic even if var u_{1i} is constant.

weeks but not on wages is available for all participants, K^* is estimated by ordinary least squares (OLS) regression of K in the reduced-form equation for weeks in equation 6.20, where the independent variables are λ, x, and z.

λ is often highly (negatively) correlated with I over the participants' sample range,[27] although $\lambda(I)$ is a nonlinear (convex) function. In addition, if $z = y$, then I is an exact linear combination of x and z, and equation 6.20 is highly multicollinear. This multicollinearity affects the reliability of individual coefficients, but not the coefficient of determination R^2 or the predicted value K^* (as long as numerical errors are not too large, which might be a problem if the independent-variables moment matrix is too nearly singular).

This predicted value is now used to compute weights K_i^*/K_i for each worker ($i \le m$). These weights are later revised by allowing for the truncation effect in weeks, but are required at this stage for estimating the predicted wage in the next step, which is required in turn for executing this weeks-truncation correction itself.

Next, first-round estimates of w^* are derived, applying weighted least squares (WLS) linear regression of $w = \ln W$ on the variables x and λ (equation 6.15) to the working sample, using the weights (K^*/K) estimated above to correct for the survey-week bias. These estimates of w^* are also revised in the final stage, but are needed for the next step.

TOBIT ANALYSIS OF SUPPLY OF WEEKS

Given the estimates of equation 6.15 above, an estimate of w_i^* may now be imputed to each participant ($i \le n$, or $K_i > 0$), although market wage data are missing for nonworking participants. The weeks supply equation in 6.19 is reproduced here, allowing for the truncation at 52 weeks:

(i) $\quad \tilde{K}_i = \gamma_2' z_i + \delta_2 w_i^* + b_4 \lambda_i + \varepsilon_i$;

(ii) $\quad K_i = \text{Min}\,(\tilde{K}_i, 52)$.

$\tilde{K}_i$ is "desired weeks supply" and $\varepsilon_i = \delta_2 v_{2i} + v_{4i}$. This truncated weeks supply equation may now be calculated by Tobin's method of estimating a linear equation with a limited dependent variable (denoted *Tobit*). This method yields maximum likelihood estimates, assuming

[27] The correlation is typically around $-.98$.

normality and homoskedastic disturbances ε_i. However, since ε_i is normal but heteroskedastic in this model (see equation 6.14), applying this method here gives only an approximation for maximum likelihood.

This equation may be chosen as a final estimate of the weeks supply equation. Alternatively, a similar equation may be estimated using only the working sample of m, and using a weighted-Tobit method with (K^*/K) as weights. One justification for the latter alternative is comparability with the hours supply and wage equations, which are estimable only for workers. Another is the assertion that, since w^* was estimated in the working sample, the imputation of w^* to nonworkers may involve biases (if transitory components in ε are important and highly correlated with v_2); therefore, the internal consistency of the equation might be improved if restricted to the working sample.

However, the Tobit step is suggested not as a vehicle for yielding final estimates, but rather as an intermediary step, for revising the weights as well as for creating a dichotomous variable that distinguishes between full-year and part-year workers. Several considerations lead to this suggestion. First, the Tobit maximum likelihood method is predicated on normality and homoskedasticity, and seems to be sensitive to deviations from these assumptions. Second, it cannot be easily incorporated into a simultaneous-equations model as part of a system to take account of relations across equations, especially since weeks and hours residuals are **highly** correlated (see Table 6.13 below). On the other hand, in specifying the supply equations within the linear simultaneous system, it would be desirable to use the Tobit estimates to allow for the effect of the upper-limit restriction on weeks, as explained below.

The Tobit analysis produces two key estimates for every individual: (1) An estimate of $\tilde{K}^*$, the predicted value of desired weeks ("the index"), as given by the deterministic part of equation 6.23; (2) the *expected value locus EK*, which is a nonlinear function of the index (and the limit). For truncation at an upper limit, EK is a concave function of $\tilde{K}^*$, smaller than $\tilde{K}^*$ and approaching the limit asymptotically from below.[28]

To introduce the effect of this truncation into the linearized supply equations, a shift is allowed in the level at the point where predicted desired weeks exceed the limit, and a change in slope is allowed with

---

[28] See Tobin (1958), Amemiya (1973a), and Sec. V.4 below.

respect to the two primary variables—the wage variable $w(=\ln W)$ and nonwage income Y. This linearization in the weeks supply approximates the expected value locus EK by two linear segments, such that the kink occurs where the individual's desired number of weeks exceeds the physical limit of 52, as predicted by the Tobit index $\tilde{K}^*$—that is, where the probability of full-year work exceeds 0.5.

The actual method for excuting this modification is simple. Define the dichotomous variable DK:

$$DK_i = \begin{cases} 0 & \text{if} & \tilde{K}_i^* \le 52 \\ 1 & \text{if} & \tilde{K}_i^* > 52 \end{cases}.$$

Then introduce (linearly) into the two supply equations these three variables:

(i) DK;   (ii) $DKW = DK \cdot w$;   (iii) $DKY = DK \cdot Y$

The corresponding coefficients are then interpreted as shifts in the level and the slopes $\partial K/\partial W$ and $\partial K/\partial Y$, respectively.

In principle, one could use the alternative dichotomous variable (and its interactions with w and Y) that distinguishes between full-year and part-year workers by the actual rather than predicted number of weeks worked, provided that these variables are treated as endogenous (associated with the endogenous variable K).[29] In the present specification, however, DK is exogenous, because the combination of exogenous variables given by the Tobit estimate $\tilde{K}^*$ is used as the criterion for defining it. DKY is also exogenous (since Y is considered exogenous), whereas DKW is an endogenous variable in the linear model, since w itself is endogenous.

An additional use of the Tobit analysis is to redefine the weights used for survey-week bias correction to be EK/K (rather than K^*/K), where EK is the estimated expected value of K. These weights seem preferable to K^*/K because the numerator of the weight equalizes or preserves the scale of the variances of residuals across individuals if the numerator's expected value is equal to that of the denominator K. But the Tobit EK is a consistent and more efficient estimate of this mean, compared with the OLS estimate K^*.

---

[29] However, this alternative method is probably inefficient, due to the increase in the number and the collinearity of the endogenous variables.

MODIFYING THE PSEUDO RESERVATION WAGE EQUATION

Equation 6.18, which is used as an alternative for estimating the coefficients β of the reservation wage equation, includes the two independent variables I and λ. As mentioned above, I and λ tend to be highly correlated negatively over the working sample range, since λ is a monotone decreasing function of I with a small degree of non-linearity.[30] To avoid this multicollinearity problem, it is preferable to substitute for I a linear function of λ, as estimated by the following regression in the working sample:

$$I_i = I_0 - I_1\lambda_i + e_i. \tag{6.24}$$

The modified equation 6.18 is now

$$w_i = (\beta_0 + \sigma_1 I_0) + \beta'_1 y_{1i} + (b_2 - \sigma_1 I_1)\lambda_i + \hat{v}_{2i}, \tag{6.25}$$

where β_0 is the constant coefficient in β; and y_1 and β_1 are, respectively, the y variables without the constant and their β-coefficients. The variable $\hat{v}_{2i}$ includes $\sigma_1 e_i$, the residual generated by the nonlinearity in $I(\lambda)$, in addition to the wage equation residual v_{2i}.[31] The coefficient b_2 is estimated separately in the market wage equation 6.15, and I_1 and I_0 are estimated separately by equation 6.24, so that σ_1 and β_0 can be estimated from the coefficient of λ and the intercept, respectively, in equation 6.25.

In modifying this equation, the function $I(\lambda)$ rather than $\lambda(I)$ should be linearized, if the same variable λ is to appear in all equations of the operational model. Omitting I as an instrument in the model involves no loss of power, since it is an exact linear combination of the other instruments x and y.

LINEAR-SYSTEM ESTIMATION

The various modifications of the basic model may now be assembled into a system of simultaneous linear equations defined for the working sample of m individuals (where $H > 0$).

Collecting all previous results and omitting the weighting operator, the linear system consists of the following four equations applicable to

[30] Estimates of the unit-normal index I typically range between -3 and $+3$, yielding a correlation coefficient of about $-.98$ to $-.99$ between λ and I.

[31] Estimation errors in $b_2\hat{\lambda}_i$ (from probit) are common to the estimated residuals in both equations.

the working sample $(i = 1, \ldots, m)$.[32]

Market wage equation:

$$\ln W_i = w_i = \alpha' x_i + b_2 \lambda_i + v_{2i}. \tag{6.26}$$

Annual hours supply equation:

$$A_i = \gamma_1' z_i + \delta_1 w_i + a_1 DK_i + a_2 DKW_i + a_3 DKY_i + b_3 \lambda_i + v_{3i}. \tag{6.27}$$

Weeks supply equation:

$$K_i = \gamma_2' z_i + \delta_2 w_i + k_1 DK_i + k_2 DKW_i + k_3 DKY_i + b_4 \lambda_i + v_{4i}. \tag{6.28}$$

Pseudo reservation wage equation:

$$\ln W_i = w_i = (\beta_0 + \sigma_1 I_0) + \beta_1' y_{1i} + (b_2 - \sigma_1 I_1) \lambda_i + \hat{v}_{2i}. \tag{6.29}$$

The endogenous variables in these four equations are W, A, K, and DKW; y_1 is the vector of exogenous variables y, omitting the constant 1; and β_1 are the corresponding coefficients, omitting the intercept β_0. In terms of the order condition for identification (exclusion restrictions), this system is identified if at least two distinct x or y variables are not included among the variables z, since each of the supply equations 6.27 and 6.28 includes two right-side endogenous variables, w and DKW (if λ is viewed as exogenous).[33]

Consistent single-equation estimates of these linear equations may now be derived inexpensively by using weighted two-stage least

---

[32] Since the recommended computer programs handle the estimation by using a *moment matrix* as an input, rather than individual observations, the variables in each observation need not be transformed for application of the weighting scheme of Sec. III, Case 2. Instead, a preliminary program creates the weighted moment matrix,

$$\hat{X}'\hat{X} = \left\{ \sum_i \left(X_{ji} X_{ki} \cdot \frac{EK_i}{K_i} \right) \right\},$$

where X contains all variables of the model, including the constant 1, and the weights EK/K are estimated by Tobit analysis above. The sums $\sum X_{ji}(EK_i/K_i)$ are thus also weighted by EK_i/K_i. The sum of the weights modifies approximately the number of observations m, to achieve correctly scaled means, covariances, and other test statistics.

[33] It is possible to treat λ as endogenous, because of its nonlinear relation to I. In this case, three variables should be excluded from z.

squares (TSLS) estimation. A more efficient set of system estimates is provided, however, by applying the weighted three-stage least squares (3SLS)[34] estimation technique. The increased efficiency results from taking into account covariances of residuals across equations to yield generalized least squares (GLS) estimates,[35] using the TSLS residuals to calculate the variance-covariance matrix.

However, the 3SLS technique should not be applied to all four equations (6.26 to 6.29) in one sweep, because of the high correlation between residuals, $\hat{v}_2$ and v_2. The difference $(\hat{v}_2 - v_2)$ consists of the following four elements: (1) $\sigma_1 e$, the nonlinearity error component of equation 6.24; (2) the error associated with the estimation of I in the probit analysis (in addition to the error in $b_2 \lambda$, which is common to both v_2 and $\hat{v}_2$); (3) differences between measurement errors in x and y, if any; (4) possibly some behavioral errors due to differences between expected actual wages and expected conceived wages used in the participation decision.

Nevertheless, these components are small relative to the cross-sectional wage residual variance $\sigma_{v_2}^2$, implying a high correlation between v_2 and $\hat{v}_2$.[36] Since equations 6.26 and 6.29 have the same dependent variable, this correlation also implies a high correlation between the deterministic parts of the two equations. In other words, the identity equation 6.5 holds with a high degree of approximation for the estimated I and the measured x and y. Since the 3SLS method is equivalent to GLS estimates of a single equation created by "stacking" all equations of the model,[37] the high correlation between these two equations would introduce high multicollinearity into the stacked equation, with the known result of drastically diminishing the accuracy of estimates in each equation separately. In addition, the adverse effects of multicollinearity would be magnified by specification errors in either or both of these two equations.

The alternative suggested here avoids this problem, by estimating separately *two systems of three equations each*, using 3SLS in each case:

1. A three-equation system consisting of 6.26 to 6.28, used mainly for efficient estimates of the wage equation 6.26, and of the residual variance matrix.

[34] See Zellner and Theil (1962).
[35] See Theil (1971).
[36] The empirically estimated correlation was .94 for the 4-equation model of Sec. V.
[37] See Theil (1971).

2. An alternative three-equation system consisting of 6.27 to 6.29 and constituting linear system estimates of the supply model—that is, the two quantity-supply equations for annual hours and weeks, and the pseudo reservation wage equation.

Since v_2 of equation 6.26 includes fewer error components than $\hat{v}_2$, the first three-equation system is used for estimating the variance-covariance matrix Σ^v (see Appendix C). Recall that Σ_i^v is heteroskedastic when the original variance matrix Σ is constant. The 3SLS method assumes constant Σ_i^v but tends to be robust against its nonconstancy. The estimated variance matrix provided as part of the 3SLS output is thus an estimate of the mean $\bar{\Sigma}^v$ among individuals in the working sample. Estimates of the underlying matrix Σ (if assumed constant; or $\bar{\Sigma}$ if allowing for original heteroskedasticity) may be derived from $\bar{\Sigma}^v$ by applying the relation

$$\hat{\Sigma} = \bar{\Sigma}^v + \hat{b}\,\hat{b}'\bar{D}. \tag{6.30}$$

Equation 6.30 aggregates 6.14 over the working sample, and $\hat{b} = (-\hat{\sigma}_1, \hat{b}_2, \hat{b}_3, \hat{b}_4)$ are estimated coefficients of the model. $\bar{D}$ is the mean of $D_i = \lambda_i^2 + \lambda_i I_i$ in the working sample.

The second system of equation 6.27 to 6.29 provides final estimates for the supply equations using the 3SLS method, which in this case allows for the covariances of the pseudo reservation wage residuals $\hat{v}_2$ with the supply residuals v_3 and v_4, as well as the covariance between the two supply residuals.

An alternative method for estimating the reservation wage equation, as explained in the next section, makes use of the results provided by these two 3SLS systems in conjunction with additional information on the total sample.

ALTERNATIVE ESTIMATE OF RESERVATION WAGE EQUATION

The coefficients α of equation 6.26 are estimated consistently and relatively efficiently by the 3SLS method described in the previous section. Using these estimates $\hat{\alpha}$, it is now possible to construct an estimate $\hat{w}_i = \hat{\alpha}'x_i$ of the predicted log wage for each individual, given his measured variables x_i, such that $\hat{w}_i$ is free from selectivity biases:

$$\hat{w}_i = \hat{\alpha}'x_i = \alpha'x_i + \varepsilon_{1i}, \qquad (i = 1, \ldots, N) \tag{6.31}$$

with ε_{1i} equal to $(\hat{\alpha} - \alpha)'x_i$, having zero mean, and uncorrelated with x_i

in the limiting distribution within the total sample of both participants and nonparticipants. Substituting from the identity equation 6.5 into 6.31 gives

$$\hat{w}_i = \sigma_1 I_i + \beta' y_i + \varepsilon_{1i} = \sigma_1 \hat{I}_i + \beta' y_i + (\varepsilon_{1i} + \varepsilon_{2i}), \quad (i = 1, \ldots, N)$$
$$(6.32)$$

where $\hat{I}_i$ is the estimated probit index and $\varepsilon_{2i} = \sigma_1(I_i - \hat{I}_i)$. Since the residuals ε_1 and ε_2 are associated with estimation errors, they tend to vanish with increased sample size. The OLS estimate of equation 6.32 in the total sample thus gives consistent estimates of σ_1 and β.

The advantages of this method, compared with the 3SLS estimates of equation 6.29, are as follows: (1) It utilizes additional information on x and y for nonworkers; (2) it is simpler to execute, since no selectivity bias corrections are required—thus obviating the need to linearize $I(\lambda)$ (when both λ and I are present in the same equation), or to weigh the moments or the observations, as in 6.29; (3) it seems more efficient, as explained below.

Substituting from 6.31 into the original wage equation 6.1 gives

$$w_i = \alpha' x_i + u_i = \hat{w}_i - \varepsilon_{1i} + u_{2i}.$$

Substituting from 6.32 gives

$$w_i = \sigma_1 \hat{I}_i + \beta' y_i + (u_{2i} + \varepsilon_{2i}). \quad (6.33)$$

Clearly, the variance of the residual $(u_2 + \varepsilon_2)$ approaches σ_2^2 as the sample size increases, and does not vanish—in contrast with the variance of $(\varepsilon_1 + \varepsilon_2)$ in 6.32. Even if wages could be measured for everybody, the OLS estimate of 6.32 would tend to be more efficient than an OLS estimate of 6.33, since both equations have the same right-side variables and $\text{var}(\varepsilon_1 + \varepsilon_2)$ tends to be smaller than $\text{var}(u_1 + \varepsilon_2)$.

The estimates of $\text{var}(\hat{\sigma}_1, \hat{\beta})$ as computed by an OLS output of equation 6.32 are biased downward considerably, since the residual variance is estimated under the assumption that observations on $\hat{w}_i$ are N independent observations, whereas in fact they are associated with only k independent estimates of α_j ($j = 1, \ldots, k$). However, the true variance of $(\varepsilon_1 + \varepsilon_2)$ can be estimated approximately—assuming ε_1 and ε_2 to be uncorrelated—by using estimates of σ_2^2 and $\text{var}\,\hat{\alpha}$ based on the 3SLS estimates of equation 6.26 to estimate $\text{var}\,\varepsilon_1$; and by estimating $\text{var}\,\varepsilon_2$ as the difference between residual variances in equations 6.26 and 6.29.

In conclusion, both simplicity and efficiency suggest the use of OLS in equation 6.32 for final estimates of the reservation wage equation. In addition, similarity of results from the two alternative methods would help to increase confidence in the internal consistency of this model (although it is not clear exactly what assumptions are tested by this comparison).

V. Estimates of the Model

V.1 introduction to the estimates

The degree of identification of the equations included in a simultaneous model depends heavily on the choice of variables, on their definition as exogenous or endogenous, and in particular, on exclusion restrictions. Strictly speaking, no variable is truly exogenous in a cross-sectional context in the long run. This is true even for a variable like age, since in the long run the age distribution is influenced by endogenous choices of birth rates (by parents), of age of marriage, and of factors affecting divorce and mortality. Other variables such as education, number and ages of children, region and type of community of dwelling and nonwage incomes clearly entail much stronger endogenous elements. Nevertheless, they are regarded as approximately exogenous in this study. Similarly, every variable should appear in each equation, if a pure literal approach to the theory is taken. It would be difficult to find a measured variable that influences only the wage rate, representing market demand, or only the reservation wage and quantity of labor (if working), representing supply. In the context of labor, the commonality of demand and supply effects is even more likely, because both deal with allocations of the same factor—time—to market work and nonmarket or leisure activities. Any variable influencing market productivity probably affects nonmarket productivity. The exclusions employed in this labor supply model are, therefore, ad hoc, rough approximations at best. Section V.2 defines and discusses the variables and the way in which they are introduced into the model.

The remainder of this section is organized in the following manner.

Section V.3 concerns reduced form estimates of the participation equation using probit analysis, and describes variables constructed by these estimates and used in subsequent steps.

Section V.4 describes briefly preliminary reduced form estimates required for subsequent sections, and discusses in more detail the analysis of the weeks supply equation by Tobin's limited dependent variable method (Tobit), in two alternative versions.

Section V.5 presents estimates of the linear system, based on modifications of the equations provided by previous steps and estimated by a weighted three-stage least squares technique. Estimated wage, hours, weeks, and reservation wage equations are presented and discussed, with a particular emphasis on the effects of age and education on market wage, and the effects of children and of the wage rate on supply. Equations for minimum supply quantities are also estimated and discussed. The residual variance structure is presented at the end, with details in Appendix C.

Finally, Section V.6 summarizes individual predictions of endogenous variables, as computed from the linear system estimates, and computes wage and income elasticities of conditional and expected (or aggregate) supplies.

V.2 DATA AND VARIABLES

The total sample on which this study is based consists of observations on 6,319 white married women with a wage-earning (nonfarm) husband present, in the 1967 Survey of Economic Opportunity (SEO). Interviews were conducted in the spring of 1967, and labor force information (hours of work and weekly earnings) reported about the week preceding the interview ("the survey week"). Other annual information, such as weeks worked, earnings, and nonwage income, was reported about the preceding calender year, 1966. The criteria for exclusions leading to the particular sample used here are described in Appendix B.

Using the coded information provided in the original files, the following variables were defined and computed for each observation (on wife):

(i) *Variables considered exogenous and common to demand (x) and the supply (y) equations*:

ED = Years of school completed.
AGE = Age in years.
AGE-45 = AGE-45 if AGE > 45; = 0 otherwise.
CENCITY = 1 if living in central city of SMSA; = 0 otherwise.
SUBURBS = 1 if living in SMSA, but not in central city; = 0 otherwise.

HLTH = 1 if, as reported, adverse health conditions affected quantity or type of work, or if health prevented work; = 0 otherwise.

CONST = 1 for everbody.

(ii) *Variables considered exogenous and assumed to affect market wage offers (demand), but not quantity of labor supplied, or reservation wage (x but not y):*

NCEN = 1 if living in north-central states; = 0 otherwise.

WEST = 1 if living in western states; = 0 otherwise.

SOUTH = 1 if living in southern states; = 0 otherwise.

SOUTH 16 = 1 if lived in a southern state at age 16; = 0 otherwise.

AGE*ED = AGE × ED

ED-7 = ED-7 if ED > 7; = 0 otherwise. (That is, years of school completed beyond 7th grade).

ED-11 = ED-11 if ED > 11; = 0 otherwise. (That is, years completed beyond 11th grade).

AGE-25 = AGE-25 if AGE > 25; = 0 otherwise.

AGE-35 = AGE-35 if AGE > 35; = 0 otherwise.

KIDSBORN = No. of live births by the wife.

(iii) *Variables considered exogenous and assumed to affect supply, but not demand (y but not x):*

EH + Y = Husband's annual earnings + regular family nonwage income in 1966 (in thousands of dollars).[38]

NOKIDS = 1 if no children under age 18 present at home; = 0 otherwise.

KIDSHOME = No. of children under age 18 living at home with married couple.

AGLSTKID = Age of youngest child living at home at last birthday (= 0 if NOKIDS = 1).

KIDS*ED = KIDSHOME × ED.

(iv) *Endogenous variables*

WEEKS = No. of weeks in 1966 in which wife worked as a civilian. The SEO weeks intervals were assigned their respective midpoints.

---

[38] See Appendix B for the definition used for nonwage income.

AHOURS = Imputed annual hours = No. of hours worked in the survey week × WEEKS.

LNWAGE = Log of [earnings from wages during the survey week ÷ hours of work during the survey week]. Computed only if AHOURS > 0. (Observation excluded if reported positive hours but zero earnings in the survey week).

DP = 1 if WEEKS > 0; = 0 if WEEKS = 0 (A dummy variable for annual participation in labor force in 1966).

A few explanations regarding these specifications are in order:

Age Variables

The age effects are nonlinear in both market wage and supply equations. "Splined" age variables (such as "AGE-45") allow for a change of slope of the wage effect at the limit point (45 years in this case), without causing a discontinuity in the function. The present specification assumes a more detailed, four-segment function (with break points at 25, 35, and 45 years of age) in the wage equation, whereas on the supply side the age effect is assumed constant up to age 45, but is allowed to be a different constant at older ages. In addition, age interacts with education on the market wage side, reflecting variations in age effects between levels of education (or equivalently, variations of productivity of schooling between age groups). Obviously, the age variables cannot distinguish, in a cross-section, between life-cycle effects and cohort effects.

Education Variables

Education is measured by years of school completed. This overlooks other important elements of education that may affect labor supply and demand, such as quality of education, time spent in school, and informal schooling and training.[39] The effects of schooling are allowed to be nonlinear, using both a spline function and interaction variables. In the market wage equation, the effect is allowed to differ in three intervals: 0–7, 8–11, and 12 or over years of school, thus producing a three-segment continuous function. This particular specification was found superior to the use of a quadratic, as well as to the use of the more common breakdown to elementary (0–8), high school (9–12) and

[39] On some of these aspects, see Welch (1966). See also Becker (1965), Mincer (1974).

college (13+). It seems that the "graduation effect" of the 8th year of grade school or the 12th year of high school causes these school years' effects to resemble more the effect at the next level of schooling than that of previous schooling at the same level. The interaction of schooling with number of children at home is taken to be important on the supply side (through the variable KIDS*ED), since the presence of children might influence the labor supply of more educated women differently than it influences the labor supply of the less educated.

Children Variables

The number and age distribution of children have been found empirically to be most important for determining the participation and labor supply of married women. Thus, on the supply side, four variables associated with children are defined. First, the dummy variable NOKIDS allows a shift of level (of quantity supplied as well as of the reservation wage) between women with and without children present in the home. Second, the age of the youngest child is assumed to have a separate important effect (on those with children; i.e., if NOKIDS = 0). Third, a linear effect of the number of children present (KIDSHOME) is assumed. Fourth, as explained above, the interaction of the number of children with mother's age modifies the effect of KIDSHOME by allowing it to vary among ages.

On the demand side, it is assumed that the number of children ever born to a woman (KIDSBORN) reflects accumulated periods of abstention from work and may be a proxy for experience and regularity of attachment to the labor force. Taken in conjunction with the children variables that appear on the supply side, its marginal effect reflects only that of children born but not present at home (mostly grown-up), and is thus associated more directly with labor demand (through labor force history) than with labor supply (through children currently present).

Location Variables

The distinction between urban, suburban, and rural (nonfarm) dwelling is assumed to be associated with tastes and home productivity, with fixed costs of labor force participation, and with consumer and labor markets segmentation, causing wage differentials between equally productive persons, as well as urban-surburban-rural differences in supply between persons receiving the same money wage offers. The dummy variables CENCITY and SUBURBS are thus present in all the equations of the model. On the other hand, the regional dummy variables, representing location in the four major regions of the U.S. (with the northeastern region as the omitted dummy variable), are assumed to influence market wages but are excluded from the supply and reservation wage equations. Regional differences in productivity and the regional segmentation of the labor market seem important, whereas sufficient variety seems to exist within each region regarding tastes, costs of participation, and consumer prices to justify the implied assumption that regional differences in supply functions are negligible.

In addition to current location, the region of location at age 16 might be another relevant factor for two reasons: first, it represents regional differences in quality of early education; and second, if it is different from current region, it represents migration effects. Both of these seem particularly relevant with respect to the dichotomy south/nonsouth. For this reason, the variable SOUTH 16 is introduced. Its total effect on wages might reflect two offsetting effects. On the one hand, quality of schooling is generally lower in the south, resulting in lower wages.[40] On the other hand its migration effect (if SOUTH = 0) is expected to reflect (as any migration effect) strong motivation and initiative and better opportunities at the region of destiny, resulting in higher average productivity and wages.

Nonwage and Husband Income

As explained in Section I, the present model is an individual model for married women, ignoring intrafamily substitution of time. Consequently, husband's earnings are assumed to influence the wife's supply decision only through the income effect, and thus their effect is assumed equal, dollar for dollar, to that of other nonwage income of the family.[41]

Health Conditions

The variable HLTH allows shifts in all the equations due to poor health (of the wife). Clearly, poor health affects productivity and wage offers (demand) as well as fixed costs, preferences, and the price of

---

[40] Interacting this variable with education might have captured this effect more appropriately.

[41] See Appendix B for its definition.

time at home (supply), through limitations on physical ability to work, affecting both market and nonmarket productivity, and through time and money requirements for health care.

Wage and Hours Variables

The 1967 SEO instructions to interviewers[42] require "hours worked last week" to include actual time spent on duty on all jobs, including overtime and excluding hours taken off or time lost, even if that time was paid for. On the other hand, on "earnings last week" the instructions stress that "normal" weekly pay should be determined, not including the effect of anything unusual, such as overtime or reduced rates paid. Since hourly wage is computed as the ratio of these two quantities, this inconsistency in treatment of extra time or time off the job may introduce large errors into hourly wage rate estimates (especially since transitory variations in hours enter only the denominator of this ratio). Since both annual hours and hourly wages are treated here as endogenous, however, the effect of these errors may reduce the efficiency of estimates and inflate residual variances but should not affect the consistency of coefficient estimates and expected predictions of the simultaneous model, unless wage rates tend to be biased in a particular direction. On the other hand, the effect of this unfortunate inconsistency in the definitions may introduce serious biases into estimates of variances and covariances of residuals.

Table 6.1 presents means of the original variables in the sample, classified by labor force status: workers (with positive hours of work in the survey week), participants (with positive workweeks in 1966, including nonworkers), and nonparticipants.[43]

Comparison of means among status groups shows the crude association of each of these variables with participation, as well as with quantity of work (since the amount of work by workers is higher, on average, than by all participants).

V.3 THE PARTICIPATION EQUATION: PROBIT ANALYSIS

Table 6.2 summarizes results of estimating the participation equation 6.6 by probit analysis, using the variable *DP* as a criterion for annual

---

[42] See 1967 SEO Codebook.

[43] Detailed tables, including variances and correlations of these variables, as well as of additional constructed or predicted variables, are filed with the author and available upon request.

TABLE 6.1: Means of Original Variables, by Labor Force Status

Variable	Workers	Total Participants	Nonparticipants	Total
number	2064	3044	3275	6319
WEEKS	41.59	35.34	0	17.02
AHOURS	1472.1	—*	0	—
LNWAGE	0.6669	—*	0	—
EH+Y	7.187	7.125	8.694	7.938
AGE	38.33	37.01	37.96	37.50
AGE-25	13.76	12.59	13.32	12.97
AGE-35	6.39	5.77	6.19	5.99
AGE-45	1.75	1.60	1.99	1.80
AGE*ED	434.3	415.8	409.1	412.3
ED	11.40	11.29	10.88	11.08
ED-7	4.47	4.38	4.06	4.21
ED-11	1.18	1.11	0.95	1.03
KIDS*ED	15.01	15.99	21.31	19.01
NOKIDS	0.391	0.349	0.222	0.283
AGLSTKID	4.83	4.50	4.14	4.32
KIDSHOME	1.33	1.43	2.00	1.725
KIDSBORN	2.17	2.22	2.73	2.48
CENCITY	0.295	0.299	0.304	0.302
SURBURBS	0.393	0.378	0.428	0.404
NCEN	0.270	0.264	0.262	0.263
WEST	0.168	0.181	0.166	0.173
SOUTH	0.314	0.317	0.307	0.312
SOUTH 16	0.321	0.319	0.302	0.310
HLTH	0.0349	0.0526	0.106	0.080

* Hours and wages for participants who are not workers are nonzero but unknown.

labor force participation. The coefficients in this table are those of the index I, and not of the probability of participation $p = P(I)$.[44,45]

Inspecting the third column of Table 6.2, which gives asymptotic t-statistics for each coefficient, the most significant effects on the

[44] A test of significance for the equation as a whole is provided by the log-likelihood ratio (LLR), where -2LLR is distributed as chi-square, yielding in this case: $\chi^2(21) = 1059.8$, which is highly significant.

[45] The effect of a variable X on the probability is not constant and is obtained by multiplying the coefficient by the normal density $f(I)$ at the relevant point, since:

$$\frac{\partial p}{\partial X} = \frac{dP}{dI} \cdot \frac{\partial I}{\partial X} = f(I) \cdot \frac{\partial I}{\partial X}.$$

TABLE 6.2: Probit Estimates of Annual Labor Force Participation (*White Married Women, 1966*)

Variable	Index Coefficient	Standard Error	t-Value
EH+Y	−0.0930	0.0057	−16.27
AGE	−0.0360	0.0170	−2.12
AGE-25	0.0036	0.0212	0.17
AGE-35	−0.0034	0.0130	−0.26
AGE-45	−0.0299	0.0115	−2.60
AGE*ED	0.00127	0.00066	1.29
ED	0.0575	0.0420	1.37
ED-7	−0.0451	0.0375	−1.20
ED-11	0.0752	0.0257	2.93
KIDS*ED	−0.00684	0.00390	−1.76
NOKIDS	1.229	0.0831	14.80
AGLSTKID	0.0824	0.0056	14.80
KIDSHOME	0.0006	0.0469	0.001
KIDSBORN	0.0411	0.0159	2.59
CENCITY	−0.0906	0.0446	−2.03
SUBURBS	−0.1000	0.0423	−2.36
NCEN	0.0478	0.0471	1.01
WEST	0.1301	0.0525	2.48
SOUTH	−0.0810	0.0726	−1.12
SOUTH 16	0.0431	0.0657	0.66
HLTH	−0.5801	0.0645	−8.99
CONST	0.4237	0.5052	0.84

participation index are the negative effect of the income variable (EH+Y), and the positive effects of the age of youngest child at home (AGLSTKID) and of having no children at home (NOKIDS). The number of children at home, other than zero, has no significant partial effect, while the number ever born has some significant positive partial effect. The adverse effect of poor health (HLTH) is also very significant.

Additional variables affecting participation significantly are: AGE, with a negative effect; AGE-45, indicating an increase in the negative age effect beyond age 45; ED-11, causing participation to increase with years of college education; CENCITY and SUBURBS both have similar negative effects, as compared with the omitted variable for rural (outside SMSA) dwelling. Among regions, the west has higher

TABLE 6.3: Means of Constructed Variables Associated with
the Participation Index, by Labor Force Status

(Standard Deviations in Parentheses)

Variables	Workers	Total Participants	Nonparticipants	Total
Index: I	0.2494 (0.5271)	0.1834 (0.5427)	−0.2800 (0.6041)	−0.0568 (0.6201)
Probability: $p = P(I)$	0.5859 (0.1801)	0.5615 (0.1856)	0.4075 (0.1736)	0.4817 (0.1953)
Conditional Density: $\lambda = f(I)/p$	0.6802 (0.2959)	0.7204 (0.3081)	1.0128 (0.4523)	0.8719 (0.4160)
Variance Truncation Factor: $D = \lambda(\lambda + I)$	0.5660 (0.1288)	0.5810 (0.1309)	0.6769 (0.0993)	0.6307 (0.1251)

labor force participation of married women than the south or the (omitted) northeast.

The lack of significant effects of some important variables is not surprising. As shown in Section II above, the participation index I is proportional to the expected relative difference between the market wage and the reservation wage (equation 6.5). Therefore a variable which has a significant effect on each of these variables in the same direction may have a small effect on the difference. As explained however, this equation was treated primarily as a reduced form equation, used to extract estimates of the index I and its related functions, and not as a structural equation for estimating individual coefficients in either the wage or the reservation wage equation.[46]

The estimated equation in Table 6.2 was employed to construct, for each individual in the total sample, the following variables: the probit index I_i; the probability of participation $p_i = P(I_i)$; the conditional density $\lambda_i = f(I_i)/P_i$, where $f(I)$ is the unit-normal density; and the variance-correction factor $D_i = \lambda_i^2 + I_i\lambda_i$. (See Lemma 1, above). Table 6.3 summarizes means and standard deviations of these constructed variables by labor force status.

[46] See above, pp. 266–267.

Comparing the probability of participation as predicted by the probit equation with actual participation, we can evaluate the predictive power of this specification: among participants, the mean predicted probability is 0.56, as against 0.41 among nonparticipants. As expected, the predicted probability is somewhat higher (0.59) among workers, due to the positive correlation between weeks worked (which is proportional to the probability of inclusion in the subsample of workers) and participation.[47]

These predictions, while not extremely powerful, are clearly unbiased, as seen by comparing the mean predicted probability of participation in the total sample (0.48167) with the actual proportion (0.48172 = 3044/6319).

The variable λ_i is used as a bias-correction variable in equations estimated for workers. The variable $D = -d\lambda/dI$ is used in computing the residual variance matrix (see Appendix C) as well as the elasticities of supply (in Section V.6).

V.4 INTERMEDIARY STEPS, REDUCED FORMS, AND TOBIT ESTIMATES OF THE WEEKS SUPPLY EQUATION

This section outlines the results of the intermediary steps in the estimation procedure,[48] which are required for the final estimates of the linear system reported in Section V.5. First, a reduced-form supply of weeks equation was estimated by OLS for all participants, using all the exogenous variables as independent variables and, in addition, using λ, as estimated in the probit step, to correct for the participation selectivity bias.[49] Using the results of this step, an estimate K_i^* of expected weeks and a weight K_i^*/K_i were computed for each participant, to be used in the next step. The predicted mean of K^* within the subgroup of survey week workers was 35.25, as compared with the mean of 35.34 among all participants, and the biased actual mean

---

[47] See Appendix A, and an estimate of this correlation in Table 6.14 below.

[48] For explanations of these steps see Sec. IV.

[49] As explained in Sec. IV, this equation exhibits high multicollinearity among the explanatory variables, due to the high correlation between λ and I over the sample range and the fact that I is a linear combination of all the other variables; indeed, the standard errors of many coefficients were relatively high, but the standard error of the estimate (15.7 weeks) and the coefficient of determination ($R^2 = .175$) obtained were not affected by this multicollinearity. (Numerical errors may be important, if the matrix is nearly singular. However, this did not seem to be a problem in the present case).

among workers of 41.59 (see Table 6.1). Thus, the selectivity bias correction embedded in these estimates appears quite satisfactory.

Using the weights K^*/K (which were later replaced by a preferred estimate from the Tobit equation), the next step consisted of estimating a reduced-form wage equation by weighted least squares (WLS) in the group of survey week workers. The estimates of expected log wage w^*, as computed on the basis of this equation, were now consistent estimates, corrected for the two types of bias: (1) the participation selectivity bias, corrected by introducing λ into the equation and; (2) the survey week bias, corrected by weighting the moments by K^*/K, which is inversely proportional to the probability $K/52$ of working during the survey week. Comparing the mean of w^* with the actual (unweighted) mean among workers, we obtained $\bar{w}^* = 0.6209$ and $\bar{w} = 0.6669$, indicating a positive relative bias of about 4.7 percent in the wage ($\exp\{\bar{w} - \bar{w}^*\} = 1.047$), associated with this survey week selectivity bias.

Since w^* could now be computed for each participant (including nonworkers), it was possible to estimate the supply equation for weeks among all participants by Tobin's maximum likelihood method for limited dependent variables (Tobit), taking into account the upper-limit truncation at 52 weeks, and substituting for w its first-stage linear estimate w^*. Table 6.4 presents these estimates within the group of 3,044 participants, of which 1,288 (42.3 percent) worked full-time in terms of annual weeks in 1966 (50–52 weeks).[50] The selectivity bias effect, represented by the coefficient of λ, is only marginally significant (at 0.1 significance level). The predicted probability of a corner solution (full-year work) computed at the point of the sample means, was 0.375, as compared with the actual proportion of 0.423.

These Tobit estimates were used for constructing new variables as follows. The underlying residual standard deviation σ_4 was estimated by maximum likelihood as part of the Tobit output ($\sigma_4 = 24.45$ in this case). For each observation, the predicted probability of falling below the limit L ($L = 51$, the midpoint of the 50–52 limit interval) is given

---

[50] Since data on weeks are grouped, the midpoint of the 50–52 group (51) was taken as the limit in estimating the Tobit equation, but the true limit 52 was used for predictions based on these estimates. The linear equation estimated represents the underlying *index* $\bar{K}^*$ of desired workweeks and not the expected value EK of weeks worked, as derived below (equation 6.33).

TABLE 6.4: Supply of Weeks: Tobit Estimates for Participants

Variable	Coefficient	Standard Error	t-Value
EH+Y	−1.96	0.45	−4.39
AGE	0.46	0.098	4.63
AGE-45	−1.10	0.28	−3.90
ED	1.67	0.49	3.40
KIDS*ED	−0.31	0.12	−2.50
NOKIDS	26.63	4.97	5.36
AGLSTKID	1.75	0.35	4.96
KIDSHOME	2.14	1.37	1.56
CENCITY	0.06	1.58	0.04
SURBURBS	−0.92	1.54	−0.59
HLTH	−20.04	3.26	−6.14
w^*	4.93	3.97	1.24
λ	11.78	7.10	1.66
CONST	−2.25	7.97	−0.28

Observations: Limit 1,288; Nonlimit 1,756.

by:

$$P\left(\frac{L - \tilde{K}^*}{\sigma_4}\right) = P(\Delta),$$

where P is again the unit-normal (left-tail) probability, $\tilde{K}^*$ is the estimated index from the equation for that observation, and $\Delta = (L - \tilde{K}^*)/\sigma_4$. The *conditional* mean of K, given that it is nonlimit, is:

$$E(K \mid K < L) = \tilde{K}^* + E(u_4 \mid u_4 < \sigma_4 \Delta) = \tilde{K}^* - \sigma_4 \cdot \frac{f(\Delta)}{P(\Delta)} = \tilde{K}^* - \sigma_4 \cdot \lambda(\Delta),$$

where $f(\Delta)$ is the unit-normal density, and $\lambda(\Delta)$ is the conditional density, as in Lemma 1. Thus, the expected value of weeks is computed for each observation as follows:[51]

$$EK = [1 - P(\Delta)]L + P(\Delta) \cdot E(K \mid K < L) = L - \sigma_4[P(\Delta) \cdot \Delta + f(\Delta)].$$
$$(6.34)$$

[51] It may be shown that $dEK/d\tilde{K}^* = P(\Delta)$, $EK < L$, $EK < \tilde{K}^*$ and EK is inversely related to the probability $P(\Delta)$, approaching the limit asymptotically as the index $\tilde{K}^*$ increases and the nonlimit probability $P(\Delta)$ decreases. See Tobin (1958), Amemiya (1973a), for proofs.

TABLE 6.5: Means of Constructed Variables Associated with the Weeks Corner Solution
(*Standard Deviations in Parentheses*)

Variable	Workers	Participants
K^*	47.32	44.93
	(12.38)	(12.99)
EK	37.41	32.51
	(10.20)	(10.33)
EK/K	1.180	1.122
	(1.02)	(0.84)
DK	0.4147	0.3525
	(0.4928)	(0.4778)
DKY	2.826	2.429
	(3.790)	(3.692)
DKW	0.2802	—
	(0.4402)	—

The expected value was used in creating the weights EK/K to replace the first-round estimated weights K^*/K.

The dummy variable DK was constructed on the basis of the computed index K^*, as explained in Section IV, thus identifying as predicted-limit observations those with the index exceeding the limit 52; or equivalently, $P(\Delta) < 0.5$. The other two constructed variables were the interactions of DK with the income variable $EH + Y$ and the wage variable $w = \log W$:

$$DKY_i = (EH + Y)_i \times DK_i$$
$$DKW_i = w_i \times DK_i.$$

Table 6.5 summarizes the means for these constructed variables for all participants and for the subsample of survey-week workers.[52]

The same weeks supply equation was estimated by a *weighted-Tobit* method, within the subsample of workers only. In Table 6.6, results

[52] DWK could not be computed for nonworking participants, since no wage rate was reported for them. Assigning this group the predicted wage, based on the final estimates (Table 6.7 below), gives 0.2349 and 0.4019 for the mean and s.d. of DKW, respectively, for total participants.

TABLE 6.6: Supply of Weeks: Weighted Tobit Estimates for
Survey-Week Workers

Variable	Coefficient	Standard Error	t-Value
EH+Y	−2.19	0.55	−4.01
AGE	0.57	0.12	4.87
AGE-45	−1.10	0.33	−3.28
ED	1.60	0.59	2.73
KIDS*ED	−0.59	0.16	−3.73
NOKIDS	25.15	5.99	4.20
AGLSTKID	1.56	0.43	3.64
KIDSHOME	5.04	1.81	2.79
CENCITY	−0.15	1.94	−0.08
SUBURBS	−3.05	1.89	−1.61
HLTH	−23.35	4.12	−5.66
w^*	12.27	4.97	2.47
λ	11.94	8.68	1.38
CONST	−12.50	9.75	−1.28

Observations: Limit 1,161; Nonlimit 903.

are reported for these alternative estimates of the truncated supply of weeks equation (using the new weights EK/K for weighting the moments).

Comparing coefficients and t-statistics in Tables 6.4 and 6.6, we observe the similarity between the two sets of estimates. The major differences are: (1) the coefficient of (expected log) wage w^* is now larger (12.3 vs. 4.9) and significant; (2) the effect of the number of children at home (KIDSHOME) is also larger and significant (5.04 weeks worked per child vs. 2.14 in Table 6.5). In all cases, however, the differences between these estimates are insignificant (at a .05 level). The estimated standard deviation $\hat{\sigma}_4$ is very similar: $\sigma_4 = 24.15$ (versus 24.45 above). These results increase our confidence in the weighting scheme and the selectivity corrections, as well as in the stability of these maximum likelihood estimates.

One additional intermediary step required for estimation of the linear system which follows is an auxiliary linear regression of the probit index I on the variable λ within the working sample, which permits the elimination of I from the pseudo reservation wage equation (to avoid high multicollinearity between λ and I). The following equation was estimated by weighted least squares (using the weights EK/K) within the working sample of 2,064 women:

$$\hat{I} = I_0 = I_1 \cdot \lambda = 1.4468 - 1.7551\lambda. \tag{6.35}$$
$$(0.0048)\ (0.0063)$$

Numbers in parentheses are standard errors of coefficients; $R^2 = 0.974$; residual variance $= 0.00770$.

V.5 LINEAR SYSTEM ESTIMATES

The model described in Section IV, equations 6.26-6.29, is reproduced here in a slightly modified form:

Market wage equation

$$w_i = \alpha_0 + \alpha'x_i + b_2\lambda_i + v_{2i} \tag{6.26'}$$

Annual hours supply equation:[53]

$$\text{AHOURS}_i = \gamma_{10} + \gamma_1'y_i + \delta_1 w_i + b_3\lambda_i$$
$$+ a_1 DK_i + a_2 DKW_i + a_3 DKY_i + v_{3i} \tag{6.27'}$$

Annual weeks supply equation:

$$\text{WEEKS}_i = \gamma_{20} + \gamma_2'y_i + \delta_2 w_i + b_4\lambda_i$$
$$+ k_1 DK_i + k_2 DKW_i + k_3 DKY_i + v_{4i} \tag{6.28'}$$

Pseudo reservation wage equation:[54]

$$w_i = (\beta_0 + \sigma_1 I_0) + \beta_1'y_i + (b_2 - \sigma_1 I_1)\lambda_i + (v_{2i} + \varepsilon_i) \tag{6.29'}$$

These equations were estimated within the working sample by weighted three-stage least squares (3SLS), using the weights EK/K estimated in the Tobit step, in two sets of three equations each: (1) equations 6.26' to 6.28', which are used for final estimates of the wage equation, as well as for estimating the variance-covariance matrix; and (2) equations 6.27' to 6.29', constituting the supply model, and used to obtain final estimates of the hours and weeks supply equations.

---

[53] γ_{10} and γ_{20} refer to the constant term in the first (annual hours) and second (annual weeks) supply equations.

[54] ε is the residual difference between equations 6.26 and 6.29, which includes errors of linearization of $I(\lambda)$ in equation 6.32 above, as well as other elements. See p. 275.

TABLE 6.7: Market Wage Equation: Weighted 3SLS Estimates

Dependent variable: $w = \log W$; *Weights: EK/K*

Variable	Coefficient	Standard Error	t-Value
AGE	0.0223	0.0096	2.32
AGE-25	−0.0155	0.0121	−1.29
AGE-35	−0.0030	0.0070	−0.42
AGE-45	−0.0122	0.0065	−1.88
AGE*ED	−0.00024	0.00381	−0.06
ED	−0.0371	0.0285	−1.30
ED-7	0.0552	0.0280	1.97
ED-11	0.0991	0.0140	7.09
KIDSBORN	−0.0457	0.0068	−6.76
CENCITY	0.1817	0.0253	7.17
SUBURBS	0.1903	0.0240	7.92
NCEN	0.0275	0.0267	1.03
WEST	0.0254	0.0298	0.85
SOUTH	−0.1710	0.0408	−4.19
SOUTH 16	0.1035	0.0370	2.79
HLTH	−0.1048	0.0505	−2.08
λ	0.1282	0.0389	3.30
CONST	−0.0151	0.3036	−0.050

No. of observations: 2,064; No. of instruments: 24.
"R^2" = [correlation $(w, \hat{w})]^2 = 0.240$; Variance of estimate: 0.1842.
Reduced form $R^2 = 0.243$.

The variables taken as exogenous (instruments) are: 1, x, y, DK, and DKY. The variables treated as endogenous are: w, AHOURS, WEEKS, DKW and λ.[55]

The Market Wage Equation

Table 6.7 presents final estimates of the wage equation (6.26′) within the three equation models 6.26′ to 6.28′.

In spite of the high significance of the equation as a whole and of some of the coefficients, these variables do not explain more than 24

[55] λ is treated as endogenous here, due to estimation errors in the probit step, and the nonlinearity of $\lambda(I)$. Note that x and y do not include the constant, and $y = z$.

percent of the logarithmic variance of hourly wage of white married women. Clearly, this is not a result of the particular exclusion restrictions employed with regard to existing variables, since R^2 in the reduced form (which includes all the excluded variables) is only marginally and insignificantly larger. These low R^2's are typical, however, for cross-sectional data on wages[56] and represent a variety of omitted individual variables, measurable and unmeasurable.

These results are not very different from estimates obtained by two-stage least squares,[57] which ignore correlations of residuals across equations. Indeed, the estimated correlations between v_2 and the residuals v_3 and v_4 of equations 6.27 and 6.28 are relatively small: $r^2_{v_2 v_3} = -.108$; $r^2_{v_2 v_4} = -0.064$.[58]

We now analyze in more detail the estimated coefficients. The effect of age on wages combines changes in productivity over the life cycle with differences in productivity among age cohorts. The slope of the age profile of log wage at each age interval is derived from the spline coefficients by accumulation; this gives:

AGE t:	up to 25	26–35	36–45	45+
SLOPE $\dfrac{\partial w}{\partial t} = \dfrac{1}{W}\dfrac{\partial W}{\partial t}$:	0.0223	0.0068	0.0038	−0.084

These point estimates of the partial effects of age describe a concave function, peaking at age 45. While the reduction in slope beyond age 45 is only marginally significant, the monotone accumulated reduction (starting at age 25) is significant. Since the interaction AGE*ED effect is negligible, the shape of this profile is similar for all education levels.

The spline function representing the schooling effect on wages indicates that the estimated slope ($\partial W/\partial ED \cdot 1/W$) is slightly negative for incomplete elementary education (0–7 years). It is positive but insignificant for 7–11 years (approximately 1.8 percent increase in wage per school year), and strongly positive and significant for college education (including high-school graduation) with an estimated slope of 0.1172 ($= -.0371 + .0552 + .0991$), equivalent to 12.4 percent per school year. The low returns to elementary and incomplete high-school

---

[56] See, for example, Mincer and Polachek (1974).

[57] Detailed results of two-stage estimates are omitted in this report.

[58] Correlations of the underlying u-variables are estimated below (Table 6.14) as 0.065 and −0.032, respectively.

education implied by these estimates are somewhat surprising, although they are not an uncommon finding.[59]

The effect of the variable KIDSBORN is to depress wage rates significantly. Since the direct effect of age is controlled for in the regression, the negative impact of the number of children ever born probably proxies smaller work experience and a history of more frequent interruptions to regular attachment to the labor force. The effects of urban dwelling (CENCITY and SUBURBS) are positive and highly significant, representing a differential of about 20 percent in wages (log $1.20 = .182$) over nonfarm rural (outside SMSA), but the difference between suburbs and central city is small and insignificant. Regional differences in wages are primarily connected with the south, with a differential of -0.171 (relative to the northeast) for migrants into the south (i.e., if SOUTH $16 = 0$). As expected, poor health produces a significant reduction in market wages.

Finally, the positive coefficient of λ indicates a significant selectivity bias in the wages of workers.[60] On average, wages of workers are estimated to be 13.7 percent higher ($e^{0.1282} = 1.137$) than those of nonparticipants who have the same values for the exogenous variables.

Supply Equations

Estimates for the annual hours and weeks supply equations are weighted 3SLS estimates in the system of equations 6.27' to 6.29' and are presented in Tables 6.8 and 6.9. First, note the similarity between the two equations: all significant coefficients have the same signs, although their magnitudes are not proportional. This verifies our theoretical analysis, which predicts the two equations to manifest similar but separate behavior. The annual hours supply is a mirror image of demand for *composite-leisure*, which is the sum of the two types of leisure, whereas the weeks supply is a mirror image of demand for one type only, namely leisure in nonwork weeks. The variation in ratios of coefficients allows for independent variation of weekly hours

---

[59] See Smith (1979) and Fuchs (1974).

[60] The coefficient is related to the reservation wage residual u_0 and the market wage residual u_2 as follows (Sec. III):

$$b_2 = -\frac{1}{\sigma_1}\sigma_{12} = -\frac{1}{\sigma_1}[\operatorname{cov}(u_0 - u_2, u_2)] = \frac{1}{\sigma_1}[\sigma_2^2 - \sigma_{02}]. \tag{6.36}$$

Hence, b_2 is positive if $\sigma_2^2 > \sigma_{02}$, or $(\sigma_2/\sigma_0) > r_{02}$. This is compatible with σ_{02} positive or negative. Estimates of these magnitudes are presented in Table 6.14 below.

TABLE 6.8: Annual Hours Supply Equation

Dependent variable: AHOURS

Variable	Coefficient	Standard Error	t-Value
EH+Y	−93.25	20.42	−4.57
AGE	8.07	3.79	2.13
AGE-45	−31.99	12.60	−2.54
ED	54.26	19.71	2.75
KIDS*ED	−24.15	7.10	−3.40
NOKIDS	927.0	216.8	4.28
AGLSTKID	58.47	15.38	3.80
KIDSHOME	222.3	88.1	2.52
CENCITY	−83.0	59.4	−1.40
SUBURBS	−140.4	57.4	−2.45
HLTH	−796.3	156.7	−5.08
$w = \log W$	690.2	325.9	2.12
DK	26.3	257.9	0.10
DKW	−682.6	625.1	−1.09
DKY	68.84	28.36	2.43
λ	609.6	328.9	1.85
CONST	−389.5	337.6	−1.15

No. of observations: 2,064; No. of instruments: 24.
"R^2" = 0.168; Variance of estimate = 524,860.
Reduced form R^2 = 0.203.

of work $H = A/K$, sometimes in an opposite direction to that of annual weeks.[61]

The squared correlations ("R^2") between the dependent variable and the estimate are 0.168 and 0.192, respectively. These compare favorably with other cross-sectional estimates based on individual observations, but indicate the importance of individual effects which are not captured by measured variables.

Individual coefficients in these equations agree with our expectations. The effect of nonwage income is negative and significant in both equations: an increase of $1,000 in husband's earnings or other family

[61] Compare, for example, studies in Cain and Watts (1973) and Cogan (Chapter 2).

TABLE 6.9: Annual Weeks Supply Equation

| Dependent variable: WEEKS | | | |
Variable	Coefficient	Standard Error	t-Value
EH+Y	−2.665	0.468	−5.69
AGE	0.243	0.087	2.79
AGE-45	−1.072	0.289	−3.71
ED	1.362	0.452	3.01
KIDS*ED	−0.423	0.162	−2.61
NOKIDS	27.61	4.97	5.56
AGLSTKID	1.849	0.353	5.24
KIDSHOME	3.363	2.018	1.67
CENCITY	−3.084	1.362	−2.26
SURBURBS	−4.851	1.315	−3.69
HLTH	−21.72	3.59	−6.05
$w = \log W$	17.129	7.450	2.30
DK	−5.27	5.90	−0.89
DKW	−3.41	14.29	−0.24
DKY	1.165	0.648	1.80
λ	24.62	7.54	3.26
CONST	−13.13	7.74	−1.70

"R^2" = 0.192; Variance of estimate = 283.08.
Reduced form $R^2 = 0.204$.

income is expected to reduce work (conditional on wife's participation) by 93.25 annual hours and 2.665 annual weeks, on average. Since average weekly hours for workers is 35.4 (Table 6.1), the effect of weeks alone implies a reduction of 94.3 annual hours. Thus, the effect on weekly hours H is negligible, and the income effect seems to be concentrated on the supply of weeks. This is, of course, in addition to the significant negative income effect on participation, estimated in the probit equation (Table 6.2).

Age effects on quantities supplied (if working) are positive up to age 45, and negative thereafter. The effect of age on labor quantities (holding wage offers constant) resembles the estimated age profile on wages (Table 6.7) and on participation (Table 6.2). This similarity of profiles probably reflects physical deterioration of aging, reducing both activity and productivity. It may also capture general differences between the prewar and the postwar cohorts (since women aged over 45 in 1966 entered the labor market before 1939).

The education effect is positive and significant in both equations, while its interaction with children at home is negative: more educated women tend to work more, in general, but this relative difference decreases with the number of children at home, and is reversed completely if more than three children are present (since the ratio of coefficients ED/KIDS*ED is 2.25 for hours and 3.22 for weeks). Once again, these effects are similar to the effects on participation (Table 6.2).

Variables associated with children are important determinants of both annual hours and weeks. The total effects are not directly visible from the coefficients, due to the complicated specification including four children variables: KIDSHOME, KIDS*ED, AGLSTKID, and NOKIDS. First, the number of children interacts negatively with mother's education. The total effect is positive if education is less than 9.2 years (for hours) or 8 years (for weeks), but it is negative if mother's years of school are higher.[62] Second, the coefficient of NOKIDS captures the difference between the supply of a woman with no children and that of a woman with one child of age less than one year. This difference is reduced by the (positive) coefficient of AGL-STKID, and disappears completely if the child is aged 16 (for hours) or 15 (for weeks).[63] In addition, this difference increases with mother's education.[64]

Table 6.10 gives examples of the combined effect of children on annual hours (measured by the difference relative to a similar woman who has no children), by number and age of children, and by mother's years of school, as computed from the point-estimates of the four relevant coefficients in Table 6.8.

To summarize, married white women with children tend to work less, and to reduce their supply with each additional child, if their

[62] The ratio of coefficients KIDSHOME/KIDS*ED are 9.20 and 7.9, respectively.

[63] Since the ratios of coefficients NOKIDS/AGLSTKID are 15.85 and 14.93, respectively.

[64] Comparing the children effects on weeks in Table 6.9 with those obtained in the two alternative Tobit estimates of the weeks supply equation (Tables 6.4 and 6.6), the direction and significance of these coefficients are quite similar. The critical ratio of coefficients NOKIDS/AGLSTKIDS is 15.2 or 16.1, and that of KIDSHOME/KIDS*ED is 6.9 or 8.5, respectively (versus 14.93 and 7.95 in Table 6.9).

TABLE 6.10: Effects of Children on Annual Hours, by Age of
Youngest Child and Mother's Education

Number of Children at Home	Age of Youngest Child	Mother's Yrs. of School		
		5	10	15
One	Less than 1	−825	−946	−1067
	5	−533	−654	−775
	10	−240	−361	−482
	15	+52	−69	−190
Two	Less than 1	−723	−965	−1207
	5	−431	−673	−915
	10	−138	−380	−622
	15	+155	−88	−330
Each additional child (except youngest)		+102	−19	−140

Note: Entries are difference in annual hours of work (rounded to integers) compared with women (with same education and other characteristics) who have no children at home. Based on coefficients in Table 6.8.

education is above 8 or 9 years. Less-educated women with children increase their supply with the number of children, but still work less than comparable women with no children at home—unless their youngest child is sufficiently old. While the effects of the presence of children and of their ages are self-evident, the negative interaction with education probably indicates a positive effect of education on home productivity in child rearing, as well as a stronger preference for quality of children of educated women.

As for other coefficients in Tables 6.8 and 6.9, the urban variables CENCITY and SUBURBS both have significant negative effects on labor supply in these equations. This may represent higher fixed costs of participation (transportation, cost of convenient housing if wife works, search costs) in urban areas. It may also reflect a discounting of the positive wage-effect due to higher consumer prices in urban areas in view of the positive urban coefficients on money wages in Table 6.7. However, our confidence for these variables is somewhat weakened by the fact that they did not have significant effects on weeks in the alternative Tobit estimates in Tables 6.4 and 6.6.[65]

[65] This difference is perhaps due to effects of multicollinearity of urban variables with the variables w and λ, both having stronger effects in this specification than in the Tobit estimates.

The significant positive coefficients of λ in these equations indicate positive correlations between individual residuals in quantity supplied conditional on participation, with the individual propensity to participate, or equivalently, with the residual $-u_1 = u_2 - u_0$, representing the difference between residuals of the wage offer and the reservation wage (see Section III).

The effect of log wage on quantity supplied is positive and significant in both the hours and the weeks equations. This implies a positively sloped and concave supply curve $A(W)$ or $K(W)$, at wages above the reservation wage, but below the wage with desired full-time work in terms of annual weeks. On the other hand, when women receive a wage higher than this corner solution wage, the response to wage increases is much smaller. In annual hours, the net response (measured by the sum of coefficients of w and DKW) is negligible (7.6 annual hours). In the weeks equation, the response decreases at these higher wages from 17.1 to 13.7 weeks (but the decrease is not significant; $t = -0.24$) with an additional decrease of the level by 5.3 weeks (implied by the coefficient of DK, also insignificant).

Since the response of weeks at the limit must be zero, and cannot be positive, these may seem to be paradoxical results. However, it must be remembered (see Section V.4) that at the predicted "corner solution wage," the probability of a corner solution becomes just higher than 0.5, not 1. The *expected value* of weeks EK at this wage is smaller than the limit, and equals (by equation 6.34, when $\Delta = 0$ and $\hat{\sigma}_4 = 24.45$): $L = \hat{\sigma}_4 f(0) = 41.2$. The estimated supply curve represents a linear approximation to the expected value locus $EK(W)$, which is positively sloped at all wages (asymptotically approaching the limit but never coinciding with it). Consequently, the coefficient of w at wages above the corner solution wage (i.e., when $DK = 1$) is expected to be positive, albeit smaller. Similarly, the coefficient of w in the hours equation should also be positive at this range, if the underlying desired hours supply is positively sloped. Since the estimated response of hours is virtually zero, however, we must conclude that at the range where $DK = 1$ (i.e., expected desired weeks greater than the physical limit), the desired supply of hours is backward-bending![66] Most studies estimate *males* supply of hours to be backward-bending; therefore, a similar behavior by married women who receive high wages and work

[66] For example, Hall, Ashenfelter, and Heckman and other studies in Cain and Watts (1973).

full-year is not surprising. The reason for a positive response of female supply to wages found in most studies is the dominance of the lower-wage section. The majority of married women who are labor force participants desire to work less than full-year at wage rates offered to them in the market and in this range the response of supply to wages is strongly positive.

Finally, the effect of husband's and family incomes on supply are also significantly smaller (the reduction measured by the coefficient of DKY) when desired weeks are above the limit. In the hours equation, the income effect changes from -93.25 to -24.4, and in the weeks equation from -2.665 to -1.500, at the point where DK becomes 1.[67]

The Pseudo Reservation Wage Equation

Table 6.11 presents estimates of equation 6.29', the pseudo reservation wage equation, as derived by weighted 3SLS in the linear system which includes the two supply equations.

Because I in this equation is represented by a linear function of λ (equation 6.35), the coefficient of λ is an estimate of $(b_2 - \sigma_1 I_1)$, and the constant coefficient an estimate of $(\beta_0 + \sigma_1 I_0)$. σ_1 and β_0 (and their standard errors) are calculated from these coefficients, using b_2 estimated from the wage equation (Table 6.7) and I_0 and I_1 from equation 6.35. The values listed in Table 6.11 for the standard errors of σ_1 and β_0 are derived by solving the following approximate equations (which assume zero covariance between different coefficients):[68]

$$\text{var} (b_2 - \sigma_1 I_1) = \text{var } b_2 + \sigma_1^2 \text{ var } I_1 + I_1^2 \text{ var } \sigma_1$$

$$\text{var} (\beta_0 + \sigma_1 I_0) = \text{var } \beta_0 + \sigma_1^2 \text{ var } I_0 + I_0^2 \text{ var } \sigma_1.$$

Second, Table 6.11 gives estimates for the pseudo reservation wage equation 6.29', where the dependent variable is w and not w_0. However, if the reservation wage W_0 could be observed, its corresponding equation among participants would be:

$$w_0 = \beta_0 + \beta_1' y + b_0 \lambda + v_0, \tag{6.37}$$

---

[67] It is possible that other variables such as education or children also have a different effect if $DK = 1$, but we omitted other interactions with DK from our specification. In order to test all these interactions it is necessary to estimate separate supply equations within the subgroup of full-year workers (correcting for the bias associated with this selection). This, however, is outside the scope of the present study.

[68] More exact approximation formulas are given in Goodman (1960).

TABLE 6.11: Pseudo Reservation Wage Equation

Dependent variable $w = \log W$

Variable		Coefficient	Standard Error	t-Value
EH+Y		0.0459	0.0101	4.55
AGE		0.00859	0.00196	4.37
AGE-45		0.00025	0.00606	0.04
ED		0.0231	0.0112	2.06
KIDS*ED		0.00411	0.00274	1.50
NOKIDS		−0.3896	0.1156	−3.37
AGLSTKID		−0.0296	0.0081	−3.63
KIDSHOME		−0.0442	0.0312	−1.42
CENCITY		0.2486	0.0264	9.43
SUBURBS		0.2502	0.0258	9.70
HLTH		0.1338	0.0791	1.69
λ	$(b_2 - \sigma_1 I_1 =)$	−0.5966	0.1719	−3.47
CONST	$(\beta_0 + \sigma_1 I_0 =)$	−0.2166	0.1938	−1.12

computed coefficients
(using equation 6.32)

I	$(\sigma_1 =)$	0.4130	(0.1004)	(4.11)
λ	$(b_2 =)$	0.1282	0.0389	3.30
CONST	$(\beta_0 =)$	−0.3809	(0.1360)	(−2.80)

No. of observations: 2,064; No. of instruments: 24.
$R^2 = 0.189$; Variance of estimate $= 0.1961$.
Note: Numbers in parentheses are approximations, assuming zero covariances between coefficients. "R^2" is the squared correlation of the estimate with the dependent variable w (not with w_0, the unobserved log reservation wage).

where $v_0 = u_0 - b_0\lambda$, and $b_0\lambda$ corrects for the participation selectivity bias. However,

$$b_0 = -\frac{\sigma_{01}}{\sigma_1} = -\frac{\operatorname{cov}(u_1 + u_2, u_1)}{\sigma_1} = b_2 - \sigma_1.^{[69]}$$

Thus, b_0 is -0.2848 (with a standard error approximately equal to $0.1072 = \sqrt{(\operatorname{var} b_2 + \sigma_1^2)}$). The negative value calculated above for b_0

[69] Since $u_0 = u_1 + u_2$, and $b_2 = -\sigma_{12}/\sigma_1$; see Sec. III.

implies a negative selectivity bias of w_0 among participants, whose reservation wage tends to be lower than its expectation based on the total population. Using these estimates, equation 6.37 provides predictions of the unobserved reservation wage, conditional on participation (see Section V.6).

The difference in "R^2" between Tables 6.11 and 6.7 (0.24 vs. 0.19) is associated with the additional error component ε_i present in equation 6.29', as compared with the wage equation 6.26'.[70] If ε is assumed uncorrelated with v_2, its variance can be estimated by the difference in residual variances between these equations.

$$\hat{\sigma}^2_\varepsilon = 0.1961 - 0.1842 = 0.0119,$$

which accounts for about 5 percent of the logarithmic variance in wages.

In interpreting coefficients in Table 6.11, it must be remembered that the reservation wage is affected positively by factors increasing the price of time at home (associated with tastes for leisure as well as nonmarket productivity), and by fixed costs of labor force participation, which affect the gap between the price of time (if not working) and the reservation wage. However, it is difficult to distinguish between these components in the combined effect of each variable on the reservation wage. It is observed that husband's earnings and income are associated with a higher wife's reservation wage, equivalent to a 4.7 percent increase per $1,000. The age variable is also positive and significant. However, since the change of slope above age 45 is negligible, its magnitude is independent of the wife's age. The reservation wage increases with mother's level of education (2.3 percent per school year), and this effect is greater the larger the number of children (as measured by the interaction coefficient KIDS*ED). As expected, women without children have much lower minimum wage demands than women with young children, but this difference decreases with the age of the youngest child (3 percent per year of his age) and also apparently decreases with the number of children. For example, if one infant (aged less than 1 year) is present, the difference in w_0 for women with ten years of schooling is $0.3896 - 0.0442 + 10 \ (0.00411) = 0.3865$. But if three children are present, with the youngest aged 10, the difference is only: $0.3896 - 3 \ (0.0442) - 10 \ (0.0296) + 30 \ (0.00411) =$

---

[70] See Sec. IV for its interpretation.

0.0903. The explanation for the decrease in the reservation wage with the number of children (above one) for women with low education, is probably related to the child-care services provided by older children in low income families. At the mean education level, however, this effect disappears.[71]

The urban variables CENCITY and SUBURBS have very strong positive effects (with an insignificant difference between them) on the reservation wage, probably combining effects of urban-rural consumer price differentials with higher fixed costs of participation.

Equations for Minimum Supply Quantities

Combining the supply equations—which give quantities supplied conditional on participation—with the reservation wage equation, we can calculate the discontinuity of supply at the point of entry. This provides a measure of the minimum supply quantities at the reservation wage. Substituting $y = z$ in equations 6.8 Section II, we have:

$$A_0 = (\gamma_1 + \delta_1\beta)'y + (\delta_1 u_0 + u_3)$$
$$K_0 = (\gamma_2 + \delta_2\beta)'y + (\delta_2 u_0 + u_4)$$

$$(6.38)$$

Among participants, an additional term appears in each equation to correct for selectivity bias $((\delta_1 b_0 + b_3)\lambda$ for hours and $(\delta_2 b_0 + b_4)\lambda$ for weeks). Tables 6.12 and 6.13 present estimates of these equations based on the linear system supply model (Tables 6.8, 6.9, and 6.11). Standard errors of coefficients were computed under the assumption of joint-normality of the coefficients γ, δ, and β, taking into account their nonzero covariances, estimated in the 3SLS system. The variable DK was assumed to be zero in both supply equations since the probability of working full-year at the point of entry is very small.[72]

If labor force participation requires fixed costs such as for travel to work, preparation, search costs, or rent differentials, then both A_0 and K_0 should be positive. But the directions of change of these quantities are ambiguous. Ceteris paribus, increased money costs tend to increase minimum supplies; increased time costs, however, while always increasing the reservation wage and resulting in a decrease in net leisure to workers, may increase or decrease minimum quantities

---

[71] Since the ratio of coefficients KIDSHOME/KIDS*ED is 10.75 and $\overline{ED} = 11.29$ among participants.

[72] The limit (52 weeks) is 3.62 standard deviations above the mean of K_0 (see Table 6.16).

TABLE 6.12: Minimum Hours Supply Equation
(*Computed from Tables 6.8 and 6.11*)

Variable	Coefficient	Approx. Std. Error*	t-Value
EH+Y	−61.63	23.55	−2.62
AGE	13.98	3.76	3.72
AGE-45	−31.81	12.96	−2.45
ED	70.19	20.32	3.45
KIDS*ED	−21.32	6.34	−3.36
NOKIDS	658.76	257.43	2.56
AGLSTKID	38.10	19.11	2.00
KIDSHOME	191.88	79.27	2.42
CENCITY	88.16	70.72	1.25
SUBURBS	31.86	74.51	0.43
HLTH	−704.14	177.44	−3.97
λ	413.52	348.3†	1.19
CONST	−651.74	365.6†	−1.78

* Approximate standard errors assume joint normality of 3SLS coefficients.
† Standard errors for these coefficients were computed assuming zero covariances.

supplied to the market, depending on the elasticity of the compensated supply curve at the point of entry.[73]

In addition to fixed costs, the quantities A_0 and K_0 vary with the variables y because these measure in part taste differences among individuals. It is not possible to distinguish cost effects from taste effects (including "derived tastes" based on productivity of nonmarket time in the home production function).[74] Since the probability and quantity of work are positively correlated in a cross-section, many of these taste factors affect the quantity supplied (if working) and the reservation wage in opposite directions; therefore, their net effects on minimum quantities are ambiguous.

In view of these arguments, it is difficult to interpret the coefficients in Tables 6.12 and 6.13. One may determine which effect is dominant by comparing these combined coefficients with the separate supply

[73] See Cogan, Chapter 7.
[74] See Becker (1965) and Michael and Becker (1973).

TABLE 6.13: Minimum Years Supply Equation
(*Computed from Tables 6.9 and 6.11*)

Variable	Coefficient	Approx. Std. Error*	t-Value
EH+Y	3.451	0.550	6.27
AGE	0.390	0.086	4.54
AGE-45	-1.068	0.296	-3.61
ED	1.758	0.464	3.79
KIDS*ED	-0.353	0.145	-2.44
NOKIDS	20.939	5.879	3.56
AGLSTKID	1.342	0.434	3.09
KIDSHOME	2.606	1.810	1.44
CENCITY	1.174	1.620	0.72
SUBURBS	-0.565	1.440	-0.39
HLTH	-19.429	4.051	-4.80
λ	19.74	8.01†	2.47
CONST	-6.61	8.51†	-0.78

* Approximate standard errors assume joint-normality of 3SLS coefficients.
† The standard errors for these coefficients were computed assuming zero covariances.

coefficients (Tables 6.8 and 6.9) and the reservation wage coefficients (Table 6.11). In most cases in which the effects are opposite in sign, the quantity effect on supply dominates the effect on the reservation wage. The only significant exception is nonwage income (EH+Y) on the minimum supply of weeks: an increase in nonwage income or in husband's earnings affects the reservation wage more than the quantity supplied, so that minimum weeks increases by 3.45 weeks per $1,000.

It is interesting to note that the effects of urban-rural differences, while quite significant in the reservation wage and the supply equations separately, become insignificant in their net effects on each minimum quantity. This seems to strengthen the interpretation of those variables as corrections for consumer-price differentials in metropolitan areas, which should increase money reservation wage and decrease supply quantities at a given money wage—but should not affect the real quantities A_0 and K_0.[75]

[75] This is contrasted with interpreting their effects as representing fixed costs, which would increase minimum quantities, in view of the estimated supply elasticities.

Table 6.14: Standard Deviations and Correlations for
Underlying Residuals

Symbol	Equation	Std. Deviation	Correlation with:			
			u_1	u_2	u_3	u_4
u_0	Reservation wage	0.5083	.560	.629	−.523	−.360
$u_1 = u_0 - u_2$	[Participation]	0.4130		−.291	−.713	−.409
u_2	Market wage	0.4400			.065	−.032
u_3	Annual hours supply	854.5				.851
u_4	Annual weeks supply	25.36				

Note: See Appendix C.

In contrast with other variables, age (below 45) and education affect positively both supply quantities and reservation wages. This is probably a result of their influence on productivity, both in the market and at home—inducing a propensity to work more if working in the market, but implying a higher alternative cost for entering the market.

The levels of the computed minimum quantities are quite large.[76] This implies that the discontinuity of supply functions is a dominant feature which should not be ignored. Empirical estimates which are based on the assumption of continuity of supply at the reservation wage are therefore likely to be extremely biased.[77]

Residual Variance Structure

The derivation of our best approximations for variances and correlations among residuals u of the underlying model is explained in Appendix C. Corrections are made, using both the 3SLS estimates and the Tobit estimates of the weeks equation (Table 6.16) to account for truncation biases both at the upper limit (for weeks) and at the lower limit (due to the participation selectivity bias). These estimates are summarized in Table 6.14 and confirm our anticipations.

[76] Means and dispersions of A_0 and K_0 are estimated below with other predictions of the model (Table 6.16).

[77] For example, Kalachek and Raines (1970), Schultz (Chapter 1), Cogan (Chapter 2), Leibowitz (1974), and Heckman (1974b). See also Cogan (Chapter 7) for similar conclusions.

The individual component in the reservation wage is positively correlated with the market wage individual component, indicating positive correlation between home and market productivity. The reservation wage error is negatively correlated with supply quantities residuals, reflecting both fixed cost and taste differences which tend to shift supply and reservation wage in opposite directions. The relative dispersion in reservation wage is higher than in market wage (holding constant all the measured explanatory variables). Market wage residuals have low correlations with both supply residuals, while the correlation between individual components in supplies of hours and weeks is quite high, as expected both from their definition and from our theory.

The variable $u_1 = u_0 - u_2$ is (negatively) associated with the unobserved individual component of participation. Its negative correlations with u_2, u_3 and u_4 thus produce positive selectivity biases in the three estimated equations for participants: market wage, hours, and weeks. On the other hand, since $\sigma_{01} > 0$, the selectivity bias in the reservation wage is negative among participants and positive among nonparticipants. Finally, the underlying dispersion (before truncation) in residual market quantities seems extremely large, with standard deviations comprising more than two thirds of actual means of hours and weeks worked. Actual dispersion is much smaller, of course, due to truncation at both limits.

V.6 PREDICTIONS OF THE ESTIMATED MODEL

Individual Predictions

Combining the estimated equations described in the previous sections, we have computed for each woman in the sample individual point estimates for the endogenous variables of the model.[78] Table 6.15 presents means and standard deviations of predicted market wage offers and reservation wages (both in logs and in absolute values) for the total sample, classified by labor force status. These predictions are based on Tables 6.7 and 6.11, and are *conditional* on actual participation. For example, the coefficient b_2 of the variable λ in the wage equation is multiplied by $\bar{\lambda}_j = -\lambda_j p_j/(1 - p_j)$ for a nonparticipant j. In the total sample group, means of conditional and unconditional predictions are essentially identical, since the mean predicted $\bar{p}$ is equal to the

---

[78] Statistics about some predicted variables have been reported above, Sec. III, Table 6.4, and Sec. V.4, Table 6.6.

TABLE 6.15: Predicted Market Wage and Reservation Wage,
by Labor Force Status
(*Means of Conditional Predictions; Standard Deviations in Parentheses*)

Variables	Symbols	Workers	Total Participants	Non-participants	Total
Market wage ($ per hour)	W^*	1.92 (0.50)	1.89 (0.50)	1.52 (0.38)	1.70 (0.48)
Log market wage:	w^*	0.621 (0.234)	0.605 (0.237)	0.393 (0.232)	0.495 (0.257)
Reservation wage:	W_0^*	1.29 (0.30)	1.29 (0.30)	2.35 (2.83)	1.84 (2.12)
Log Reservation wage:	w_0^*	0.233 (0.233)	0.230 (0.226)	0.777 (0.310)	0.513 (0.386)
Percent with $W^* > W_0^*$	W_0^*	99.6	99.4	0.85	48.3
No. of observations		2064	3044	3275	6319
Percent of total		32.7	48.2	51.8	100.0

actual proportion participating. (See Section V.3). Therefore, the conditional estimates are also unbiased; but they are much more powerful. Indeed, the classification of the sample into participants and nonparticipants by comparing conditional predictions of market and reservation wage conforms to the actual classification in all but 46 cases (0.73 percent), as against 2,667 (42.2 percent) misclassified by unconditional predictions. The only comparison that can be made between predictions and actual data concerns market wage in the group of survey-week workers. The actual mean wage in this group is biased upward, however, due to the *survey-week selectivity bias*, which implies a higher probability of inclusion for women who supply more weeks, and have` higher-than-expected wages. The mean wage in this group was $2.17, as compared with the mean of conditional predictions of $1.92 in Table 6.15.[79] The effect of the *participation selectivity bias* is determined by comparing these mean wages with the mean of unconditional

---

[79] Using log wage, the predicted geometric mean for workers is $1.86, as compared with the actual geometric mean $1.95.

predictions for this group: \$1.75 (0.534 in logs). The correlation in the worker's group between predicted and actual (log) wage is 0.476 (0.467 with unconditional predicted log wage).

Among nonparticipants, the predicted reservation wage is, on average, more than 50 percent higher than the predicted wage offer, with a large relative dispersion of reservation wages within the group.

Table 6.16 presents statistics on predicted supply variables, conditional on participation, for the group of participants. These predictions were computed as follows. Annual hours were computed using the coefficients of Table 6.8. The value of λ_1 was computed from probit estimates (as in Table 6.3), and DK_1 computed using the Tobit estimates (as in Table 6.5). The wage variable was log actual wage for workers, and predicted log wage w^* for participants who are not survey-week workers. In cases where hours computed were estimated as negative (only 19 cases), the value 0 was assigned.

Annual weeks were computed similarly, using coefficients from Table 6.9 except that estimated weeks K^* were truncated at 52 weeks (this truncation reduced $\bar{K}^*$ by 0.19 weeks). The computation of minimum hours and weeks was based on Tables 6.12 and 6.13, except that negative values of A_0 were changed to 0 (20 cases for A_0, no case for K_0).

TABLE 6.16: Predicted Supply Variables for
Participants
(*Means of Conditional Predictions; Standard
Deviations in Parentheses*)

Variable	Symbol	Survey-Week Workers	Total Participants
Annual hours	A^*	1171	1099
		(391)	(397
Annual weeks	K^*	33.1	31.2
		(10.1)	(10.1)
Minimum hours	A_0	872	820
		(344)	(345)
Minimum weeks	K_0	25.8	24.5
		(7.2)	(7.6)
Price of time at zero hours		0.423	0.453
(\$ per hour)	PT_0	(0.277)	(0.284)

The variable PT_0 denotes the wage rate at which the supply curve intersects the wage axis, choosing the higher intersection point between the hours and the weeks supply equations.[80] This is the marginal price of time at the point of entry, after incurring fixed time and money costs of participation, but before working. It is *not* the price of time at home, corresponding to the nonparticipation alternative—unless no fixed costs exist.[81] Algebraically, if PT_0 corresponds to zero hours (rather than weeks), then:

$$\delta_1(w_0^* - \log PT_0) = A_0,$$

$$PT_0 = \exp\left[w_0^* - \frac{A_0}{\delta_1}\right].$$

Inspecting the predictions listed in Table 6.16, we observe relatively large discontinuities of both supply curves at the reservation wage. In fact, minimum supply quantities constitute about three-quarters of predicted actual work. This is also reflected in the large discrepancy between the price of time at zero hours and the predicted reservation wage ($0.45 vs. $1.29 for participants). These results again emphasize the importance of taking supply discontinuities into account in estimating labor supply.

Comparing the means of predicted hours (for workers) and predicted weeks (for both groups of participants), with means of actual quantities worked (in Table 6.1), our estimates tend to be biased downward. The average prediction for weeks worked is 31.2, compared to the actual mean 35.3, for all participants. The larger discrepancies in the group of workers, however, is a result of the survey-week bias, as explained above, since the selection into the group is positively associated with K.

The remaining bias is probably due to two factors; first, the non-linearity of the equations, associated with the corner solution for weeks; and second, the transitory effects in the residuals for weeks. As explained in Appendix A, the weighting scheme uses the weights EK/K^{t-1}, where K^{t-1} is weeks worked in previous year (1966). If there exists transitory year-to-year variation in weeks worked, then the

---

[80] In almost all cases, this corresponds to the annual hours supply curve, indicating a positive number of weeks worked at this wage.

[81] In this case PT_0 is equal to the reservation wage, and minimum supply is zero.

probability of inclusion among the survey-week workers is $K^t/52 \neq K^{t-1}/52$, and the weights tend to overcompensate for these probabilities. The higher the relative variance of the transitory component in the weeks residuals, the more downward biased are the weighted estimates.[82]

The correlations between predicted and actual supply quantities are as follows: for annual weeks, 0.398 among all participants, and 0.387 among workers, and for annual hours, it is 0.360 among workers.

The results reported in Tables 6.3, 6.5, 6.15, and 6.16 thus summarize individual predictions for all the endogenous variables of the model.

Wage and Income Elasticities of Supply

Next, we estimate wage and nonwage-income elasticities of supply, as predicted by the equations and estimated at the means of exogenous variables. Equations 6.27' and 6.28' above give the forms of supply equations, conditional on participation. Denoting the deterministic part of the equations by A^* and K^*, respectively, the elasticities of conditional quantities with respect to the wage (that is, for an exogenous shift in the expected wage offer, equivalent to a change of the constant term α_0) are:

$$\eta_{A^*W} = \frac{\delta_1 + a_2 DK}{A^*}; \qquad \eta_{K^*y_1} = \frac{y_1(\gamma_{21} + k_3 DK)}{K^*}. \qquad (6.39)$$

Assuming the first exogenous variable y_1 to be nonwage income $(EH + Y)$, the corresponding income elasticities of supply are:

$$\eta_{A^*y_1} = \frac{y_1(\gamma_{11} + a_3 DK)}{A^*}; \qquad \eta_{K^*y_1} = \frac{y_1(\gamma_{21} + k_3 DK)}{K^*}. \qquad (6.40)$$

Equations 6.39 and 6.40 assume that DK is given (either 1 or 0), such that individuals do not move from a (predicted) part-year work $(K^* < 52)$ to a predicted corner solution $(K^* = 52; DK = 1)$ as a result of the infinitesimal change in wage or in income, respectively. The compensated wage elasticities, corresponding to a pure substitution effect, are derived by Slutsky's equation.[83]

$$\eta^c_{A^*W} = \eta_{A^*W} - W(\delta_{11} + a_3 DK) = \eta_{A^*W} - \frac{A^*W}{y_1}\eta_{A^*y_1}, \qquad (6.41)$$

---

[82] The relative transitory component in weeks is estimated as 0.175. See Chapter 3.
[83] See Hanoch (Chapter 3).

and since

$$\frac{\partial K^c}{\partial W} = \frac{\partial K}{\partial W} - A \frac{\partial K}{\partial y_i},$$

$$\eta^c_{K^*w} = \eta_{K^*w} - \frac{A^*W}{K^*}(\gamma_{21} + k_3 DK) = \eta_{K^*w} - \frac{A^*W}{y_1} \eta_{K^*y_1}.$$

$$(6.42)$$

Table 6.17 presents estimates of these elasticities, computed at the means for participants. In part I, the elasticities are conditional on $DK = 0$ (i.e., no corner solution in weeks). In part II, elasticities given in equations 6.39 and 6.40 are computed at the mean $\overline{DK}$, which predicts the proportion of individuals working full year. Since both wage and income effects on annual supplies are smaller if $DK = 1$ ($a_2, k_2 > 0$; a_3 and $k_3 < 0$; see Tables 6.8 and 6.9), these average elasticities are smaller in magnitude.

Each elasticity of weekly hours $H^* = A^*/K^*$ is computed as the difference between those for annual hours and weeks. They are smaller in magnitude than those of annual supplies, and in part II even

TABLE 6.17: Elasticities of Supply Conditional on Participation
(*At Means of Participants*)

| | Elasticity with Respect to: | | |
| | Wage | | Nonwage |
	Noncompensated	Compensated	Income
I. *Assuming no Corner Solution* ($K < 52$):			
Annual hours	0.640	0.811	−0.616
Annual weeks	0.554	0.724	−0.614
Weekly hours	0.096	0.087	−0.002
II. *Average, allowing for Corner Solution in weeks:*			
Annual hours	0.417	0.543	−0.456
Annual weeks	0.515	0.660	−0.524
Weekly hours	−0.098	−0.117	0.068

Note: Using means of participants (and using for the wage rate predicted wage conditional on participation) gives: $\bar{A}^* = 1077.6$; $\bar{K}^* = 30.9$; $\overline{DK}^* = 0.3525$.

opposite in sign. This is in accordance with our theory outlined in Chapter 3 since the supply of weekly hours is derived as a ratio of two supply functions and is therefore not a mirror image of a demand function for leisure.

Thus, if wage offers increase by 1 percent, existing participants increase annual hours, on average, by 0.417 percent, and annual weeks by 0.515 percent. This results in a slight decline (0.1 percent) in weekly hours, although if predicted (with better than equal odds) to work part-year only, weekly hours increase by 0.1 percent. Income elasticities of both annual supplies are negative, and are essentially the same (if $DK = 0$), implying that no response to income is expected in weekly hours by participants. The low elasticities for weekly hours may reflect, however, demand restrictions which tend to fix weekly hours, allowing supply responses to be expressed mainly in participation and in weeks worked.

The next set of estimates are elasticities of *expected* (or aggregate) hours and weeks in the total sample population. The participation index I (equation 6.5) is proportional to the difference between expected log wage w^* and log reservation wage w_0^*. Therefore, the probability of participation $p(I)$ and the selectivity bias variable $\lambda(I)$, vary with changes in expected wage, as well as with nonwage income (through its effect on the reservation wage, β_1). As a result, the elasticity of *expected* supply, which also estimates the elasticity of aggregrate supply in this population, consists of three elements: (1) the change in participation; (2) the change in quantity supplied by existing participants (i.e., conditional on participation); and (3) the change in average quantity supplied due to changes in the composition of participants, i.e., due to the fact that new participants tend to supply smaller quantities than existing participants on average.

Mathematically, the total wage elasticity of expected supply of annual hours $EA = P(I)EA^*$ is derived as follows:

$$\eta_{EA,w} = \frac{1}{P(I)} \frac{\partial P(I)}{\partial w^*} + \frac{1}{EA^*} \left[\frac{\partial EA^*}{\partial w^*} + \frac{\partial EA^*}{\partial EDK} \cdot \frac{\partial EDK}{\partial w^*} \right]$$

$$+ \frac{1}{EA^*} \cdot \frac{\partial EA^*}{\partial \lambda} \cdot \frac{\partial \lambda}{\partial w^*}, \quad (6.43)$$

where the three terms correspond to the three elements mentioned above. Computing the values of each term separately we have:

(i) $\dfrac{1}{p}\dfrac{\partial p}{\partial w^*} = \eta_{PW} = \dfrac{1}{P(I)} \cdot \dfrac{1}{\sigma_1} \cdot f(I) = \dfrac{\lambda(I)}{\sigma_1}$,   since $I = \dfrac{1}{\sigma_1}(w^* - w_0^*)$

and $\lambda = \dfrac{f(I)}{P(I)}$;

(ii) $\dfrac{1}{EA^*}\dfrac{\partial EA^*}{\partial w^*} = \eta_{A^*w}$, as in equation 6.36

$\dfrac{\partial EA^*}{\partial EDK} = a_1 + a_2 w^* + a_3 y_1$, by equation 6.27′ (Table 6.8)

$\dfrac{\partial EDK}{\partial w^*} = \dfrac{\partial}{\partial w^*} P\!\left(\dfrac{\bar{\bar{K}}T^* - 52}{\sigma_4}\right) = \dfrac{1}{\sigma_4} f\!\left(\dfrac{\bar{\bar{K}}T^* - 52}{\sigma_4}\right) \cdot \dfrac{\partial \bar{\bar{K}}T^*}{\partial w^*}$,

where $\bar{\bar{K}}T^*$ is the expected (Tobit) desired supply of weeks, computed from Table 6.4 in V.4 using the total sample means, and $\partial \bar{\bar{K}}T^*/\partial w^*$ ($=4.93$) is the wage coefficient in this Tobit equation.

(iii) $\dfrac{\partial EA^*}{\partial \lambda} = \delta_1 b_2 + b_3$, by equation 6.27′ (Table 6.9);

$\dfrac{\partial \lambda}{\partial w^*} = \dfrac{\partial \lambda}{\partial I} \cdot \dfrac{\partial I}{\partial w^*} = \dfrac{-\lambda(I + \lambda)}{\sigma_1} = \dfrac{-D}{\sigma_1}$ (See Section III)

The first term in equation 6.43 is the wage elasticity of participation. The second term is the elasticity of conditional supply, given participation, where the second term in the brackets is the additional effect of the increased probability of a corner solution in weeks due to increased wages, as derived from the Tobit analysis of Section V.4. The third term is the effect on λ, through changes in the mean supply residual among participants, which results from the effect of the wage rate on participation.

The income elasticity of expected supply is derived similarly, where the effect of $y_1 = EH + Y$ on I and $\lambda(I)$ is through the effect of income on the reservation wage:

$$\eta_{EA} = \dfrac{1}{P(I)}\dfrac{\partial P(I)}{\partial w_0^*}\dfrac{\partial w_0^*}{\partial y_1} + \left[\eta_{A_1^* y_1} + \dfrac{1}{EA^*}\dfrac{\partial EA^*}{\partial EDK}\dfrac{\partial EDK}{\partial y_1}\right]$$

$$+ \dfrac{1}{EA^*} \cdot \dfrac{\partial EA^*}{\partial \lambda} \cdot \dfrac{\partial \lambda}{\partial w_0^*} \cdot \dfrac{\partial w_0^*}{\partial y}. \qquad (6.44)$$

The individual elements are computed as follows:

(i) $\dfrac{\partial P(I)}{\partial w_0^*} = \dfrac{1}{\sigma_1} f(I); \dfrac{\partial w_0^*}{\partial y_1} = \beta_1$ (Table 6.11)

Hence $\eta_{py_1} = \dfrac{-\lambda\beta_1}{\sigma_1}$;

(ii) $\eta_{A^*y_1}$ is the conditional elasticity in equation 6.40;

$\dfrac{\partial EDK}{\partial y_1} = \dfrac{1}{\sigma_4} f\left(\dfrac{\bar{\bar{K}}T^* - 52}{\sigma_4}\right) \dfrac{\partial \bar{\bar{K}}T^*}{\partial y_1}$, and $\dfrac{\partial \bar{\bar{K}}T^*}{\partial y_1}$ $(= -1.96)$ is the coefficient of $EH + Y$ in Table 6.4.

(iii) $\dfrac{\partial \lambda}{\partial I} \cdot \dfrac{\partial I}{\partial w_0^*} = \dfrac{D}{\sigma_1}$, since $\dfrac{\partial I}{\partial w_0^*} = \dfrac{-1}{\sigma_1}$,

(other terms are equal to those in equation 6.43).

In both equations 6.43 and 6.44, the wage w^* which enters the computed expected hours EA^* and expected desired weeks $\bar{\bar{K}}T^*$ (in Tobit equation) is the expected wage *conditional on participation*, as given in equation 6.26.[84]

Table 6.18 presents estimates of these total expected elasticities, broken down by the three types of effects, as estimated at the means of the total sample.[85]

The wage elasticities of expected or aggregate supplies are primarily affected by changes in participation, with the conditional elasticity (which is conventionally taken as "the supply elasticity") in part II amounting to only one-third (for hours) or one-half (for weeks) of the total aggregate change.

Elasticity of participation is approximately 2, but the reduction in average quantities (part III) reduces the net participation effect to 0.957 for hours and 0.546 for weeks (I minus III). The participation effects of nonwage income are also large, with the conditional elasticity of participants comprising only 62 percent (for hours) and 76 percent (for weeks) of the aggregate effect, with net participation effect equal to -0.348 for hours and -0.198 for weeks.[86]

[84] Similar formulas apply with respect to weeks expected supply, replacing EA^*, δ_1, b_3 and a_j $(j = 1, 2, 3)$ by EK^*, δ_2, b_4, and k_j, respectively.

[85] At these means, the participation index I is equal to the mean predicted $\bar{I}$ (Table 6.3), since I is a linear function of the variables. But λ, p, D, and DK are nonlinear, and therefore were computed at the mean $\bar{I}$.

[86] The effects associated with the corner solution variable DK are quantitatively minor (0.012 is the largest effect, on η_{A^*w}).

TABLE 6.18: Elasticities of Expected Supplies
(At Means of Total Sample)

| | Elasticity with Respect to: | |
	Wage	Nonwage Income
I. Participation	2.022	−0.736
II. Supply Quantities for Given Participants:		
Annual hours	0.481	−0.571
Annual weeks	0.567	−0.643
(Weekly hours)	(−0.086)	(0.075)
III. Effect of Changing Participation on Conditional Supplies:		
Annual hours	−1.065	0.388
Annual weeks	−1.476	0.538
IV. Total Elasticities of Expected Supply (I + II + III):		
Annual hours	1.438	−0.919
Annual weeks	1.113	−0.841

Note: Using means of the exogenous variables gives: $EA = 471.8$, $EK = 13.57$ ($\bar{p} = 0.4773$; $EDK = 0.3315$; $EA^* = 988.5$; $EK^* = 28.43$; $\tilde{KT}^* = 43.16$).

Regarding weekly hours, the elasticity of conditional supply (holding constant λ) in part II is computed as the difference between elasticities of annual hours and of weeks and gives results similar to those in Table 6.17, part II. But for expected supplies, this computation is not valid, since $EH = E(A/K) \neq EA/EK$.

The following generalized results seem to be valid:[87] (1) aggregate

[87] The mean predictions and elasticities given in this section are of less general value, as they stand, than equation estimates presented in previous sections, because they depend on the particular SEO sample used here, and represent predictions for a hypothetical population for which this is a random sample with equal selection probabilities. They are not corrected for the actual sampling proportions of SEO, which tended to overrepresent certain low-income groups. Therefore, means and elasticities based on these means may be biased relative to the existing population of white married women as defined. The coefficients in estimated equations, however, are not biased by variable sampling proportions, and should be taken as representative for this group. Given extraneous information about means and distributions in the actual population, the corresponding correct predictions may be calculated, using the equations estimated in previous sections, in combination with the methodology applied here.

labor supply of married women is elastic ($\eta > 1$) with respect to wages; (2) aggregate supply is negatively related to nonwage income (including husband's earnings) with an elasticity less than 1; (3) elasticities of expected annual hours of work are larger than those of weeks; and (4) the effects of wages and incomes on participation are quite important by themselves, as well as in their net contribution to the total effect on expected aggregate supply.

ACKNOWLEDGMENTS

I am indebted to Finis Welch who encouraged and supported this work, and discussed it with me regularly. Zvi Griliches, James P. Smith and Michael Ward read various parts of the manuscript and provided extensive written comments. Richard Buddin assisted me throughout the study, carrying out the programming and computations and helping with comments and suggestions. I had fruitful discussions with Ed Leamer, James P. Smith, Michael Ward and especially John Cogan. Many others at Rand and UCLA and members attending workshops at the Hebrew University, Harvard University, CORE (Belgium), and the National Bureau of Economic Research (Stanford), where these findings were presented at an earlier stage, helped with questions, comments, and suggestions that shaped this final chapter.

All errors and omissions are my own responsibility, of course.

APPENDIX A

SURVEY-WEEK SELECTIVITY BIAS AND ITS CORRECTION BY WEIGHTING

Denote the joint density function corresponding to the random variables v_i of equations 6.15 to 6.17 by $g^i(v_i)$. The function $g^i(\ )$ differs among individuals (see equation 6.13), and corresponds to the u_{1i}-truncated joint-normal distribution of u_i where $u_{1i} \le \sigma_1 I_i$. For each participant ($i \le n$ in the sample), v_i have zero means:

$$Ev_i = \int_g^i g^i(v_i)v_i \, dv_i = 0, \tag{A.1}$$

as shown in equations 6.9 and 6.12. Denote by ε_i the reduced-form residual for K_i: $\varepsilon_i = \delta_2 v_{2i} + v_{4i}$ and $K_i = K_i^* + \varepsilon_i$ in equation 6.20. Among participants, ε_i has zero mean and zero correlations with the exogenous variables, including K_i^*, since each ε_i is a linear function of v_i. Also, ε_i are independent across individuals. The covariances of ε_i with v_i are given by:

$$
\begin{aligned}
E\varepsilon_i v_i &= \delta_2 E v_{2i} v_i + E v_{4i} V_i \\
&= \delta_2(\Sigma_2 - b_2 b D_i) + (\Sigma_4 - b_4 b D_i) \\
&= (\delta_2 \Sigma_2 + \Sigma_4) - (\delta_2 b_2 + b_4) b D_i, \tag{A.2}
\end{aligned}
$$

by equation 6.14. The *conditional density* g^{ci} of v_i, given that $H_i > 0$, is derived by applying Bayes' formula to the corresponding joint density g^i, using equation A.1:

$$
\begin{aligned}
g^{ci}(v_i \mid H_i > 0) &= \frac{(K_i/52)g^1(v_i)}{\int (K_i/52)g^i(v_i) \, dv_i} = \frac{(K_i^* + \varepsilon_i)g^i(v_i)}{\int (K_i^* + \varepsilon_i)g^i(v_i) \, dv_i} \\
&= \frac{(K_i^* + \varepsilon_i)g^i(v_i)}{K_i^* \int g^i(v_i) \, dv_i + E\varepsilon_i} = \frac{1}{K_i^*}(K_i^* + \varepsilon_i)g^i(v_i),
\end{aligned}
$$

where the last equality follows, since $\int g^i(v_i) \, dv_i = 1$ (g^i being a true density) and $E\varepsilon_i = 0$.

The *conditional expectation* of v_i under $H_i > 0$ is therefore

$$E(v_i \mid H_i > 0) = \int v_i g^{ci}(v_i \mid H_i > 0) \, dv_i$$

$$= \frac{1}{K_i^*} \left[K_i^* \int v_i g^i(v_i) \, dv_i + \int \varepsilon_i v_i g^i(v_i) \, dv_i \right]$$

$$= E \frac{\varepsilon_i v_i}{K_i^*} = \frac{i}{K_i^*} [(\delta_2 \Sigma_2 + \Sigma_4) - (\delta_2 b_2 + b_4) b D_i], \tag{A.3}$$

where these equalities follow, since K_i^* is exogenous, $E v_i = 0$ ($i \leq n$, equation A.1), and the last equality uses equation A.2 above. More explicitly, the biases (expected values of v_i) in equations 6.15 to 6.18, if applied to survey-week workers, are

$$E(v_{2i} \mid H_i > 0) = (\delta_2 \sigma_2^2 + \sigma_{24}) \cdot \frac{1}{K_i^*} - (\delta_2 b_2^2 + b_2 b_4) \cdot \frac{D_i}{K_i^*},$$

$$E(v_{3i} \mid H_i > 0) = (\delta_2 \sigma_{23} + \sigma_{34}) \cdot \frac{1}{K_i^*} - (\delta_2 b_2 b_3 + b_3 b_4) \cdot \frac{D_i}{K_i^*},$$

$$E(v_{4i} \mid H_i > 0) = (\delta_2 \sigma_{24} + \sigma_4^2) \cdot \frac{1}{K_i^*} - (\delta_2 b_2 b_4 + b_4^2) \cdot \frac{D_i}{K_i^*}. \tag{A.4}$$

Expressions for the conditional variance matrix of v_i may also be derived but are quite tedious.

The biases are inversely proportional to K_i^*, and are present in any of these equations if the corresponding residual v_{ji} is correlated with the weeks residual $\varepsilon_i = \delta_2 v_{2i} + v_{4i}$. One seemingly feasible method of modifying the model to eliminate these biases is analogous to the treatment of the participation bias under Case 1 in Section III. The variables $1/K^*$ and D/K^* may be estimated separately[88] and then introduced into the equations linearly where their corresponding coefficients (defined in equation A.4) are to be estimated, along with the other coefficients, by linear methods. The implied residuals (e.g., in the wage equation) $\tilde{v}_2$ are:

$$\tilde{v}_{2i} = v_{2i} - (\delta_2 \sigma_2^2 + \sigma_{24}) \frac{1}{K_i^*} + (\delta_2 b_2^2 + b_2 b_4) \frac{D_i}{K_i^*},$$

and may be shown to have zero means, and to be uncorrelated with the

---

[88] Using the exact functional relation $D(I)$ on the probit estimates of I, and estimating K^* in a reduced-form equation.

exogenous right-side variables within the selective group of survey-week workers.

However, this suggested modification turns out to be self-defeating, because it introduces severe multicollinearity into the equations. K_i^* is a linear combination of all the exogenous variables (including λ_i), as shown in equation 6.20. D_i is a function of λ_i or, equivalently, a function of the index $I_i = (1/\sigma_1)(\alpha' x_i - \beta' y_i)$, again combining all the exogenous variables. Clearly, the pair of variables $1/K^*$ and D/K^* are bound to be highly collinear with the other variables in each equation (and may be highly correlated with each other), and to make the estimates of coefficients quite unreliable.

A much simpler alternative route is available for eliminating or drastically reducing these survey-week biases. The sample moments in the biased sample of m survey-week workers may be weighted by the inverse of the selection probabilities $K/52$, so that the weighted moments become consistent estimates of the corresponding moments among all participants. To preserve the scale of these moments, and thus to avoid additional heteroskedasticity,[89] the moments are weighted by K^*/K (or by EK/K, where EK is the estimated expected value of K, which takes into account the corner-solution restriction $K \leq 52$). Since K is measured and K^* (or EK) may be estimated approximately, this weighting scheme is feasible. The same effect may be achieved alternatively by weighting the observations rather than the moments—that is, transforming all the variables (including the constant) through multiplication by the factor $\sqrt{(K_i^*/K_i)}$ for each $i = 1, \ldots, m$. Replacing each variable χ_i by the transformed variable $\hat{\chi}_i = \sqrt{(K_i^*/K_i)} \cdot \chi_i$ gives a set of equations completely analogous to 6.15 to 6.20, in terms of the transformed variables, and applicable to the selective subsample $\{i \leq m\}$. None of the variables is now exogenous, since the endogenous variable K enters the definition of each transformed variable. Nevertheless, applying familiar linear methods to these equations yields consistent estimates of the parameters.[90]

These informal statements may now be clarified by a more formal treatment, although a complete analysis is tedious. Consider, for

---

[89] Since some heteroskedasticity is already present, by equation 6.14. A correction for this is costly, and quantitatively of minor consequence.

[90] Except for a slight bias, due to the difference in transitory effects in K between adjacent years, if the K used for weighting is measured in the preceding year. See below, equation A.8.

example, the weeks supply equation in 6.19, where the method is most likely to produce inconsistencies since the transformation involves the same endogenous variable K as does the dependent variable. In compact form, the equation is

$$K_i = K_i^* + \varepsilon_i.$$

Using equations A.3 and A.4 above, $E(\varepsilon_i \mid H_i > 0)$ is seen to be generally nonzero. Also,

$$E(\varepsilon_i K_i^* \mid H_i > 0) = K_i^* E(\varepsilon_i \mid H_i > 0) = E\varepsilon_i^2 > 0,$$

implying that least-squares estimates of this equation within the sample of m are inconsistent. The transformed equation, using the proposed weighting scheme, is derived by multiplying each variable by $\sqrt{K_i^*/K_i}$ for each $i \leq m$:

$$\hat{K}_i = \hat{K}_i^* + \hat{\varepsilon}_i. \tag{A.5}$$

A necessary and sufficient condition for consistency of the OLS estimate of equation A.5 is $E\hat{\varepsilon}_i \hat{K}_i^* = 0$ (*not* $E\hat{\varepsilon}_i = 0$, since $\hat{K}^*$ is no longer exogenous; $\hat{K}^* = (K^*)^{3/2} K^{-1/2}$). This moment is now evaluated, using methods analogous to equations A.3 and A.4.

$$E(\hat{\varepsilon}_i \hat{K}_i^* \mid H_i > 0) = E\left(\frac{K_i^*}{K_i} \cdot \varepsilon_i K_i^* \mid H_i > 0\right)$$

$$= \frac{\displaystyle\int \frac{K^{*2}}{K_i} \cdot \varepsilon_i \cdot \frac{K_i}{52} \cdot g^i(v_i) \, dv_i}{\displaystyle\int (K_i/52) g^i(v_i) \, dv_i}$$

$$= \frac{K_i^{*2} E\varepsilon_i}{K_i^* + E\varepsilon_i} = K_i^* E\varepsilon_i = 0. \tag{A.6}$$

Equation A.6 shows that the weighting scheme applied in equation A.5 eliminates the bias, and provides consistent estimates of this equation. Moreover, it preserves the scale of the moments, since $E(\hat{\varepsilon}_i \hat{K}_i^* \mid H_i > 0) = E(\varepsilon_i K_i^*)$, where the last term is the unconditional expectation among all participants. Similar evaluation of other equations and moments clearly gives analogous results, since K is eliminated between the weights K^*/K and the probability $K/52$.

Next, consider the effects of transitory components. Assume

$$K_i^t = K_i^* + \varepsilon_i^p + \varepsilon_i^t$$

and

$$K_i^{t-1} = K_i^* + \varepsilon_i^p + \varepsilon_i^{t-1}, \tag{A.7}$$

where K^* and ε^p are constant (between the two adjacent years), and ε^t, ε^{t-1} are transitory and assumed uncorrelated with each other and with the permanent component ε_i^p.

Repeating the derivation in equation A.6 for this case, using $(K^t/52)$ for the selection probability and (K^*/K^{t-1}) for weights, and remembering that the measured weeks variable is K^{t-1}, gives

$$E(\hat{\varepsilon}_i \hat{K}_i \mid H_i > 0) = K_i^* E\left[\frac{K_i^t(\varepsilon_i^p + \varepsilon_i^{t-1})}{K_i^{t-1}}\right]$$

$$= K_i^* E\left[\varepsilon_i^p + \varepsilon_i^{t-1} + \frac{(\varepsilon_i^t - \varepsilon_i^{t-1})(\varepsilon_i^p + \varepsilon_i^{t-1})}{K_i^{t-1}}\right],$$

by substitution from equation A.7 and some manipulation. Hence,

$$E(\hat{\varepsilon}_i \hat{K}_i^* \mid H_i > 0) = K_i^* E\left[\frac{(\varepsilon_i^t - \varepsilon_i^{t-1})\varepsilon_i^p + \varepsilon_i^{t-1})}{K_i^{t-1}}\right]$$

$$\cong - \text{var } \varepsilon_i^{t-1}, \tag{A.8}$$

where the last equality is an approximation derived by replacing expectations by probability limits. On the other hand, the bias in the same original unweighted equation is given by

$$E(\varepsilon_i K_i^* \mid H_i > 0) = E[(\varepsilon_i^p + \varepsilon_i^{t-1}) \cdot K_i^t]$$

$$= E(\varepsilon_i^p + \varepsilon_i^{t-1})(\varepsilon_i^p + \varepsilon_i^t)$$

$$= \text{var } \varepsilon_i^p. \tag{A.9}$$

Since the weeks permanent residual variance is estimated to account for most of the total variance of K_i,[91] the bias in the unweighted weeks equation (A.9) is larger than in equation A.8. Applying a similar analysis to other equations and moments tends to give similar results.

---

[91] The proportion of the permanent component was estimated as 0.825 in Chapter 3.

APPENDIX B

SAMPLE DEFINITIONS AND EXCLUSIONS

(i) *Sample exclusions:*

The original 1967 sample of SEO units was first narrowed down to 9,770 married, spouse present households, by the following exclusions (based mainly on husband):

- Farm households
- Husband younger than 18 or older than 61
- Husband salaried self-employed, other self-employed, working without pay, or work class data missing
- Husband attending school or in military
- Husband not working (during survey, or during nonwork weeks in 1966), or working part-time, because he was ill, disabled, unable to work, going to school, in armed forces or in institution, keeping house, or if reason for part-time work missing
- Business or farm income not reported

The final sample used here consisted of 6,319 white married women defined by using the following additional exclusions:

- Missing value for hours worked last week
- Missing value for earnings last week
- Missing state in which lived at age 16
- Missing number of children ever born, number of children at home, or age of youngest child at home
- Wife with positive hours worked but zero earnings last week
- Missing weeks worked
- Wife in military

(ii) *Definition of nonwage income included:*

Interest, dividends, rental income, other regular income (annuity payments, royalties, private welfare or relief, etc.), and work-related income (social security or railroad retirement benefits, government pensions, veteran pensions, private employer pensions, workmen's compensation, illness or accident insurance benefits, unemployment insurance benefits, and public welfare assistance).

APPROXIMATING THE RESIDUAL VARIANCE STRUCTURE

The residual variance matrix as estimated in the 3SLS system (equations 6.3, 6.4, 6.5) gives biased estimates for the corresponding elements of the underlying variance matrix Σ, because of two types of truncation bias: (1) the participation selectivity bias, truncating the distribution of the participation residual $u_1 = u_0 - u_2$ at $u_1 \leq w^* - w_0^*$ for participants; and (2) the weeks corner solution of full-year (52 weeks), truncating the weeks residual u_4 at $u_4 \leq 52 - \tilde{K}^*$.

A full joint treatment of these two truncation biases was not pursued in this model, however. Instead, the effect of the weeks truncation was introduced only into the weeks and hours supply equations, linearizing the effects through the variable DK and its interactions with w and $EH + Y$. This seemed sufficient for providing consistent estimates of relevant coefficients, but not of variance estimates—especially in the weeks equation itself.

On the other hand, the Tobit analysis in Section V.4 does provide an estimate of the variance σ_{44}^v ($= 582.016$) which is corrected for the truncation effect in weeks (as against the corresponding estimate, 273.16, in the 3SLS estimate of equation 6.5). For this reason, the Tobit estimate of σ_{44}^v—and for the sake of consistency also the Tobit coefficient of λ, estimating $b_4 = (-\sigma_{14}/\sigma_1)$ ($= 10.37$)—were chosen as point estimates of these parameters.

These were combined with estimates of other parameters from the 3SLS system (equations 6.3 to 6.6), given as follows:

(i) $\sigma_1 = -b_1 = 0.4130$; $b_2 = (-\sigma_{12}/\sigma_1) = 0.1282$; $b_3 = (-\sigma_{13}/\sigma_1)$ $= 609.6$ (from coefficients in Tables 6.11, 6.7, and 6.8, respectively).

(ii) The variances: $\sigma_{22}^v = 0.1843$; $\sigma_{33}^v = 518435$; and the correlations: $r_{23}^v = -0.0645$; $r_{24}^v = -0.108$; $r_{34}^v = 0.854$, computed from residuals of the first 3SLS system (equations 6.3 to 6.5).

Combining these estimates gives Σ^v matrix for residuals $v_{ji} = u_{ji} - \lambda_i b_j$ $(i = 1 \cdots n; j = 2, 3, 4)$ (equation 6.12). The corresponding section of the underlying variance matrix Σ of Table 6.14 is now estimated by using equation 6.13 as follows:

$$\sigma_{jk} = \sigma_{jk}^v + b_j b_k \bar{D} \qquad (j, k = 2, 3, 4),$$

where $\bar{D}$ is the mean of $D_i = \lambda_i (I_i + \lambda_i)$ ($\bar{D} = 0.566$ for workers; Table 6.3), to correct for the selectivity bias truncation.

Estimates associated with $u_0 = u_1 + u_2$ (first row in Table 6.14) were computed from these: $\sigma_{0j} = \sigma_{1j} + \sigma_{2j}$ $(j = 1, \ldots, 4)$; $\sigma_0^2 = \sigma_1^2 + \sigma_2^2 + 2\sigma_{12}$. (Table 6.14 is given in correlation form: $r_{jk} = \sigma_{jk}/\sigma_j \sigma_k$; $j, k = 0, \ldots, 4$.).

CHAPTER 7

LABOR SUPPLY WITH COSTS
OF LABOR MARKET ENTRY

JOHN COGAN

THE RAND CORPORATION

I. INTRODUCTION

Recent empirical research on married women's labor supply has considerably enhanced knowledge of the role that economic and demographic factors play in shaping labor market behavior of this demographic group. There are, however, several factors that have received only superficial attention. One in particular is the costs of work. Despite its potential empirical importance, the existence of either fixed or variable costs of work is typically assumed away in empirical analyses. In this chapter I develop a simple model of labor supply with time and money costs of labor market entry, and develop a statistical procedure for estimating labor supply functions when these costs are not directly observable in the data.

In previous theoretical work, the costs of labor market entry have been treated in much the same manner as a fixed license fee in traditional consumer theory (Cogan, 1977; Hanoch, Chapter 3). In this treatment, the individual supplier of labor is assumed to incur a fixed time and/or money cost upon entry into the labor market. These components of the total cost of labor market participation are assumed to be unalterable through market exchange. As a departure from reality, this assumption is quite striking. Individuals can and do choose between time and money costs of labor market entry. The purchase of automobiles (in part) for transportation to and from work, the use of formal child-care arrangements by working women, and household migration are all evidence of this choice. The model developed in

Section II of this paper incorporates the trade-off between time and money costs by allowing individuals to choose between the two at given rates of exchange.

Section III describes alternative strategies for estimating labor supply functions when the costs of entry are observed in the data and when they are not. In this section, the latter strategy is applied to data from the Michigan Panel of Income Dynamics to estimate the parameters of married women's wage, labor force participation, and hours worked parameters. The estimated parameters are then used to infer the costs of labor market participation.

The major conclusions drawn from these estimates are in two areas; the magnitude and effects of entry costs on labor market behavior, and the choice of statistical procedures used in estimating married women's labor supply functions.

In the first area, the existence of costs of participation imparts a discontinuity in the labor supply function, reflecting the fact that women will not be willing to work below some minimum number of hours. The estimated discontinuity is large, at the sample means about 1,100 hours per year, slightly over half-time work. The discontinuity reflects the importance of entry costs in determining married women's labor supply behavior. It is at least a partial explanation for the fact that relatively few observations on married women lie in the range of 1 to 800 hours worked per year. The estimated costs of work are also large, almost $1,000 per year. This is about 16 percent of the average earnings of working women in the data. Preschool children appear to be the most important source of work costs. An additional preschool-age child increases the annual costs of participation by over $300.

Incorporating costs of labor market participation appears to increase significantly the ability of labor supply models to explain variation in hours worked among working women. Using the same data and identical specifications of the labor supply function, the variation in hours worked among these women explained by the entry cost model is more than double that explained by the approach developed by Heckman (1974b), which ignores costs of work. Parameter estimates between the two procedures are dramatically different. The constraint of no discontinuity imposed by the Heckman procedure results in parameter estimates that are between two and five times as large as those of the entry cost model. These systematic and large differences are evidence of the importance of incorporating the discontinuity in the supply function in estimating married women's labor supply functions.

II. A SIMPLE GRAPHICAL EXPOSITION

This section provides a simple graphical exposition of the effects of time and money costs of labor market entry on married women's labor supply. This exposition extends the traditional treatment by incorporating the fact that women can and do choose between time and money costs of work. In a larger study upon which this paper is based (Cogan, 1977), I explored the implications of a model that treated the time and money costs of labor market entry as fixed and unalterable through market exchange. The major implication which emerged from that analysis was that the existence of either fixed time or money costs severs the link between the woman's reservation wage and the value of her time at full-time leisure and, as a consequence, produces a discontinuity in her labor supply function at the reservation wage. In addition, increases in either type of cost raise reservation wages and reduce the probability that the woman will work. But although increases in time costs reduce hours of work conditional upon working, increases in money costs increase hours of work conditional upon working.

Although in the short run both the time and money cost components of the total cost of labor market entry may be viewed as fixed, both casual empiricism as well as previous detailed empirical analysis suggest the individuals can and do choose between time and money costs, and that this choice depends upon their market earning capacity. In the literature on household location the importance of individual household member's earning capacity in determining the distance the household locates from the jobs of its members has long been recognized (see, for instance, Alonzo, 1964 and Kain, 1962). Indeed, the negatively inclined rent gradient observed for residential housing is empirical evidence that households choose between time and money costs of work. For married women, child-care arrangements for preschool children are an important cost of work. An increase in a working woman's wage rate might, in the short run, not induce her to alter her child-care arrangements, but over time one would expect her to substitute toward arrangements that are less intensive in her time. Since in cross-sections, differences in labor supply resulting from differences in wage rates are likely to reflect, in part, different chosen combinations of time and money costs of work, it is important to incorporate the choice between these two dimensions of the cost of work into labor supply analysis.

To develop a model of endogenous time and money costs of labor market entry, I begin by assuming that the individual faces an exogenously given locus of points representing all possible combinations of time and money costs of work. The locus of points that represents all the alternative *minimum* entry cost combinations defines the individual's entry cost curve. Denoting dollars expended in entering the market as X^* and time "lost" in entering the market as L^*, the entry cost curve is depicted in Figure 7.1 by GG'. The entry cost curve indicates that the individual could choose to incur the entire cost of entry in terms of time (L_0^*) or in terms of money (X_0^*) or any convex combination of the two.

The slope of the entry cost curve is the rate at which the individual can transform time cost into money cost on the margin or, equivalently, it is the marginal cost of labor market entry time. Convexity of the entry cost curve implies that the marginal cost of entry time rises as the individual attempts to purchase more and more substitutes for her time.

As is shown in Appendix A, convexity of the entry cost curve is a necessary condition for an interior solution in the choice between time

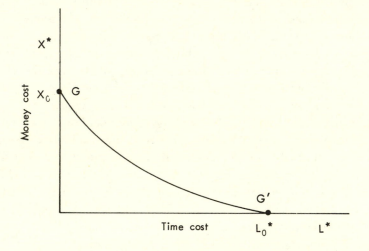

FIGURE 7.1   Entry cost curve

and money costs. There are, however, many examples of other empirical phenomena that would give rise to a convex entry cost curve. One rather obvious example is the rising rent gradient, as the marginal cost of constant quality housing rises as one moves closer to the central business district. Moving closer to one's job may be viewed as substituting money costs for time costs in getting to work. Thus, with a rising rent gradient, the cost of this substitution on the margin rises as one attempts to reduce time cost in getting to work by moving closer to the central city.

The nature of the individual's choice between time and money costs, as well as the choice of how much time to allocate to market work is easily described once the individual's preferences and remaining constraints are specified. For simplicity, assume that the individual's preferences are discribed by the utility function.

$$U = U(X, L), \tag{7.2.1}$$

where X is a composite commodity and L is leisure time.[1] The individual's income is allocated between consumption (X) and money costs of work (X^*)

$$X = Wh + V - X^*, \tag{7.2.2}$$

where W is the wage rate, h denotes hours of work, and V is nonwage income. The composite good is considered the numeraire commodity $(P_X \equiv 1)$. The individual is assumed to allocate the available time to him (H) among leisure (L), market work (h), and time lost in getting to work (L^*). That is,

$$H = L + h + L^*. \tag{7.2.3}$$

The individual's entry cost curve is given by

$$X^* = G(L^*, Z), \tag{7.2.4}$$

where, in accordance with our previous discussion, $g_{L^*} < 0$ and $g_{L^*L^*} > 0$. The variable Z is a shift parameter.

For the analysis that follows, I shall ignore the possibility of corner solutions for the individual's time and merely assume the existence of an interior solution. This is done solely for expository convenience. The decision of whether to participate in the labor market is dealt with later.

[1] The utility function is assumed to possess the usual properties, namely, it is assumed to be twice continuously differentiable and quasi-concave.

The necessary conditions for a relative maximum are equations $7.2.2 = 2.4$ and

$$U_X - \lambda = 0, \tag{7.2.5}$$

$$U_L - \lambda W = 0, \tag{7.2.6}$$

$$W + g_{L^*} = 0, \tag{7.2.7}$$

where λ is the marginal utility of full income. These conditions describe the nature of the equilibrium. Equations 7.2.5 and 7.2.6 combine to yield the familiar result that the individual, in equilibrium, equates the marginal rate of substitution between income and leisure to the market wage rate. Equation 7.2.7 indicates that the individual will substitute money cost of entry for time cost up to the point where the marginal time cost of entry equals the return to that time, which, in turn, equals the wage rate. The working individual's equilibrium is graphically depicted in Figure 7.2.

In Figure 7.2 the point (V_0, H) is the individual's initial endowment. Given a wage rate of W and an entry cost opportunity curve GG', the individual chooses to spend $V_0 - V_1$ dollars and forego $H_0 - L_1$ hours of leisure to get to work. The amount of time the individual spends at market work at this wage is given by $L_1 - L_2$.

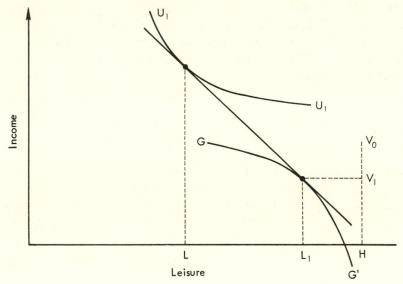

FIGURE 7.2   Equilibrium allocation of time with endogenous time and money costs of participation

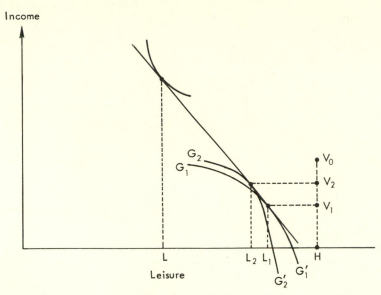

Income

Leisure

FIGURE 7.3   Compensated effect of a rise in the marginal time cost of entry

In examining the impact of variations in entry costs on the individual's equilibrium position, it is useful to decompose the total effect into a "pure price effect" and a "wealth effect." As is conventional, the pure price effect holds the individual's real wealth constant, but allows the marginal time cost of entry to vary. The "wealth effect," on the other hand, holds the marginal time cost of entry constant, but allows the total cost to vary.

The pure price effect is described with the aid of Figure 7.3. An increase in the marginal cost of entry time implies that the slope of GG' becomes steeper at every quantity of leisure. If the total cost of entry is held constant, then it must be true that the new equilibrium time and money cost combination lies along the given wage line. Together these considerations imply that the pure price effect may be obtained by rotating the entry cost curve clockwise by some arbitrary amount. In Figure 7.3, G_1G_1' denotes the initial entry cost curve. G_2G_2' denotes the entry cost curve associated with a higher marginal cost of entry time, but with the same total costs of entry.

As Figure 7.3 indicates, the pure price effect of an increase in the marginal cost of entry time results in a larger proportion of the given

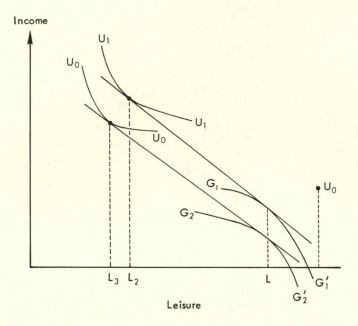

FIGURE 7.4   Effect of an increase in the total costs of labor market entry

total cost of entry being incurred in the form of time. The quantity of leisure demanded does not change and hence the quantity of labor supplied declines by an amount equal to the increase in time spent getting to work. Thus, for compensated changes in the marginal cost of entry time it is true that

$$\frac{dh}{dg_{L*}} = -\frac{dL^*}{dg_{L*}}.$$

(7.2.8)

The effect of an increase in the total cost of entry, holding the marginal cost of entry time constant, is illustrated in Figure 7.4 by a vertical displacement downward in the entry cost curve from $G_1 G_1'$ to $G_2 G_2'$. Since the marginal cost of entry time is unaltered, the amount of time devoted to obtaining entry into the labor market will not be altered. The increased entry cost lowers the worker's net wealth and, as a consequence, the quantity of leisure demanded falls and the quantity of labor supplied to the market increases.

The total effect of a rise in the wage rate above the initial equilibrium wage is[2]

$$\frac{dh}{dW} = \left(\frac{\partial h}{\partial W}\right)^c + \frac{\partial h}{\partial V} \frac{\partial L^*}{\partial W}. \qquad (7.2.9)$$

Equation 7.2.9 decomposes the total own-wage effect into three terms. The first two are the conventional Hicks–Slutsky substitution and income effects. The third term results from the substitution of money costs for time costs of entry induced by the higher wage. As the wage rate rises, the return to reducing time "lost" in entering the labor market rises. The individual will respond by purchasing more substitutes for her time and will continue to do so until the marginal cost of an additional substitute equals her higher wage. Thus, $\partial L^*/\partial W$ in equation 7.2.9 is negative and the own-wage effect allowing for substitutability between time and money costs of work exceeds the own-wage effect of the conventional labor supply model which ignores the cost of work (see Kosters, 1966).

This result has two immediate implications. First, if the degree of substitutability between time and money in getting to work increases over time, then we would expect labor supply functions to become more elastic over time. Second, attempts to estimate compensated labor supply functions directly with cross-sectional data, such as that of Ashenfelter and Heckman (1973), will be deficient unless one can first identify the parameters of the entry cost curve.

The effect of a rise in nonwage income on hours of work is identical to the effect obtained in the conventional labor supply model, if it is assumed that the marginal cost of entry time does not change with nonwage income.

It is important to recognize that the incorporation of time and money costs of participation alters the interpretation of estimated labor supply parameters only if these costs cannot be observed in the data. To illustrate, the labor supply function is written as

$$h = g[W, V - X^* + W(L_0 - L^*), Z], \qquad (7.2.10)$$

where Z is a vector of tastes on nonmarket productivity variables and the equilibrium costs of work function as

$$X^* = X(W, V, Z), \qquad (7.2.11)$$

$$L^* = Z(W, V, Z). \qquad (7.2.12)$$

[2] All derivations are performed in Appendix A.

The derivatives of the labor supply function (7.2.10) reflect only the parameters of the underlying utility function. If one could estimate 7.2.10, the coefficients would be interpreted as estimates of these partial derivatives. An interpretation of estimated labor supply parameters when the costs of work cannot be observed in the data can be obtained by substituting equations 7.2.11 and 7.2.12 into 7.2.10. The resulting equation, which is termed the quasi-reduced form labor supply function, may be written as

$$h = \gamma(W, V, Z), \tag{7.2.13}$$

and its partial derivatives include not only those of the g function but also those of the X and L functions. Thus, if equation 7.2.13 could be estimated, the coefficients would be interpreted as reflecting not only the parameters of the underlying utility function but also of the effects of variation in the costs of work.

To aid in describing behavior, the concept of reservation hours is introduced. Reservation hours are defined as the minimum number of hours the individual is willing to work. The typical individual's reservation hours may be found by choosing a wage such that the individual is indifferent between working and not and solving for the interior solution to the hours of work function. This solution is graphically depicted in Figure 7.5.

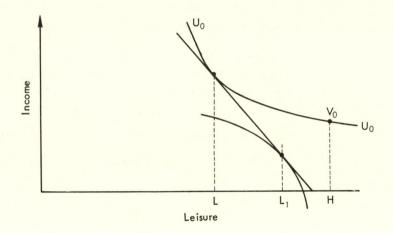

FIGURE 7.5   Reservation hours of work of a representative woman

In Figure 7.5 the individual's reservation hours are given by $L_1 - L$. As the figure suggests, the individual's reservations hours are determined by her tastes for leisure, the parameters of the entry cost curve she faces, and her level of nonwage income.

The effects of changes in tastes and nonwage income on reservation hours are, in general, theoretically indeterminant. The direction of the effects of changes in the parameters entry cost curve are, on the other hand, unambiguous. As is rather obvious from the graph in Figure 7.5, an increase in the marginal cost of entry time, holding the total entry cost constant, necessarily reduces the individual's reservation hours. Increases in total entry cost, holding the marginal time cost constant, necessarily raises reservations hours.

III. ESTIMATION STRATEGIES

INTRODUCTION

To estimate labor supply functions when there are costs of labor force participation, one of two empirical strategies may be followed. The choice between them depends on the data available. If information on the time and money costs of labor market entry incurred by participants is available, then these costs can be used to estimate the structural parameters of not only the labor supply function but also of costs of work functions. Tests of the degree of the long-run substitutability between time and money costs may also be made. If information on the time and money costs of work is not available, then one can only obtain estimates of a quasi-reduced form labor supply function. Both estimation strategies are discussed fully in this section. The reader interested only in the development of the estimation procedure used to obtain the estimates in this paper may skip the section on estimating the structural model.

ESTIMATION OF THE STRUCTURAL MODEL

In the previous approaches to formulating empirical models of married women's labor supply behavior, the labor supply decision is expressed in terms of market wage and shadow wage functions.[3] If the market wage offer exceeds the shadow price of time at full-time leisure, the

---

[3] See Cogan (Chapter 2) for an analysis of alternative approaches to estimating married women's labor supply function in the absence of participation costs.

woman does not enter the labor market. Otherwise, she is a participant and supplies an amount of labor such that on the margin her shadow price of time equals her market wage. With the introduction of costs of labor market entry, the reservation wage no longer equals the shadow price of time at full-time leisure and, consequently, the latter price no longer plays a role in determining the labor force participation decision. Hence, an alternative formulation of the empirical model is required.

Following the analysis of the preceding section, married woman's labor supply decision is characterized in terms of two hypothetical variables: reservation hours (h_0) and "notional" hours (h_n). The woman's reservation hours are simply the minimum number of hours the woman is willing to work. Notional hours are the number of hours the woman would choose to work if she were required to spend at least some positive amount of time in the labor market. The notional hours function is simply the hours of work function extrapolated down to the wage axis. Assuming an upward sloping supply curve, a woman participates in the labor force if her notional hours exceed her reservation hours. Since for working women the requirement that the woman spend at least some portion of her time in the labor market is irrelevant, it is true for these women that notional hours equal actual hours of work. If a woman's notional hours are less than her reservation hours, she will choose not to work and her observed hours of work are zero.

In general, we may write the notional hours equation for the ith observation as

$$h_{n_i} = \eta(W_i, L_i^*, X_i^*, Z_{1_i}, \varepsilon_{1_i}), \qquad (7.3.1)$$

where W_i is the market wage offer; L and X denote the time and money costs of participation respectively; Z_1 is a vector of variables that reflect the woman's tastes for nonmarket activities, her nonmarket productivity, nonwage income, and the prices of related goods; and ε_1 is a random deviation reflecting unobserved factors that affect hours of work.

Equation 7.3.1 is applicable under the assumption of fixed time and money costs of participation or under the assumption that individuals can choose between time and money costs. Under the fixity assumption, the partial derivatives of equation 7.3.1 measure the full change in hours of work as the woman adjusts to her equilibrium. If, on the other hand, the woman is able to substitute between time and money costs in response to exogenous forces then these partial derivatives measure only the effects associated with partial adjustment.

The reservation hours equation may be written as

$$h_{0_i} = \Delta(L_i^*, X_i^*, Z_{1_i}^*, \varepsilon_{0_i}), \tag{7.3.2}$$

where ε_0 captures the effects of unobservable factors that operate through the cost of work or tastes for nonmarket activities. It should be noted that theory implies some restrictions on equation 7.3.2. A particularly important one is that if there are no costs of participation ($L_i^* = X_i^* = 0$), then reservation hours must be identically zero. This, of course, assumes that the utility function exhibits diminishing marginal rates of substitution throughout. Thus, a natural procedure for testing for the existence of participation costs in the data is available. The test has as its null hypothesis that $\Delta(\cdot)$ is zero for all observations.

The equations describing the costs of work facing the ith individual are given by

$$L_i^* = \theta(W_i, Z_{0_i}, \varepsilon_{3_i}), \tag{7.3.3}$$

$$X_1^* = \phi(W_i, Z_{2_i}, \varepsilon_{4_i}), \tag{7.3.4}$$

where Z_{0_i} and Z_{2_i} are vectors of measurable variables that reflect differences in participation costs constraints among individuals. The random deviations ε_3 and ε_4 reflect the effects of unmeasurable differences in constraints among individuals. Under the assumption that individuals choose between time and money costs, the partial derivatives of θ and ϕ with respect to the wage rate W are negative and positive, respectively. Under the assumption of fixed costs of participation these derivatives are zero. Thus, if the partial derivatives of equations 7.3.3 and 7.3.4 could be estimated, the fixity assumption could be tested directly against the data.

To complete the model, a market wage offer equation is written for the ith observation as

$$W_i = \alpha(Z_{3_i}, \varepsilon_{2_i}) \tag{7.3.5}$$

and added to the model.

If the endogenous variables h_n, h_0, W, L^*, and X^* could be observed for all individuals, then the parameters of equations 7.3.1–3.5 could be estimated with two- or three-stage least squares. Unfortunately, these variables are not observed for all individuals. Reservation hours is a hypothetical variable and cannot be observed for *any* individual in the data; notional hours and wage offers cannot be observed for nonworkers, and the time and money costs of participation can, in principle, only be observed for working individuals. Without these data, an alternative estimation approach is required.

To develop such an alternative, the functional form of equations 7.3.1–3.5, the structure of disturbances, and the relationship between the hypothetical endogenous variables and their respective observed values in the data must be specified. For convenience, let us assume that each endogenous variable may be expressed as a linear function of its determinants.

For the ith observation, then, we have

$$h_{n_i} = \eta_1 W_i + \eta_2 L_i^* + \eta_3 X_i^* + \bar{\eta}_4' \bar{Z}_{1_i} + \varepsilon_{1_i} \tag{7.3.6}$$

$$h_{0_i} = \Delta_1 L_i^* + \Delta_2 X_i^* + \Delta_3' Z_{1_i} + \varepsilon_{0_i}, \tag{7.3.7}$$

$$L_i^* = \theta_1 W_i + \theta_2 Z_{2_i} + \varepsilon_{3_i}, \tag{7.3.8}$$

$$X_i^* = \phi_1 W_i + \phi_2' Z_{2_i} + \varepsilon_{4_i}, \tag{7.3.9}$$

$$W_i = \alpha_0' Z_{3_i} + \varepsilon_{2_i}, \tag{7.3.10}$$

where as a matter of notation, the bars over the coefficients and variables indicate that they are vectors rather than scalars. The random disturbances are assumed to be distributed with mean vector zero and unknown but constant variance-covariance matrix.

The relationship between the hypothetical left-hand side variables and their corresponding observed values can be described once we have specified the nature of the labor force participation decision. Assuming that the labor supply function is upward rising throughout, ($\eta_1 > 0$), the woman will be observed to be working if the solution to the notional hours equation exceeds her reservation hours. That is, if

$$h_{n_i} = \eta_1 W_i + \eta_2 L_i^* + \eta_3 X_i^* + \eta_4' Z_{1_i} + \varepsilon_{1_i}$$
$$> \Delta_1 L_i^* + \Delta_2 X_i^* + \Delta_3' Z_{1_i} + \varepsilon_{0_i} = h_{0_i}. \tag{7.3.11}$$

Using equations 7.3.6–3.10, the participation decision may be expressed in terms of only the exogenous variables of the system. Substituting these relations into 7.3.11, the condition for participation may be written compactly as

$$\prod Z' > V, \tag{7.3.12}$$

where

$$Z_i = (Z'_{0_i}, Z'_{1_i}, Z'_{2_i}, Z'_{3_i}),$$

$$V_i = (\Delta_1 - \eta_2)\varepsilon_3 + (\Delta_2 - \eta_3)\varepsilon_{4_i} + [-\eta_1 + \theta_1(\Delta_1 - \eta_2) + \phi_1(\Delta_2 - \eta_3)]\varepsilon_{2_i}$$

$$\Pi = \left\{ \begin{array}{l} \theta_2(\eta_2 - \Delta_1) + \phi_2(\eta_3 - \Delta_2) \\ \eta_4 - \Delta_3 \\ \eta_1 + \theta_1(\eta_2 - \Delta_1) + \phi_1(\eta_3 - \Delta_2) \end{array} \right\}.$$

For a woman who participates in the labor force her notional hours of work equal her actual hours of work and her wage offer can be observed. With detailed household survey data, the time and money costs may also, in principle, be observed for these women. For nonparticipants, on the other hand, actual hours of work are zero and the hypothetical notional hours variable cannot be observed. Also, nonparticipants reject wage offers and choose not to incur any time and money of labor market entry. Hence, W_i, L^*, and X^* cannot be observed for these individuals.

The failure to be able to observe for nonworkers results in a censored data problem. However, since the relation determining the point of censoring is known, the likelihood function for the data can be ascertained and maximum likelihood used to estimate the structural parameters. As a matter of notation, the reduced form of the equations 7.3.6–3.10 are

$$h_{n_i} = \beta'_1 Z_i + U_{1_i}, \tag{7.3.13}$$

$$h_{0_i} = \beta'_0 Z_i + U_{2_i}, \tag{7.3.14}$$

$$L_i^* = \beta'_3 Z_{4_i} + U_{3_i}, \tag{7.3.15}$$

$$X_i^* = \beta'_4 Z_{4_i} + U_{4_i}, \tag{7.3.16}$$

$$W_i = \alpha'_0 Z_{3_i} + \varepsilon_{2_i}. \tag{7.3.17}$$

The probability that h_{n_i} is zero and that L_i^*, X_i^*, and W_i are not observed is simply the probability that the woman does not participate in the labor force. Using equation 7.3.12, the probability of nonparticipation is

$$Pr(P = 0) = Pr(V > \Pi'Z) = \int_{\pi'Z_i/\sigma_n}^{\infty} f(t)\, dt = 1 - P\left(\frac{\Pi'Z}{\sigma_v}\right),$$

$$f(t) = \frac{1}{\sqrt{2\pi}} e^{-\frac{1}{2}t^2} \tag{7.3.18}$$

For workers in the sample we know that reservation hours are less than notional hours; that is,

$$h_{n_i} - \beta_0' Z_i > U_{2_i}. \tag{7.3.19}$$

Hence, the appropriate density measure for h_{n_i}, L_i^*, X_i^*, and W_i among the workers in the samples is given by

$$\int_{-\infty}^{h_i - \beta_0 Z_i} f(h_i - \beta_i' Z_i, L_i^* - \beta_3' Z_{4_i}, X_i^* - \beta_4' Z_{4_i}, W_i - \alpha_0' Z_{3_i}, U_{2_i}) \, dU_{2_i}. \tag{7.3.20}$$

Using 7.3.18 and 7.3.20, the likelihood function for a sample consisting of n observations, S of whom do not work is

$$L = \prod_{i=1}^{S} \left[1 - P\left(\frac{\Pi Z_i}{\sigma_v}\right) \prod_{i=S+1}^{N} \int^{h_i - \beta_0' Z_i} f(h_i - \beta_i' Z_i, L_i^* \right. $$
$$\left. - \beta_3' Z_{4_i}, X_i^* - \beta_4' Z_{4_i}, W_i - \alpha_0' Z_{3_i}, U_{2_i}) \right] dU_{2_i}. \tag{7.3.21}$$

Assuming, of course, that the structural parameters can be identified, optimizing 7.3.21 yields consistent estimates of these parameters. While in theory optimizing 7.3.21 is a straightforward task, in practice it is likely to be quite difficult and costly. The derivatives of the log likelihood function are highly nonlinear and the possibility of multiple roots cannot be dismissed. Given the dimensionality of the density function $f(\cdot)$, and the problem of multiple roots, the cost of finding the maximum likelihood estimator is likely to be prohibitive. This, coupled with the fact that information on the time and money costs of participation contained in currently available data files is at best sketchy, suggests that perhaps an alternative approach might be preferred.

A QUASI-REDUCED FORM MODEL AND
THE CONDITIONAL MAXIMUM LIKELIHOOD ESTIMATOR

One such approach is to ignore the available information on time and money participation costs and estimate a quasi-reduced form labor supply function. Substituting relations 7.3.15 and 7.3.16 into the reservation and notional hours functions yields these quasi-reduced form equations. Along with the wage equation they are

$$h_{n_i} = \gamma_0' Z_i + \gamma_{1_i} W_i + V_{1_i}, \tag{7.3.22}$$

$$h_{0_i} = \beta' Z_i + V_{0_i}, \tag{7.3.23}$$

$$W_i = \alpha' Z_3 + \varepsilon_{2_i}. \tag{7.3.24}$$

The likelihood function for the quasi-reduced form equations may be derived in a manner identical to the derivation of 7.3.21. Although the resulting likelihood function is much simpler than 7.3.21 it still involves manipulating the trivariate normal distribution and, hence, is also likely to be quite expensive to optimize. If, however, consistent estimates of the parameters of the wage equation could be obtained, then this information might be used to reduce the dimensionality of the likelihood function and as a result reduce its cost. To see how, consider the estimation of the reduced form of the hours of work equation. Substituting the wage equation into the hours of work equation, we obtain

$$h_{n_i} = \gamma_0' Z_i + \gamma_1 \alpha_0' Z_2 + V_{2_i}, \tag{7.3.25}$$

where

$$V_{2_i} = V_{1_i} + \gamma_0 \varepsilon_{2_i}.$$

Equations 7.3.25 and 7.3.23 combine to form the censored regression model analyzed independently by Nelson (1974) and Olsen (1974). The likelihood function in terms of equations 7.3.23 and 7.3.25 is

$$L = \left\{ \prod_{i=1}^{S} 1 - P\left[\frac{\gamma_0 \alpha_0' Z_{2_i} + (\gamma_1' - \beta_0') Z_i}{\sigma_v^*}\right] \right.$$
$$\left. \times \prod_{i=S+1}^{N} \int_{-\infty}^{h_i - \beta_0 Z_i} f(h_i - \gamma_0 \alpha_0' Z_{2_i} - \gamma' Z_i, V_{0_i}) \, dV_{0_i} \right\}, \tag{7.3.26}$$

where

$$\sigma_v^* = (\sigma_{v_1}^2 + \sigma_{v_2}^2 - 2\sigma_{v_1 v_2})^{\frac{1}{2}}.$$

If there is at least one element in Z_2 that is not contained in Z, one can obtain consistent estimates of the reduced form parameters β_0', $\gamma_0 \alpha'$, σ_{v_1}, σ_{v_2} and $\sigma_{v_1 v_2}$ by optimizing the likelihood function 7.3.26.[4] Suppose that the parameter vector α_0 were known with perfect certainty prior to estimation, clearly this prior information would serve to identify γ_0 along with the remaining parameters of 7.3.22 and 7.3.23. Optimizing 7.3.26 subject to the known values of the elements α would, of course, yield consistent estimates of these remaining parameters. Now, suppose that instead of knowing with perfect certainty, we had a consistent estimate of α which we shall denote as $\hat{\alpha}$. In this

---

[4] This is a necessary condition for identification of the elements of the parameter vector B_0.

instance, optimizing 7.3.26 subject to $\hat{\alpha}$ would yield consistent estimates of the parameters β_0, γ_0, σ_{v_1}, σ_{v_2}, and $\sigma_{v_1 v_2}$.

IV. Empirical Results

THE DATA

The data used for the empirical analysis is taken from the 1976 survey of the Michigan Panel of Income Dynamics (IDP). The original IDP sample contained over 5,800 families. Of these, 2,700 were white families in which both the husband and wife were present at the time of the interview. Only these families are included in our analysis. Further exclusions were made because either spouse reported self-employment or farm income and because of missing or incomplete information on the core variables used in the analysis, such as education level, age, husband's earnings, etc. Finally, observations on women who were in school, reported being permanently disabled, or retired at the time of the interview were deleted from the sample. The remaining sample used for the analysis of this paper contains 1,584 families. In this sample, 1,003 of the wives reported doing some market work in 1975 and 581 did no market work. Table 7.1 provides the means and standard deviations of all the variables used in the empirical analysis which follows.

SPECIFICATION OF THE EMPIRICAL MODEL

To estimate the fixed cost model, relatively simple specifications of the notional hours, reservation hours, and market wage functions are adopted. The hours of work equation assumes the form

$$h_{N_i} = \gamma_0 + \gamma_1 N(W_i) + \gamma_2 Y_{H_i} + \gamma_3 E_i + \gamma_4 A_i + \sum_{i=1}^{3} \gamma_{4+j} C_j + u_{1_i}, \quad (7.4.1)$$

where $N(W_i)$ is the natural logarithm of the wife's wage; Y_H is the husband's annual earnings; E is the wife's education level; A is the wife's age; C_1, C_2 and C_3 are variables measuring the presence and age composition of children in the home. C_1 is the number of preschool children in the home (age 0–5), C_2 is the number of elementary school age children in the home (age 6–13), and C_3 is the number of high-school age children in the home (age 14–18).

The dependent variable is annual hours of work. This variable deserves some comment. Presumably, the major source of fixed costs

TABLE 7.1: Sample Statistics

| Variable | Workers | | Nonworkers | |
	Mean	Standard Deviation	Mean	Standard Deviation
Wife's education	12.75	2.29	11.59	2.24
Wife's age	34.92	11.1	37.44	11.91
Log of wife's prior labor market experience	2.10	.786	1.486	.872
No. of children age 0–5	.342	.63	.621	.814
No. of children age 6–13	.502	.859	.700	.931
No. of children age 14–18	.290	.700	.341	.680
Southwest residence	.48	.50	.46	.50
Husband's earnings ($)	12,358	7,826	14,334	10,794
No. of observations	1,003		581	

of work are transportation costs to and from work, child-care arrangements, and expenses such as clothing and utensils necessary in the performance of the job. The ideal measure of labor supply to capture the effects of these costs, especially the first two, is hours worked per day. Unfortunately, existing household survey data files do not provide information on this dimension of labor supply. The choice of annual hours of work is made primarily on the grounds that it is the best practical alternative to the ideal measure. Also, because it is the most comprehensive measure of labor supply, it is the most commonly used one and facilitates comparisons with estimates from earlier studies. It may be argued that the major sources of the costs of work are more properly treated as variable costs with respect to annual hours. This is true, especially if most of the variation in annual hours worked was the result of variations in days worked per year. But, even in this instance the annual hours of work function should exhibit a discontinuity. One can imagine that the annual hours of work supplied is the result of a joint decision between hours worked per day and days worked per year. Fixed costs would generate a discontinuity in the hours per day function. A discontinuity in the annual hours function would arise if the reservation price for days worked per year were below that of hours worked per day.[5] Otherwise, the discontinuity in the annual hours function would be unimportant, equaling the minimum hours worked per day. Clearly, the importance of costs of work could be more properly addressed by estimating these functions separately, and the possible inappropriateness of the combined measure, annual hours of work, should be kept in mind.

The reservation hours equation assumes the form

$$h_{0_i} = \delta_0 + \delta_2 Y_{H_i} + \delta_3 E_i + \delta_4 A_i + \sum_{j=1}^{3} \delta_{4+j} C_j + M_{0_i}. \qquad (7.4.2)$$

Although one may have intuitive feelings about the effects of each of these variables on reservation hours, the theory developed in the preceding section offers little insight into their expected effects.

Together equations 7.4.1 and 7.4.2 imply a reservation wage equation of the form

$$N(W_{R_i}) = \beta_0 + \beta_2 Y_{H_i} + \beta_3 E_i + \beta_4 A_i + \sum_{j=1}^{3} \beta_{4+j} C_j + \varepsilon_{1_i}, \qquad (7.4.3)$$

where

$$\beta_K = \frac{1}{\gamma_1} (\delta_K - \gamma_K) \qquad K = 0, 4$$

and

$$\varepsilon_{1_i} \sim N(0, \sigma_1^2).$$

The specification of the wage offer equation is

$$N(W_i) = \alpha_0 + \alpha_1 X_i + \alpha_2 SW + \alpha_3 E + \alpha_4 A_i + \varepsilon_{0_i}, \qquad (7.4.4)$$

where

$$\varepsilon_0 \sim N(0, \sigma_0^2),$$

and where E is the level of education completed by the wife, X is the natural logarithm of her prior labor market experience, SW is a

[5] This argument has been formalized in a slightly different context by Hanoch (Chapter 3).

dummy variable which assumes a value of one if the woman resides in the southwestern region of the U.S., and A is her age. This specification was arrived at after some preliminary specification search over a subset of residence variables.[6]

In order to implement the conditional maximum likelihood estimation procedure developed in the preceding section it is necessary first to have consistent estimates of the market wage parameters.

To estimate the parameters of the wage offer equation without selectivity bias, the approach suggested by Heckman (Chapter 5) was adopted. This approach, which utilizes the subsample of labor force participants, requires an estimate of the inverse of Mill's ratio for each observation.[7] Heckman suggests using probit analysis applied to the labor force participation decision to estimate Mill's ratio. Given the assumed forms of the labor supply, reservation wage, and market wage equation, there exists a unique labor force participation function. The theory implies that the woman will participate if

$$h_{N_i} > h_{0_i} \qquad (7.4.5)$$

or, equivalently if

$$N(W_i) > N(W_{R_i}). \qquad (7.4.6)$$

Using equations 7.4.3 and 7.4.4, the participation condition may be rewritten as

$$(\alpha_0 - \beta_0) + \alpha_1 X_i + \alpha_2 SW_i + (\alpha_3 - \beta_3)E_i + (\alpha_4 - \beta_4)A_i$$
$$- \beta_2 Y_{H_i} - \sum_{j=1}^{3} \beta_{4+j} C_j > \varepsilon_{1_i} - \varepsilon_{0_i} \quad (7.4.7)$$

Denoting the right- and left-hand sides of 7.4.7 by I and v, respectively, we may write the probability of participating as

$$P = Z\left(\frac{I}{\sigma_v}\right), \qquad (7.4.8)$$

where $Z(\cdot)$ is the unit normal cumulative distribution function and $\sigma_v = (\sigma_1^2 + \sigma_0^2 - 2\sigma_{10})^{1/2}$.

---

[6] We initially considered five region variables, southwest, west, north-central, northeast, and southeast. The latter three were not significantly different from western residence and were dropped from the equation.

[7] Mill's ratio is defined as the cumulative frequency at τ divided by the density at τ.

TABLE 7.2: Estimates of Reduced Form Labor Force Participation
Index

Variable	Coefficient	Standard Error
Constant	.0085	.294
Southwest residence	.0843	.079
Age	−.0538	.046
Log of experience	.7894	.054
Education	.1145	.019
Husband's earnings ($1,000s)	−.0254	.0046
Children age 0–5	−.5352	.059
Children age 6–13	−.0686	.041
Children age 14–17	.0706	.057
−2 × log likelihood		510.12
Sample proportion of participants		.633
Estimated probability of participation of sample means		.663
Estimated mean probability of participating		.637

With probit analysis one may estimate the parameters of the labor
force participation index, I/σ_v. Estimates of this index can, in turn, be
used to compute the density of the unit normal at I/σ_v and calculate
the inverse of Mill's ratio for each observation. The Probit Function is
useful not only in providing estimates of Mill's ratio, but also in
providing "reduced form" estimates of the labor force participation
function.[8]

REDUCED FORM LABOR FORCE PARTICIPATION AND WAGE ESTIMATES

Table 7.2 provides probit estimates of the parameters of the reduced
form labor force participation index. These estimates conform closely

[8] The relationship between the labor force participation parameters and those of index
is given by

$$\frac{\partial B}{\partial X_K} = \frac{1}{\sigma_V \sqrt{2\pi}}\, \theta_K e^{-1/2(I/\sigma_v)^2}$$

where θ_K denotes the Kth parameter of the labor force participation index. To obtain
the parameters of the participation function at the sample means from index parameters
reported in Table 7.2, simply multiply each coefficient by .3.

to those of earlier studies (Heckman, 1974b; Cogan, Chapter 2; Schultz, Chapter 1). The wife's prior labor market experience and education both have a positive and significant effect on her probability of participating. At the sample means, an additional year of prior experience raises the probability of her participating by 4 percentage points. Likewise, an additional year of education increases the probability of her participating by 4 percentage points. Her age, her husband's earnings and the number of preschool children negatively affect the probability of her participating. The age effect may reflect life-cycle behavior or differences across age cohorts, as the two cannot be separated with a single cross-section of data. Elementary school age children appear to affect the wife's labor force participation negatively but the effect is not statistically significant. High-school age children, on the other hand, positively influence the wife's participation. Though their effect is not significant, high-school age children appear to be a net substitute for the mother's time in the home.

WAGE OFFER EQUATION ESTIMATES

Estimates of the wage offer equation are reported in Table 7.3. For comparative purposes, ordinary least squares estimates of the wage offer equation are also presented. The parameters of each equation offer no surprises. The coefficients on education and prior labor market experience are as usual positive and significant, and age is negative and significant.

Comparisons of corresponding parameter estimates across equations are of interest because they reveal the empirical importance of "selectivity bias" in wage equation estimates. The estimates in the first column are free of selectivity bias; those in the third column are not. The selectivity bias term (the coefficient on the inverse of Mill's ratio) is relatively large, 8 percent, though not statistically significant. The sign of the selectivity bias term is positive, indicating that working women on average receive higher wage offers than nonworking women. Consistent with my earlier findings using a different data set (Chapter 2, using the National Longitudinal Survey of Married Women), the selectivity bias appears to have a quantitatively small impact on the education coefficient. Likewise, the estimated effects of age and region of residence are only negligibly altered.

The major effects of the selectivity bias are on the estimated effect of prior labor market experience and the constant term. The ordinary least squares estimate of the experience effect is 16 percent lower than the selectivity bias free estimate, and the constant term is only slightly more than one-half as large (in absolute value).

A good summary measure of the overall quantitative importance of the selectivity bias is the magnitude of the overstatement in predicted wage offers if selectivity bias is ignored. At the sample means, the overstatement is only 5 percent. It should be noted that the magnitude of the selectivity bias in predicted wages varies inversely with the labor force participation rate. The participation rate in this sample is relatively high, 66 percent. This should be kept in mind when comparing the results of Table 7.3 with those reported in other studies, especially those which use earlier data where the labor force participation rate among married women is much lower.

HOURS OF WORK ESTIMATES

Table 7.4 reports the conditional maximum likelihood estimates of the parameters of the hours of work and reservation hours functions. The coefficients are qualitatively similar to those found in previous empirical studies of married women's labor supply. The labor supply function is upward rising, children of all ages deter the wife's work, and the effect declines with the age of the children. Age and education (holding the market wage constant) are associated with reductions in work, and the husband's earnings has a negative effect on the wife's amount of work.

In the reservation hours equation children of all ages and the wife's education reduce the minimum number of hours the woman is willing to work, while her age and her husband's income increase the minimum hours worked. The coefficients on the children variables are of particular interest because children are likely to be important sources of the costs of work, both monetary and psychic. In an earlier paper (Cogan, 1977), I demonstrated that an increase in time costs would reduce the women's reservation hours if the wage elasticity of the compensated labor supply function at the reservation hours were less than unity. This elasticity evaluated at the mean reservation hours in the data is .79. Thus, the coefficients on the children variables are consistent with children increasing the time costs of work and younger children being associated with larger time costs than older children.

The discontinuity in the labor supply function is large. Measured at the sample means the discontinuity is 1,151 hours. The discontinuity

TABLE 7.3: Wage Equation Parameter Estimates

Variable	Censored Sample Regression Estimates		Ordinary Least Squares Estimates	
	Coefficient	Standard Error	Coefficient	Standard Error
Constant	−.212	.136	−.113	.105
Education	.096	.007	.092	.007
Log of experience	.251	.042	.213	.026
Southwest residence	−.081	.028	−.085	.029
Age	−.007	.003	−.005	.002
Inverse of Mill's ratio	.088	.076	—	—
R^2	—		.243	
F	64.31		80.03	

TABLE 7.4: Parameter Estimates of Fixed Cost Model

Variable	Hours of Work Equation		Reservation Hours Equation	
	Coefficient	Standard Error	Coefficient	Standard Error
Constant	2139.78	161.87	1862.57	196.39
Log wife's wage	881.66	208.03	—	—
Age	−6.54	2.68	2.91	4.20
Education	−108.16	20.20	−57.57	28.59
Husband's earnings ($1,000)	−8.51	3.00	.35	4.08
Children age 0–5	−302.61	44.19	−135.67	68.71
Children age 6–13	−107.09	24.20	−83.99	27.79
Children age 14–17	−51.21	30.72	−67.45	35.20
Index of hours and sample means	1292.98		1151.5	
Standard deviation	629.84		689.93	
Correlation between disturbances		.89		
Log likelihood function		554.26		

has an important behavioral implication which is ruled out by labor supply models that ignore fixed costs of work. When the typical woman enters the labor force she does so by supplying a large number of hours, working slightly over half-time. But, increases in her wage rate given that she is in the labor force, generate only modest increases in her hours worked. To illustrate, consider a representative woman in the data who is offered a wage of $2.70 per hour. This is less than her reservation wage, which at the sample means is $2.94 per hour, and she will choose not to work. A 10% increase in her wage offer, to $2.97, will induce her to enter the labor force. In doing so she will jump in, and work 1,162 hours during the year. A further 10% increase in her wage, $3.27 per hour, would induce her to supply only an additional 83 hours during the year. This interpretation suggests that the large elasticities of married women's hours of work equations reported in earlier studies that ignore the discontinuity (Heckman, 1974b; Rosen, 1976) result primarily from variations in hours worked among women entering the labor force and not from variations in hours worked among working women.

The estimated labor supply parameters may be used to infer the costs of work incurred by married women upon entry into the labor force and how these costs differ across women according to their demographic characteristics. To illustrate, consider the graph in Figure

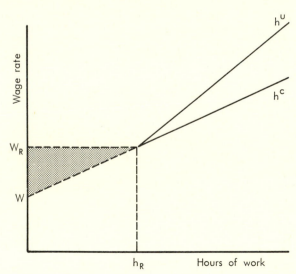

FIGURE 7.6   Inferring the costs of work

7.6. This graph depicts a representative woman's compensated (h^c) and uncompensated (h^u) labor supply functions, her reservation wage (W_R), and reservation hours (h_R). The compensated labor supply function is extrapolated down to the wage axis.[9] The total minimum compensation necessary to just induce the woman to enter the labor market is $W_R \times h_R$. This compensation may be decomposed into two components; the value of foregone leisure time spent at market work, and the time and money costs of work. The area under the compensated labor supply function from zero hours to her reservation hours measures the value of the foregone leisure time spent at market work. The remainder, the area under the reservation wage and above her compensated labor supply function (the shaded triangle) measures the value of the time and money costs of work. Variations in demographic characteristics will produce shifts in the labor supply function and the reservation wage, resulting in a new triangle. The costs associated with these variations may be inferred by calculating the difference between the shaded areas.

To estimate the fixed cost of work, the compensated labor supply function is needed. The form of the uncompensated empirical labor supply function (equation 7.4.1) implies a unique form of the compensated labor supply function. Using equation 7.4.1, the slope of the compensated labor supply function at a point is

$$\left(\frac{\partial h}{\partial W}\right)^c = \frac{\gamma_1}{W} - h\gamma_2 \tag{7.4.9}$$

Equation 7.4.9 is a first-order differential equation whose general solution is

$$h_N^c = e^{-\gamma_2 W} \int_{W*}^{W} \frac{\gamma_1}{\tau} e^{\gamma_2 \tau} \, d\tau + c e^{-\gamma_2 (W - W^*)}. \tag{7.4.10}$$

The particular solution may be obtained by substituting the estimated values of h_R and W_R into equation 7.4.10 and evaluating 7.4.10 with numerical methods.

Table 7.5 reports the annual costs of work implied by the labor supply parameter estimates. The costs for workers and nonworkers are calculated at their respective sample means. As expected, nonworking women do not work in part because they face higher costs of work

---

[9] Note that if there are only money costs of work W^* is the value of the nonworking women's time.

TABLE 7.5: Estimated Annual Costs of Work

Total Annual Cost	
Workers	$949.70
Nonworkers	$1022.62
Full sample	$974.29
Change in Total Costs of Work Resulting from Unit Change in	
Number of children 0–5	$380.16
Number of children 6–13	41.75
Number of children 14–17	−52.29
Wife's education	123.12
Wife's age	24.80

than working women. The differential is small, about $50. However, the total annual cost of work for both groups is large, almost $1,000. The annual cost of work, expressed as a percentage of the average working women's earnings, is 16 percent.

Table 7.5 also reports the effects of demographic characteristics on the annual costs of work. Of particular interest is the effect of additional children, since the costs of formal and informal child-care arrangements are likely to be a large component of costs of work. An additional child of preschool age raises the cost of work markedly, almost $400 at the sample means. The increase in cost associated with an additional child of elementary school age is rather small. Perhaps surprisingly, children of high-school age reduce the costs of work. It appears that high-school age children are a good substitute for the mother's time in the performance of household chores and care for younger children.

The wife's education is positively related to the costs of work and its effect is large. An additional year of education is associated with a cost increase of over $120. Michael (1973) has argued that education raises nonmarket productivity. If so, and if more highly educated women have better allocative skills, one might expect more highly educated women to incur a lower cost of work. However, balanced against this is the idea that more highly educated women tend to attach a higher value to their nonmarket time and, hence, value the time lost in getting to work at a higher rate. Also it seems likely that highly educated women would tend to enter occupations which require a greater expenditure on items, such as clothes etc., relative to women with low levels of education.

The effect of age on the cost of work is large but it is not clear how it is to be interpreted. Ten years of age is associated with a $240 increase in the cost of work at the sample means (the mean age in the sample is 36). Whether this difference reflects life-cycle variations or cohort differences cannot be answered with cross-sectional data alone.

Given the magnitude of the estimated discontinuity in the labor supply function, it is natural to ask what biases are introduced when the labor supply function is assumed to possess no discontinuity. In his seminal work Heckman (1974b) proposed a maximum likelihood estimator for labor supply parameters under the assumption of no discontinuity. Without detracting from Heckman's original contribution, it should be noted that the assumption of no discontinuity results in a restriction on the parameters, namely, that the parameters of the reservation wage function are proportional to the corresponding parameters of the labor supply function. If this restriction fails to hold in the data and a discontinuity exists, one would expect Heckman's approach systematically to overestimate (in absolute value) the true population parameters. This is illustrated in Figure 7.7. The function h^T represents the true labor supply function with fixed costs of work. The function is discontinuous at the reservation wage to reflect the effects of these costs. Imposing a constraint of zero discontinuity on data that has at least some nonworkers will result in an estimated labor supply function that looks like the restricted model and the effect of wages on hours worked will be overstated. Intuitively, the estimated wage effect will be some weighted average of the size of the discontinuity and the slope of the true labor supply function. In general this result will hold for all the estimated parameters.

To provide some empirical evidence on the size of the bias in parameters estimated under the assumption of no discontinuity, Table 7.6 compares the labor supply parameters of the fixed cost model with those of Heckman's constrained model (hereafter termed the constrained model) estimated on the same data.

The differences between corresponding parameters of the fixed cost model and the constrained model are striking. The constrained model results in a substantial overstatement in all the estimated parameters (except for the coefficient on children age 14–17) relative to the fixed

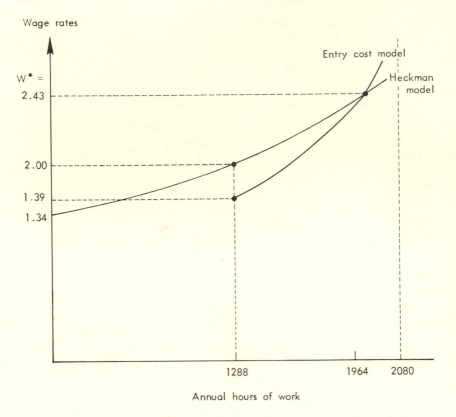

FIGURE 7.7   Average married women's estimated labor supply functions

cost model. The size of the overstatement is large. The own-wage
effect is three times as large in the former approach, the effect of age
four times as large, the effects of education and husband's income
more than twice as large, and the effect of preschool age almost twice
as large. It appears that the imposition of the zero discontinuity
constraint leads to severe biases in the estimated parameters of the
hours of work function.

To assess further the comparability of the two approaches several
summary statistics were computed. A pseudo R^2 was calculated among
the subsample of workers by taking the ratio of the explained variance,
measured by the expected value locus, to the total variance. The
pseudo R^2 for the fixed cost model was .276 and for the constrained
model was .101.

TABLE 7.6: Comparisons of Estimated Hours of Work Parameters

Variable	Constrained Model	Fixed Cost Model
Constant	1684.87	2139.78
	(223.93)	(161.87)
Log wife's wage	2845.45	881.66
	(166.63)	(208.03)
Age	−26.48	−6.54
	(2.96)	(2.68)
Education	−227.45	−108.16
	(22.55)	(20.20)
Husband's earnings	−22.8	−8.51
($1,000)	(3.68)	(3.00)
Children age 0–5	−568.72	−302.61
	(46.51)	(44.19)
Children age 6–13	−122.87	−107.09
	(32.53)	(24.20)
Children 14–17	500	−51.21
	(166.63)	(30.72)
σ_h	1007.05	629.84

The mean hours worked among both labor force participants and nonparticipants is 858.62. The mean expected hours of work predicted by the fixed cost model is 858.82, and the expected hours of work predicted by the constrained model is 726.85.

Finally, if the discontinuity in the labor supply function is important in the data, the constrained model would be expected systematically to underpredict hours worked among low wage workers and overpredict hours worked among high wage workers. In Figure 7.7, let W denote the wage at which the estimated labor supply functions of the two models intersect. To determine whether the constrained model systematically mispredicts hours worked in the expected manner, the mean residual above and below $\tilde{W}$ was computed for both models. For workers whose wage is above $\tilde{W}$ the mean residual of the fixed cost model is −69.33 and the mean residual of the constrained model is −82.83. For workers with wages below $\tilde{W}$ the difference between the models is even more dramatic. The mean residual of the fixed cost model is 15.72 while that of the constrained model is over 10 times as large, 171.65.

It is apparent from these summary statistics that the fixed cost model fits the data more accurately than the constrained model. When combined with the large and systematic differences in estimated labor supply function parameters, they suggest that imposition of a zero discontinuity constraint in the labor supply function does injustice to the data. Fixed costs appear to be important in determining labor supply behavior among married women, and ignoring their effect is likely to give very misleading parameter estimates.

CONCLUSIONS

This paper has presented a model of labor supply with time and money costs of labor market entry and used the model to estimate married women's labor supply functions and the total annual costs of labor market work. The existence of costs of labor market entry imparts a discontinuity in the labor supply function at the reservation wage. The estimated size of the discontinuity is large, over 1,100 hours per year at the sample means of the data. The large discontinuity reflects high costs of work, which at the sample means are around $1,000 per year: about 16 percent of the average earnings of working women in the data. Young children in the home, especially those of preschool age, are the most important source of the costs of work identified in this study. An additional child in this age range adds over $300 to the annual costs of work. Another finding is that incorporating fixed costs into the empirical analysis significantly improves the ability of labor supply models to explain observed hours of work. Moreover, models of labor supply that ignore the discontinuity in the labor supply function give seriously biased estimates of the parameters that underlie married women's labor supply behavior.

ACKNOWLEDGMENTS

The author would like to thank Bill Gould, Reuben Gronau, Giora Hanoch, Randal Olsen, William Rodgers, Sherwin Rosen, Kenneth

Mauer, James P. Smith, Michael P. Ward, and Finis Welch for their comments and suggestions. The research assistance of Frank Berger is also gratefully acknowledged. Financial assistance was provided by grants from the Department of Health, Education and Welfare and the Department of Labor. I, of course, assume responsibility for all errors.

APPENDIX A

DERIVATION OF THE ENTRY COST MODEL

The entry cost model is summarized by the following four equations:[10]

$$U = U(X, L), \tag{A.1}$$

$$X = Wh + V - X^*, \tag{A.2}$$

$$H = L + h + L^*, \tag{A.3}$$

$$X^* = G(L^*, \alpha). \tag{A.4}$$

Assuming an interior solution, we may substitute equations A.3 and A.4 into A.2 to obtain the full wealth constraint

$$WH + V = X + W(L + L^*) + G(L^*, \alpha). \tag{A.5}$$

Maximizing A.1 subject to A.5, the necessary conditions for an interior relative maximum are

$$U_X - \lambda = 0, \tag{A.6}$$

$$U_L - \lambda_W = 0, \tag{A.7}$$

$$W - g_L^* = 0, \tag{A.8}$$

$$WH + V - X - W(L + L^*) - G(L^*, \alpha) = 0, \tag{A.9}$$

where λ is the Lagrangian multiplier.

Totally differentiating equation A.6 through A.9 yields the displacement system, written in matrix form as

$$
\begin{bmatrix}
0 & -1 & -W & 0 \\
-1 & U_{XX} & U_{XL} & 0 \\
-W & U_{LX} & U_{LL} & 0 \\
0 & 0 & 0 & -g_{L^*L^*}
\end{bmatrix}
\begin{bmatrix}
d\lambda \\
dX \\
dL \\
dL^*
\end{bmatrix}
=
\begin{bmatrix}
-dV - h\,dW + g_\alpha\,d\alpha \\
0 \\
\lambda\,dW \\
dW + g_{L^*\alpha}\,d\alpha
\end{bmatrix}.
\tag{A.10}
$$

[10] All terms are defined in the text.

Denoting the cofactors of the displacement system of the conventional labor supply model[11] as A_{ij}, and those of the displacement system (A.10) as A_{ij}^*, the relationships among the corresponding cofactors of the two systems are given by

$$A_{4.4}^* = |A|,$$
$$|A^*| = |A| \, g_{L^*L^*},$$
$$A_{1.3}^* = -g_{L^*L^*} A_{1.3}, \qquad\qquad (A.11)$$
$$A_{3.3}^* = -g_{L^*L^*} A_{3.3},$$
$$A_{4.3}^* = A_{3.4}^* = A_{1.4}^* = 0.$$

Using the relationships given in A.11, and noting that $dh = dL - dL^*$, the partial derivatives of hours worked with respect to wages and income are

$$\frac{dh^*}{dW} = \left(\frac{\partial h}{\partial W}\right)^c + h\frac{\partial h}{\partial v} - \frac{\partial L^*}{\partial W}, \qquad\qquad (A.12)$$

where

$$\frac{\partial L^*}{\partial W} = -\frac{1}{g_{L^*L^*}} < 0$$

and

$$\frac{\partial h^*}{\partial V} = \frac{\partial h}{\partial V}. \qquad\qquad (A.13)$$

The utility-compensated effect of a change in the marginal cost of entry time, or, equivalently, the effect of a change in the marginal cost of entry time holding the total cost of entry constant, is obtained by setting $g_\alpha = 0$ and examining the effect of a change in $g_{L^*\alpha}$. This "pure price effect" is given by

$$\left.\frac{dL}{d\alpha}\right|_{g_\alpha = 0} \equiv \frac{dL}{dMC_{L^*}} = 0 \qquad\qquad (A.14)$$

and

$$\left.\frac{dL^*}{d\alpha}\right|_{g_\alpha = 0} \equiv \frac{dL^*}{dMC_{L^*}} = -\frac{g_{L^*\alpha}}{g_{L^*L^*}}. \qquad\qquad (A.15)$$

If $g_{L^*\alpha} > 0$, then the marginal cost of entry time increases with α and,

---

[11] It should be noted that the partial derivatives of the supply function in the conventional labor supply model are those of the supply function in a regime of fixed costs of labor market entry.

since $g_{L^*L^*} > 0$, the hours of work decline with increases in the marginal cost of entry time.

The effect of a change in the total cost of entry, holding the marginal cost of entry time constant, is obtained by setting $g_{L^*\alpha} = 0$. This pure-wealth effect is given by

$$\frac{dL}{d\alpha}\bigg|_{g_{L^*\alpha}} \equiv \frac{dL}{dC}\bigg|_{MC_{L^*}} = -g_\alpha \frac{A^{1.3}}{|A|} = -g_\alpha \frac{\partial L}{\partial V}, \qquad (A.16)$$

$$\frac{dL^*}{d\alpha}\bigg|_{g_{L^*\alpha}=0} \equiv \frac{dL^*}{dC}\bigg|_{MC_{L^*}} = \frac{A^{1.4}}{A} = 0. \qquad (A.17)$$

Hence

$$\frac{dh}{d\alpha}\bigg|_{g_{L^*\alpha}} \equiv \frac{\partial h}{\partial C}\bigg|_{MC_{L^*}} = \frac{\partial h}{\partial V}\bigg|_{MC_{L^*}}. \qquad (A.18)$$

The effect of a rise in entry costs on the reservation wage may be obtained by solving for the effect of a change in entry costs on hours and allowing for the wage rate to rise such that the change in utility equals zero. Using equations A.12 and A.18, we may write

$$\frac{dh_0}{dC} = \left(\frac{\partial h}{\partial W}\right)^c + h_0 \frac{\partial h}{\partial V} - \frac{\partial L^*}{\partial W} dW - \frac{\partial h}{\partial C} dC. \qquad (A.19)$$

If utility is held constant, it must be true that

$$h_0 \, dW + g_\alpha \, d\alpha = 0$$

or, equivalently,

$$\frac{dW}{dC} = \frac{1}{h_0}.$$

Using these relations in equation A.19, we obtain

$$\frac{dh_0}{dC} = \left[\left(\frac{\partial h_0}{\partial W}\right)^c - \frac{\partial L^*}{\partial W}\right]\frac{1}{h_0} > 0. \qquad (A.20)$$

APPENDIX B

The proof of this assertion is straightforward. The likelihood function conditional upon the known value of α may be written as

$$L(\gamma_0, \beta_0, \sigma_{v_1}, \sigma_{v_2}, \sigma_{v_1 v_2} \mid \alpha, \chi), \tag{B.1}$$

where χ is used to denote the data. The normal equations are defined in vector notation as

$$\frac{\partial \log L}{\partial \theta} = g(\theta \mid \alpha, \chi_t) = 0, \tag{B.2}$$

where

$$\theta = (\beta_0, \gamma_0, \sigma_{v_1}, \sigma_{v_2}, \sigma_{v_1 v_2}).$$

The solution to the normal equations that corresponds to the global maximum of the likelihood function yields a consistent estimate of the parameter vector θ.[12]

The likelihood function conditional upon an estimated $\hat{\alpha}$ may be written compactly as

$$L^*(\gamma_0, \beta_0, \sigma_{v_2}, \sigma_{v_1 v_2} \mid \hat{\alpha}, \chi) \tag{B.3}$$

and its normal equations are defined as

$$\frac{\partial \log L^*}{\partial \theta} = g^*(\theta \mid \hat{\alpha}, X_t) = 0. \tag{B.4}$$

The solution to 3.30 that corresponds to the global maximum of the likelihood function (3.29) defines what we shall call the "conditional maximum likelihood estimator."

Since the solution to B.3 at the global maximum is a consistent estimator of θ, to prove the consistency of the conditional maximum likelihood estimator, it suffices to show that the normal equations B.4 converge to those of B.2 and that the likelihood function B.3 converges to B.1. A theorem by Mann and Wald (1943) guarantees the

---

[12] See Olsen (1974) or Amemiya (1973a).

convergence of these two functions. The Mann–Wald theorem states that if $f(\cdot)$ is a continuous function and X_n converges in probability to X, then $f(X_n)$ converges in probability to $f(X)$.[13] The regularity conditions on the likelihood function B.1, in particular that of the density function possessing derivatives up to at least the third order, insures the continuity of both equations B.4 and B.3.

Therefore, since $\hat{\alpha} \xrightarrow{P} \alpha$ it follows that

$$g^*(\theta \mid \hat{\alpha}, \chi_t) \to g(\theta \mid \alpha, \chi_t) \quad \text{and} \quad L^*(\theta \mid \hat{\alpha}, \chi_t) \xrightarrow{P} L(\theta \mid \alpha, \chi_t).$$

Hence, the conditional maximum likelihood estimator converges to the maximum likelihood estimator and is consistent if the maximum likelihood estimator is consistent.

The generality of this result should be noted. It implies that a two-step procedure may be used to estimate consistently the parameters of simultaneous equation versions of nonlinear models, wherein the right-hand-side endogenous variable possesses the same distribution as the dependent variable. The first step is to obtain consistent estimates of the reduced form parameters of the right-hand-side endogenous variable. The second step is to maximize the likelihood function corresponding to the reduced form of the equation of interest, subject to the conditional parameters estimated in the first stage. The Mann–Wald theorem on convergence implies that the two-step procedure will yield consistent estimates of the structural parameters if the likelihood function satisfies the regularity conditions.

---

[13] Actually, Mann and Wald state their theorem under more general conditions, by assuming $f(\cdot)$ to be Borel measurable by placing restrictions on the set of admissible discontinuities.

BIBLIOGRAPHY

Aigner, Dennis, "An Appropriate Economic Framework for Estimating a Labor Supply Function from the SEO File," mimeo, University of Wisconsin, November 1971.

Alonzo, W., *Location and Land Use: Toward a General Theory of Land Rent*, Cambridge: Harvard University Press, 1964.

Amemiya, Takeshi, "Multiple Regression and Simultaneous Equation Models When the Dependent Variables are Truncated Normal," Technical Report #82, Institute for Mathematical Studies in the Social Sciences, Stanford University, January 1973(a).

―――, "Regression Analysis When the Dependent Variable is Truncated Normal," *Econometrica*, 41: 16, November 1973(b), 997–1016.

Ashenfelter, Orley and James Heckman, "Estimating Labor Supply Functions," in *Income Maintenance and Labor Supply*, G. Cain and H. Watts (eds.), Chicago: Markham Press, 1973, Chapter 7.

Barzel, Y., "The Determination of Daily Hours and Wages," *Quarterly Journal of Economics*, 87: 1973, 220–238.

Becker, Gary S., *Human Capital: A Theoretical and Empirical Analysis*, National Bureau of Economic Research, New York: Columbia University Press, 1954.

―――, "A Theory of the Allocation of Time," *The Economic Journal*, 75: 299, September 1965, 493–517.

―――, "A Theory of Marriage: Part Two," *Journal of Political Economy*, 82: 2, Part II, March/April 1974, 511–526.

Benham, Lee, "Benefits of Women's Education with Marriage," *Journal of Political Economy*, 82: 2, Part II, March/April 1974, 51–71.

Ben-Porath, Yoram, "Labor Force Participation Rates and the Supply of Labor," *Journal of Political Economy*, 81: 3, May/June 1973, 697–704(a).

―――, *First Generation Effects of Second Generation Fertility*, R-1259-NIH, The Rand Corporation, Santa Monica, Ca., December 1973(b).

Berkson, J., "Application of the Logistic Function to Bio-Assay," *Journal of the American Statistical Association*, 39: 1944, 357–365.

Berkson, J., "Maximum Likelihood and Minimum χ^2 Estimates of the Logistic Function," *Journal of the American Statistical Association*, 50: 1955, 130–161.

Blinder, A. and Y. Weiss, "Human Capital and Labor Supply: A Synthesis," National Bureau of Economic Research, Working Paper 67, January 1975 (unpublished).

Boskin, M. J., "The Economics of Labor Supply," in *Income Maintenance and Labor Supply*, G. Cain and H. Watts (eds.), Chicago: Markham Press, 1973, Chapter 4.

Bowen, William G. and T. Aldrich Finnegan, *The Economics of Labor Force Participation*, Princeton, N.J.: Princeton University Press, 1969.

Break, George, F., "Income Taxes and Incentives to Work: An Empirical Study," *American Economic Review*, 47: 5, September 1957, 529–549.

Brown, A. and A. Deaton, "Models of Consumer Behavior: A Survey," *Economic Journal*, 82: 328, December 1972, 1145–1236.

Brumberg, Richard and Franco Modigliani, "Utility Analyses and the Consumption on Function," in *Post-Keynesian Economics*, Kenneth K. Kurihara (ed.), Princeton, N.J.: Princeton University Press, 1962.

Brumm, Harold, "Comment on 'Shadow Prices, Market Wages and Labor Supply,'" *IDA*, June 1976.

Burkhauser, Richard V. and John A. Turner, "A Time Series Analysis on Social Security and Its Effect on the Market Work of Men at Younger Ages," *Journal of Political Economy*, 86: 4, August 1978, 701–715.

Cain, Glen G., *Labor Force Participation of Married Women*, Chicago: University of Chicago Press, 1966.

Cain, Glen G., *et al.*, "The Labor Supply Response of Married Women, Husband Present," *Journal of Human Resources*, 9: 2, Spring 1974, 201–222.

Cain, Glen G. and Harold Watts (eds.), *Income Maintenance and Labor Supply: Econometric Studies*, Chicago: Markham Press, 1973.

Cogan, John F., *Labor Supply with Time and Money Costs of Participation*, R-2044-HEW, The Rand Corporation, Santa Monica, Ca., October 1977.

Cox, D. R., *The Analysis of Binary Data*, London: Methuen, 1970.

Cragg, J., "Some Statistical Models for Limited Dependent Variables with Applications to the Demand for Durable Goods," *Econometrica*, 39: 5, September 1971, 829–844.

Cramer, H., *Mathematical Methods of Statistics*, Princeton, N.J.: Princeton University Press, 1963.

Danforth, John P., "Expected Utility, Infinite Horizon, and Job Search," Discussion Paper No. 74–42, University of Minnesota, Minneapolis, June 1974.

DaVanzo, Julie, Dennis De Tray, and David Greenberg, *Estimating Labor Supply Responses: A Sensitivity Analysis*, R-1372-OEO, The Rand Corporation, Santa Monica, Ca., December 1973.

Dhrymes, P. J., "Alternative Asymptotic Tests of Significance and Related Aspects of 2 SLS and 3 SLS Estimated Parameters," *Review of Economic Studies*, 36 (2): 106, April 1969, 213–226.

Diewert, W., "Applications of Duality Theory," in *Frontiers of Quantitative Economics*, M. Intrilligator and D. Kendrick (eds.), Vol. II, Amsterdam: North Holland Publishing Co., 1975, 106–171.

Feldstein, Martin S., "Social Security, Induced Retirement, and Aggregate Capital Formation," *Journal of Political Economy*, 82: 4, September/October 1974, 905–926.

Finnegan, T. A., "Hours of Work in the United States: A Cross-Sectional Analysis," *Journal of Political Economy*, 70: 5, October 1962, 452–470.

Fisher, Irving, "The Theory of Interest," *Reprints of Economic Classics*, New York: Augustus M. Kelley, 1965.

Fleisher, Belton M., Donald O. Parsons, and Richard D. Porter, "Asset Adjustments and Labor Supply of Older Workers," in *Income Maintenance and Labor Supply*, G. Cain and H. Watts (eds.), Chicago: Markham Press, 1973, Chapter 8.

Fuchs, V., "Recent Trends and Long-run Prospects for Female Earnings," *American Economic Review*, papers and proceedings, Vol. 64, May 1974, 236–242.

Garfinkel, Irwin, "On Estimating the Labor Supply Effects of a Negative Income Tax," in *Income Maintenance and Labor Supply*, G. Cain and H. Watts (eds.), Chicago: Markham Press, 1973, Chapter 6.

Ghez, Gilbert and Gary Becker, "The Allocation of Goods and Time Over the Life Cycle," National Bureau of Economic Research, New York: Columbia University Press, 1975.

Glejser, H., "A New Test for Heteroskedasticity," *Journal of the American Statistical Association*, 64: 325, March 1969, 316–323.

Goldberger, A. S., "Maximum Likelihood Estimation of Regression Models Containing Unobservable Variables," *International Economic Review*, 13: 1, February 1972(a).

———, "Structural Equation Methods in the Social Sciences," *Econometrica*, 40: 6, November 1972(b), 979–1002.

Goodman, L., "On the Exact Variance of Products," *Journal of the American Statistical Association*, 55: 292, December 1960, 708–713.

Green, Christopher and Alfred Tella, "Effect of Nonemployment Income and Wage Rates on the Work Incentives of the Poor," *Review of Economics and Statistics*, November 1969.

Greenberg, David H., *Problems of Model Specification and Measurement: The Labor Supply Function*, R-1085-EDA, The Rand Corporation, Santa Monica, Ca., December 1972.

Greenberg, David H. and Marvin Kosters, *Income Guarantees and the Working Poor: The Effect of Income Maintenance Programs on the Hours of Work of Male Family Heads*, R-579-OEO, The Rand Corporation, Santa Monica, Ca., December 1970.

Griliches, Zvi, "Errors in Variables and Other Unobservables," Harvard Discussion Paper No. 333, December 1973.

Griliches, Zvi and W. M. Mason, "Education, Income, and Ability," *Journal of Political Economy*, 80: 3, Part II, May/June 1972, 74–103.

Gronau, Reuben, "The Effect of Children on the Housewife's Value of Time," *Journal of Political Economy*, 81: 2, Part II, March/April 1973(a), 168–199.

———, "The Intrafamily Allocation of Time: The Value of the Housewife's Time," *American Economic Review*, 63: 4, September 1973(b).

———, "Wage Comparisons—A Selectivity Bias," *Journal of Political Economy*, 82: 6, November/December 1974, 1119–1145.

Grossman, M., "On the Concept of Health Capital and the Demand for Health," *Journal of Political Economy*, 80: 2, March/April 1972, 223–255.

Hall, Robert, "Wages, Income, and Hours of Work in the U.S. Labor Force," in *Income Maintenance and Labor Supply*, G. Cain and H. Watts (eds.), Chicago: Markham Press, 1973, Chapter 3.

Hanoch, Giora, "The 'Backward-Bending' Supply of Labor," *Journal of Political Economy*, 73: 6, December 1965(a), 636–642.

———, "Personal Earnings and Investment in Schooling," unpublished Ph.D. dissertation, University of Chicago, 1965(b).

Hause, John C., "Earnings Profile: Ability and Schooling," *Journal of Political Economy*, 80: 3, Part II, May/June 1972, 108–138.

Heckman, James, "Three Essays in the Supply of Labor and the Demand for Goods," unpublished Ph.D. dissertation, Princeton University, May 1971.

———, "Effects of Child Care Programs on Women's Work Effort," *Journal of Political Economy*, 82: 2, Part II, March/April 1974(a), 136–163.

———, "Shadow Prices, Market Wages, and Labor Supply," *Econometrica*, 42: 4, July 1974(b), 679–694.

———, "Estimates on Human Capital Production Functions Embedded in a Life Cycle Model of Labor Supply," National Bureau of Economic Research, 1974(c) (unpublished).

———, "The Common Structure of Statistical Models of Truncation, Sample Selection and Limited Dependent Variables and a Simple Estimator for Such Models," *The Annals of Economic and Social Measurement*, December 1976.

———, "Dynamic Models of Female Labor Supply," unpublished paper, University of Chicago, March 1977.

———, "Heterogeneity and State Dependence in Dynamic Models of Labor Supply," unpublished manuscript, University of Chicago, 1978.

Heckman, James and Thomas MaCurdy, "A Dynamic Model of Female Labor Supply," *Review of Economic Studies*, November, 1978.

Heckman, James and Solomon Polachek, "The Functional Form of the Income-Schooling Relationship," National Bureau of Economic Research, New York, October 1972.

Hicks, J., *Value and Capital: An Inquiry into Some Fundamental Principles of Economic Theory*, 2nd ed., Oxford: Clarendon Press, 1946.

Hotelling, H., "Demand Functions with Limited Budgets," *Econometrica*, 3: 1935, 66–78.

Internal Revenue Service. *Statistics of Income-Individual Tax Returns*, Washington, D.C., 1966–1972.

Jevons, S., *The Theory of Political Economy*, London: The Macmillan Co., 1871.

Johnson, N. and S. Kotz, *Distributions in Statistics: Continuous Multivariate Distributions*, New York: Wiley, 1972.

Johnston, J., *Econometric Methods*, 2nd ed., New York: McGraw-Hill, 1972.

Kain, J., "The Journey-to-Work as a Determinant of Residential Location," *Papers of the Regional Science Association, IX*, Philadelphia: University of Pennsylvania, 1962.

Kalachek, E. and F. Raines, "Labor Supply of Low Income Workers," in *President's Commission on Income Maintenance Programs, Technical Studies*, Alfred J. Tella (ed.), 1970.

Kosters, Marvin, "Income and Substitution Effects in a Family Labor Supply Model," P-3339, The Rand Corporation, Santa Monica, Ca., December 1966.

———, "Effects of an Income Tax on Labor Supply," in *The Taxation of Income from Capital*, Arnold Harberger and Martin Bailey (eds.), Washington, D.C.: The Brookings Institution, 1969.

Landsberger, Michael, "Children's Age as a Factor Affecting the Simultaneous Determination of Consumption and Labor Supply," *Southern Economic Journal*, 40: October 1973, 279–288.

Leibowitz, Arleen, "Women's Allocation of Time to Market and Nonmarket Activities," unpublished Ph.D. dissertation, Columbia University, 1972.

———, "Home Investments in Children," *Journal of Political Economy*, 82: 2, Part II, March/April 1974, 111–131.

Lewis, H. G., "Hours of Work and Hours of Leisure," *Proceedings of the IRRA*, 1956.

———, *Unionism and Relative Wages*, Chicago: University of Chicago Press, 1963.

———, "Income and Substitution Effects in Labor Force Participation and Hours of Work," Discussion Paper No. 18, Center for Economic Research, University of Minnesota, June 1972.

———, "Comments on Selectivity Biases in Wage Comparisons,"

Journal of Political Economy, 82: 6, November/December 1974, 1145–1155.

Linder, Steffan, *The Harried Leisure Class*, New York: Columbia University Press, 1970.

Lindsay, C., "Measuring Human Capital Returns," *Journal of Political Economy*, 79: 6, November/December 1971, 1195–1216.

Long, Clarence D., *The Labor Force under Changing Income and Employment*, National Bureau of Economic Research, Princeton, N.J.: Princeton University Press, 1958.

Malinvaud, E., *Statistical Methods of Econometrics*, 2nd ed., Amsterdam: North Holland Publishing Co., 1970.

Mann, H. B. and A. Wald, "On Stochastic Limit and Order Relationships," *Annals of Mathematics and Statistics*, 14: 1943, 217–226.

McCall, John J., "Economics of Information and Job Search," *Quarterly Journal of Economics*, 84: 1, February 1970, 113–126.

——, "Probabilistic Microeconomics," *Bell Journal of Economics and Management Science*, 2: 2, Autumn 1971, 306–327.

Metcalf, Charles E., "Predicting the Effects of Permanent Programs from a Limited Duration Experiment," *Journal of Human Resources*, 9, Fall 1974, 530–555.

Michael, Robert, "Education in Nonmarket Production," *Journal of Political Economy*, 81: 2, Part I, March/April 1973, 306–327.

Michael, R. T. and G. S. Becker, "On the New Theory of Consumer Behavior," *Swedish Journal of Economics*, 4, 1973.

Mincer, Jacob, "Labor Force Participation of Married Women," in *Aspects of Labor Economics*, H. G. Lewis (ed.), Natural Bureau of Economic Research, Princeton, N.J.: Princeton University Press, 1962, 63–105.

——, *Schooling, Experience and Earnings*, National Bureau of Economic Research, New York: Columbia University Press, 1974.

Mincer, Jacob and Solomon Polachek, "Family Investments in Human Capital: Earnings of Women," *Journal of Political Economy*, 82: 2, Part II, March/April 1974, 76–108.

Morgan, J. M. (ed.), *Five Thousand American Families—Patterns of Economic Progress*, I and II, Survey Research Center, Institute for Social Research, University of Michigan, 1974.

Munnell, Alicia H., *The Effect of Social Security on Personal Savings*, Cambridge, Mass.: Ballinger, 1974.

Muth, R., "Household Production and Consumer Demand Functions," *Econometrica*, 34: 3, July 1966, 699–708.

Nelson, Forrest D., "Censored Regression Models with Unobserved Stochastic Censoring Thresholds," Working Paper No. 63, Computer Research Center for Economics and Management Science, Cambridge, Mass., December 1974.

Nerlove, Marc and James Press, *Univariate and Multivariate Log-Linear and Logistic Models*, R-1306-EDA/NIH, The Rand Corporation, Santa Monica, Ca., December 1973.

Nerlove, Marc and T. P. Schultz, *Love and Life Between the Censuses: A Model of Family Decision Making in Puerto Rico, 1950–1960*, RM-6322-AID, The Rand Corporation, Santa Monica, Ca., September 1970.

Okner, Benjamin, "Constructing a New Data Base from Existing Microdata Sets: The 1966 Merge File," *Annals of Economic and Social Measurement*, 1: 3, July 1972, 325–342.

Olsen, Randall J., "An Econometric Model of Family Labor Supply," Methods Workshop Paper, University of Chicago, 1974 (and dissertation, 1977).

————, "The Analysis of Two Variable Models When One of the Variables is Dichotomous," Yale University, unpublished discussion paper, September 1975.

Parkinson, C. Northcote, *The Law and the Profits*, Ballantine Books, 1960.

Pechman, Joseph A., *Federal Tax Policy*, The Brookings Institution, W. W. Norton and Co., 1971.

Projector, Dorothy S., *Survey of Changes in Family Finances*, Board of Governors of the Federal Reserve System, 1968.

Robbins, Lionel, "On the Elasticity of Demand for Income in Terms of Effort," *Econometrica*, 10: June 1930, 123–129.

Rosen, Harvey S., "Taxes in a Labor Supply Model with Joint Wage-Hours Determination," *Econometrica*, 44: 3, May 1976, 485–508.

Rosen, S., "On the Interindustry Wage and Hours Structure," *Journal of Political Economy*, 77: 2, March/April 1969, 249–273.

————, "Learning and Experience in the Labor Market," *Journal of Human Resources*, 7: 3, Summer 1972, 326–342.

————, "Comment on Heckman's Paper," *Journal of Political Economy*, 82: 2, Part II, March/April 1974, 164–169.

Rosenbaum, S., "Moments of a Truncated Bivariate Normal Distribution," *Journal of the Royal Statistical Society*, 23: 2, 1961, 405–409.

Rothenberg, T. and C. Leenders, "Efficient Estimation of Simultaneous Equation Systems," *Econometrica*, 32: 1, January 1964, 57–76.

Roy, R., "La distribution de revenu entre les divers biens," *Econometrica*, 15: 3, July 1947, 205–225.

Samuelson, P., *Foundations of Economic Analysis*, Cambridge: Harvard University Press, 1947.

Schoenberg, E. G. and Paul H. Douglas, "Studies in the Supply Curve of Labor," *Journal of Political Economy*, 45: 1937, 45–79.

Schultz, T. Paul, *Long Term Change in Persons Income Distribution: Theoretical Approaches, Evidence and Explanations*, P-4667, The Rand Corporation, Santa Monica, Ca., January 1972.

———, *Fertility Determinants: A Theory, Evidence and an Application to Policy Evaluation*, R-1016-RF/AID, The Rand Corporation, Santa Monica, Ca., January 1974.

———, "The Influence of Fertility on the Labor Force Participation of Married Women," Yale University, unpublished discussion paper, March 1976.

Scitovsky, T., *Welfare and Competition: The Economics of a Fully Employed Economy*, Chicago: D. Irwin, Inc., 1951.

Shea, J. R. Spitz and F. Zeller, *Dual Careers: A Longitudinal Study of Labor Market Experience of Women*, Columbus, Ohio: Center for Human Resource Research, The Ohio State University, May 1970.

Slutsky, E., "Sulla teoria del bilancio del consomatore," *Giornale degli economisti*, 51: 1915, 19–23. (English translation in *Readings in Price Theory*, G. Stigler and K. Boulding, eds., Chicago: Chicago University Press, 1952.)

Smith, James P., "The Life Cycle Allocation of Time in a Family Context," unpublished Ph.D. dissertation, University of Chicago, 1972.

———, *Family Decisionmaking Over the Life Cycle: Implications for Estimating Labor Supply*, R-1121-EDA, The Rand Corporation, Santa Monica, Ca., 1973.

———, "On the Labor-Supply Effects of Age-Related Income

Maintenance Programs," *Journal of Human Resources*, 10, Winter 1975, 25–43.

———, "The Convergence to Racial Equality in Women's Wages," in *Women in the Labor Market*, Cynthia Lloyd (ed.), New York: Columbia University Press, 1979.

Stigler, George, "Information in the Labor Market," *Journal of Political Economy*, Supplement 70: 2, Part II, October 1962, 94–105.

Survey of Consumer Finances 1970, Survey Research Center, Institute for Social Research, University of Michigan, Ann Arbor, 1971.

Sweet, James A., *Women in the Labor Force*, New York: Seminar Press, 1973.

Tella, Alfred, Dorothy Tella, and Christopher Green, "Hours of Work and Family Income Response to Negative Income Tax Plan," mimeo, 1971.

Theil, H., *Principles of Econometrics*, New York: Wiley, 1971, 628–636.

Tobin, James, "The Application of Multivariate Probit Analysis to Economic Survey Data," Cowles Foundation Discussion Paper No. 1, December 1955.

———, "Estimation of Relationships for Limited Dependent Variables," *Econometrica*, 26: 1, January 1958, 24–36.

U.S. Bureau of the Census, *Census of Population: 1970*, I, *Characteristics of the Population*, GPO, Washington, D.C., 1973.

U.S. Office of Economic Opportunity, *Survey of Economic Opportunity, 1967* (a magnetic tape file of data collected for OEO by the Census Bureau); also *1967 SEO Codebook* (xerox copy).

Wald, A., "A Note on the Consistency of the Maximum Likelihood Estimate," *Annals of Mathematics and Statistics*, Vol. 20, 1949, 595–601.

Wales, Terrence J., "Estimation of a Labor Supply Curve for Self-Employed Business Proprietors," *International Economic Review*, 14: 1, February 1973, 49–68.

Weiss, Y., "On the Optimal Lifetime Pattern of Labour Supply," *Economic Journal*, 82: 328, December 1972, 1293–1315.

Welch, Finis, "Measurement of the Quality of Schooling," *American Economic Review*, 56: 2, 1966, 379–392.

———, "Education in Production," *Journal of Political Economy*, 78: 1, January/February 1970, 35–59.

———, "Black–White Differences in the Return to Schooling," *American Economic Review*, 63: 5, December 1973, 893–907.

Wu, D., "Alternative Tests of Independence Between Stochastic Regressions and Their Disturbances," *Econometrica*, 41: July 1973, 733–750.

Zellner, A. and H. Theil, "Three-Stage Least Squares: Simultaneous Estimation of Simultaneous Equations," *Econometrica*, 30: 1, January 1962, 54–78.

Zeman, Morton, "A Quantitative Analysis of White–Nonwhite Income Differentials in the United States," unpublished Ph.D. dissertation, University of Chicago, September 1955.

INDEX

SELECTED LIST OF RAND BOOKS

Armor, David J., J. Michael Polich, and Harriet B. Stambul. *Alcoholism and Treatment.* New York: John Wiley and Sons, 1978.

Arrow, Kenneth J. and Marvin Hoffenberg. *A Time Series Analysis of Interindustry Demands.* Amsterdam, The Netherlands: North-Holland Publishing Company, 1959.

Aumann, R. J., and L. S. Shapley. *Values of Non-Atomic Games.* Princeton, New Jersey: Princeton University Press, 1974.

Coleman, James S., and Nancy L. Karweit. *Information Systems and Performance Measures in Schools.* Englewood Cliffs, New Jersey: Educational Technology Publications, 1972.

Dantzig, George B. *Linear Programming and Extensions.* Princeton, New Jersey: Princeton University Press, 1963.

Dorfman, Robert, Paul A. Samuelson, and Robert M. Solow. *Linear Programming and Economic Analysis.* New York: McGraw-Hill Book Company, 1958.

Downs, Anthony. *Inside Bureaucracy.* Boston, Massachusetts: Little, Brown and Company, 1967.

Fishman, George S. *Spectral Methods in Econometrics.* Cambridge, Massachusetts: Harvard University Press, 1969.

Hirshleifer, Jack, James C. DeHave, and Jerome W. Milliman. *Water Supply: Economics, Technology, and Policy.* Chicago, Illinois: The University of Chicago Press, 1960.

Hitch, Charles J., and Roland McKean. *The Economics of Defense in the Nuclear Age.* Cambridge, Massachusetts: Harvard University Press, 1969.

Jorgenson, D. W., J. J. McCall, and R. Radner. *Optimal Replacement Policy.* Chicago, Illinois: Rand McNally & Company; Amsterdam, The Netherlands: North-Holland Publishing Company, 1967.

McCall, John J. *Income Mobility, Racial Discrimination, and Economic Growth.* Lexington, Massachusetts: D. C. Heath and Company, 1973.

Meyer, John R., John F. Kain, and Martin Wohl. *The Urban Transportation Problem.* Cambridge, Massachusetts: Harvard University Press, 1965.

Mitchell, Bridger, Willard G. Manning, Jr., and Jan Paul Acton. *Peak-Load Pricing: European Lessons for U.S. Energy Policy.* Cambridge, Massachusetts: Ballinger Publishing Company, 1978.

Park, Rolla Edward. *The Role of Analysis in Regulatory Decision-Making.* Lexington, Massachusetts: D. C. Heath and Company, 1973.

Pascal, Anthony H. (ed.) *Racial Discrimination in Economic Life.* Lexington, Massachusetts: D. C. Heath and Company, 1972.

Sharpe, William F. *The Economics of Computers,* New York: Columbia University Press, 1969.

LIBRARY OF CONGRESS CATALOGING IN PUBLICATION DATA

Main entry under title:

Female labor supply.

    (A Rand Corporation research study)
    Bibliography: p.
    Includes index.
    1. Women—Employment—Addresses, essays, lectures.
2. Women—Employment—Mathematical models—Addresses,
essays, lectures.   I. Smith, James P., 1943-
II. Cogan, John F.   III. Series: Rand Corporation.
Research study.
HD6053.F4   331.4'12   79-3230
ISBN 0-691-04223-3